FORMULA 1
CAR BY CAR 1990-99

Published in March 2021

ISBN 978-1-910505-62-5

Published by Evro Publishing
Westrow House, Holwell, Sherborne, Dorset DT9 5LF, UK

Edited by Mark Hughes
Designed by Richard Parsons

Printed and bound in Bosnia and Herzegovina by GPS Group

www.evropublishing.com

The author

Peter Higham is a freelance writer who has worked in the motor racing media for over 30 years. A motor racing enthusiast since watching the 1973 Silverstone International Trophy on television, Higham joined Haymarket Publishing in 1986 to work in *Autosport*'s advertising department and remained with the company for nearly 30 years. Part of the launch publishing team for football monthly magazine *FourFourTwo*, he was involved with the LAT Photographic business for 17 years and Publishing Director of Haymarket Consumer Media's motor racing publications during the 2000s.

He has written eight previous books, including the first four titles in the *Formula 1 Car by Car* series covering the 1950s, 1960s, 1970s and 1980s. He has been a columnist for *Autosport* and *Motor Sport* and was instrumental in running the prestigious Autosport Awards for over 25 years.

The photographs

All of the photographs in this book have been sourced from Motorsport Images (www.motorsportimages.com). This London-based archive is the largest motoring and motorsport picture collection in the world with over 23 million colour images and black and white negatives dating back to 1895. It includes the collections of LAT Images and Sutton Images as well as the work of Rainer Schlegelmilch, Ercole Colombo and Giorgio Piola.

Motorsport Images also photographs today's Formula 1 World Championship, with full-time photographers and digital technicians at every race. Other events covered include the WRC, World Endurance Championship, Le Mans 24 Hours, IndyCar, NASCAR, ALMS, GP2 Series, GP3 Series, World Series by Renault, DTM and National Championships including BTCC and British F3. As part of Motorsport Network, Motorsport Images supplies all of the company's leading media, including *Autosport* and *GP Racing*.

The cover

The main image on the front shows Nigel Mansell's Williams FW14B-Renault during the 1992 Monaco GP. The cars in the inset photos on the front are (from left) 1990 McLaren MP4/5B-Honda (Ayrton Senna, Japanese GP), 1995 Benetton B195-Renault (Michael Schumacher, German GP), 1996 Williams FW18-Renault (Damon Hill, Belgian GP) and 1998 McLaren MP4-13-Mercedes (Mika Häkkinen, Japanese GP). The photos on the back depict (from top left to bottom right) 1993 Williams FW15C-Renault (Alain Prost, Australian GP), 1994 Ferrari 412T1B (Gerhard Berger, Australian GP), 1996 Benetton B196-Renault (Jean Alesi, Portuguese GP) and 1997 Williams FW19-Renault (Jacques Villeneuve, Argentinian GP).

FORMULA 1
CAR BY CAR 1990-99

PUBLISHING

Peter Higham

CONTENTS

INTRODUCTION **6**

ACKNOWLEDGEMENTS **7**

BIBLIOGRAPHY **7**

1990 SENNA REGAINS HIS CONTROVERSIAL CROWN **8**

1991 McLAREN WITHSTANDS WILLIAMS'S ACTIVE EFFORT **40**

1992 MANSELL AND WILLIAMS FW14B DOMINATE **76**

1993 PROST RETURNS TO CLAIM HIS FOURTH TITLE **106**

1994 SCHUMACHER INHERITS SENNA'S TRAGIC MANTLE **134**

1995 MICHAEL SCHUMACHER IN A CLASS OF HIS OWN **166**

1996 DAMON HILL EMULATES HIS FATHER AS CHAMPION **194**

1997 JACQUES DENIES MICHAEL AS RENAULT BOWS OUT **220**

1998 McLAREN'S FIRST WORLD TITLE IN SEVEN YEARS **248**

1999 HÄKKINEN FINALLY RETAINS HIS CROWN **274**

INDEX **300**

INTRODUCTION

The continuing rivalry between Ayrton Senna and Alain Prost opened this decade, with the Brazilian winning the 1990 and 1991 titles and Prost clinching his fourth in 1993 before retiring from the sport. Nigel Mansell finally won the crown in 1992 and both Damon Hill and Jacques Villeneuve also achieved singleton championships for Williams, in 1996 and 1997 respectively. The decade ended with Mika Häkkinen and Michael Schumacher to the fore, both as two-time World Champions.

The World Championships of 1990, 1994 and 1997 were all decided controversially when the top two protagonists crashed into each other. Furthermore, 1994 was a tragic campaign with a series of accidents that reminded everyone of the dangers of the sport and hastened an enhanced drive for safety.

Technical innovation flourished early in the 1990s although Max Mosley, the new president of the Fédération Internationale de l'Automobile, already wanted to ban what he saw as electronic driver aids before Senna and Roland Ratzenberger were killed at Imola in 1994. Banned in 1983, refuelling was reintroduced in 1994 despite concerns about its safety.

Normally aspirated engines were used throughout the 1990s with the existing 3.5-litre units replaced by a 3-litre maximum in 1995. Honda remained the most powerful engines in 1990 but was superseded in the power stakes by Renault in 1992. The French V10s remained the engine of choice until Renault withdrew at the end of the 1997 campaign. That coincided with Mercedes-Benz adding reliability to power and McLaren used the Ilmor-developed units to win the last two drivers' titles of the decade.

Having under-achieved for most of the 1980s, Ferrari reorganised under the leadership of Luca di Montezemolo. Jean Todt's management, the engineering skills of Ross Brawn and Rory Byrne and Michael Schumacher's talents in the cockpit were all added but the drivers' title continued to remain elusive. The 1999 constructors' championship was tangible reward for the investment, however, and a rare era of total domination would soon follow.

One noticeable change through the decade was the size of grids. The 1990 season began with 35 cars, necessitating a pre-qualifying session on the Friday morning. Economic reality – in a period of recession – saw famous and not-so-famous teams go to the wall before a franchise system limited the number of teams from 1996.

Nigel Mansell and Ayrton Senna go wheel-to-wheel for the length of Barcelona's pit straight in 1991

KEY TO 'DRIVER PERFORMANCE' CHARTS

Qualifying positions are included in superscript next to the race result. When a driver led a Grand Prix across the line, this is indicated by that result being underlined and in bold.

R	Retired
NC	Not classified
DSQ	Disqualified
DNS	Did not start
DNP	Did not take part in qualifying
DNQ	Did not qualify
NPQ	Did not pre-qualify
FL	Fastest lap
NT	No time recorded in qualifying

THE GRAND PRIX KEY IS AS FOLLOWS:

A	Austria
AUS	Australia
B	Belgium
BR	Brazil
CDN	Canada
D	Germany
E	Spain
EU	Europe
F	France
GB	Britain
H	Hungary
I	Italy
J	Japan
LUX	Luxembourg
MAL	Malaysia
MC	Monaco
MEX	Mexico
P	Portugal
PAC	Pacific
RA	Argentina
RSM	San Marino
USA	United States
ZA	South Africa

ACKNOWLEDGEMENTS

Many thanks to Eric Verdon-Roe and Mark Hughes of Evro Publishing for commissioning the *Formula 1 Car by Car* series, and to Mark for editorial management and to Richard Parsons for design. All of the photographs come from the vast archives of Motorsport Images, and I am indebted to Kevin Wood, Tim Wright, Craig Woollard, Catherine Benham, Jade Gallagher and Paul Duncan for making so much material available online. Also, thanks Kathy Ager for all her work on this series of books. Finally, welcome to Florence and thanks to Françoise, Joe, Luc and Sofia for their encouragement and support.

BIBLIOGRAPHY

MAGAZINES AND ANNUALS
Autocourse (Icon Publishing, Malvern, UK)
Autosport (Autosport Media UK, Richmond, UK)
F1 Racing (now GP Racing, Autosport Media UK, Richmond, UK)
Motor Sport (Motor Sport Magazine, London, UK)
Motorsport News (Kelsey Media, Yalding, UK)

BOOKS
A-Z of Grand Prix Cars by David Hodges (Crowood, Marlborough, UK, 2001)

Autocourse Grand Prix Who's Who Fourth Edition by Steve Small (Icon Publishing, Malvern, UK, 2012)

Ferrari: Men From Maranello by Anthony Pritchard (Haynes, Sparkford, UK, 2009)

Grand Prix Databook by David Hayhoe and David Holland (Haynes, Sparkford, UK, 2006)

The History of the Grand Prix Car 1966–91 by Doug Nye (Hazleton, Richmond, Surrey, UK, 1992)

A Record of Grand Prix and Voiturette Racing Volume 13 by Paul Sheldon with Duncan Rabagliati (St Leonards Press, Shipley, West Yorkshire, UK, 2002)

A Record of Grand Prix and Voiturette Racing Volume 14 by Paul Sheldon and David Smith (St Leonards Press, Shipley, West Yorkshire, UK, 2010)

SELECTED WEBSITES
www.autosport.com
www.formula1.com
www.grandprix.com
www.motorsportmagazine.com
www.oldracingcars.com

Ayrton Senna crashed into Alain Prost at the start of the Japanese Grand Prix to clinch his second world title

1990

SENNA REGAINS HIS CONTROVERSIAL CROWN

Ayrton Senna made a winning start in Phoenix while Jean Alesi further enhanced his reputation

Alain Prost switched to Ferrari and challenged for the title

The acrimony between Alain Prost and Ayrton Senna continued into 1990 despite the Frenchman moving from McLaren-Honda to Ferrari. Their two-way title fight came to a head at Suzuka once more where Senna drove Prost off the road at the first corner in a controversial high-speed accident. That confirmed Senna's second world title but the move was widely criticised.

The 3.5-litre maximum engine capacity meant that multi-cylinder engines were required to be competitive, with Honda V10 and Ferrari V12 to the fore. Two years' notice had to be given for rule changes but the Formula 1 Commission cited safety when Jean-Marie Balestre, president of the Fédération Internationale du Sport Automobile, announced changes on 6 May 1989 with larger cockpit dimensions and improved side protection around the shoulders and feet of the driver. Crash tests were now for the whole monocoque and fuel tanks. Three million French Francs were to be invested in medical facilities at international circuits following the injuries Philippe Streiff sustained in 1989. A medical helicopter now had to be present before any track action could take place.

Zakspeed and Rial withdrew in the winter but 35 entries remained so pre-qualifying was still required. That involved the twin entries from AGS, EuroBrun and Larrousse, plus the singleton Coloni, Life and Osella, competing in an

World Champions in Australia: James Hunt, Jackie Stewart, Denny Hulme, Nelson Piquet, Juan Manuel Fangio, Ayrton Senna and Jack Brabham

hour-long session at 8am on Friday from which the fastest four would progress to qualifying, with participants reviewed after the French GP. For the first time, teams had to nominate reserve drivers (a maximum of one per car) at the start of the season. In addition to reserves, just one driver change per car was allowed during the season, with claims of *force majeure* considered on a case-by-case basis. A 'tyre war' raged between Goodyear and Pirelli. While Akron dominated, the Italians occasionally perfected their qualifying rubber.

The United States GP moved to the start of the season while the Brazilian GP returned to a redeveloped (if slightly shabby) Interlagos. Donington Park owner Tom Wheatcroft announced the non-championship Donington 200 Gold Cup for Easter Monday with support from the Formula One Constructors' Association, but it was cancelled on 9 February due, according to a statement from Wheatcroft, 'to a lack of support from some teams', and continued: 'Donington feels it would be very unfair to mislead the public that there would be a full Grand Prix field in attendance.' In November 1988, the Singaporean tourist board announced its intention to organise a GP in 1990. Renovation of the old street circuit at Thomson Road and the Sentosa Island resort were considered before a site near the Tanah Merah Country Club was identified. Like Donington, Singapore would have to wait for F1.

Tyrrell's anhedral front wing was a major innovation

HONDA MARLBORO McLAREN

The fallout following the 1989 Japanese GP dominated much of the close season. Ayrton Senna was fined $100,000 and handed a six-month suspended sentence by FISA's Court of Appeal for claiming that the 1989 championship had been 'manipulated'. FISA initially refused McLaren's World Championship entry or to issue Senna with a super licence. A period of terse negotiations ensued until the deadline for driver nominations on 15 February, with Senna omitted, and then included, in the official entry list.

As Alain Prost would not stay at McLaren if Senna, who had one more year left on his contract, remained, Ferrari's Gerhard Berger had been announced at the 1989 British GP as the Frenchman's replacement on a three-year contract. Tyrrell driver Jonathan Palmer signed as reserve driver in February with F3000 hopeful Allan McNish also on the driver strength. Senna's race engineer, Steve Nichols, followed Prost to Maranello and Gordon Murray transferred to McLaren's new road car project. Dave Ryan, who had been with the team since 1974, was promoted to team manager in May. McLaren lured Ferrari engineers Henri Durand and Gordon Kimball (to engineer Senna's car) to Woking in June and July respectively, while Tim Wright looked after Berger's car.

Senna first drove the new McLaren MP4/5B at Silverstone on 20 February. Chief designer Neil Oatley and his team introduced a taller monocoque to comply with the new cockpit dimensions and to accommodate the lanky Berger, with Hercules Aerospace of Utah supplying the carbon-fibre as before. The fuel capacity was increased by 1.5 gallons and air now exited the narrow and reprofiled sidepods

to the rear. The undertray had five arches and extended to the back of the rear wing, although a shorter version was used at the Hungarian GP. The 3,498cc Honda engine, now designated RA100E, remained exclusive to McLaren and was driven through a heavily modified version of the six-speed transverse gearbox that had been introduced at the 1989 British GP. Such was the rate of development that there were at least six distinct iterations of the powerful 72-degree V10 during 1990 alone.

Berger qualified on pole position for his first McLaren race at Phoenix after a misfire and rain ruined Senna's practice. The Brazilian immediately put the winter behind him. Third into the first corner and second when Berger spun backwards into the tyres, he passed Jean Alesi for victory after a hard-fought lap 34. Berger changed his rear wing and set the fastest lap before his clutch failed.

Senna soon regained his qualifying mastery and annexed pole for ten of the remaining 15 races. Victory was lost at his home race when he hit Satoru Nakajima's Tyrrell while lapping it, leaving him to finish third after changing a damaged front wing; Berger started and finished second despite understeer. As the Austrian barely fitted into the cockpit, he had a new chassis with a raised dashboard for Imola, where Senna led another qualifying 1–2 only for a wheel rim to fail after three laps. Having led before his tyres degraded, Berger faded to second at the finish.

Senna led all the way from pole in Monaco, slowing down in the closing stages as a precaution; Berger collided with Prost at the original start and finished third in the spare car, which had been set up for Senna. More comfortable thanks to further cockpit

Gerhard Berger, McLaren MP4/5B-Honda (Italian GP)

Ayrton Senna, McLaren MP4/5B-Honda (Australian GP)

modifications, Berger won on the road in Canada but had been penalised 60sec for jumping the start and stole fourth on adjusted times on the very last lap; Senna eased to his 23rd GP win by 10.497sec despite losing first gear. Senna dominated the Mexican GP before a tyre with a slow puncture finally disintegrated while Berger, who started from pole, finished third behind the Ferraris after changing a blistered tyre.

Third in France (where Berger led) and at Silverstone (following a spin), Senna won at Hockenheim despite Alessandro Nannini's resistance and then in Hungary he recovered from a puncture and heavy contact with the Benetton driver to finish second, just 0.288sec behind Thierry Boutsen. Senna dominated the Belgian GP where Berger completed a McLaren 1–3. After the McLaren-Hondas finished second (Senna) and third (Berger) in the Portuguese GP when it was red-flagged, Senna qualified on pole position for the 50th time in his career in Spain although both he and Berger retired from the race.

And so to the penultimate race in Japan, where Prost needed to win to maintain his lingering title hopes. Senna argued throughout the meeting that pole position should be on the cleaner left-hand side of the track, and after he duly set the fastest time he was incensed when stewards refused his request in a stormy drivers' briefing on Sunday morning. Predictably, Prost made the better start so Senna, fuming at another perceived injustice, crashed into his rival at high speed at the first corner, claiming it was a legitimate passing manoeuvre. The World Championship was won but it tarnished a

season in which Senna had otherwise excelled. Berger now led but threw away victory by spinning in the same corner next time around.

Senna dominated the final race in Adelaide until a gearbox glitch caused him to crash; Berger finished fourth as McLaren-Honda retained the constructors' title for the third consecutive season.

SCUDERIA FERRARI

Alain Prost announced he was quitting McLaren in July 1989 and ignored interest from Benetton and Williams to sign with Ferrari on 6 September 1989. Nigel Mansell had already re-signed by that time, with number one status assured. That clause was renegotiated and Mansell soon regretted that amendment. Prost won the internal battle between the drivers as the Englishman's Ferrari love affair turned sour. Gianni Morbidelli joined as test and reserve driver in November.

Cesare Fiorio remained as sporting director. With technical director John Barnard's departure to Benetton, Enrique Scalabroni arrived from Williams as chief designer in September 1989 and Steve Nichols from McLaren in January 1990, initially in charge of Ferrari's on-track operations but soon responsible for chassis design. Peter Windsor became managing director of the Guildford Technical Office on 1 November 1989. Race engineer Giorgio Ascanelli also moved to Benetton and was replaced by Luigi Mazzola on Prost's car with Maurizio Nardon working with Mansell. Umberto Banassi was the new chief mechanic following Joan Villadelprat's departure to Tyrell.

Nigel Mansell, Ferrari 641 (Brazilian GP)

Prost drove Barnard's ground-breaking Ferrari 640 at Fiorano on 23–24 November and was quickest in pre-season tests at Estoril and Paul Ricard. Unveiled at Maranello at the start of February, the new Ferrari 641 was a logical development of the 640. Scalabroni marginally lengthened the monocoque with fuel capacity raised from 205 to 220 litres in a longer and taller central tank with ancillaries on either side. Suspension from the 640 was retained while detail changes were made to the aerodynamics, especially at the rear. The gearbox was modified so sequential down-shifts were no longer required. Ferrari remained with Goodyear, although Prost secretly tried Pirelli tyres in the summer.

The season began badly with Mansell in gearbox trouble from the start of practice in Phoenix, where both retired from points positions, Mansell's 641 catching fire when his broken clutch ruptured the oil

Alain Prost, Ferrari 641 (United States GP)

tank. New AP clutches were fitted for the Brazilian GP and fortunes for the team improved with Prost inheriting victory after Senna tripped over a backmarker and Mansell finishing fourth despite illness and a slow pitstop.

Scalabroni used the seven weeks before the San Marino GP to introduce the revised Ferrari 641/2, which had a rounded nose as part of one-piece bodywork, although the drivers complained of increased buffeting. The front wings were now fitted directly to the chassis with enlarged water radiators in revised sidepods. A new rear diffuser introduced on Prost's car in Belgium became standard thereafter. Paolo Massai's engine department produced a lighter, high-revving development of the 65-degree V12 engine, now designated 037, that was not raced until Hungary. The 641/2 handled well and top-end power was on a par with the Honda V10. However, making qualifying tyres last a lap was an early problem and Ferrari lacked Honda's low-speed torque.

Having sprained his wrist in testing, Mansell survived a couple of moments at Tamburello to challenge Gerhard Berger's McLaren-Honda for the lead of the San Marino GP until his engine failed, while Prost finished a gripless fourth. The Frenchman qualified second in Monaco but caused a red flag when he was hit by Berger on the opening lap at Mirabeau; both Ferraris retired from the restarted race with electronic issues. New rear suspension was introduced in Canada, where Mansell was third and Prost fifth. Only 13th on the grid in Mexico, Prost took advantage of Senna's slow puncture and subsequent blow-out to lead a welcome Ferrari 1–2 in the race; Mansell spun with five laps to go and drove around the outside of Berger at the Peraltada to retake second.

Alain Prost, Ferrari 641/2 (Italian GP)

That success in Mexico masked tensions as Scalabroni and Fiorio were in dispute about the need for a totally new car in 1991 and aerodynamicist Henri Durand had already left. Scalabroni was summoned to Maranello on the Tuesday following the Mexican GP with his immediate departure confirmed. 'I regret that one very good designer and one very, very good aerodynamic guy have left,' the unhappy Prost told the press.

Prost pursued the Leyton House-Judds of Ivan Capelli and Maurício Gugelmin – surprise leaders of the French GP – to steal victory three laps from the end and claim Ferrari's 100th victory in a World Championship race. The increasingly frustrated Mansell started from pole in France and at Silverstone but retired from both. Having agitated for a move for much of 1990, Mansell had gearbox failure when running second in front of his home crowd and immediately announced that he would retire at the end of the season. Prost scored his third successive win to briefly take the points lead.

Prost's title challenge faltered with an uncompetitive fourth in Germany and clutch failure in Hungary, where Mansell collided with Berger. At the start of the Belgian GP, the Englishman was nudged into the pit wall, prompting a red flag, and after restarting in the ill-handling spare his pointless run continued while Prost finished second. Testing at Monza before the Italian GP, Prost walked away from a huge accident when something broke at the first Lesmo, going on to finish second in the race with Mansell fourth.

Mansell led another qualifying 1–2 at Estoril. Ferrari had launch control for the first time and Prost initially made a great start. Mansell was slow off the line and squeezed his team-mate towards the pit wall, forcing Prost to lift, so they were only third and fifth by the end of lap one. Armed with the best car that day, Mansell eventually passed Senna to win for the only time in 1990. Third-placed Prost was furious that team orders had not been imposed to help his title challenge. 'Ferrari does not deserve to be World Champion,' he told French radio. 'It is a team without directive and without strategy.'

Prost led another Ferrari 1–2 at Jerez to extend the title fight to Suzuka, where he qualified second. Senna was incensed when the stewards refused to move his pole position to the racing line so Prost made the better getaway. Rather than cede the corner, Senna crashed into his rival at high speed, eliminating both cars and thereby clinching the title in dubious circumstances. Mansell led from lap two only for the driveshaft to fail as he rejoined from his tyre stop. After Mansell (despite a spin) and Prost finished 2–3 in Australia, Prost and Ferrari ended the season as runners-up in their respective championships.

Nigel Mansell, Ferrari 641/2 (Monaco GP)

BENETTON FORMULA

Benetton Formula's only victory of 1989 had come by default and Ford demanded change if it was to retain exclusive works support. That came in the form of John Barnard, who signed a five-year contract as technical director from 1 November 1989, the day after his Ferrari deal expired, with plans to establish the Benetton Advanced Research Group in Godalming, Surrey. Commercial director Flavio Briatore turned to a fallen star for Alessandro Nannini's team-mate with Nelson Piquet accepting a performance-related deal worth $100,000 per championship point scored. Ferrari race engineer Giorgio Ascanelli arrived on 15 November and Lotus's Mike Coughlan joined Barnard's staff. Italian rumours of a switch from Goodyear to Pirelli tyres proved a year premature. Cosworth Engineering, which designed and built the Ford HB engine, was sold to Vickers in March 1990.

For the first time since acquiring Toleman, Benetton kept the same engine for a second season. Cosworth's compact V8 gave away 40bhp to its rivals so Benetton normally adopted a low-downforce set-up. Better fuel consumption meant the cars were lighter than their rivals at the start of a race, giving improved early pace and tyre longevity that allowed Benetton to run non-stop when others needed new rubber.

Benetton began the year with updated B189B cars that featured new wings and a revised undertray. Piquet scored points in Phoenix and Interlagos but Nannini finished both races outside the top six.

Nannini tested the new B190 at Silverstone before the start of the

Nelson Piquet, Benetton B189B-Ford (United States GP)

European season. With Benetton's 'active' suspension programme cancelled, chief designer Rory Byrne opted for push-rod suspension all round, replacing the B189B's pull-rod front. Dave Wass was responsible for the suspension and revisions to the six-speed gearbox. The B189 had been overly sensitive so particular attention was paid to the aerodynamics with an unusual rear diffuser that curled upwards at the exit. A high airbox replaced the side intakes and a new monocoque was required due to altered cockpit regulations.

Three B190s were sent to Imola, where Nannini recovered from a heavy crash at Tamburello on Friday to finish third, setting the fastest lap as he withstood Alain Prost's late pressure. Piquet spun when he clashed with Tyrrell's Jean Alesi early in the race and finished fifth

Alessandro Nannini, Benetton B189B-Ford (United States GP)

Nelson Piquet, Benetton B190-Ford (Australian GP)

despite evil handling thereafter. Neither finished at Monaco, where Piquet was black-flagged after being push-started following a spin at the Loews Hairpin. With the B190 improving with every race, Nannini led during the pitstops in Canada only to hit a luckless groundhog that damaged a front wing and punctured a tyre. While Nannini crashed during his subsequent recovery drive, Piquet passed Prost's Ferrari to claim second and stand on the podium for the first time since 1988. Fourth in Mexico, Nannini lost a podium finish in France when the engine failed with five laps to go. Piquet ran second in Mexico before changing tyres and inherited fourth in France following Nannini's late demise.

An upgraded Series IV version of Cosworth's HB engine, with revised electronics and new internals, was raced for the first time at Silverstone, where Piquet snatched fifth on the penultimate lap. Nannini was mighty at Hockenheim despite crashing on Friday afternoon: he charged from ninth on the grid to lead for 16 laps when Ayrton Senna pitted and went on to finish second, splitting the McLaren-Hondas after running non-stop with a broken exhaust and worn tyres. Nannini was unlucky not to do even better in Hungary, where he challenged for the lead before being hit when an overly optimistic Senna tried to take second, while Piquet finished third despite an electrical issue and moment on the grass.

Both scored points at Spa-Francorchamps, where the non-stopping Nannini briefly challenged Senna for the lead, but lack

Alessandro Nannini, Benetton B190-Ford (Italian GP)

Roberto Moreno, Benetton B190-Ford (Australian GP)

of grip forced him wide at Eau Rouge with three laps to go and he dropped to fourth as a consequence. Pointless after a troubled Italian GP, both drivers were unable to make their tyres last in Portugal, where they lay fifth (Piquet) and sixth (Nannini) when the race was stopped. The B190 was better suited to Jerez and Piquet led during the pitstops before his engine misfired, which promoted Nannini to third. The popular Italian had already re-signed for 1991 but this proved to be his last GP: shortly after, on 12 October, his right arm was severed below the elbow in a helicopter accident near his parents' house at Bellosguardo.

Despite that setback, Benetton finished the year on a high with Roberto Moreno, a great friend of Piquet, replacing Nannini for the last two races. They benefited from the first-corner accident at Suzuka with Piquet leading an emotional Moreno in a joyous 1–2 finish. Piquet took full advantage when Senna crashed in Australia to win a second successive GP. That late-season success earned Piquet a share of third in the championship with Benetton-Ford also third in the constructors' standings.

CANON WILLIAMS TEAM

Championship runners-up in 1989, Williams and Renault now aimed to build on that promising first season together. Thierry Boutsen was in the final year of his contract but the team delayed taking up Riccardo Patrese's option, which expired on 31 August 1989, while courting Alain Prost. When the Frenchman eventually chose Ferrari,

Williams's driver line-up remained unchanged.

Patrick Head and his team modified the 1989 car as the FW13B with longer sidepods, revised bodywork and new rear wing. The push-rod front suspension had the rockers mounted higher and the pull-rod rear was also modified. New mono-shock front suspension with single transverse damper was tried at the Silverstone FOCA test and in subsequent practice sessions but was not raced. The FW13Bs' pace fluctuated from circuit to circuit and tyre wear was an issue.

Bernard Dudot's engine department at Viry-Châtillon introduced the new RS02 version of its 67-degree V10 engine which was 9lb lighter than its predecessor and now gear-driven. The alternator and oil filter were moved to reduce its length and height by 20in and 6in respectively, improving weight distribution and lowering the centre of gravity. It had plenty of torque and a smooth power curve but lacked the ultimate top-end power of Honda or Ferrari.

Boutsen began 1990 by finishing third in Phoenix (despite his engine cutting out) and fifth in Brazil when delayed by a slow pitstop. Having lost his nosecone against the back of Olivier Grouillard's Osella-Ford on lap one in Phoenix and denied fourth by late engine failure in Brazil, Patrese ended his seven-year winless streak with a finely judged victory at Imola, where Boutsen led but blew his engine by selecting the wrong gear. Boutsen was fourth in Monaco and challenged for a podium in Montréal before crashing into Nicola Larini's Ligier-Ford.

Larger water radiators were fitted for the Mexican GP, where Patrese qualified on the front row but chose tyres that were too

Thierry Boutsen, Williams FW13B-Renault (Japanese GP)

Riccardo Patrese, Williams FW13B-Renault (Monaco GP)

hard and finished ninth after a spin, with Boutsen a distant fifth. Patrese was sixth in France, having led during the pitstops, and became the first driver to start 200 GPs next time out at Silverstone only to be punted out of the race when hit by Alessandro Nannini. Under pressure to retain his place in the team, Boutsen survived blistered tyres to finish second at Silverstone and set the fastest lap in Germany, where both cars scored.

Recently fired by Leyton House, Adrian Newey arrived at the end of July and new aero parts were available at just about every subsequent race as he improved the FW13B. There was a new undertray in Germany that Newey further revised for Hungary, where Boutsen and Patrese qualified 1–2. Running non-stop at the Hungaroring, the Belgian withstood pressure throughout to lead from start to finish and beat Ayrton Senna by 0.288sec, with Patrese fourth. Both retired by half-distance in Belgium, Boutsen having run third, and Patrese finished fifth in Italy.

Patrese had a messy Portuguese GP weekend. Frank Williams and mechanic Len Jones were hurt when Patrese's car caught fire in the pits on Saturday, and the Italian then set the fastest lap as he recovered to finish seventh following a botched pitstop, spin and unscheduled second stop. Boutsen retired from the third GP in a row. Patrese set further fastest laps in Spain and Japan and both drivers scored points at the final three races of the season, albeit without challenging for victory. Boutsen and Patrese ended up sixth and seventh in the final standings while Williams-Renault slipped to fourth in the constructors' championship.

TYRRELL RACING ORGANISATION

Jean Alesi further enhanced his reputation as Tyrrell's resurgence continued, with an innovative new design from engineering director Harvey Postlethwaite and aerodynamicist Jean-Claude Migeot. Satoru Nakajima brought much-needed sponsorship from Epson and PIAA with his two-year contract announced at the Tokyo Motor Show in October 1989. The Tyrrell 019, a development of the 018, was most notable for its raised nose and low front wings, the result of work in Southampton University's wind tunnel. 'Aerodynamically, the car is very different,' Migeot explained at launch. '[The] anhedral wing concept… gives us a step forward in increased aerodynamic efficiency and handling characteristics.' Push-rod suspension was retained with a single damper at the front. The Ford Cosworth DFR V8 lacked power but this was a compact and nimble car that handled very well. Alesi had the benefit of Brian Hart's development unit, which produced 625bhp, while Nakajima's engines were prepared by Langford & Peck. Tyrrell signed a two-year contract with Pirelli tyres so late that the team had not even tested the Italian rubber before the first race.

With Brabham in turmoil, Sergio Rinland joined the technical department on the eve of the season but left after just three weeks when the Chessington team's participation was confirmed. He was replaced by EuroBrun's George Ryton. Ken Tyrrell remained as chairman with his son Bob having day-to-day responsibilities as managing director. Joan Villadelprat arrived from Ferrari as team manager and Tyrrell hired the independent TAG/McLaren Marketing Services to assist with sponsorship acquisition.

Jean Alesi, Tyrrell 018-Ford (United States GP)

Satoru Nakajima, Tyrrell 018-Ford (Brazilian GP)

With the 019 due for the start of the European season, Tyrrell arrived in Phoenix with three old 018s. Alesi qualified fourth, took the lead after a blistering start and led Ayrton Senna's McLaren-Honda for 34 glorious laps. When Senna finally got past, Alesi briefly retook the position before settling for a fine second place. Nakajima, who had a heavy testing shunt at Jerez on 15 February, finished sixth to complete a great day. Alesi collided with Andrea de Cesaris at the start of the Brazilian GP and lost sixth to Nelson Piquet's more powerful Benetton-Ford on the last lap. Nakajima dented local hopes when he crashed into race leader Senna while being lapped.

Nakajima wrote off the original 019 in another sizable accident on the opening lap of the San Marino GP but Alesi's new 019 finished sixth despite colliding with Piquet. In another eye-catching display, Alesi used the new car's impeccable handling to qualify third and finish second in Monaco. Now third in the championship, it seemed inconceivable that the occasionally over-aggressive Alesi would not score another point all year. There were spectacular performances such as running third in Canada and Italy and qualifying fourth in Spain but luck normally deserted him on Sundays and there were too many accidents. He crashed into Alessandro Nannini's stationary Benetton-Ford in Canada, collided with Pierluigi Martini's Minardi while lapping him in Hungary, spun out of third at Monza, clashed with Gerhard Berger's McLaren at the start in Spain and missed the Japanese GP through whiplash suffered in a head-on crash during Friday qualifying. A misfiring seventh in Mexico was Alesi's best result after Monaco.

Nakajima suffered a barren mid-season run with a lacklustre 11th

Jean Alesi, Tyrrell 019-Ford (Australian GP)

Satoru Nakajima, Tyrrell 019-Ford (Mexican GP)

LEYTON HOUSE RACING

Property tycoon Akira Akagi acquired the Bicester-based March F1 team in May 1989 and renamed it Leyton House. Technical director Adrian Newey did not waver from his design principles despite a disappointing 1989 season and the start to the new campaign was even more difficult.

Ivan Capelli and Maurício Gugelmin re-signed for a third successive season. Arrows chief mechanic Harry Mendel joined as team manager only to be replaced in May by Charlie Moody, who had been running the test team. Managing director Ian Phillips contracted viral meningitis at the Brazilian GP and was off work for five months so finance director Simon Keeble took temporary control. No longer in charge when well enough to return in August, Phillips left after the final race of 1990 as politics permeated this once unified team.

Gustav Brunner joined in October 1989 and immediately redesigned the CG891's front suspension to improve traction. These changes were incorporated into the new Leyton House CG901, which had a new monocoque and exhausts that exited above a rear diffuser with five arches rather than three. John Judd's narrow 78-degree EV V8 engines were retained with a development version from Rochdale-based Scott Russell Engines tested. Newey used the one-third scale wind tunnel at Southampton University to develop the car's aerodynamics but this data did not correlate with findings from Leyton House's own facility in Brackley.

The CG901 had pronounced understeer and a dire lack of grip at the start of the year as both drivers struggled. Gugelmin did not

in Mexico a rare finish but finally scored a point with a steady sixth after a race of attrition in Italy. Affected by 'flu, he did not start the Portuguese GP after crashing in the warm-up but returned to claim another sixth in Japan.

Alesi's early form meant that Tyrrell-Ford finished fifth overall for a second successive season, although much of the campaign was overshadowed by discussions about the Frenchman's future. Under contract with Tyrrell until the end of 1991, F1's hottest property nonetheless signed a two-year contract with Williams on 2 February. By mid-season, he had decided to replace Nigel Mansell at Ferrari if he could negotiate his release from Tyrrell and sort out the Williams situation. The matter was resolved on 18 September when Tyrrell announced that Alesi would be joining Ferrari in 1991.

Maurício Gugelmin, Leyton House CG901-Judd (United States GP)

Ivan Capelli, Leyton House CG901-Judd (French GP)

qualify for four of the opening six races with Capelli joining him on the sidelines in Brazil and Mexico. Furthermore, the Italian wrote off a new chassis during testing on 3 May at Imola when he barrel-rolled at Piratella corner due to a mechanical failure. His tenth place in Canada, when lapped three times, was the team's best finish during this desperate time.

The wind tunnel problem was narrowed down to an anomaly in Southampton and, having identified the problem, Newey redesigned the undertray, diffuser (with lower arches) and sidepods for the French GP. With pre-qualifying an ever-more-likely prospect, there were wholesale changes in the design department in the week before that race. Newey was dismissed and Tim Holloway returned to the March Group he had originally joined in 1975. Having flown to Japan to meet Akagi, Lola's Chris Murphy replaced Newey as technical director. 'Adrian was very good at aerodynamics but Chris is more of an all-rounder,' Keeble told *Autosport*'s Joe Saward at Paul Ricard. Newey later told *The Guardian* in 2011, 'I was fired but I'd already made up my mind I was going – because once a team gets run by an accountant, it's time to move.'

Although the stiffly sprung CG901 remained overly sensitive at bumpier tracks, Newey's changes transformed it at super-smooth Paul Ricard. After qualifying seventh and tenth, Capelli and Gugelmin chose to race non-stop and *Motor Sport*'s Denis Jenkinson feared sunstroke when they ran 1–2 as rivals pitted for new rubber. Alain Prost (Ferrari) finally passed Gugelmin, whose engine then failed in front of the pits, but Capelli, incredibly, led for 45 laps before a fuel pick-up problem slowed him and allowed Prost to snatch victory with three laps to go. The exhausted Capelli held off Ayrton Senna's closing McLaren to retain second place, giving the team its first points since the opening race of 1989.

While Gugelmin did not start the British GP because of fuel pump failure before the formation lap, Capelli, with his car handling beautifully, lay third when he had to drop out with 15 laps to go. He was seventh in Germany and Belgium but retired from the remaining races, losing a points finish at Monza to engine failure. Eighth following a spin in Hungary, Gugelmin adopted a non-stop strategy to finish sixth at Spa-Francorchamps and score his only point of 1990. Paul Ricard apart, this had been another troubled campaign for the turquoise cars.

CAMEL TEAM LOTUS

Twelve years had passed since Lotus last won the World Championship and the team had been in decline since Ayrton Senna's departure at the end of 1987. When Peter Warr left in 1989, the Chapman family appointed Tony Rudd as executive chairman, with Colin Chapman's son Clive as his assistant. Lotus responded to its underwhelming 1989 season with new engines and drivers but the colours remained the same. At a press conference during the 1989 Italian GP weekend, W. Duncan Lee, director of sponsorships for R.J. Reynolds, announced a one-year extension to Camel's sponsorship, with power coming from Mauro Forghieri's Lamborghini 3512 engine, the 80-degree V12 that had been used exclusively by Larrousse in 1989.

Nelson Piquet left on the expiry of his lucrative two-year contract and Satoru Nakajima took his backing to Tyrrell, to be replaced by Derek Warwick and former test driver Martin Donnelly. Johnny Herbert signed as reserve driver in January. Chief designer Mike Coughlan left in the spring with Frank Coppuck, nephew of Gordon Coppuck, his replacement.

The first engine was delivered to Hethel in September and Warwick and Donnelly tested it in the back of a converted Lotus 101 at Snetterton on 13–14 November. Technical director Frank Dernie described the new Lotus 102 as 'an evolutionary progression on last year's car' when it was launched in February, adding, 'We've tried to keep the strong points of the 101 and delete the weak ones.' The carbon-fibre/Nomex monocoque was revised with higher sides to accommodate its taller drivers. The wheelbase was extended by just 2in despite the length of the V12, thanks to the transverse six-speed gearbox which had Lamborghini internals and a Lotus casing. Pull-rod front/push-rod rear suspension was retained. The engine was heavier and thirstier than the Judd so a higher and much wider fuel tank was required – and weight was an issue.

Warwick's unstinting optimism immediately lifted the team's morale only for the pre-season feel-good factor to wane. The 102 was a handful, especially in fast corners, due to a chronic lack of grip and chassis flex. The gearbox was unreliable and Forghieri's advice regarding the oil capacity required for his engine initially went unheeded. That led to two engine failures on the first day of testing at Estoril and the 4-litre oil tanks had to be enlarged before the first race. The monocoque and gearbox casing were eventually stiffened and a new arched diffuser used by Warwick in Canada was adopted on both cars thereafter.

Two 102s and a spare 101B were sent to Phoenix for a troubled weekend that saw Donnelly left on the dummy grid and Warwick eliminated after just six laps, then both retired in Brazil. The oil system was further revised and front aerodynamics improved for Imola, where they finished in an improved seventh (Warwick) and eighth (Donnelly), the latter having recovered from spinning at Tosa on lap one. Warwick lost fifth in Monaco when he spun in the closing stages as his brakes snatched before surviving a similar problem and loose undertray to claim sixth in Canada.

Both finished outside the points at the next two races, with understeer adding to the woes in France, and suffered double

Derek Warwick, Lotus 102-Lamborghini (Monaco GP)

engine failure at Silverstone as rumours of the team's sale and Camel's dissatisfaction circulated. Eighth in Germany, Warwick responded to news that Camel would spend its money elsewhere in 1991 by finishing a lonely fifth in Hungary, with Donnelly seventh.

They collided at the first start in Belgium before crashes punctuated the next three races. Warwick survived a huge accident exiting the Parabolica at the end of lap one of the Italian GP and earned the applause of the *tifosi* by crawling from the wreckage and running to the pits to take the spare car for the restart. Donnelly was not so lucky at Jerez. Having re-signed for Lotus in the morning,

his car was shattered in a 140mph accident behind the pits during Friday qualifying. The Ulsterman was thrown into the middle of the track still strapped to his seat and only quick trackside treatment saved his life. Herbert replaced Donnelly for the last two races but neither Lotus finished them following yet more mechanical failures.

Lotus-Lamborghini were eighth in the constructors' standings after a dispiriting campaign. The cost of failure was already apparent: Camel's announcement in Hungary was compounded when Lamborghini terminated its engine supply for 1991. Team Lotus was on the brink of extinction.

Martin Donnelly, Lotus 102-Lamborghini (Belgian GP)

Johnny Herbert, Lotus 102-Lamborghini (Australian GP)

Bernd Schneider, Arrows A11-Ford (United States GP)

Alex Caffi, Arrows A11B-Ford (Canadian GP)

FOOTWORK ARROWS RACING

Arrows restructured its management team during the winter of 1989/90 following the team's sale to Wataru Ohashi's Footwork Corporation by Jackie Oliver and Alan Rees, who remained as managing director and team principal respectively. They were joined on the board by Footwork's Yoshihiko Nagata and John Wickham, who had managed the company's F3000 operation. In addition to Footwork's red-and-white colours, USF&G Asset Management and Camozzi remained as secondary sponsors. At the team's official presentation in Tokyo on 5 February, Ohashi revealed an exclusive four-year contract for Porsche engines from 1991 at a reputed cost of $35 million.

In the meantime, James Robinson updated Ross Brawn's existing chassis as the Arrows A11B with tall central fuel tank, revised aerodynamics and new suspension. Brian Hart prepared the old-fashioned Ford DFR V8 engines. Alan Jenkins joined from Onyx before the Canadian GP as the new technical director, with Robinson now reporting to him. Unfortunately, the A11B lacked low-speed grip and Arrows even struggled to qualify at some circuits, including double DNQs at Imola and Adelaide. New wings and aerodynamics were tried during the season following wind tunnel work at Southampton University and Cranfield but to no avail.

With the departures of Derek Warwick and Eddie Cheever, Michele Alboreto was confirmed as team leader in September but failed to rebuild his reputation. When he finished races, he struggled to break into the top ten, and was also unable to qualify for the Monaco GP. A lapped ninth in Portugal was his best result and there were tenth places in Phoenix, France and Spain.

Michele Alboreto, Arrows A11B-Ford (Japanese GP)

It was a surprise when Arrows paid highly rated Alex Caffi's Scuderia Italia release clause and announced him as Alboreto's team-mate on 22 November 1989. Paul Warwick, Gregor Foitek and Bertrand Gachot had all tested on Silverstone's south circuit on 10 October and the well-backed Satoru Nakajima had also been in the frame before he chose Tyrrell. Caffi's season began badly when he broke his collarbone in a cycling accident just before the opening round in Phoenix so Osella reserve Bernd Schneider stood in, driving a 1989-specification A11. The German struggled to fit in the cockpit, crashed in the wet Saturday session and collided with Alessandro Nannini at the first corner.

Caffi returned in Brazil, where he retired through exhaustion, followed by non-qualification at Imola. He raised moods somewhat by finishing fifth in a race of attrition in Monaco, lapped twice and with only one other finisher behind him. Thereafter he out-raced Alboreto and scored eight top-ten finishes but also failed to qualify in Mexico and Australia. He sprained his left ankle in the crash with Aguri Suzuki that stopped the Portuguese GP and was not fit for the following week's race in Spain, where Schneider again deputised but crashed on Friday morning and did not qualify.

MOTOR RACING DEVELOPMENTS (BRABHAM)

Brabham's winter was spent amid legal dispute and seeking new owners. Representing the McKeever Group, former Onyx Grand Prix men Mike Earle and Jo Chamberlain plus businessman Romeo

Gregor Foitek, Brabham BT58-Judd (United States GP)

Casola were placed in control in the New Year only to be dismissed a month later by Brabham's Swiss owners. The team's future remained in doubt throughout the close season. Talks with Kohji Nakauchi's Middlebridge Group began in November 1989 and were finally concluded on 5 March, just four days before first practice in Phoenix.

With the team in disarray, chief designer Sergio Rinland switched to Tyrrell only to return three weeks later once Middlebridge's take-over was completed. Team manager Dave Stubbs left to run Paul Stewart Racing's new F3000 operation. Brabham exercised options on both Martin Brundle and Stefano Modena at the 1989 United States GP although Brundle moved to Tom Walkinshaw's sports cars operation instead. Bernd Schneider could not agree terms and Gregor Foitek outbid Luis Pérez Sala to sign a two-race deal on 15 February.

Stefano Modena, Brabham BT58-Judd (United States GP)

David Brabham, Brabham BT59-Judd (Australian GP)

Tim Densham arrived from Lotus as Modena's race engineer.

Brabham's reprieve only came after the FOCA freight had departed for Phoenix so sporting director Herbie Blash arranged alternative transport for three Brabham BT58-Judd CV V8s and agreed a tyre contract with Pirelli in the paddock. The unsponsored cars arrived on Thursday, Modena qualified tenth on Saturday and finished fifth on Sunday. 'It's absolutely fantastic to have scored points,' was his post-race reaction, 'I was just happy to be here.' Foitek crashed heavily after hitting Olivier Grouillard during that race and both Brabham drivers retired from the Brazilian GP.

Despite Rinland's brief absence, the new Brabham BT59 was ready for the Imola test at the beginning of May. This interim car was

Stefano Modena, Brabham BT59-Judd (Hungarian GP)

described as a 'BT58½' with the old longitudinal gearbox and pull-rod rear suspension initially retained under extended rear bodywork. A new six-speed transverse gearbox, push-rod rear suspension and Penske dampers were introduced on the spare car in France and gradually used thereafter, forming the definitive BT59. The new gearbox proved unreliable and several selector variations were tried before the old longitudinal units were refitted for the final race. Power now came from the newer 78-degree Judd EV V8 that Leyton House had used exclusively in 1989. Smaller than its predecessor, the BT59 featured a slender airbox with horizontal inlet that was reminiscent of the Williams FW13. The fuel tank was lower and squatter than before and half-length sidepods housed two water radiators in the left and oil to the right.

Modena suffered brake issues and spun during the San Marino GP and was an early retirement in Monaco. Increasingly frustrated as the season progressed, he managed only two top-ten results in the BT59, seventh in Canada and ninth after a spin at Silverstone. With Foitek's short-term deal expired, Sir Jack Brabham was at Chessington on 30 April for the announcement of his third son David as the Swiss driver's replacement from Imola. 'It's almost unbelievable to have another Brabham in a Brabham,' the three-time champion said. 'I'm very excited.' Unfortunately, David Brabham failed to qualify six times and finished just once when 15th in France, as he struggled with uncompetitive machinery and having to learn many of the circuits.

Money was in short supply during 1990 and a delay in acquiring the Chessington factory saw them briefly locked out in the summer.

ESPO LARROUSSE F1 (LOLA)

Bolstered by recent investment from Kazuo Ito's ESPO Group, Larrousse renewed its contracts with Lola and Lamborghini and continuity was rewarded with the best season in the team's history. Lamborghini's Mauro Forghieri concentrated on improving the bulky V12 engine's reliability over the winter. Larrousse opted for youth when it confirmed Éric Bernard and Aguri Suzuki, and they began 1990 driving little-changed Lola LC89s in Phoenix, where the Frenchman finished eighth despite a spin, and at Interlagos.

Lola designer Chris Murphy admitted that the new Lola 90-Lamborghini was 'a logical development of the 1989 chassis' when it was introduced at the Imola test in April. The front wing and exhausts were revised, airbox and radiators were new and the gearbox was redesigned to save weight. The fuel tank was an inch longer so capacity for the thirsty V12 could be increased. Digital instruments were introduced on the fifth chassis to be built.

After being blighted by teething troubles at Imola, Bernard came from the penultimate row to finish sixth in Monaco, having barged past Gregor Foitek's Onyx at the chicane in the closing stages. Bernard was ninth in Canada despite bruising from a practice accident and another robust duel with Foitek. A retiree at the first four races, Suzuki finally finished a race that weekend, albeit delayed by changing his front wing following contact with Pierluigi Martini's Minardi at the start.

Éric Bernard, Lola LC89-Lamborghini (United States GP)

Aguri Suzuki, Lola LC89-Lamborghini (United States GP)

Aguri Suzuki, Lola 90-Lamborghini (Australian GP)

Éric Bernard, Lola 90-Lamborghini (British GP)

fourth on Friday morning at the Hungaroring, the brakeless Bernard scored another point thanks to finishing sixth. A slow pitstop restricted him to ninth in Belgium and he retired from the remaining five championship rounds.

Having crashed with Alex Caffi to trigger the red flag in Portugal and finished sixth at Jerez, the increasingly impressive Suzuki sent the Suzuka locals into delirium by surviving a race of attrition to claim third, and become the first Japanese driver to score an F1 podium finish. Both retired in Australia in a downbeat finale as Larrousse nonetheless claimed sixth in the constructors' standings. That success proved short-lived for FISA stripped the team of its 1990 constructors' points in the spring due to an administrative error stating that Larrousse, rather than Lola, had built the cars.

Both retired early in Mexico, Suzuki having been hit by compatriot Satoru Nakajima, but they finished seventh and eighth in France. Normally the fastest pre-qualifiers so far, Larrousse escaped that unwanted session with a fine double result at Silverstone: eighth on the grid, Bernard passed Nelson Piquet's Benetton on the penultimate lap to snatch fourth while Suzuki recovered from a puncture to score his first point with sixth place. Rocked by Murphy's defection to Leyton House, neither Lola-Lamborghini finished in Germany as Suzuki began a four-race run of DNFs that included crashing during the warm-up and into Piquet at the original start of the Belgian GP. A surprise

ÉQUIPE LIGIER GITANES

Guy Ligier announced an all-new driving line-up on 16 November 1989 after René Arnoux's retirement and the release of Olivier Grouillard despite the two years left on his contract. Philippe Alliot returned following a partial season in 1986 and Ferrari-contracted Nicola Larini preferred Ligier to Scuderia Italia. A karting world champion in 1988, teenager Emmanuel Collard signed a two-year contract as test driver. State-owned sponsorship continued from Gitanes, LOTO and Elf.

Claude Galopin returned after spells with GDBA and AGS to

Nicola Larini, Ligier JS33B-Ford (Italian GP)

Philippe Alliot, Ligier JS33B-Ford (Italian GP)

engineer Alliot's car but efforts to hire Chris Murphy as technical director were unsuccessful. With state-of-the-art facilities at the Magny-Cours base, Richard Divila updated the 1989 design as the JS33B with almost 80lb saved. Ford DFR V8 engines were retained and push-rod front suspension revised. New rear suspension (also push-rod/double wishbone), sidepods and nose were all part of a major upgrade at Imola. A new transverse gearbox was introduced in practice for the British GP and raced from the Italian GP following an extensive development programme.

Both drivers set promising times during pre-season testing but Larini's winter was interrupted by a bout of chicken pox and a couple of nasty accidents. He lost control on oil in Paul Ricard's high-speed Signes corner before Christmas and suffered suspension failure at Estoril in February, both without injury.

Ligier struggled from the start with Alliot excluded in Phoenix after a mechanic crossed the track during qualifying following a crash. The Frenchman lined up a season-best tenth at Interlagos but both cars finished outside the points in that race and the next, Alliot ninth at Imola. Ligier's heavy testing schedule resulted in a new front wing at Monaco where both suffered gearbox failure and another double retirement followed in Montréal.

Larini finished every remaining race of the season without scoring, seventh in Spain and Japan his best results. Twelfth on the grid in Australia, he recovered from a spin to record his seventh top-ten finish of a consistent if disappointing campaign. Alliot was ninth in France, disqualified for a push start in Germany and did not qualify in Belgium. Having suffered a high-speed shunt with Andrea de Cesaris (Dallara) during Portuguese practice, Alliot then crashed following contact with race leader Nigel Mansell. He spun out of the Spanish GP, crashed twice during Japanese qualifying and was a lapped finisher in the last two races of the year.

Ligier's pointless first half of 1990 led to both of its cars having to pre-qualify in Germany and Hungary, the team finishing 1–2 in both sessions before Monteverdi's closure ended that early-Friday chore for the rest of the year. Alliot shaded his team-mate in qualifying but crashed too often, whereas Larini had a strong finishing record (13 of 16 races). But neither driver scored a point and both were released at the end of the season.

SCM MINARDI TEAM

Pierluigi Martini signed a one-year contract extension on 19 September 1989 and former reserve driver Paolo Barilla was preferred to Marco Apicella as his team-mate. Aldo Costa remained as technical director but aerodynamicist Nigel Cowperthwaite left before the start of the season. The Englishman was replaced by René Hilhorst, a professor at the École Nationale Supérieure de l'Aéronautque et l'Espace in Toulouse.

Minardi decided against using Carlo Chiti's bulky flat-12 Subaru engine after testing was blighted by poor reliability so Heini Mader-prepared Ford DFR V8s were ordered. Three Minardi M189s were sent to Phoenix and Interlagos, including a brand-new chassis with modified front suspension for Martini. He used Pirelli's sticky rubber to qualify in a shock second place in America but made a poor start and faded to seventh by the finish. Braking issues restricted him to ninth in Brazil. Barilla struggled to fit in the M189 and retired from both races.

Costa and Vincenzo Emiliani aimed for improved rigidity with the new Minardi M190, which Martini tested at Imola in April. The monocoque, engine mountings, gearbox casing, bodywork and wings were all new while, as was the fashion at the time, push-rod suspension was retained. After the promise of the M189, the M190 proved an unreliable disappointment due to poor straight-line speed and pronounced understeer.

Barilla did not qualify six times during the European season and

Pierluigi Martini, Minardi M189-Ford (Brazilian GP)

Paolo Barilla, Minardi M189-Ford (United States GP)

Pierluigi Martini, Minardi M190-Ford (Australian GP)

Paolo Barilla, Minardi M190-Ford (Mexican GP)

Gianni Morbidelli, Minardi M190-Ford (Australian GP)

only started the San Marino GP when Martini withdrew following a huge accident at Acque Minerali on Friday. Barilla was dropped for the last two races after a run of three successive DNQs. His replacement was Ferrari reserve Gianni Morbidelli, who spun out of the Japanese GP and broke his gearbox in Australia.

Test driver Apicella was placed on standby for the Monaco GP in case Martini did not recover from heel injuries suffered at Imola. Martini was fit enough to qualify eighth on his return in Monaco and seventh in Mexico but he rarely finished when hindered by the durability of Pirelli's race tyre. In addition to mechanical woes, Martini was hit by Aguri Suzuki at the start in Canada and by Jean Alesi while being lapped in Hungary. He suffered whiplash in Spain when he crashed into David Brabham during qualifying but completed the season with top-ten finishes in Japan and Australia.

Although Martini had begun 1990 from the front row, neither he nor his team scored a point all year.

FONDMETAL OSELLA

Enzo Osella secured his small team's immediate future by selling 51 per cent to title sponsor Fondmetal Wheels in November 1989. Majority shareholder Gabriele Rumi confirmed a singleton entry for the combative Olivier Grouillard, who tested at Vallelunga and Jerez during the winter. Bernd Schneider signed as reserve driver in February when Zakspeed quit F1. Mader continued to prepare the Ford DFR V8 engines at the start of the year although Osella later switched to Tickford units.

Olivier Grouillard, Osella FA1Me-Ford (Australian GP)

Grouillard had a pair of old Osella FA1M-Fords to choose from at the opening two races of the season. He used Pirelli qualifiers to start the United States GP from an unrepresentative eighth on the grid – Osella's best-ever qualifying performance. Unfortunately, Grouillard crashed into Riccardo Patrese and then Gregor Foitek in Phoenix and Michele Alboreto in Brazil, breaking his suspension during both races.

Technical director Antonio Tomaini's new Osella FA1Me was introduced at Imola. Unaltered behind the driver, it had its front shock absorbers now mounted on top of the monocoque with sidepods shorter and higher than before. Gradual developments included a taller airbox in Monaco, revised rear suspension and slightly raised front wings from Montréal and new exhausts and undertray at Silverstone. This evolutionary car proved a handful and Grouillard failed to qualify in Monaco as driveshaft failures halted progress. Last in Canada and Mexico, he failed to pre-qualify in France and Hungary and did not qualify for either the British or German GPs.

A new diffuser was introduced at the Belgian GP with the sidepods and radiators reduced in size. The changes seemed to work as he qualified for the next two races and finished 16th (and last) at Spa-Francorchamps. A non-qualifier when deprived of Pirelli's newest compound in Portugal and following mechanical issues in Japan, he made the field in Australia only to be criticised as 'a mobile chicane' while being lapped on the way to another last-place finish, seven laps behind after two tyre stops. Osella failed to score a championship point for the sixth successive season.

Olivier Grouillard, Osella FA1M-Ford (United States GP)

BMS SCUDERIA ITALIA (DALLARA)

Beppe Lucchini's BMS Scuderia Italia planned to keep an unchanged driver line-up for the new season. Andrea de Cesaris remained for a second season and it was thought that Alex Caffi would stay, only for the promising youngster to sign for Footwork Arrows instead. Bertand Gachot was considered before Emanuele Pirro was announced in January. Team manager Patrizio Cantú left to form the Crypton Engineering F3000 team and was replaced by Pierpaolo Gardella, formerly Marco Piccinini's assistant at Ferrari. Mario Tolentino moved to Lamborghini so Christian Vanderpleyn joined Gian Paolo Dallara's design department on 7 December 1989. That did not last long for Vanderpleyn returned to Coloni at the Canadian GP.

The new Dallara F190 was revealed on 29 January in a vineyard

Andrea de Cesaris, Dallara F190-Ford (German GP)

Gianni Morbidelli, Dallara F190-Ford (United States GP)

Emanuele Pirro, Dallara F190-Ford (San Marino GP)

at Monticelli Brusati, near the team's Brescia base. It had a new monocoque and push-rod suspension was now employed at the front with pull-rods to the rear. Heini Mader continued to prepare the Ford DFR V8 engines and Pirelli supplied the tyres. After the relative promise of F189, the F190 was unreliable, slow in a straight line and handled badly in fast corners. Scuderia Italia sunk without a trace and did not score a point all season.

Although de Cesaris used Pirelli qualifiers to line up third for the opening race in Phoenix, he only finished twice, 13th in Mexico and 10th in Italy (having held up second-placed Alain Prost while being lapped). His engine failed when running fifth in the United States and

he crashed into Jean Alesi at the start of the Brazilian GP. De Cesaris injured his wrist during practice in Monte Carlo but ran as high as sixth before the throttle linkage broke. His underweight car was disqualified from 15th in France and he even failed to qualify for the German GP. He spun when the throttle stuck open on the opening lap in Portugal and without excuse in Japan.

Pirro missed the first two races due to hepatitis so was replaced by débutant Gianni Morbidelli, who failed to qualify following a couple of crashes in America and was last in Brazil having lost five laps in the pits. Pirro returned at Imola but had an equally frustrating season, retiring from all but three races, tenth in Hungary his best result. He did qualify an excellent ninth in Monaco but could not take the restart as his engine refused to fire. He crashed into Michele Alboreto's Arrows in Canada, exited the French GP in a wild spin when his brake disc shattered on the main straight, was concussed in the start-line pile-up in Germany, spun out of the Italian GP, and dislocated his finger in a practice shunt in Japan. It had been a bruising campaign from team and drivers alike.

AUTOMOBILES GONFARONAISE SPORTIVE (AGS)

'It was a miserable season for AGS,' Nigel Roebuck wrote in *Autosport*'s review of the year, 'who ran two of the prettiest cars in the business, but also two of the slowest.'

The season began with some optimism as majority shareholder Cyril de Rouvre sought to stabilise matters and reorganise. The team moved from Gonfaron to the nearby refurbished Circuit du Var. AGS used its factory opening in February to announce the Ted Lapidus fashion company as its new title sponsor. At the same time, Hugues de Chaunac and Claude Rouelle arrived from perennial French F3 champions ORECA as sporting director and research and development chief respectively, but both had quit by the end of June. Michel Costa returned following a brief sojourn at Coloni while Henri Cochin assumed team manager duties. AGS founder Henri Julien and former driver Philippe Streiff were retained as consultants while drivers Gabriele Tarquini and Yannick Dalmas remained despite the travails of 1989. Heini Mader was entrusted with preparation of the Ford Cosworth DFR V8 engines.

AGS began 1990 with the heavy old JH24 chassis fitted with new front suspension that featured a single centrally mounted damper. Neither driver pre-qualified in Phoenix but Dalmas bumped Tarquini on Friday morning in Brazil and then qualified last for AGS's first start since the 1989 French GP. He retired when his suspension failed, the legacy of contact with Aguri Suzuki in the warm-up.

Costa's compact new AGS JH25-Ford was launched at Paul Ricard before the end of April. It retained the mono-shock front suspension, push-rod suspension all round, a thin 'needle' nose, and diminutive sidepods that tapered to the rear. The six-speed Hewland gearbox was fitted longitudinally and plans for a transverse unit were shelved. Sadly, the JH25 proved no more competitive and neither AGS pre-qualified at the next four races, Dalmas missing the San Marino GP meeting entirely after injuring his hand in a testing shunt at Imola.

With former Leyton House March engineer Peter Wyss now

with the team, both cars made it through pre-qualifying in France, where Dalmas scraped into the field and finished 17th, five laps down. Tarquini finally qualified for two of the next three races, his first GP starts for over a year. A revised floor and diffuser were introduced at Monza as AGS's fortunes marginally improved. Dalmas qualified for the next three races and in Spain he finished ninth, a result that meant AGS did not have to pre-qualify at the start of 1991. Tarquini ended three successive DNQs to line up 22nd (a season best for AGS) for the Spanish GP but crashed into Stefano Modena's Brabham after five laps; that Dalmas also qualified at Jerez prompted champagne in the AGS garage. Neither driver made the grade at Suzuka and Dalmas ended his full-time F1 career with another DNQ in Australia, where Tarquini retired when last but one to close another chastening campaign.

Yannick Dalmas, AGS JH24-Ford (Brazilian GP)

Gabriele Tarquini, AGS JH24-Ford (United States GP)

Yannick Dalmas, AGS JH25-Ford (Italian GP)

Gabriele Tarquini, AGS JH25-Ford (Monaco GP)

Claudio Langes, EuroBrun ER189B-Judd (Hungarian GP)

EUROBRUN RACING

Paolo Pavanello and Walter Brun persevered with their F1 ambitions despite a wretched 1989. They expanded to a two-car team once more despite rumoured Middle Eastern sponsorship failing to materialise. Brun announced Roberto Moreno as lead driver on 12 December 1989 with newcomer Claudio Langes his unexpected team-mate when confirmed on 26 January. Moreno was reunited with his F3 race engineer Kees van der Grint who joined in February.

George Ryton's EuroBrun ER189 had been introduced at the 1989 German GP and was updated for the new season, complete with new rear suspension and repositioned shock absorbers. Ryton moved the steering rack on the ER189B to comply with footwell regulations that were introduced for the European season before leaving to join Brabham. Mono-shock front suspension was tried on Moreno's car in France.

A deal to use Neotech's new 70-degree V12 engine for both F1 and sports cars was announced in December 1989. Designed by ex-Porsche/BMW engineer Rolf-Peter Marlow and built at Neotech's Austrian factory, the four-valves-per-cylinder unit ran on the dyno in

October 1988 and was tested in a Porsche 962 at the Österreichring in March. Sufficient finance could not be raised so EuroBrun continued with old Judd CV V8s. Pirelli tyres were retained.

Moreno qualified for two of the opening three races and finished 13th in Phoenix despite pitting after the parade lap to change a flat battery. A pre-qualifier at every race until France, Moreno did not make it through that session again as a lack of testing saw EuroBrun become increasingly uncompetitive. Langes was out of his depth and was only allowed limited mileage to save money. Eliminated in pre-qualifying at the opening four races, Langes quit when he learned that Mark Blundell and Marco Greco had been approached to replace him in Canada. Blundell turned down the opportunity and the Brazilian's super-licence application was refused so the disgruntled Langes continued to fulfil EuroBrun's commitments, failing to pre-qualify for the next ten races. EuroBrun withdrew at the end of the European season, having started just 14 of the 46 GPs it had entered during three seasons in F1.

MONTEVERDI ONYX FORMULA ONE

Onyx Grand Prix had graduated to F1 in 1989 and a turbulent first season culminated in Mike Earle leaving the team he had founded. Majority shareholder Jean-Pierre van Rossem of the Moneytron investment company wanted to hire a race-winning lead driver and to find a long-term engine partner. There were suggestions of a lucrative offer being made to Alain Prost when he announced he was leaving McLaren and Thierry Boutsen was mentioned in despatches before Stefan Johansson and J.J. Lehto signed one-year contract extensions before the end of the 1989 season.

Porsche were building a new V12 engine for 1991 and van Rossem chased the deal only for Footwork Arrows to announce its partnership on 5 February 1990. At the Ritz Hotel in Paris 18 days later, van Rossem told the assembled press that the team

Roberto Moreno, EuroBrun ER189-Judd (United States GP)

J.J. Lehto, Onyx ORE1-Ford (United States GP)

Stefan Johansson, Onyx ORE1-Ford (Brazilian GP)

was for sale. Onyx was acquired by Peter Monteverdi and a Swiss consortium that included Ferrari importer Karl Foitek, whose son had just signed a short-term deal with Brabham. Earle returned as team principal but Monteverdi was no easier to work for than van Rossem. Cutbacks followed by the end of April and Earle walked out when Monteverdi announced plans to relocate to Switzerland.

With all the close-season turmoil, the Onyx ORE1-Ford DFRs were virtually unchanged at the start of the year and neither qualified in Phoenix or at Interlagos as accidents and mishaps interrupted their weekends. Monteverdi fired technical director Alan Jenkins, who disagreed about the development budget, then company secretary Johan Denekamp left on 2 April, and Johansson was released the following day after refusing to take a pay cut. The former Ferrari driver took legal action and Monteverdi was placed with an injunction preventing the team from moving to Switzerland until the claim was settled. With finances in short supply, Gary Brabham and Luis Pérez Sala could not bring sufficient sponsorship and it was no surprise when Gregor Foitek was announced as Lehto's team-mate from Imola, with engine preparation switched from Brian Hart to Swiss-based Heini Mader. The changes were also cosmetic as Moneytron's pink trim was now replaced by lime green stripes.

The cars were renamed Onyx ORE2-Fords but little changed for the San Marino GP, where both qualified among the tail-enders and Lehto finished last. Foitek challenged Éric Bernard's Lola for sixth in Monaco after faster cars had retired before they clashed at the chicane during the closing stages; Foitek spun and stalled but was classified seventh nonetheless. Both Onyx drivers retired in Mexico and Foitek was a brakeless 15th in Mexico.

They failed to qualify in France and Britain while engineer Ken Anderson was among the last Onyx employees to leave as Monteverdi finally moved to a new base in Switzerland. The cars were officially renamed as Monteverdi ORE2-Fords when they arrived at Hockenheim with Peter Monteverdi himself now engineering Foitek's car. Having scraped onto the back row, Foitek spun in the stadium and Lehto was unclassified.

Neither qualified in Hungary, where Lehto's differential was fitted the wrong way around and Foitek quit the team during a session when his suspension failed. A one-off deal was agreed

with Eric van de Poele to replace Foitek at Spa-Francorchamps but, in dispute with Goodyear, the team failed to arrive. Faced with a $250,000 fine as a result, Monteverdi withdrew from F1 and closed the team. He announced that he would return as Monteverdi F1 Swiss Team but that did not happen.

J.J. Lehto, Onyx ORE2-Ford (Monaco GP)

Gregor Foitek, Monteverdi ORE2-Ford (Hungarian GP)

Bertrand Gachot, Coloni C3B-Ford (Italian GP)

SUBARU-COLONI/COLONI RACING

The prototype of the Subaru 1235 engine was revealed to the press in Milan's Hotel Michaelangelo on 7 September 1988 and Minardi tested it during 1989. An antiquated flat-12 'boxer' configuration was chosen for the latest design from Carlo Chiti's Motori Moderni concern. The 3,498cc unit had five valves per cylinder, an aluminium alloy block and Magneti Marelli/Weber fuel injection, with a Bosch system planned.

Minardi turned down the opportunity to use the unreliable

Bertrand Gachot, Coloni C3B-Subaru (Brazilian GP)

engine so Subaru acquired a majority stake in Enzo Coloni's impoverished team by Christmas. Former Subaru rally driver Yoshio Takaoka was appointed as president with Coloni retained as vice president. Engineers Christian Vanderpleyn and Michel Costa had left in August 1989 so it was Englishman Paul Burgess who reworked the already uncompetitive Coloni C3 to accommodate the bulky flat-12 and Motori Moderni six-speed transverse gearbox. The engine was overweight, 10 per cent wider than a Ford V8, and its 600bhp was less than any rival apart from the Life W12. Coloni switched to Goodyear tyres and cut back to a singleton entry. Bertrand Gachot had hoped to secure a drive with BMS Scuderia Italia but was confirmed by Coloni in January.

'It will be very difficult in the beginning,' Gachot told *Autosport*, 'but there is undoubtedly a lot of potential.' A V12 engine was already on the drawing boards before the start of the season but never appeared. The Coloni C3B-Subaru was late and only completed five laps of pre-season testing at Firebird Raceway in Arizona. It was unreliable and slow so Gachot failed to pre-qualify for the first eight GPs, despite the return of Vanderpleyn as race engineer in Canada.

Confusion reigned during the summer, Coloni left in May but was back in charge when Subaru withdrew after the British GP. A Langford & Peck-prepared Ford DFR was installed for the subsequent German GP but Gachot's pre-qualifying misery continued. The wheelbase was extended for Spa-Francorchamps,

Gary Brabham, Life F190 (Brazilian GP)

Bruno Giacomelli, Life F190 (Belgian GP)

Bruno Giacomelli, Life F190-Judd (Spanish GP)

where Gachot made it through pre-qualifying for the first time, the withdrawal of Life Racing Engines making that hour-long session unnecessary for the last two races. Unfortunately, Saturday was as good as it got for Gachot could not coax the Coloni into any race during a hopeless campaign.

LIFE RACING ENGINES

Bologna-based businessman Ernesto Vita chose the English translation of his surname when launching Life Racing Engines at the end of 1987, hoping to interest a customer team in his unusual W12 (or broad arrow '12') engine. The designer was distinguished engineer Franco Rocchi, who had had been a cornerstone of Ferrari's engineering department for three decades after joining the embryonic company in 1949 and had remained a consultant with the *Scuderia* until 1982. The four-valves-per-cylinder 3,493cc W12 had three banks of four cylinders set at 60 degrees, which allowed it to be as short as the most compact V8, albeit taller. A design office was established at Reggio Emilia with a factory in Formigine, just three miles north of Fiorano, where the new engine was unveiled in October 1988.

No customer could be found so Vita acquired Lamberto Leoni's unraced FIRST 189 chassis that Richard Divila had designed for 1989. Two of Rocchi's former Ferrari colleagues were also involved: Walter Salvarini designed the six-speed gearbox and Gianni Marelli

converted the unique chassis to accommodate the W12. The overly complicated engine was underpowered, heavy and unreliable so the Life proved a total disaster from the moment it first turned a wheel.

Gary Brabham signed a two-year contract in January 1990 with Franco Scapini, who did not qualify for a super licence, as test driver. The renamed Life F190 was ready in February but the first test at Vallelunga was an unfortunate foretaste of its future; Brabham completed a single lap and Scapini just two. Brabham failed to pre-qualify for the United States and Brazilian GPs – having completed a total of four laps – and then quit.

There was talk of Bernd Schneider replacing the Australian but it was Bruno Giacomelli, who had not raced in F1 since 1983, who made a surprise return. With money and spares in short supply, organisation negligible and just one chassis and engine, Giacomelli did not pre-qualify for the next ten races as the engine broke time and again. Vita sold 67 per cent of his company to Verona entrepreneur Daniele Battaglino and gave up on Rocchi's W12 engine.

Three Judd CV engines were acquired from Leyton House and the F190 was converted back to V8 power in the Portuguese GP paddock. It was only fired up during the closing stages of pre-qualifying and the engine cover flew off on Giacomelli's first lap out of the pits. It was little better at Jerez as Giacomelli failed once more on Life's final appearance before the team closed its doors.

DRIVER PERFORMANCE

DRIVER	CAR-ENGINE	USA	BR	RSM	MC	CDN	MEX	F	GB	D	H	B	I	P	E	J	AUS
Michele Alboreto	Arrows A11B-Ford	21 10	23 R	29 DNQ	27 DNQ	14 R	17 17	18 10	25 R	19 R	22 12	26 13	22 12	19 9	26 10	25 R	27 DNQ
Jean Alesi	Tyrrell 018-Ford	4 2	7 7	—	—	—	—	—	—	—	—	—	—	—	—	—	—
	Tyrrell 019-Ford	—	—	7 6	3 2	8 R	6 7	13 R	6 8	8 11	6 R	9 8	5 R	8 8	4 R	7 DNS	5 8
Philippe Alliot	Ligier JS33B-Ford	NT DNQ	10 12	17 9	18 R	17 R	22 18	12 9	22 13	24 DSQ	21 14	27 DNQ	20 13	21 R	13 R	21 10	19 11
Paolo Barilla	Minardi M189-Ford	14 R	17 R	—	—	—	—	—	—	—	—	—	—	—	—	—	—
	Minardi M190-Ford	—	—	27 11	19 R	29 DNQ	16 14	27 DNQ	24 12	28 DNQ	23 15	25 R	28 DNQ	28 DNQ	28 DNQ	—	—
Gerhard Berger	McLaren MP4/5B-Honda	1 R FL	2 2 FL	2 2	5 3	2 4 FL	1 3	2 5	3 14	2 3	3 16	2 3	3 3	4 4	5 R	4 R	2 4
Éric Bernard	Lola LC89-Lamborghini	15 8	11 R	—	—	—	—	—	—	—	—	—	—	—	—	—	—
	Lola 90-Lamborghini	—	—	14 13	24 6	23 9	25 R	11 8	8 4	12 R	12 6	15 9	13 R	10 R	18 R	17 R	23 R
Thierry Boutsen	Williams FW13B-Renault	9 3	3 5	4 R	6 4	6 R	5 5	8 R	4 2	6 6 FL	1 1	4 R	6 R	7 7	7 4	5 5	9 5
David Brabham	Brabham BT59-Judd	—	—	30 DNQ	25 R	30 DNQ	21 R	25 15	28 DNQ	21 R	28 DNQ	24 R	29 DNQ	26 R	27 DNQ	23 R	25 R
Gary Brabham	Life F190	34 NPQ	NT NPQ	—	—	—	—	—	—	—	—	—	—	—	—	—	—
Alex Caffi	Arrows A11B-Ford	—	25 R	28 DNQ	22 5	26 8	29 DNQ	22 R	17 7	18 9	26 9	19 10	21 9	17 13	—	24 9	29 DNQ
Ivan Capelli	Leyton House CG901-Judd	26 R	29 DNQ	19 R	23 R	24 10	27 DNQ	7 2	10 R	10 7	16 R	12 7	16 R	12 R	19 R	13 R	14 R
Yannick Dalmas	AGS JH24-Ford	32 NPQ	26 R	—	—	—	—	—	—	—	—	—	—	—	—	—	—
	AGS JH25-Ford	—	—	NT DNP	32 NPQ	32 NPQ	31 NPQ	26 17	32 NPQ	29 DNQ	27 DNQ	29 DNQ	24 NC	25 R	24 9	29 DNQ	28 DNQ
Andrea de Cesaris	Dallara F190-Ford	3 R	9 R	18 R	12 R	25 R	15 13	21 DSQ	23 R	30 DNQ	10 R	20 R	25 10	18 R	17 R	26 R	15 R
Martin Donnelly	Lotus 102-Lamborghini	19 DNS	14 R	12 8	11 R	12 R	12 8	17 12	14 R	20 R	18 7	22 12	11 R	15 R	23 DNS	—	—
Gregor Foitek	Brabham BT58-Judd	23 R	22 R	—	—	—	—	—	—	—	—	—	—	—	—	—	—
	Onyx ORE2-Ford	—	—	24 R	20 7	21 R	23 15	29 DNQ	30 DNQ	—	—	—	—	—	—	—	—
	Monteverdi ORE2-Ford	—	—	—	—	—	—	—	—	26 R	30 DNQ	—	—	—	—	—	—
Bertrand Gachot	Coloni C3B-Subaru	35 NPQ	33 NPQ	31 NPQ	34 NPQ	33 NPQ	33 NPQ	34 NPQ	34 NPQ	—	—	—	—	—	—	—	—
	Coloni C3B-Ford	—	—	—	—	—	—	—	—	33 NPQ	32 NPQ	30 DNQ	30 DNQ	30 DNQ	30 DNQ	30 DNQ	30 DNQ
Bruno Giacomelli	Life F190	—	—	33 NPQ	35 NPQ	35 NPQ	35 NPQ	NT NPQ	35 NPQ	35 NPQ	35 NPQ	33 NPQ	33 NPQ	—	—	—	—
	Life F190-Judd	—	—	—	—	—	—	—	—	—	—	—	—	NT NPQ	—	33 NPQ	—
Olivier Grouillard	Osella FA1M-Ford	8 R	21 R	—	—	—	—	—	—	—	—	—	—	—	—	—	—
	Osella FA1Me-Ford	—	—	23 R	28 DNQ	15 13	20 19	31 NPQ	27 DNQ	27 DNQ	31 NPQ	23 16	23 R	27 DNQ	21 R	27 DNQ	22 13
Maurício Gugelmin	Leyton House CG901-Judd	25 14	30 DNQ	13 R	29 DNQ	28 DNQ	28 DNQ	10 R	15 DNS	14 R	17 8	14 6	10 R	14 12	12 8	16 R	16 R
Johnny Herbert	Lotus 102-Lamborghini	—	—	—	—	—	—	—	—	—	—	—	—	—	15 R	—	18 R
Stefan Johansson	Onyx ORE1-Ford	27 DNQ	27 DNQ	—	—	—	—	—	—	—	—	—	—	—	—	—	—
Claudio Langes	EuroBrun ER189-Judd	33 NPQ	34 NPQ	—	—	—	—	—	—	—	—	—	—	—	—	—	—
	EuroBrun ER189B-Judd	—	—	32 NPQ	33 NPQ	34 NPQ	34 NPQ	33 NPQ	33 NPQ	34 NPQ	34 NPQ	32 NPQ	32 NPQ	32 NPQ	32 NPQ	—	—
Nicola Larini	Ligier JS33B-Ford	13 R	20 11	21 10	17 R	20 R	24 16	19 14	21 10	22 10	25 11	21 14	26 11	23 10	20 7	18 7	12 10
JJ Lehto	Onyx ORE1-Ford	NT DNQ	28 DNQ	—	—	—	—	—	—	—	—	—	—	—	—	—	—
	Onyx ORE2-Ford	—	—	26 12	26 R	22 R	26 R	30 DNQ	29 DNQ	—	—	—	—	—	—	—	—
	Monteverdi ORE2-Ford	—	—	—	—	—	—	—	—	25 NC	29 DNQ	—	—	—	—	—	—
Nigel Mansell	Ferrari 641	17 R	5 4	—	—	—	—	—	—	—	—	—	—	—	—	—	—
	Ferrari 641/2	—	—	5 R	7 R	7 3	4 2	1 18 FL	1 R FL	4 R	5 17	5 R	4 4	1 1	3 2	3 R	3 2 FL
Pierluigi Martini	Minardi M189-Ford	2 7	8 9	—	—	—	—	—	—	—	—	—	—	—	—	—	—
	Minardi M190-Ford	—	—	10 DNS	8 R	16 R	7 12	23 R	18 R	15 R	14 R	16 15	15 R	16 11	11 R	11 8	10 9
Stefano Modena	Brabham BT58-Judd	10 5	12 R	—	—	—	—	—	—	—	—	—	—	—	—	—	—
	Brabham BT59-Judd	—	—	15 R	14 R	10 7	10 11	20 13	20 9	17 R	20 R	13 17	17 R	24 R	25 R	22 R	17 12
Gianni Morbidelli	Dallara F190-Ford	28 DNQ	16 14	—	—	—	—	—	—	—	—	—	—	—	—	—	—
	Minardi M190-Ford	—	—	—	—	—	—	—	—	—	—	—	—	—	—	20 R	20 R
Roberto Moreno	EuroBrun ER189-Judd	16 13	32 NPQ	—	—	—	—	—	—	—	—	—	—	—	—	—	—
	EuroBrun ER189B-Judd	—	—	25 R	30 DNQ	27 DNQ	30 DNQ	32 NPQ	31 NPQ	32 NPQ	33 NPQ	31 NPQ	31 NPQ	31 NPQ	31 NPQ	—	—
	Benetton B190-Ford	—	—	—	—	—	—	—	—	—	—	—	—	—	—	9 2	8 7
Satoru Nakajima	Tyrrell 018-Ford	11 6	19 8	—	—	—	—	—	—	—	—	—	—	—	—	—	—
	Tyrrell 019-Ford	—	—	20 R	21 R	13 11	9 R	15 R	12 R	13 R	15 R	10 R	14 6	20 DNS	14 R	14 6	13 R
Alessandro Nannini	Benetton B189B-Ford	22 11	15 10	—	—	—	—	—	—	—	—	—	—	—	—	—	—
	Benetton B190-Ford	—	—	9 3 FL	16 R	4 R	14 4	5 16	13 R	9 2	7 R	6 4	8 8	9 6	9 3	—	—

DRIVER PERFORMANCE CONTINUED

DRIVER	CAR-ENGINE	USA	BR	RSM	MC	CDN	MEX	F	GB	D	H	B	I	P	E	J	AUS
Riccardo Patrese	Williams FW13B-Renault	12 9	4 13	3 1	4 R	9 R	2 9	6 6	7 R	5 5	2 4 FL	7 R	7 5	5 7 FL	6 5 FL	8 4 FL	6 6
Nelson Piquet	Benetton B189B-Ford	6 4	13 6	–	–	–	–	–	–	–	–	–	–	–	–	–	–
	Benetton B190-Ford	–	–	8 5	10 DSQ	5 2	8 6	9 4	11 5	7 R	9 3	8 5	9 7	6 5	8 R	6 1	7 1
Emanuele Pirro	Dallara F190-Ford	–	–	22 R	9 R	19 R	18 R	24 R	19 11	23 R	13 10	17 R	19 R	13 15	16 R	19 R	21 R
Alain Prost	Ferrari 641	7 R	6 1	–	–	–	–	–	–	–	–	–	–	–	–	–	–
	Ferrari 641/2	–	–	6 4	2 R	3 5	13 1 FL	4 1	5 1	3 4	8 R	3 2 FL	2 2	2 3	2 1	2 R	4 3
Bernd Schneider	Arrows A11-Ford	20 12	–	–	–	–	–	–	–	–	–	–	–	–	–	–	–
	Arrows A11B-Ford	–	–	–	–	–	–	–	–	–	–	–	–	–	29 DNQ	–	–
Ayrton Senna	McLaren MP4/5B-Honda	5 1	1 3	1 R	1 1 FL	1 1	3 20	3 3	2 3	1 1	4 2	1 1	1 1 FL	3 2	1 R	1 R	1 R
Aguri Suzuki	Lola LC89-Lamborghini	18 R	18 R	–	–	–	–	–	–	–	–	–	–	–	–	–	–
	Lola 90-Lamborghini	–	–	16 R	15 R	18 12	19 R	14 7	9 6	11 R	19 R	11 R	18 R	11 14	15 6	10 3	24 R
Gabriele Tarquini	AGS JH24-Ford	31 NPQ	31 NPQ	–	–	–	–	–	–	–	–	–	–	–	–	–	–
	AGS JH25-Ford	–	–	NT NPQ	31 NPQ	31 NPQ	32 NPQ	28 DNQ	26 R	31 NPQ	24 13	28 DNQ	27 DNQ	29 DNQ	22 R	28 DNQ	26 R
Derek Warwick	Lotus 102-Lamborghini	24 R	24 R	11 7	13 R	11 6	11 10	16 11	16 R	16 8	11 5	18 11	12 R	22 R	10 R	12 R	11 R

FORMULA 1 RACE WINNERS

ROUND	RACE (CIRCUIT)	DATE	WINNER
1	Iceberg United States Grand Prix (Phoenix)	Mar 11	Ayrton Senna (McLaren MP4/5B-Honda)
2	Grande Prêmio do Brasil (Interlagos)	Mar 25	Alain Prost (Ferrari 641)
3	Gran Premio di San Marino (Imola)	May 13	Riccardo Patrese (Williams FW13B-Renault)
4	Grand Prix de Monaco (Monte Carlo)	May 27	Ayrton Senna (McLaren MP4/5B-Honda)
5	Grand Prix Molson du Canada (Montréal)	Jun 10	Ayrton Senna (McLaren MP4/5B-Honda)
6	Gran Premio de México (México City)	Jun 24	Alain Prost (Ferrari 641/2)
7	Rhône-Poulenc Grand Prix de France (Paul Ricard)	Jul 8	Alain Prost (Ferrari 641/2)
8	Foster's British Grand Prix (Silverstone)	Jul 15	Alain Prost (Ferrari 641/2)
9	Grosser Mobil 1 Preis von Deutschland (Hockenheim)	Jul 29	Ayrton Senna (McLaren MP4/5B-Honda)
10	Magyar Nagydíj (Hungaroring)	Aug 12	Thierry Boutsen (Williams FW13B-Renault)
11	Grand Prix de Belgique (Spa-Francorchamps)	Aug 26	Ayrton Senna (McLaren MP4/5B-Honda)
12	Coca Cola Gran Premio d'Italia (Monza)	Sep 9	Ayrton Senna (McLaren MP4/5B-Honda)
13	Grande Premio de Portugal (Estoril)	Sep 23	Nigel Mansell (Ferrari 641/2)
14	Gran Premio Tio Pepe de España (Jerez)	Sep 30	Alain Prost (Ferrari 641/2)
15	Fuji Television Japanese Grand Prix (Suzuka)	Oct 21	Nelson Piquet (Benetton B190-Ford)
16	Foster's Australian Grand Prix (Adelaide)	Nov 4	Nelson Piquet (Benetton B190-Ford)

DRIVERS' CHAMPIONSHIP

	DRIVERS	POINTS
1	Ayrton Senna	78
2	Alain Prost	71 (73)*
3=	Gerhard Berger	43
	Nelson Piquet	43 (44)*
5	Nigel Mansell	37
6	Thierry Boutsen	34
7	Riccardo Patrese	23
8	Alessandro Nannini	21
9	Jean Alesi	13
10=	Ivan Capelli	6
	Roberto Moreno	6
	Aguri Suzuki	6
13	Éric Bernard	5
14=	Satoru Nakajima	3
	Derek Warwick	3
16=	Alex Caffi	2
	Stefano Modena	2
18	Maurício Gugelmin	1

*Best 11 results count

CONSTRUCTORS' CHAMPIONSHIP

	CONSTRUCTORS	POINTS
1	McLaren-Honda	121
2	Ferrari	110
3	Benetton-Ford	71
4	Williams-Renault	57
5	Tyrrell-Ford	16
6*	Lola-Lamborghini	11 *
7	Leyton House-Judd	7
8	Lotus-Lamborghini	3
9=	Arrows-Ford	2
	Brabham-Judd	2

*Stripped of its points due to incorrect entry but kept championship position

Ayrton Senna celebrates victory in the Belgian Grand Prix

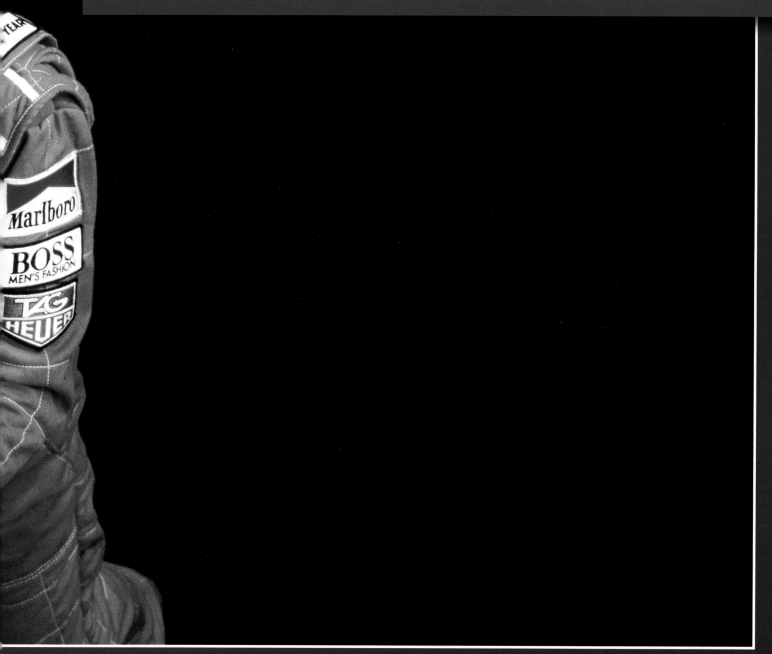

1991
McLAREN WITHSTANDS WILLIAMS'S ACTIVE EFFORT

Adrian Newey, Nigel Mansell and Patrick Head confer in Hungary

Formula 1 in 1991 was a period of great technological innovation as Williams perfected its semi-automatic gearbox and developed computer-controlled suspension. However, poor early reliability of the gearbox and Ayrton Senna's unbeaten opening four races proved insurmountable for Nigel Mansell. In the power race, Renault also surpassed both Honda and Ferrari with Elf's potent brew a significant factor.

Most teams followed Tyrrell's 1990 lead with differing interpretations of the high nose/anhedral wing by the time the definitive 1991 cars appeared. A multi-cylinder engine remained necessary to be truly competitive and there were new V12s from Honda, Porsche and Yamaha and V10s from privateers Ilmor and Judd, with varying degrees of success. Pirelli scored a lucky 1–2 in Canada but were soundly beaten by Goodyear elsewhere so withdrew at the end of the season.

The Fédération Internationale du Sport Automobile (FISA) made late rule changes once more: the front wing was 10cm narrower, the crucial skirts on the front endplates had to be 25cm above the ground, and the rear wing was 10cm further forward. The mandatory crash test was 20 per cent more stringent with particular attention paid to the roll hoop, footwell and fuel tank protection; the fuel tank had to be between driver and engine, while the oil tank was not allowed within the survival cell.

The first change to the points system since 1961 was ratified on 13 February, with ten points to the winner and no dropped scores. New powers were handed to the three stewards at each GP to improve driving standards. Those who caused an accident or held up cars while being lapped could be penalised with ten-second stop-go penalties, or time added to their race time if it occurred in the last 12 laps.

There were two new circuits on the calendar. Political pressure in France resulted in the oldest GP moving to

Nigel Mansell gives Ayrton Senna a lift after the British Grand Prix

the refurbished but underwhelming Circuit de Nevers at Magny-Cours. Jerez was on the verge of signing a new five-year agreement to host the Spanish GP when the race was awarded to the new Circuit de Catalunya at Montmeló, north of Barcelona; FISA president Jean-Marie Balestre had laid the foundation stone on 17 February 1989 and the circuit was ready just in time for the race. A modified Silverstone opened on 9 January with new sections from Maggots to Chapel, at the south of the circuit, and a complex behind the pits. Phoenix also had a new layout but proved disappointing once more. There was talk of staging the 1992 race in the city zoo or Papago Park but F1 did not return to Arizona. The Australian GP was stopped due to heavy rain after just 14 laps.

There were a number of disturbing aspects to the United States GP weekend. In addition to attempted sabotage on Leyton House, the hotel rooms of both Ayrton Senna and Alain Prost were burgled and pre-qualifying was interrupted by an apparent suicide attempt, when a man on crutches lay down on the track with drivers having to take avoiding action.

The IndyCar World Series organised a race in Surfers Paradise on Australia's Gold Coast and Balestre promised sanctions against drivers, suppliers and manufacturers who took part: 'Only the FISA is permitted to stage and control international championships.' A threat to ban Goodyear was later withdrawn. His FISA presidency ended on 9 October 1991 when challenger Max Mosley defeated him by 43 votes to 29.

Michael Schumacher made his Formula 1 début in Belgium

The Iraqi Army invaded neighbouring Kuwait on 2 August 1990 and the resulting Gulf War, which ended on 28 February 1991, was a factor in a new world recession. Many F1 teams struggled to survive and the economic mood in the pitlane was further dampened when European commissioner for social affairs Vaso Papendreoiu proposed a Europe-wide ban on cigarette advertising.

The Australian Grand Prix was abandoned after just 14 laps

HONDA MARLBORO McLAREN

Despite winning both titles for their three seasons together so far, McLaren-Honda introduced yet another engine configuration for 1991. Allan McNish shook down the prototype Honda RA121E at Silverstone on 28 June 1990. Design work on this 60-degree V12 was begun at Tokagi in 1989 and it tested on the dyno that October. The rev limit was increased and 680bhp was claimed from the 3,493cc unit.

Gerhard Berger remained under contract but Ayrton Senna considered an offer from Williams before agreeing a one-year extension (with an option for 1992) on the Friday of the 1990 Belgian GP. 'When you are dealing in such important decisions,' he said a day later, 'and when you have to discuss with a man like Ron [Dennis], it gets very complex. I'm not any less easy than him.' In turn, Dennis said, 'We are both very strong negotiators. Ayrton is an extremely clever guy. What I can genuinely say is that the outcome was very good for both sides.' McNish and Jonathan Palmer were regular test drivers while Indycar star Michael Andretti signed a one-year testing agreement as they evaluated a future together.

There were changes among the race engineers. Gordon Kimball moved to Benetton so James Robinson arrived from Arrows to work with Senna. Tim Wright switched to Peugeot in sports cars and was replaced by Lotus's Steve Hallam. Akimasa Yasuoka headed Honda's F1 programme from round three with Osamu Goto reassigned to the company's research and development department in Japan although Dennis persuaded him to move to Woking in the spring.

Senna spent the winter in Brazil as normal while Berger, McNish and Palmer put mileage on the V12 in a converted MP4/5B. The new McLaren MP4/6-Honda first appeared at Estoril in March, with Senna trying the new engine for the first time since October – and criticising its lack of development: 'I don't know what they have been doing since, but there is not enough progress and not enough power.' In contrast, the drivers praised the chassis, the work of Neil Oatley's design group. Ex-Ferrari aerodynamicist Henri Durand's influence on the MP4/6 was evident in the long nose and extended front wing skirts but the raised-nose fashion was not followed. The monocoque was stiffened, with coil springs and shock absorbers now mounted on top, and the number of components reduced for simplicity. David North was responsible for the transmission and transverse gearbox while a semi-automatic unit was tried on the spare car in Hungary. The radiators were moved forward in longer sidepods and fuel capacity increased due to the V12's increased consumption. The new package was heavier than its predecessor and incorrect fuel

Ayrton Senna, McLaren MP4/6-Honda (United States GP)

Gerhard Berger, McLaren MP4/6-Honda (Japanese GP)

read-outs cost Senna at Silverstone and Hockenheim.

Despite his fears, Senna won the first four races from pole position, leading all the way in Phoenix, Interlagos and Monaco, and passing Riccardo Patrese as the Imola track dried. Senna's first Brazilian GP victory of his career came despite being stuck in sixth gear and suffering cramp during the closing stages, his raw emotions revealed in the documentary *Senna*. That winning run (and seven consecutive pole positions) ended in Canada, where Williams-Renault dominated. Having retired when third in Montréal, Senna required stiches to a head wound following a jet-ski accident in Brazil and he rolled at Peraltada during Mexican qualifying. He was a distant third in Mexico and France as McLaren-Honda's formed dipped and Williams surged. Slightly more comfortable than he had been in the MP4/5B, Berger was third in Brazil and second at Imola, despite spinning on the formation lap. However, cruel unreliability during the first half of 1991 included a spate of engine failures and a couple of crashes in Monaco.

Four successive race wins shifted the power to Williams and British GP winner Nigel Mansell gave Senna a lift back to the pits after the Brazilian ran dry on the last lap. At least the under-fire Berger was second at Silverstone, his first finish since April, and fourth at the next two races. Senna escaped a 180mph roll during testing at Hockenheim on 19 July and his championship lead shrank to just eight points when he ran out of fuel once more in the German race.

Senna had a lighter chassis and heavily revised engine in Hungary, the V12 featuring variable-length induction trumpets and able to rev to 14,800rpm, with an improved mid-range power curve. Senna qualified on pole and, wearing a black armband after the death of Soichiro Honda, withstood Williams-Renault's pressure to win and re-establish his championship momentum. Another pole position and victory followed for Senna in Belgium despite having just two operational gears by the finish, while Berger supported in second

place after a slow pitstop and subsequent spin.

Senna was second in Italy and Portugal, where Mansell was disqualified following his disastrous pitstop. They went wheel-to-wheel for the length of the pit straight at Barcelona but Senna faded to fifth having spun and changed his blistered tyres. On the front row for both Iberian races (on pole in Spain), Berger lost potential second places when his engine failed on both occasions.

With two races to go, Mansell needed to beat Senna in Japan to maintain his title hopes. Berger led a McLaren qualifying 1–2 and eased away from Senna and Mansell before his tyres deteriorated. Mansell spun out on lap ten to confirm Senna as World Champion. The Brazilian slowed at the final corner to hand Berger his first McLaren victory. Senna won the curtailed Australian GP with Berger third (despite three spins in the monsoon) as McLaren-Honda added another constructors' title to Senna's crown.

CANON WILLIAMS TEAM

Williams sought Jean Alesi throughout 1990 but he was announced as a Ferrari driver on 18 September 1990. Frank Williams was in the Isle of Man that day as he tried to persuade Nigel Mansell to reverse his decision to retire and return to Williams. After more talks with Williams himself plus technical director Patrick Head and commercial head Sheridan Thynne, Mansell a signed a two-year contract on 1 October, with number one status guaranteed and exclusive use of a spare car. Riccardo Patrese remained in the second car and test driver Mark Blundell was replaced by Damon Hill in February. Hill spent much of 1991 developing Williams's computer-controlled 'reactive' suspension, which was tried in practice in Australia.

Renault agreed a two-year engine-contract extension with exclusivity in 1991. Canon remained as title sponsor, a two-year

Nigel Mansell, Williams FW14-Renault (Japanese GP)

subsidiary deal was agreed with Camel cigarettes (in place of Barclay), and Labatt's beer and Elf oil remained as associate partners. Team manager Michael Cane left while Alan Challis, chief mechanic for 11 years, took up a new factory post. They were replaced by Peter Windsor and Dickie Stanford respectively. Developments at the factory included a new electronics research and development department and half-scale wind tunnel.

Mansell's FW13B was fastest at Paul Ricard in January while Patrese first tried the latest 3,493cc Renault RS03 engine, which was marginally shorter and now featured four pneumatically controlled valves per cylinder. Use of magnesium helped save weight, the oil sump was revised, and the Magneti Marelli management system was smaller. A high-revving version (RS03B) with new cylinder heads and valve gear was introduced in Italian GP qualifying but was not enough of an advantage to be raced.

The new Williams FW14-Renault delighted Mansell on first acquaintance at a wet Silverstone on 21 February. With Head leading the design team and Adrian Newey responsible for the aerodynamics, it had an electro-hydraulic semi-automatic transverse gearbox and raised nose, with front wing endplates that curved inside the wheels. Conventional push-rod suspension was retained with dampers and springs mounted on top of the nose at the front. The carbon-fibre/Aramid monocoque doubled for the bodywork. Williams began the year with Brembo calipers but braking issues led to a switch to AP at Monza. Mansell interrupted the final Ricard test to fly back to London to receive the Order of the British Empire (OBE) from HM The Queen at Buckingham Palace on Tuesday 26 February.

The FW14 was immediately quick but Williams could not exploit that advantage due to its initially unreliable gearbox: Mansell retired from the opening three races while Patrese finished just once. In Phoenix, Mansell's gearbox failed and Patrese had an electronic glitch that caused him to spin before being hit by Roberto Moreno's Benetton. Williams used just five gears in Brazil, where Mansell shadowed Senna before another gearbox malfunction sent him spinning out, but Patrese qualified and finished second. Initially quicker than Mansell in qualifying, Patrese started from the front row at Imola and led the opening wet laps before a misfire ruined his race. Laid low by 'flu, Mansell was punted out of the race on the opening lap. Senna 30 points, Mansell zero.

Mansell opened his account in Monaco by snatching second from Alain Prost's Ferrari at the chicane; Patrese crashed on Stefano Modena's oil when challenging for second. Patrese led a Williams 1–2 in qualifying in Canada and Mansell dominated the race until the final lap, when his engine stalled at the hairpin while he was acknowledging the crowd and the FW14 coasted to a halt; he was classified sixth due to distance covered, while Patrese finished second. Mexico saw another Williams qualifying 1–2 with Patrese on pole and in the race the Italian passed an out-of-sorts Mansell to score a dominant victory with his team-mate second.

With reliability added to speed, Mansell won the next three races. He twice passed Prost in France, led all the way at Silverstone, and headed another 1–2 at Hockenheim – and achieved the latter two victories from pole position. Patrese finished only fifth at Magny-Cours from pole following more gearbox issues, collided with

Riccardo Patrese, Williams FW14-Renault (German GP)

Gerhard Berger at the start of the British GP when he cut across the McLaren-Honda, and came second in Germany.

McLaren-Honda fought back in Hungary, where brakes troubled both Mansell and Patrese as they finished 2–3. Belgium was disastrous as Mansell retired from the lead and Patrese, who was demoted to 17th on the grid when his reverse gear was found not to work, only finished fifth. In Italy, Patrese took the lead from Senna into the Ascari chicane only to spin at the same place a lap later following another gearbox problem. Mansell then pressured Senna into overcooking his tyres to claim victory.

The Estoril race proved pivotal when Mansell pitted from the lead on lap 30 and his loose right-rear wheel fell off as he accelerated away. His mechanics broke the rules by refitting the wheel in the pitlane so he was disqualified. Patrese qualified on his fourth pole of the season and eased to another victory following Mansell's second costly Portuguese pitstop drama in three years. Although Mansell sprained an ankle on the Friday before the Spanish GP while playing football for the press against photographers, he maintained lingering title hopes by leading a Williams 1–3 in the race.

With victory required in Japan, Mansell's challenge ended when he spun out while chasing Senna on lap ten; Patrese finished third. The conditions for the Australian GP were appalling and second-placed Mansell crashed on his 15th lap, just as the red flag was waved. With results declared after 14 laps, Mansell was classified second and Patrese fifth. While the team's drivers were second and third in the standings, Williams-Renault lost the constructors' title by just 14 points.

SCUDERIA FERRARI

Ferrari endured a shambolic campaign as it pressed the self-destruct button. With Alain Prost in the last year of his deal, Ferrari beat Williams and Tyrrell to sign Jean Alesi on a three-year contract that was announced on 18 September 1990. Andrea Montermini joined Gianni Morbidelli as a test driver in January. Having previously shunned commercial sponsorship (bar Marlboro paying its drivers), Ferrari denied Minardi its title partner when Pioneer electronics agreed a five-year deal. Luigi Mazzola continued to engineer Prost's car while Giuseppe Pedrotta replaced Maurizio Nardon when Alesi's race engineer joined the Il Barone Rampante F3000 team after the Italian GP.

With reputation enhanced by the Tyrrell 019-Ford, Jean-Claude Migeot returned in October 1990. Steve Nichols tidied up the existing design as the Ferrari 642, which appeared at January's Paul Ricard test. The stiffened carbon-fibre monocoque was moulded at the Guildford Technical Office with footwell strengthened to pass the more rigorous crash test. The tapered sidepods were lower and the semi-automatic gearbox was placed longitudinally under revised rear bodywork that improved airflow to the centrally mounted rear wing. A transverse gearbox, active suspension and traction control were under development at Fiat's Turin research and development facility under the direction of Amedeo Visconti. With the best technical package at the end of 1990 and quickest in every major winter test, Ferrari travelled to Phoenix as favourites.

In America, Alesi's late gearbox failure handed second place to

Alain Prost, Ferrari 642 (United States GP)

Prost, but the Ferrari 642 was no match for the new McLaren-Honda. With Prost vocal and his already frosty relationship with sporting director Cesare Fiorio deteriorating, work immediately began on a new car and engine. Both drivers scored points in Brazil and Migeot revised the aerodynamics before for the San Marino GP with longer sidepods, new airbox and altered rear undertray. At Imola, where the improved car had been quick in testing, the track was very wet at the start and the race proved a disaster for Ferrari as Prost crashed on the parade lap and Alesi out-braked himself at Tosa on lap three. Alesi finished third in Monaco with Prost dropping from second to fifth after a pitstop to correct faulty suspension.

With scathing headlines in the Italian press, Ferrari president Piero

Fusaro fired Fiorio on 14 May. Enzo's son Piero Ferrari led a new management group including Lancia's Claudio Lombardi as general manager, Marco Piccinini liaising with the governing body (as he had done in 1988) and FISA press officer Francesco Longanesi looking after the partners.

Modifications in Canada included new front suspension, Penske shock absorbers and front endplates that channelled air around the wheels, but both cars retired from that race and the next.

The new Ferrari 643 finally ran at Fiorano on 27 June with Montermini behind the wheel. Nichols evolved John Barnard's original 639 concept still further and Migeot's influence was obvious in the higher nose and front wings. Following back-to-back tests at Imola,

Jean Alesi, Ferrari 642 (Mexican GP)

Alain Prost, Ferrari 643 (Spanish GP)

Jean Alesi, Ferrari 643 (Portuguese GP)

two 643s were sent to the French GP and brought a brief upturn in fortunes, with Prost second after challenging for the lead and Alesi fourth. At Silverstone Prost inherited third when Ayrton Senna ran out of fuel but Alesi lost a podium when he hit Aguri Suzuki's Lola while lapping it. Alesi used hard tyres at Hockenheim to run non-stop and finish third but Prost was eliminated when Senna eased him off the road at the first chicane; the Frenchman earned a one-race suspended ban when he criticised FISA for not punishing the McLaren driver.

An engine with variable-length intake trumpets and an improved power curve was introduced in Hungary, where Alesi finished fifth but Prost had an engine issue. Both had costly engine failures

Gianni Morbidelli, Ferrari 643 (Australian GP)

in Belgium, Alesi having established a commanding lead. Off the ultimate pace at Monza, Prost was third while Alesi matched that result in Portugal despite a botched pitstop.

With Prost increasingly unhappy and Alesi unsettled by rumours about his future, they struggled for grip in Spain but finished second and fourth respectively. Fourth in Japan, Prost was sacked on 29 October after one complaint too many. 'Ferrari has terminated my contract,' Prost's statement read, 'and the matter is now in the hands of my lawyers.' He was replaced at Adelaide by Morbidelli, who scored half a point for sixth place when the race was stopped; Alesi crashed in the heavy rain.

Prost was fifth in the championship and Ferrari third despite its first winless F1 campaign since 1986.

CAMEL BENETTON FORD

R.J. Reynolds director of sponsorships W. Duncan Lee and Benetton's Flavio Briatore used the 1990 Hungarian GP to announce a two-year sponsorship for the Camel cigarette brand. 'I think it is very good news for Benetton,' Briatore said. 'The package is strong. Benetton needs a lot of money to become a winning team.' Japan's ambitious new Autopolis racing complex provided additional support.

Benetton's technical team was restructured under John Barnard, with Mike Coughlan promoted to chief designer when Rory Byrne, Pat Symonds, Dave Wass and Willem Toet joined Reynard's F1 project. With a new factory being built in a disused quarry at Enstone,

Roberto Moreno, Benetton B190B-Ford (United States GP)

Gordon Message looked after the move and was replaced as team manager by Tyrrell's Joan Villadelprat. Nelson Piquet remained under contract and Roberto Moreno signed a one-year deal before Christmas, having been preferred to Aguri Suzuki. Benetton finalised a lucrative three-year contract with Pirelli on 30 November.

Buoyed by success late in 1990 and with the Series V Ford HB engine now developing over 700bhp, a title challenge was expected. As the B191 was delayed, modified B190Bs were used for the first two races. Piquet had a couple of near misses on the way to third in Phoenix and finished fifth in his home GP; Moreno hit Riccardo Patrese's spun Williams in America and finished seventh despite complaining of understeer in Brazil.

Launched in London on 27 March, the Benetton B191 looked conventional with high nose and low-slung wing supported by curved struts, manual six-speed transverse gearbox and passive push-rod suspension. However, Barnard adopted complex new carbon-fibre manufacturing techniques that rendered load-bearing bulkheads and brackets unnecessary. The British weather and shortage of spares delayed the B191's shakedown until 4 April, when Moreno completed just four laps of Silverstone.

With a largely unsorted car at Imola, they qualified in the midfield before Piquet spun at Tosa on lap two and Moreno ran third before his engine failed. Piquet qualified fourth in Monaco but was hit by Gerhard Berger at the first corner and made it to Mirabeau before pulling off, while Moreno finished a steady fourth. Rumours of a rift between Barnard and Briatore dominated paddock gossip in Canada, where Piquet inherited victory when Nigel Mansell stopped on the last lap. Barnard and Briatore met after the race and the Englishman's departure was announced the following Friday due to 'a basic contrast of ideas in the running of the company on a day-to-day basis'. Briatore was promoted to managing director and Gordon Kimball, who had left McLaren in the winter, replaced Barnard as technical director. Coughlan moved to Tyrrell and chief mechanic Nigel Stepney became Lotus team manager.

Moreno finished fifth in Mexico, then uncompetitive rubber and illness ruined his French GP while a late tyre stop dropped Piquet out of the points. Further restructuring followed before the British GP with the sale of 35 per cent of the team to Tom Walkinshaw, who

Nelson Piquet, Benetton B190B-Ford (United States GP)

Nelson Piquet, Benetton B191-Ford (Australian GP)

Roberto Moreno, Benetton B191-Ford (Belgian GP)

became responsible for all matters except sponsorship and marketing, these remaining Briatore's domain. The Scot set about reorganising the engineering department: Byrne, Symonds, Toet and Wass all returned in October when Reynard cancelled its F1 project, Byrne to run Benetton's research and development department. TWR's Ross Brawn replaced Kimball as the team's third technical director of the year on 19 November.

After Piquet's fifth place at Silverstone, neither driver scored at troubled weekends in Germany and Hungary. Matters improved at Spa-Francorchamps, where Piquet and Moreno finished 3–4, but it was the performance of Jordan débutant Michael Schumacher that stole the headlines that weekend. Briatore released Moreno with

immediate effect on 3 September and Schumacher duly signed until the end of 1995. Moreno and Eddie Jordan took legal action and Alex Zanardi had a Benetton seat fitting in case Schumacher was prevented from racing. Moreno eventually negotiated a $500,000 settlement and Jordan's case was unsuccessful, so Schumacher made his controversial switch at the Italian GP.

Schumacher immediately impressed and outqualified Piquet at four of the five remaining races. At Monza, he ran as high as fourth before a vibration restricted him to fifth at the finish, with Piquet sixth. They swapped finishing positions at Estoril despite both needing two tyre stops. Neither scored in Japan and Piquet survived a lurid spin to claim fourth in the Australian downpour on his last F1 appearance.

Michael Schumacher, Benetton B191-Ford (Portuguese GP)

TEAM 7UP JORDAN

Eddie Jordan Racing had been winning in the junior categories since 1981. The team's Martin Brundle challenged Ayrton Senna for the 1983 British F3 Championship and Johnny Herbert clinched that title in 1987. Team and driver graduated to F3000 in 1988 and won on début at Jerez. Rumours of Jordan's F1 plans had begun by the time Herbert was seriously injured at Brands Hatch that autumn.

Jean Alesi won the 1989 F3000 championship in Irishman Eddie Jordan's Camel-sponsored Reynard 89D-Mugen and the designer of that car, Gary Anderson, began work at Jordan Grand Prix's Silverstone base on 29 January 1990. Reynard colleagues Andrew Green and Mark Smith were recruited to focus on suspension and gearbox respectively. Anderson adopted a straight-forward approach, wanting Jordan's first F1 car to be easy to work on. Trevor Foster, EJR team manager since 1989, fulfilled the role for the F1 operation and chief mechanic John Walton arrived from Benetton.

Rather that arrange for cheaper Cosworth DFR engines, Jordan met Ford's Michael Kranefuss over breakfast before the 1990 United States GP and a supply of Ford HB Series IV engines was announced in June, to the dismay of established teams in the midfield. Design of the carbon-fibre monocoque was finalised in July and the first tub was completed by Precision Composites in October. Anderson used the wind tunnel at Southampton University to design sleek bodywork with a distinctive twin-arched diffuser, tapered rear end and anhedral front wing. The transverse six-speed gearbox had

Hewland ratios, while mono-shock front suspension and twin-damper rear unusually had carbon-fibre push-rods. Goodyear agreed to supply tyres in another significant early development. The impressive Jordan 191 had mild slow-speed understeer but it was easy to drive and superb in fast corners.

John Watson was chosen to shakedown the unpainted Jordan 191-Ford at a wet Silverstone on 28 November 1990 with 20 laps that were trouble-free other than a spin. Bertrand Gachot, who was a client of Eddie Jordan Management, was announced as a driver a week later and Ian Phillips, who had recently left Leyton House, joined as commercial director before Christmas.

Gachot set promising testing times at Paul Ricard before Jordan dropped another bombshell at the team launch in February by landing Pepsi-Cola brand 7Up as title sponsor, a proposed deal with Camel having fallen through. Secondary deals were gradually agreed with Fuji Film, Denim, Unipart, Tic-Tac and Philips Car Stereo during an impressive first year commercially. Bernd Schneider was to be Gachot's team-mate but lost his backer so Andrea de Cesaris was confirmed two weeks before the United States GP. Both drivers developed into regular contenders for points and seemed relaxed in the team's jovial atmosphere.

De Cesaris failed to pre-qualify in America after missing a gear and over-revving his engine but Jordan eased through that session everywhere else. Gachot ran as high as sixth in Phoenix and both retired from the midfield at the next two races, de Cesaris having

Michael Schumacher, Jordan 191-Ford (Belgian GP)

Bertrand Gachot, Jordan 191-Ford (Monaco GP)

Roberto Moreno, Jordan 191-Ford (Portuguese GP)

Andrea de Cesaris, Jordan 191-Ford (Portuguese GP)

lost points at Imola when his gear linkage broke. The drivers had feisty reputations so some repair work was required: the Italian wrote off his monocoque in Brazil when he spun following engine failure and Gachot spun and hit the wall at Tamburello during the San Marino GP at Imola.

Promise finally turned to tangible success in Canada with de Cesaris fourth and Gachot fifth, despite another spin. In Mexico, Gachot spun out of fifth position and de Cesaris pushed his broken car across the line to claim another fourth place. The Italian came from the back following a spin in France to claim sixth and allow Jordan to escape pre-qualifying. Gachot was sixth at the next two races while de Cesaris, who had a huge crash during the British GP when his rear suspension failed exiting Abbey, finished fifth in Germany. Tyre issues ruined the Hungarian GP although Gachot set the fastest lap after pitting.

That was Gachot's last appearance for the team as he was jailed at Southwark Crown Court on 20 August for an altercation with a London taxi driver the previous December. The 18-month sentence (later halved with six months suspended) caused protests and indignation at the next race, the Belgian GP at Spa-Francorchamps, where T-shirts and banners demanded 'Free Gachot'.

Jordan signed Mercedes-Benz sports car star Michael Schumacher as Gachot's replacement following a test at Silverstone. Having not raced at Spa before, Schumacher shocked the establishment by qualifying seventh only for his clutch to fail on the opening lap. De Cesaris climbed through the field and challenged for the lead before losing oil pressure, which caused the engine to blow up three laps

from a second-place finish. Jordan tried to sign Schumacher but the German instead made a controversial move to Benetton, so legal proceedings overshadowed the following race at Monza.

A deal was reached with Moreno in the early hours of Friday morning in Italy and the deposed Benetton driver qualified ninth but spun out of the race after two laps. Neither driver scored in Portugal and Moreno was replaced for the last three races by Alex Zanardi, the F3000 star finishing ninth in Spain and Australia. Having crashed into Ayrton Senna during qualifying and Karl Wendlinger during the race in Japan, de Cesaris was eighth when the Australian GP was stopped. It was a downbeat end to the year but the precocious newcomers were an excellent fifth overall in the final constructors' points.

Alex Zanardi, Jordan 191-Ford (Japanese GP)

Stefano Modena, Tyrrell 020-Honda (Japanese GP)

BRAUN TYRRELL HONDA

Tyrrell seemed to enter 1991 in its most competitive state for over a decade. Satoru Nakajima remained under contract and his presence helped secure championship-winning Honda V10 engines. Ken Tyrrell agreed terms with Stefano Modena in Portugal on the day after Jean Alesi's Ferrari move was announced. 'I am very pleased to have been offered the chance to drive for the Tyrrell team,' Modena said. 'I feel the combination of the Tyrrell chassis, the Honda engine and Pirelli tyres will be very competitive.' The tie-up with TAG/McLaren Marketing Services delivered new sponsorship from Braun (electrical appliances) and Calbee (snack food). Engineering director Harvey

Satoru Nakajima, Tyrrell 020-Honda (Italian GP)

Postlethwaite was contracted until 31 July but Jean-Claude Migeot returned to Ferrari. Mike Coughlan joined in August to engineer Nakajima's car. Joan Villadelprat left and was replaced as team manager by Lotus's Rupert Manwaring.

Modena first drove the new Tyrrell 020-Honda on Silverstone's south circuit on 17 December 1990. Chief designer George Ryton evolved the promising 019 while retaining its anhedral front wing and mono-shock front suspension. The V10 was larger (and heavier) than the Ford DFR but a new transverse gearbox allowed the wheelbase to stay unchanged. January testing times at Jerez and Kyalami were promising and early gearbox problems were rectified so race wins were predicted. However, the 020's weight distribution affected handling and caused understeer, and tyres proved increasingly inadequate, so early positivity soon ebbed away.

The season began well as Modena and Nakajima finished 4–5 in Phoenix but both retired in Brazil. A new undertray was introduced for the Imola test, where Modena crashed heavily on 3 April. Come the race, transmission failures denied both Tyrrells when well-placed, Nakajima running fourth and Modena while third late in the race. In Monaco, Modena qualified and ran second for an impressive 42 laps before a huge engine failure in the tunnel sent shrapnel through the floor. The Italian inherited second place in Canada when Nigel Mansell retired on the last lap, allowing Pirelli runners to finish 1–2.

Nine days after that fine result, news broke that Postlethwaite was moving to Sauber Mercedes as the Swiss/German partners evaluated

F1. Postlethwaite was immediately placed on gardening leave and Tyrrell's downward spiral began. Tyre issues blighted the next four races. Nakajima, who had narrowly missed Andrea de Cesaris's crashing Jordan-Ford at Silverstone, announced his intention to retire and Modena appeared to lose interest.

The Italian spun twice during the Hungarian GP, then ran sixth in Belgium until sidelined by an oil fire. Neither driver figured at the remaining European races. With Honda having already chosen an alternative partner for its V10s in 1992 and Braun reconsidering its sponsorship, Ryton introduced revised suspension for much-needed back-to-back tests at Silverstone before the last two races. This improved the 020's balance and Modena finished sixth in Japan despite being hit by a bird in the closing stages, while Nakajima crashed. In Australia, Modena qualified ninth and lay tenth when the race was stopped, but Nakajima ended his F1 career in the wall. After such pre-season expectation, sixth in the constructor's standings with just 12 points represented a meagre return.

MINARDI TEAM

Giancarlo Minardi's long association with Ferrari included borrowing a Ferrari 312T for Giancarlo Martini (Pierluigi's uncle) to drive in the British non-championship races of 1976 and using its F2 engine in 1977. Pierluigi Martini's qualifying performance for the 1990 United States GP prompted Fiat's Gianni Agnelli to ask why the works cars of Alain Prost and Nigel Mansell had been outqualified by the minnows from Faenza. Ferrari had not supplied another team with engines in

modern F1 so the announcement on 5 April 1990 that Minardi would have Ferrari V12 power in 1991 and 1992, with six engines per race meeting, was a major surprise.

Technical director Aldo Costa and aerodynamicist René Hilhorst designed the Minardi M191, which first ran at Fiorano on 8 January 1991. The Tyrrell-inspired step under the nose raised the pedals by two inches and long, tapered sidepods had air exits at the side and rear. The V12, the first of which had been delivered in August, was driven through a longitudinal six-speed gearbox, which was placed under extra strain by a succession of clutch failures. Minardi switched from Pirelli to Goodyear at Ferrari's behest.

Pierluigi Martini re-signed at the end of September 1990 and Gianni Morbidelli, who had completed 1990 with the team, was confirmed a fortnight later. At the last two races of 1990 the Minardi-Fords had small Pioneer logos and negotiations with the prospective title sponsor continued during the winter. Pioneer eventually chose to support Ferrari so money was in short supply in Faenza, restricting testing and gradually delaying engine payments.

Beginning the season with 1990-specification Ferrari engines and excessive oversteer, the Minardis had teething troubles at the opening two races, engine failure with five laps to go in Phoenix depriving Martini of sixth place. New rear suspension produced for the Imola test in April improved handling but progress that week was halted when Martini crashed. With newer engines and revised aerodynamics for the San Marino GP, Minardi enjoyed its best weekend of the year. Both drivers qualified in the top ten and Martini finished in a vital fourth position despite losing his clutch.

Pierluigi Martini, Minardi M191-Ferrari (Australian GP)

Gianni Morbidelli, Minardi M191-Ferrari (Japanese GP)

Roberto Moreno, Minardi M191-Ferrari (Australian GP)

Minardi did not build on that promise. Last in Monaco after losing oil throughout and having just one operational gear at the finish, Martini became the first driver to incur FISA's new ten-second stop-go penalty when he held up Stefano Modena while being lapped. Martini finished seventh from the pitlane in Canada and Morbidelli took that position in Mexico.

Morbidelli's Minardi hit Lotus mechanic Pete Vale in the crowded Magny-Cours pitlane during Friday practice, breaking Vale's ankle. Fitted with new undertrays, both cars crashed into rivals in the race although Martini finished ninth, and repeated that result at Silverstone. Another engine upgrade, first used in Germany, saw Martini qualify in the top ten at six of the remaining eight races as progress was made, although failures made tangible results scarce, such as when Martini lost gears in Belgium with points in prospect. A strong weekend in Portugal saw Martini equal Minardi's best-ever finish with fourth and Morbidelli ran as high as sixth before fading.

The team-mates collided during the closing stages of a disappointing Spanish GP and retired in Japan, Martini having been fifth when the electrics died. Morbidelli drove for Ferrari in Australia as Alain Prost's replacedment so Roberto Moreno was a one-off substitute. Both Minardi-Ferraris struggled in the downpour with Martini one of those to crash and cause the race to be red-flagged.

Martini's fourth places in San Marino and Portugal were enough for Minardi to claim seventh overall but 1991 had been a cash-strapped disappointment with the team's survival in jeopardy.

BMS SCUDERIA ITALIA (DALLARA)

Without a top-six finish in 1990, BMS Scuderia Italia looked to re-establish itself in the F1 midfield. Emanuele Pirro remained for a second season with the team and J.J. Lehto replaced Andrea de Cesaris. F3000's Andrea Montermini was named as test driver, a role he also performed for Ferrari.

The relationship with Dallara Automobili continued for a fourth season and a supply of Ford HB engines was hoped for until Jordan Grand Prix's surprise announcement in June. John Judd's Rugby-based Engine Developments was developing a new V10 engine and an exclusive arrangement was confirmed at the 1990 Hungarian GP. 'This was a very compact, sensible power unit, produced with minimal fuss on a budget that wouldn't have kept Honda in cam covers for the season,' wrote David Tremayne in *Autocourse*. A little longer than the previous V8, the 72-degree Judd GV V10 developed 660bhp at 13,500rpm at the start of the year and its wide power curve was appreciated by the drivers. With Pirro racing at Macau, Lehto gave the Judd V10 its first track mileage in a modified Dallara F190 at Vallelunga in November 1990, although running was limited by an installation issue and poor weather. Tests continued at Misano in December before the new Dallara F191-Judd was launched at Scuderia Italia's Brescia factory on 9 January.

The F191 was the work of Nigel Cowperthwaite, who had replaced Christian Vanderpleyn as chief designer, and Gian Paolo Dallara's team at Varano. This was a neat, conventional car with attractive raised nose and push-rod suspension all-round (rather than the F190's pull-rod rear), with inboard springs and dampers. The transverse six-speed Dallara/Hewland gearbox was new, with the rear wing attached to it. The team remained contracted to Pirelli so performance was increasingly masked by inadequate rubber, especially in race conditions. Dallara's technical department was augmented by the arrival of former Lamborghini chief technical officer Paolo Stanzani.

A promising first test at Paul Ricard was curtailed on 18 January when Lehto wrote off the prototype F191 after something broke at the penultimate corner on his first lap that day. Further mileage at Monza on 26–28 January was followed by a six-day Pirelli test at Estoril in February where the Dallara-Judds caused a surprise

J.J. Lehto, Dallara F191-Judd (San Marino GP)

Emanuele Pirro, Dallara F191-Judd (Belgian GP)

by dominating – Pirro quickest and Lehto second.

The cars qualified for the United States GP in an excellent ninth (Pirro) and tenth (Lehto) although both retired early, then Pirro finished 11th in Brazil after losing his front wing at the first corner. At Imola, Pirro's race car caught fire during pre-qualifying and he was bumped by Lehto in the final seconds. Without a finish so far, Lehto climbed through the field in the wet opening laps and with nine laps to go took third, a vital podium finish behind the McLaren-Hondas that meant Scuderia Italia would not have to pre-qualify after the British GP. Lehto ran as high as sixth in Monaco before becoming stuck in top gear while Pirro withstood cramp to finish in that position to score Scuderia Italia's last points of the season.

When Lehto lost fourth place in Canada through engine failure, it marked the start of a run of eight retirements in nine races, interrupted only by eighth in Spain despite contact with Martin Brundle's Brabham. In the same period, Pirro impressively qualified seventh in Hungary and had six top-ten finishes, with a best of eighth in Belgium, but he failed to pre-qualify in Mexico and France. Scuderia Italia's drivers collided at the chicane on lap two of the Japanese GP while trying to avoid Andrea de Cesaris's spinning Jordan-Ford, but both finished the curtailed Australian GP, Pirro seventh and Lehto 12th.

The early-season points finishes were enough for Dallara-Judd to claim eighth in the constructors' standings.

TEAM LOTUS

Having lost Camel and Lamborghini in the autumn of 1990, Team Lotus spent an anxious winter restructuring and looking for money.

Peter Collins and Peter Wright, who had been running Lotus Engineering since 1988, were appointed as consultants in August 1990 and they were joined by German F3 entrant Horst Schübel when a management buyout was announced in December, with Keke Rosberg's protégé Mika Häkkinen the unexpected choice as driver. The convalescing Martin Donnelly remained under contract and was included on the official F1 entry list when it closed at midnight on 15 February, although he never raced in F1 again.

Collins became managing director and Wright restructured the technical department while Schübel looked for sponsors. With the future uncertain for much of the winter, there were inevitable departures. Derek Warwick decided to lead the Tom Walkinshaw's Jaguar sports car team, technical director Frank Dernie moved to Ligier, and engineer Steve Hallam joined McLaren. Enrique Scalabroni replaced Dernie before Christmas although he left after just nine months in the role. Chief designer Frank Coppuck was responsible for detailed work on the new Lotus 102B while Judd EV V8 engines were acquired from Brabham. Aerodynamicist Dr John Davis was seconded from Lotus Engineering in the New Year. Team manager Rupert Manwaring moved to Tyrrell and Greg Field, who had worked with Collins at Benetton, helped with logistics until Nigel Stepney replaced Manwaring in July. Tony Rudd retired after

Mika Häkkinen, Lotus 102B-Judd (Monaco GP)

Julian Bailey, Lotus 102B-Judd (Monaco GP)

Michael Bartels, Lotus 102B-Judd (German GP)

53 years in the industry, 22 of which had been with Lotus.

A two-year-old type 101 chassis was modified to test the Judd engine, which David Brabham shook down on 23 January with Häkkinen taking over to gain F1 mileage. Having needed to work day and night following its late start, the Lotus 102B-Judd was ready for Julian Bailey to drive at Silverstone on 25 February at the start of a three-day test while Häkkinen pounded round in the 101 test chassis. Despite its old designation, 90 per cent of the 102B was new or modified, and its rear bulkhead was reworked to fit the Judd engine. Russian aviation manufacturer Sukhoi advised on new composites for the revised monocoque. The pull-rod front/push-rod rear suspension layout was revised and six-speed transverse Lotus/Lamborghini gearbox retained while AP supplied carbon discs and pads.

Coppuck and Davis used London's Imperial College wind tunnel to revise the aero both over and under the car before Williams's quarter-scale wind tunnel was acquired. A new white and British Racing Green colour scheme was unveiled at that test with limited backing from Tamiya (models), Komatsu (industrial machinery) and Tommy Hilfiger (clothing) plus plenty of space to sell. With Donnelly sidelined, Lotus considered Bernd Schneider and Johnny Herbert to lead the team before Bailey agreed a short-term deal. Coppuck engineered Bailey's car as he had at Tyrrell during the 1988 season.

That Lotus was on the grid at all was a success, although it scored points at just one GP during a transitional campaign. Against better-funded and quicker rival cars, the impressive Häkkinen only failed to qualify once (following mechanical woes in France) and starred elsewhere. With the team in mourning following the death of mechanic

David Jacques following an accident at the hotel when testing at Imola, Häkkinen lifted spirits by coming from the last row to finish fifth in the race, just his third GP start. He was ninth in Mexico despite losing his clutch and finished another five races outside the top ten.

Bailey did not qualify for three of his four races before his funds ran out. The exception was San Marino where he took sixth on the last lap to complete a double points score for Hethel. Herbert replaced Bailey in Canada, where the car broke on its out lap during Saturday qualifying; Lotus was fined $5,000 for fetching the stranded machine's qualifying tyres during the session. That unlucky DNQ was followed by seven performances that re-established Herbert's reputation, with two tenth places and an unlapped seventh at Spa-Francorchamps. Herbert missed the German, Hungarian, Italian and Spanish GPs due to pre-existing Japanese F3000 commitments. Michael Bartels, who was also represented by Rosberg, used backing from *Auto Motor und Sport* and Marlboro to secure the drive at those races. With track time during the Hockenheim test limited by engine problems, Bartels failed to qualify on each occasion and did not return to F1.

Looking for a multi-cylinder engine partner, Lotus further modified a chassis as the 102C to test Isuzu's V12 engine (the P799WE) that Herbert drove at Silverstone on 6–7 August. This was a four-year-old research and development exercise that is said to have been 'discovered' by road car stylist Peter Stevens on a visit to the Japanese manufacturer. The engine was displayed at the 1991 Tokyo Motor Show but it never raced.

Johnny Herbert, Lotus 102B-Judd (Belgian GP)

MOTOR RACING DEVELOPMENTS (BRABHAM)

Brabham looked to rebuild following Middlebridge's takeover. Keen to render its calamitous association with Zakspeed to history, the Yamaha Motor Company planned a new V12 engine and a partnership appeared to suit both parties. However, this proved an even more difficult campaign for beleaguered Brabham.

An old Brabham BT58Y ('Y' for Yamaha) was fitted with an updated eight-cylinder Yamaha OX88 and Bosch telemetry for the Silverstone FOCA test in July 1990 to acquire data as the V12's specification was finalised. After Silverstone, the BT58Y was

Mark Blundell, Brabham BT59Y-Yamaha (United States GP)

Martin Brundle, Brabham BT59Y-Yamaha (Brazilian GP)

dispatched to Yamaha's test track at Sugo where local F3000 star Ukyo Katayama continued the programme.

Norio Shimizu had already embarked on the new V12 by that time and a three-year contract, exclusive for 1991, was soon confirmed. Yamaha and Porsche both unveiled new V12 engines during the 1990 Japanese GP weekend with the bulky German unit in stark contrast to the compact Yamaha OX-99. The Japanese company's 3,498cc 70-degree V12 retained five valves per cylinder – a configuration pioneered by Yamaha in motorcycle engines – and used carbon-fibre, aluminium alloy, titanium and magnesium to reduce weight. Yamaha formed Ypsilon Technology to service the engines at a factory in Milton Keynes that had previously been

home to the Nimrod Aston Martin sports car team.

Eight months after quitting Brabham due to monies owed by previous management, Martin Brundle rejoined in October 1990. Mark Blundell raced for Middlebridge's F3000 team in 1989 and signed a one-year contract on 17 December 1990. Renowned F3 and sports car entrant David Price joined as team manager that month but left after four races due to a disagreement. He was replaced by former RAM Racing owner John MacDonald from the French GP. Brabham retained Sergio Rinland as chief designer with Tim Densham and Andy Brown, who arrived from Leyton House, engineering Blundell and Brundle respectively.

The Japanese-owned team attracted a portfolio of sponsors from that country, including Mitsukoshi World Motors (a subsidiary of Japan's oldest company), Autobacs (a car accessory retailer), Yamazen (industrial machinery), Sunitomo Marine (insurance) and Kyosho (radio-controlled models). Brabham continued with Pirelli tyres for a third successive season.

A new car was not scheduled until Imola so Brabham began 1991 with modified Brabham BT59Y-Yamahas featuring an interim transverse gearbox. Testing was blighted by valve-gear failures so revs were cut to improve reliability, inevitably compromising performance. Officially launched on the eve of the season in an unfamiliar dark blue, white and red livery, the BT59Y was an overweight compromise. Brundle started from a surprise 12th in Phoenix and finished 11th after clipping a wall; Blundell spun out of the race on a patch of oil. The drivers qualified on the final row

Martin Brundle, Brabham BT60Y-Yamaha (Belgian GP)

Mark Blundell, Brabham BT60Y-Yamaha (Italian GP)

in Brazil before running at the back until Blundell retired, leaving Brundle to finish last.

The new BT60Y was completed just in time for the San Marino GP after a problem with the monocoque had been rectified, and Brundle completed nine laps of Silverstone's south circuit before two BT60Ys were freighted to Imola. This was a distinctive design with conical-shaped raised nose and low front wing. Complicated sidepods that split the air were replaced by more conventional arrangements at the French GP, where a new undertray was also introduced. The new transverse gearbox had Xtrac internals. Push-rod suspension was adopted all round with a single shock absorber at the front. Active suspension and semi-automatic gearbox were also under development. The car was finished in an altogether more 'Brabham-like' navy blue and white.

Both finished outside the points at Imola after Brundle was delayed by first-lap contact with Nigel Mansell. At Monaco, Brundle was excluded from the meeting for missing the weighbridge on Thursday and Blundell, who again crashed on oil during that race, failed to qualify for the Canadian GP as mechanical failures ruined the weekend. They retired from the next three races although Blundell ran seventh in Mexico, where Brundle lost a wheel when it was incorrectly attached at a pitstop. The lack of points so far consigned Brabham to another half season of pre-qualifying.

Compromised by an unsuitable tyre compound at Hockenheim after their mid-race pitstops, Brundle finished 11th and Blundell 12th, the latter having spun in the first corner. Brundle qualified tenth in Hungary and ran as high as seventh before stopping when he lost feeling in his right foot.

Now aware that Yamaha would not be supplying its engines in 1992, Brabham scored its first point of the year in Belgium, Blundell recovering from a poor start to finish sixth while Brundle lost a wheel after placing ninth. They set third and fifth fastest race laps in Italy only for their tyres to degrade alarmingly. Both suffered rear suspension failures in Portugal, Brundle's occurring during pre-qualifying, as worrying breakages continued.

Having already arranged alternative employment for 1992, Brundle ran sixth in Spain before clashing with J.J. Lehto and finished fifth at Suzuka. Blundell did not pre-qualify in front of Yamaha's home crowd due to an oil leak and Brundle was frustrated

in Australia as he sat in the pits with a brake issue and was bumped from qualifying. With heavy rain turning the race into a dangerous lottery, Blundell survived a couple of spins to be classified at the conclusion of a disheartening campaign for all concerned. Blundell was released at the end of the year as Brabham sought paying drivers for 1992.

Brabham's year was further complicated when it began to move out of its works in Cox Lane, Chessington from August with a new 30,000sq ft factory secured at Sherbourne House, Tilbrook, on the outskirts of Milton Keynes. Yamaha took over the team's long-time base with Brabham sporting director Herbie Blash remaining to run the renamed Activa Technology.

LARROUSSE F1 (LOLA)

Larrousse always wanted to move from the Paris suburb of Antony to a purpose-built facility at a racetrack. Plans to relocate in Rouen fell through when the old circuit was not redeveloped so Larrousse looked south. A new factory at Signes, adjacent to Circuit Paul Ricard, was opened during the 1990 French GP weekend with relocation completed at the end of the year. Plans to build its own chassis in 1991 were shelved due to the move so the Lola contract was extended for a final year.

Having enjoyed its most successful season so far, Larrousse experienced a series of blows as it prepared for 1991. At the 1990 Italian GP came the announcement that Lamborghini would not supply engines, deciding instead to partner with fierce rivals Ligier. With the economic outlook worsening, the ESPO Corporation withdrew its support so Gérard Larrousse spent the winter in fruitless merger talks with AGS and in Japan looking for money.

A supply of Brian Hart-tended Ford DFRs was agreed in October and Éric Bernard and Aguri Suzuki (with some Toshiba backing) were confirmed as drivers in February. Just a week after that announcement, FISA stripped Larrousse of its 1990 constructors' points for incorrectly stating in its championship entry that it, rather than Lola, was the constructor. That denied the team $2 million FOCA travel money and left it obliged initially to pre-qualify, jeopardising sponsorship deals. That Ligier inherited Larrousse's travel fund compounded the sense of injustice. Faced with closure,

Aguri Suzuki, Lola L91-Ford (San Marino GP)

Éric Bernard, Lola L91-Ford (Italian GP)

Gérard Larrousse met with Jean-Marie Balestre on 25 February and a compromise was reached: the points were lost but his team would not have to pre-qualify.

That meeting delayed the launch of the new Lola L91-Ford until 27 February. Mark Williams and Bruce Ashmore developed Chris Murphy's successful 1990 car with Lola founder Eric Broadley and Larrousse technical director Gérard Ducarouge also credited. It was a well-balanced car although its power deficit required a low-downforce set-up that compromised grip. Larrousse's impecunious state resulted in minimal testing or development. Parts were used beyond their normal life so reliability was poor, especially with the six-speed gearbox.

Given the winter's FISA sanction, Suzuki's point for finishing sixth

Bertrand Gachot, Lola L91-Ford (Australian GP)

in Phoenix was popular and Bernard qualified 11th in Brazil. Suzuki's fuel pump failed on the way to the grid at Interlagos and he retired from the next eight races. Ninth in Monaco was Bernard's first finish and he claimed sixth after a strong run in Mexico amid rumours of imminent closure. Larrousse, who had visited Ligier with Ducarouge in the hope of forming a French 'super team', wrote an open letter to prime minister Édith Cresson that was published in *Le Journal du Dimanche*, bemoaning Ligier's state backing while France's top team in 1990 and 1991 got nothing. 'Not only does one team have the unconditional support of all the big companies,' he wrote, 'which are more or less controlled by the government but... it discourages other businesses interested in us.'

Larrousse eased short-term pressure from his creditors by entering *redressement judiaciare* (France's equivalent of receivership) before the French GP, where the team welcomed new backing from MVS Venturi, the sports car company. Furthermore, the team's future was secured by a three-year agreement with the Doi Group that was announced at the German GP. That Yasuhiro Doi's Central Park was the prime sponsor of Lamborghini's Modena Team added irony to welcome financial injection. Ligier had wanted to rehire Ducarouge for some time and, with Larrousse's immediate future assured, the designer returned to the team that had sacked him in 1981. He was replaced as Larrousse technical director by Michel Tétu.

Bernard challenged for seventh in France before the transmission failed and the Lola grew less competitive as rivals developed their cars. Suzuki was fined $10,000 for colliding with Jean Alesi's Ferrari while being lapped at Silverstone. Thereafter the retirements were only interrupted when the cars failed to qualify, which was Suzuki's fate at four of the last six races. Mourning the death of long-term sponsor Charles-Pierre André in a road accident, Bernard failed to qualify in Portugal and broke his left leg at Suzuka when he crashed during Friday practice.

Larrousse considered Roberto Moreno and Maurizio Sandro Sala as Bernard's replacement before choosing Bertrand Gachot for the Australian GP, the Franco-Belgian having recently been released from jail following an incident with a London taxi driver. Gachot complained of erratic handling as both Lola-Fords failed to qualify for the final race of the season.

Lola ended its five-year association with Larrousse in December as it looked to enter F1 as a works entity in its own right in 1993. Larrousse went before a French court on 11 December to prove it had sufficient funding to be released from receivership and continue trading into 1992.

LEYTON HOUSE RACING

Following two disappointing seasons, Leyton House Racing (formerly March) signed a five-year deal to use Ilmor Engineering's forthcoming V10 engine in April 1990. Based in Brixworth, Northamptonshire, Ilmor had been founded in 1984 by former Cosworth engineers Mario Ilien and Paul Morgan, hence the name, with backing from US racing mogul Roger Penske. Exclusive to Leyton House in 1991,

the Ilmor 2175A was a 3,498cc 72-degree aluminium alloy V10 with four valves per cylinder, titanium conrods and Zytek engine management. The intention had been to sell naming rights to a manufacturer but 'LH10' on the cam covers referred to Leyton House's funding.

Team owner Akira Akagi re-signed Ivan Capelli and Maurício Gugelmin, predicting 'we will begin to realise the full potential of the team in 1991'. Capelli, who was on Williams's radar in case Nigel Mansell did not return, first tested the prototype of this lightweight, short-stroke unit in a converted CG901 in October 1990 at Donington Park. Testing continued throughout the winter although gearbox, cooling and lubrication issues restricted mileage. Gordon Coppuck formed a design agency in 1990 and joined Leyton House as a consultant in the spring. Most recently team manager of the Suzuki 500cc team, John Gentry replaced Andy Brown as Gugelmin's race engineer. Simon Keeble and Mike Smith became joint managing directors following the departure of erstwhile MD Ian Phillips in December 1990.

Chris Murphy's new Leyton House CG911 was among the new cars that bucked the trend when it first ran at Silverstone in February. While the front of the monocoque was raised as was the fashion, it did not have a Tyrrell-like anhedral front wing. Murphy and chief designer Gustav Brunner opted for an uncomplicated car that was easy to work on during a race weekend and that performed at a variety of circuits. Brunner concentrated on the new

Maurício Gugelmin, Leyton House CG911-Ilmor (Australian GP)

Ivan Capelli, Leyton House CG911-Ilmor (Monaco GP)

Karl Wendlinger, Leyton House CG911-Ilmor (Japanese GP)

transverse six-speed gearbox, which caused problems during testing and at early races, leading to questions about the sub-contracted manufacturer's build quality. The new car continued its predecessor's trait of being a handful on bumpy circuits.

Having tested at Arizona's Firebird Raceway prior to the United States GP, this opening race was overshadowed by an attempted sabotage of the cars in the early hours of Saturday morning, with wires and brake lines cut. 'It's clearly a malicious attack,' a frustrated Murphy told *Autosport*. 'They knew how to upset a racing car, but only in an annoying way.'

Early reliability was poor with Capelli retiring from the first nine races and Gugelmin's seventh place in France the only finish (although he was classified 11th at Imola after his engine failed in the closing laps). The Brazilian showed that the CG911 had pace by qualifying eighth at Interlagos only to suffer burns when his fire extinguisher discharged during the warm-up, forcing him to quit the race after nine painful laps. Recriminations followed the first two disappointing races, with Keeble dismissed and Smith put in sole charge. 'Just five months after the last *coup d'état*,' *Autosport* reported, 'the top management has again been disrupted by another upheaval.' Brunner replaced Murphy as technical director and the demoted Englishman left by the end of the European season. Yasutada Oda transferred from Akagi's Japanese operation as chief executive.

Capelli ran fifth at Imola and fourth in Canada before a puncture-induced spin and engine failure respectively ended the chance of points. A fundamental flaw in the front suspension was discovered during Silverstone's FOCA test and Leyton House was more competitive at the subsequent French GP, where Gugelmin qualified ninth and finished seventh despite a 10sec penalty and $10,000 fine for blocking race leader Nigel Mansell. They retired from the next two races, Gugelmin having started ninth at Silverstone. Finally in Hungary, Leyton House enjoyed its most competitive weekend of 1991 as Capelli reminded everyone why he had been so sought-after in 1988. He completed every session in the top ten, qualified ninth and achieved his first race finish of the year in sixth place.

A double engine failure tempered optimism in Belgium but both cars finished the next two races, albeit outside the points. Capelli lost possible scores in Italy (blistered tyres) and Portugal (loss of nosecone). They qualified in the top ten at Estoril where Gugelmin

started and finished seventh. Problems were not confined to the track by this time for the workforce was drastically cut as Akagi was investigated by the Japanese authorities. Leyton House's owner was arrested in September due to alleged financial malpractice, throwing the future of the team into doubt. Ilmor reacquired the rights to its engine and removed Leyton House's LH10 identification from the cam covers at the Spanish GP.

Gugelmin finished seventh in Spain and eighth in Japan, by which time he had a new team-mate. Needing finance to complete the season, the team accepted Mercedes-Benz's proposal to replace Capelli with Karl Wendlinger. Too tall for the cockpit, the Austrian Mercedes junior driver crashed into Andrea de Cesaris on lap two of his début. As rain decimated the Australian GP field, Gugelmin crashed into the pitlane while trying to pass Stefano Modena's Tyrrell after 13 laps. He hit the inside of the pit wall and scattered debris, leaving two marshals needing treatment in the medical centre. Wendlinger started last, pitted to cure an engine complaint and lay 20th when the race was stopped.

Leyton House scored a single point during another under-achieving campaign and was 12th in the final standings.

FOOTWORK PORSCHE

Porsche was responsible for the successful turbocharged engines for McLaren-TAG during the mid-1980s so its F1 return was greeted with anticipation. A normally aspirated V12 was designed for the 3.5-litre formula in 1987 but McLaren chose Honda as its partner. Work continued nonetheless and director of engineering Ulrich Bez visited the 1989 German GP to speak to prospective clients, with up to five teams chasing the deal.

Moneytron Onyx were left disappointed on 5 February 1990 when Footwork's Wataru Ohashi announced an exclusive three-year contract with Porsche (with an option on 1994). Bernd Schneider drove an Arrows A11C-Porsche test chassis at Weissach in October 1990, a week before the engine was launched at the Japanese GP, where Michele Alboreto and Alex Caffi were confirmed for 1991. Schneider was named as reserve driver and Sauber Mercedes team manager Max Welti arrived in the New Year as Porsche's project manager. Arrows team manager since the start, Alan Rees became financial director early in the season and was replaced by John Wickham. USF&G ended its association with the team but Blaupunkt signed a three-year contract as associate sponsor.

Veteran engineer Hans Mezger, who had worked for Porsche since 1956 and was responsible for the TAG turbo, opted for a 3,499cc 80-degree V12 with four valves per cylinder. The most novel feature was the central drivetrain with power taken from the middle of the crankshaft to reduce vibration. Fitted with a Bosch Motronic engine management system, this was an antiquated and bulky design that weighed 418lb as opposed to the Honda V12's 352lb. Power of 650bhp at 12,000rpm was claimed – but the works Hondas were developing 780bhp.

Conrod failures and gearbox problems stymied pre-season progress and Footwork's cars were the slowest at both Paul Ricard and Estoril. Given Porsche's reputation, this lack of performance – even in the heavy old A11C – was the most surprising story of the winter. The first two races were a disaster. Having scraped into the field on the final row in Phoenix, Alboreto had gearbox failure after a frustrating afternoon among the tailenders, while Caffi's oversteering car was a non-qualifier. Both A11Cs DNQ'd in Brazil.

Alboreto gave the new FA12 its shakedown on Silverstone's south circuit on 14 April before it was sent to Imola for the following week's FOCA test. Technical director Alan Jenkins had a new interpretation of the high-nose concept with a needle-thin central pillar suspending a full-width front wing. There were no front bulkheads thanks to the complex use of composites. The rest of the

Michele Alboreto, Footwork A11C-Porsche (Brazilian GP)

design was conventional with push-rod suspension, side-mounted water radiators and a tapered rear end.

Things started badly for the FA12 and got worse. Testing at Imola on 20 April, Alboreto wrote off the prototype in a violent, fiery accident at Tamburello when the front wing support broke. Having cracked a couple of ribs and with 15 stiches in a deep cut to his right calf, Alboreto was forced to race an old A11C. Caffi's FA12 was only completed on Thursday morning of the San Marino GP where a plethora of new-car issues ruined practice. Neither qualified on another embarrassing weekend and they blew three engines at the following test at Paul Ricard.

In Monaco, Caffi crashed head-on at the swimming pool during

Alex Caffi, Footwork A11C-Porsche (United States GP)

Alex Caffi, Footwork FA12-Porsche (San Marino GP)

Stefan Johansson, Footwork FA12-Porsche (Canadian GP)

Michele Alboreto, Footwork FA12-Ford (Spanish GP)

Alex Caffi, Footwork FA12-Ford (Spanish GP)

Michele Alboreto, Footwork FA12-Porsche (Monaco GP)

Stefan Johansson, Footwork FA12-Ford (British GP)

Saturday practice and was ruled out for the rest of the weekend. Still limping from his Imola injuries, Alboreto qualified the spare A11C on the last row before switching to a newly completed FA12 that had yet another engine failure when last. Footwork's cursed luck continued: Caffi broke his jaw when a passenger in a road accident so was replaced by Stefan Johansson in Canada, where Footwork finally had a full complement of FA12s; both cars qualified for the first time but retired. With oil-scavenge issues preventing long runs on either car in Mexico, the 'flu-ridden Alboreto qualified last, stalled on the grid and ran at the back before losing oil pressure; Johansson failed to qualify.

Now in danger of having to pre-qualify, the team took action before the French GP: 'Formula 1 partners Footwork and Porsche are not satisfied with the racing capacity of the Footwork-Porsche programme. Therefore, both parties have decided to implement a temporary halt to their racing programmes. This will allow full concentration of all available forces to develop the reliability and competitiveness, avoiding the "testing in public" of the past. It is hoped that the Footwork-Porsche combination will be back in action before the end of the season.' Alboreto, Johansson and Schneider tested the Porsche-powered FA12 for the rest of the summer but Dr Bez left Porsche and its withdrawal was confirmed on 18 October.

Hart DFRs were mounted in modified FA12s and the lower engine required a series of transfer gears to connect it to the gearbox. This system was so fragile that failures were frequent and the 1990 gearbox, which fitted directly to a DFR, was even tried. Caffi was fit enough to visit June's Silverstone FOCA test but Footwork kept Johansson for Magny-Cours and Silverstone, prompting unsuccessful legal action on Caffi's behalf on the first day of French GP practice. Blighted by the weak transfer gears, Johansson failed to qualify for either race while Alboreto retired from both.

Caffi returned at Hockenheim but neither driver made the field at the next four races. Admitting he was out of practice following his enforced lay-off, Caffi failed to pre-qualify in Portugal and Spain while Alboreto recorded the team's first finish of the year when 15th at Estoril. Gradually improving, Caffi bumped his team-mate for the final grid slot in Japan and finished tenth – Footwork's best result of 1991. Both were still running when the Australian GP was stopped.

ÉQUIPE LIGIER GITANES

Guy Ligier's close relationship with François Mitterand's French government seemed to guarantee a healthy budget irrespective of how bad the results were. After a points-free 1990, wholesale changes were made for yet another transitional season. Ligier already had Renault engines for 1992–94 so a one-year contract was agreed with Lamborghini, a deal made sweeter still because it denied French rivals Larrousse. Ligier was the 11th best team in 1990 so did not qualify for FOCA travel assistance, but FISA stripped Larrousse of its 1990 constructors' points and Ligier was the beneficiary once more.

Thierry Boutsen wanted to stay with Williams but signed a two-year contract with Ligier in October 1990 after Nigel Mansell reversed his decision to retire. A week later, new F3000 champion Érik Comas agreed a two-year deal while Lotus's Frank Dernie arrived as technical director in November. By that time, Michel Beaujon, Claude Galopin and Richard Divila were finishing designs for the Ligier JS35-Lamborghini. Snow delayed the planned shakedown test at Magny-Cours so Boutsen and Comas first drove the JS35 at Paul Ricard on 11 February. This was an entirely conventional design with raised wing, push-rod suspension and transverse six-speed gearbox. However, the V12's large oil tank made the JS35 a cumbersome beast.

The opening six races were a crushing disappointment with Comas, who struggled to adapt to qualifying tyres all year, a non-qualifier in America and Mexico. Boutsen finished seventh at Imola and Monaco and Comas eighth in Canada but drastic action was required. Galopin and Divila were sacked after two races while Beaujon was reassigned to engineer Comas and run the research and development department.

Dernie set about revising the JS35 with higher sidepods and new undertray. Boutsen drove the JS35B at Silverstone on 25 June but his optimism proved misplaced at the subsequent French GP. With Mitterand and seven cabinet ministers in attendance, Comas finished only 11th and Boutsen 12th after both pitted twice to reattach loose bodywork. Comas did not qualify at Silverstone and recovered from a huge barrel roll at Hockenheim's Ostkurve during Saturday practice to scrape into the German GP field. Boutsen had a new rear wing in Germany and finished ninth.

Boutsen's engine failed four laps from the end of another lacklustre run in Hungary, although there had been better news

Érik Comas, Ligier JS35B-Lamborghini (Portuguese GP)

Thierry Boutsen, Ligier JS35-Lamborghini (Monaco GP)

off the track. Ligier had wanted to re-sign former technical director Gérard Ducarouge for some time and his shock arrival from Larrousse was announced before the Hungarian GP. Ducarouge became managing director for race operations and fabrication with Dernie focusing on the 1992 car and restructuring for the long-term.

The on-track misery continued with both drivers struggling to break into the top ten as a lack of grip and balance prevailed. The increasingly forlorn Comas ran as high as sixth during the early wet laps at Barcelona before the track dried, restoring his overweight JS35B to its gripless self once he changed to slick tyres. Boutsen was ninth in Japan and ran into Satoru Nakajima in Australia, leaving France's national team without a point to its name for the second successive season.

AUTOMOBILES GONFARONAISE SPORTIVE (AGS)

AGS was in a financial quagmire throughout its final F1 season. Title sponsor Ted Lapidus did not renew, team owner (and mayor of Chaumont in the Haute-Marne) Cyril de Rouvre decided not invest any more of his own money and year-long merger talks with Larrousse proved unsuccessful. The lack of money was crippling and technical director Michel Costa's new AGS JH26 never made it further than a wind-tunnel model. AGS persevered with the JH25 with modified suspension and aerodynamics. Heini Mader continued to

prepare the Ford DFR engines and a transverse gearbox was tested.

Gabriele Tarquini remained for a third season and crashed heavily, without injury, after a rear-end failure during testing at Paul Ricard. Andrea de Cesaris tried the JH25 at the Circuit du Var in January and signed an option with AGS before choosing to move to the new Jordan team. Left with a late vacancy, AGS hired Stefan Johansson for the first two races but he did not qualify for them. Tarquini finished a distant eighth in Phoenix despite tyre vibration, oversteer and a misfire, then spun out of the Brazilian GP on the opening lap.

With his team in financial meltdown on its return to Europe, de Rouvre called in the receiver (redressement judiaciare), giving AGS six months to settle its debts and find new investment. Daniel Djeliri, a senior manager in de Rouvre's other businesses, replaced Henri Cochin as team manager after a dispute over the latter's negotiations with Larrousse. By the end of April, de Rouvre had sold a majority shareholding to touring car entrant Gabriele Rafanelli and Patrizio Cantú, the former Scuderia Italia team manager bringing personnel from his Crypton Engineering F3000 set-up. Former Champ Car rookie of the year Fabrizio Barbazza was hired as Tarquini's team-mate and Christian Vanderpleyn returned once more as the new driver's race engineer. Both drivers failed to qualify for three of the next four races, with Tarquini's 20th on the grid in Monaco the exception; his gearbox broke after nine laps.

Vanderpleyn scrapped the JH26 in May and Modena Team's Mario Tolentino was hired to work on a new design, with race

Gabriele Tarquini, AGS JH25B-Ford (French GP)

Fabrizio Barbazza, AGS JH25-Ford (Monaco GP)

Stefan Johansson, AGS JH25-Ford (United States GP)

Olivier Grouillard, AGS JH27-Ford (Spanish GP)

Gabriele Tarquini, AGS JH27-Ford (Portuguese GP)

Fabrizio Barbazza, AGS JH27-Ford (Spanish GP)

engineer Peter Wyss moving in the opposite direction. In the meantime, Vanderpleyn upgraded the JH25 to B-specification, which was introduced at the French GP with revised suspension and a new colour scheme, but without discernible improvement. Non-qualifiers at Magny-Cours and Silverstone, AGS dropped into pre-qualifying from the following race in Germany. Tarquini escaped that session at Hockenheim (only to fail to qualify) but otherwise both AGS-Fords were early-Friday casualties, including at Spa-Francorchamps where Tarquini suffered whiplash in a 10G accident following suspension failure at Blanchimont.

After a week working day and night, the AGS crew completed the first JH27 in time for the Italian GP but Tarquini did not complete a lap before the Ford engine cut out. There were two examples of

Tolentino's conventional design in Portugal, where Tarquini was third in pre-qualifying but failed to qualify after hitting Aguri Suzuki's Lola on his final run. With AGS's future in doubt (despite satisfying the courts of its seven-year business plan) and negotiations with Larrousse restarted, Tarquini was allowed to leave before the Spanish GP and swapped seats with Fondmetal's Olivier Grouillard. The JH27s were the slowest cars in pre-qualifying at Jerez, after which AGS closed down rather than spend the $1 million required to continue in Japan and Australia.

FONDMETAL

It was all change at Osella in the close season. Founder Enzo Osella and technical director Antonio Tomaini both left and ambitious owner Gabriele Rumi renamed the concern after his Fondmetal wheels brand. The workforce was expanded and a new factory opened in December at Palosco, 120 miles east of Osella's base at Volpiano. Furthermore, Rumi changed the team's design philosophy by establishing a studio in England's 'motorsports valley' at Bicester. Having sold March F1 to Leyton House, founder Robin Herd formed Robin Herd Limited with former March men Tino Belli, Tim Holloway and Les McTaggart all involved. With Herd now a sleeping partner, the company was renamed Fomet 1 in November 1990 following agreement to supply Fondmetal's new F1 contender. Olivier Grouillard re-signed in November with ex-Ferrari designer Nino Frison named as technical director. Harlow-based Brian Hart prepared the Ford DFR engines from Monaco.

Olivier Grouillard, Fomet FA1Me-Ford (United States GP)

Fondmetal wanted to run two cars but reckoned a switch from Pirelli to Goodyear was vital. The American company only had capacity to supply one car so a singleton entry was confirmed with intended second driver Paul Belmondo announced as reserve in the New Year. Waiting for the new car to be completed, Grouillard started the year with the redesignated Fomet FA1Me predictably uncompetitive, failing to pre-qualify in the USA and Brazil.

Designed by Belli, Holloway and Riccardo Rosa, the new Fomet F1-Ford was unveiled at Palosco on 16 April. A reshaped monocoque, made in modified old moulds, tapered upward at the front to raise the nose and a more compact fuel tank improved airflow behind the driver. The front shock absorbers were mounted on the monocoque and the DFR V8 was driven through a transverse Xtrac gearbox. Advanced Composites of Derby supplied the carbon-fibre elements and the suspension was fabricated at Superpower Engineering in Milton Keynes with the car assembled at Palosco. It ran during the Imola test, where Richard Divila, who had worked with Grouillard at Ligier, joined as race engineer.

With the new car failing to pre-qualify at its first three races, Divila gradually reorganised the race team and progress was finally seen by mid-season. A new rear diffuser was introduced in Canada and Grouillard pre-qualified in Mexico and France, starting from a stunning tenth in México City but sidelined from both events by terminal oil leaks. Grouillard failed to pre-qualify in Britain and Germany when forced to use old-specification engines and was a DNQ in Hungary after two days of accidents and engine woes.

Holloway became race engineer at the Belgian GP, Divila having

Olivier Grouillard, Fomet F1-Ford (Italian GP)

been replaced after a disagreement with Rumi, and Grouillard had a new chassis. He not only qualified but also finished the race, tenth despite understeer and falling fuel pressure. Unfortunately, the new chassis was written off in a huge testing accident at Monza when launched over the kerbs at the first chicane. Forced back into the old chassis, Grouillard had engine failure late in the Italian GP.

With his relationship with Rumi increasingly strained, Marlboro-sponsored Grouillard attended a Camel press function after not pre-qualifying at Estoril – and was fired. Gabriele Tarquini replaced him and finished in Spain and Japan outside the top ten but failed to pre-qualify in Australia.

The contract with Herd's agency expired on 31 October and was not renewed as Rumi considered his options.

Gabriele Tarquini, Fomet F1-Ford (Japanese GP)

Nicola Larini, Lambo 291 (Brazilian GP)

MODENA TEAM

Mexican Fernando González Luna of González Luna Associates (GLAS) announced his intention to enter F1 in September 1989 with Lamborghini Engineering of Novara commissioned to supply both chassis and engine. Giovanni Aloi signed as test driver with Mauro Baldi favoured as his team-mate. Lamborghini technical director Mauro Forghieri began work on chassis and engine with Dallara's Mario Tolentino hired at the start of 1990.

A one-third scale model was completed in March and wind-tunnel testing began at Pininfarina's facility in Turin with the prototype ready to be launched on the Wednesday before the 1990 Mexican GP. The car was in transit to México City when news broke that Luna had disappeared and finances had collapsed. Lamborghini persevered nonetheless and Baldi shook down the Lambo 290 at Imola on 2 July. Lamborghini managing director Daniele Audetto

Eric van de Poele, Lambo 291 (German GP)

searched for a replacement client and Milan-based industrialist Sergio Patrucco, whose plan to invest in Larrousse fell through in 1989, led a consortium that took over the project on 10 September 1990.

Eric van de Poele, who had backing from long-term sponsors LeasePlan, signed an option with Patrucco's Modena Team until 31 October with Nicola Larini announced as team leader that month. Van de Poele was confirmed on 14 November, despite being slower than Marco Apicella (who signed as test driver) during a test at Estoril. Tolentino, who began the year engineering Larini's car, left after a couple of races so Forghieri was seconded to the team until Peter Wyss was poached from AGS in July. Dave Morgan was van de Poele's race engineer, as he had been during the 1990 F3000 season.

There was a welcome injection of cash when Yasuhiro Doi's Central Park company acquired a 40 per cent stake in the team in February. An evolution of the original car, the Lambo 291, was presented to the press at Mugello before testing there and at Monza. The bulky engine and angular monocoque, which initially failed its crash test, resulted in a large car and the tall van de Poele found the cockpit cramped so it had to be modified. The suspension was via push-rods all round and the radiators were mounted at an angle in distinctive curved sidepods.

A couple of favourable early results masked the Lambo 291's true level of competitiveness. Quick enough in a straight line, it was overweight, lacked grip and was terrible on bumpy tracks, so both drivers struggled to pre-qualify during the first half of the season. That said, Larini was seventh in the opening race at Phoenix when three laps down and van de Poele lined up 21st on the grid for the San Marino GP, in which he ran as high as fifth before running out of fuel as he entered his last lap, so was classified ninth. Neither

Pedro Chaves, Coloni C4-Ford (United States GP)

pre-qualified again until the German GP, including Larini's exclusion in Mexico when his rear wing was too high. The results at Phoenix and Imola allowed Modena Team to escape pre-qualifying thereafter, although the recalcitrant and underdeveloped Lambo 291 meant van de Poele was a DNQ on each occasion he tried and Larini only made it onto the grid at another four races. A finisher in 16th place in Hungary and Italy, he crashed at the first corner in Germany and hit Jean Alesi in the Australian rain.

Lamborghini did not want to build a chassis for 1992 so Patrucco was looking for a new partner by mid-season. With Lamborghini engine and gearbox confirmed for 1992, Patrucco held talks with Larrousse, Coloni and Reynard before trying to buy Ferrari's Guildford Technical Office. Sergio Rinland was hired to design a new chassis and worked at the GTO for just two days before the deal fell through. Modena Team sent a skeleton crew to the final two GPs and closed down after a single, disappointing campaign.

COLONI RACING

Coloni's spectacularly unsuccessful appearances continued into a final deflating campaign. Having tested at Estoril before the 1990 Portuguese GP, Pedro Chaves brought a limited budget from Mateus (wine) and Galp (fuel) and signed in December. Hopes to field a second car for Andrea de Cesaris fell through.

With finances stretched, the team persevered with Ford DFR engines as Enzo Coloni acted as team manager and race engineer. The 'new' Coloni C4 was scarcely altered from the C3 with design credited to the 'Coloni Technical Department and University of Perugia'. Chaves completed a brief shakedown at Magione on 25

February before the C4 was sent to Phoenix. Without any in-season testing, this was an unequal struggle even after Brian Hart DFRs were secured from Canada. Chaves failed to pre-qualify for every race until the end of the European season, the car not even leaving the pitlane in Italy. A Langford & Peck DFR was fitted for Chaves's home race at Estoril but blew up after six laps. Chaves quit on the Thursday before the Spanish GP and no one wanted to endure the inevitable failure to pre-qualify, so the car remained in the pits for the weekend.

Having considered not going to the last two long-haul races, Coloni sold a controlling interest to shoe manufacturer Andrea Sassetti that was announced at the Spanish GP. Rather than incur fines for non-participation, the team soldiered on with reigning Japanese F3 Champion Naoki Hattori behind the wheel. On the only F1 appearances of his career, Hattori did not pre-qualify in Japan and Australia when at least 4.8sec too slow.

Naoki Hattori, Coloni C4-Ford (Australian GP)

DRIVER PERFORMANCE

DRIVER	CAR–ENGINE	USA	BR	RSM	MC	CDN	MEX	F	GB	D	H	B	I	P	E	J	AUS
Michele Alboreto	Footwork A11C-Porsche	25 R	29 DNQ	30 DNQ	–	–	–	–	–	–	–	–	–	–	–	–	–
	Footwork FA12-Porsche	–	–	–	25 R	21 R	26 R	–	–	–	–	–	–	–	–	–	–
	Footwork FA12-Ford	–	–	–	–	–	–	25 R	26 R	27 DNQ	28 DNQ	31 NPQ	27 DNQ	24 15	24 R	27 DNQ	15 13
Jean Alesi	Ferrari 642	6 12 FL	5 6	7 R	9 3	7 R	4 R	–	–	–	–	–	–	–	–	–	–
	Ferrari 643	–	–	–	–	–	–	6 4	6 R	6 3	6 5	5 R	6 R	6 3	7 4	6 R	7 R
Julian Bailey	Lotus 102B-Judd	30 DNQ	30 DNQ	26 6	27 DNQ	–	–	–	–	–	–	–	–	–	–	–	–
Fabrizio Barbazza	AGS JH25-Ford	–	–	28 DNQ	28 DNQ	27 DNQ	30 DNQ	–	–	–	–	–	–	–	–	–	–
	AGS JH25B-Ford	–	–	–	–	–	–	28 DNQ	29 DNQ	33 NPQ	33 NPQ	34 NPQ	31 NPQ	–	–	–	–
	AGS JH27-Ford	–	–	–	–	–	–	–	–	–	–	–	–	31 NPQ	32 NPQ	–	–
Michael Bartels	Lotus 102B-Judd	–	–	–	–	–	–	28 DNQ	30 DNQ	–	28 DNQ	–	29 DNQ	–	–	–	–
Gerhard Berger	McLaren MP4/6-Honda	7 R	4 3	5 2 FL	6 R	6 R	5 R	5 R	4 2	3 4	5 4	4 2	3 4	2 R	1 R	1 1	2 3 FL
Éric Bernard	Lola L91-Ford	19 R	11 R	17 R	21 9	19 R	18 6	23 R	21 R	25 R	21 R	20 R	24 R	27 DNQ	23 R	NT DNP	–
Mark Blundell	Brabham BT59Y-Yamaha	24 R	25 R	–	–	–	–	–	–	–	–	–	–	–	–	–	–
	Brabham BT60Y-Yamaha	–	–	23 8	22 R	29 DNQ	12 R	17 R	12 R	21 12	20 R	13 6	11 12	15 R	12 R	30 NPQ	17 17
Thierry Boutsen	Ligier JS35-Lamborghini	20 R	18 10	24 7	16 7	16 R	14 8	–	–	–	–	–	–	–	–	–	–
	Ligier JS35B-Lamborghini	–	–	–	–	–	–	16 12	19 R	17 9	19 17	18 11	21 R	20 16	26 R	17 9	20 R
Martin Brundle	Brabham BT59Y-Yamaha	12 11	26 12	–	–	–	–	–	–	–	–	–	–	–	–	–	–
	Brabham BT60Y-Yamaha	–	–	18 11	NT DNQ	20 R	17 R	24 R	14 R	15 11	10 R	16 9	19 13	19 12	11 10	19 5	28 DNQ
Alex Caffi	Footwork A11C-Porsche	28 DNQ	27 DNQ	–	–	–	–	–	–	–	–	–	–	–	–	–	–
	Footwork FA12-Porsche	–	–	29 DNQ	NT DNQ	–	–	–	–	–	–	–	–	–	–	–	–
	Footwork FA12-Ford	–	–	–	–	–	–	–	32 NPQ	32 NPQ	29 DNQ	33 NPQ	33 NPQ	31 NPQ	26 10	23 15
Ivan Capelli	Leyton House CG911-Ilmor	18 R	15 R	22 R	18 R	13 R	22 R	15 R	16 R	12 R	9 6	12 R	12 8	9 17	8 R	–	–
Pedro Chaves	Coloni C4-Ford	32 NPQ	33 NPQ	34 NPQ	33 NPQ	34 NPQ	32 NPQ	34 NPQ	34 NPQ	34 NPQ	34 NPQ	34 NPQ	33 NPQ	34 NPQ	NT DNP	–	–
Érik Comas	Ligier JS35-Lamborghini	27 DNQ	23 R	19 10	23 10	26 8	27 DNQ	–	–	–	–	–	–	–	–	–	–
	Ligier JS35B-Lamborghini	–	–	–	–	–	–	14 11	27 DNQ	26 R	25 10	26 R	22 11	23 11	25 R	20 R	22 18
Andrea de Cesaris	Jordan 191-Ford	31 NPQ	13 R	11 R	10 R	11 4	11 4	13 6	13 R	7 5	17 7	11 13	14 7	14 8	17 R	11 R	12 8
Bertrand Gachot	Jordan 191-Ford	14 10	10 R	12 R	24 8	14 5	20 R	19 R	17 6	11 6	16 9 FL	–	–	–	–	–	–
	Lola L91-Ford	–	–	–	–	–	–	–	–	–	–	–	–	–	–	30 DNQ	–
Olivier Grouillard	Fomet FA1Me-Ford	33 NPQ	34 NPQ	–	–	–	–	–	–	–	–	–	–	–	–	–	–
	Fomet F1-Ford	–	–	32 NPQ	34 NPQ	31 NPQ	10 R	21 R	31 NPQ	31 NPQ	27 DNQ	23 10	26 R	32 NPQ	–	–	–
	AGS JH27-Ford	–	–	–	–	–	–	–	–	–	–	–	–	–	33 NPQ	–	–
Maurício Gugelmin	Leyton House CG911-Ilmor	23 R	8 R	15 12	15 R	23 R	21 R	9 7	9 R	16 R	13 11	15 R	18 15	7 7	13 7	18 8	14 14
Mika Häkkinen	Lotus 102B-Judd	13 R	22 9	25 5	26 R	24 R	24 9	27 DNQ	25 12	23 R	26 14	24 R	25 14	26 14	21 R	21 R	25 19
Naoki Hattori	Coloni C4-Ford	–	–	–	–	–	–	–	–	–	–	–	–	–	31 NPQ	32 NPQ	–
Johnny Herbert	Lotus 102B-Judd	–	–	–	–	30 DNQ	25 10	20 10	24 14	–	–	21 7	–	22 R	–	23 R	21 11
Stefan Johansson	AGS JH25-Ford	29 DNQ	28 DNQ	–	–	–	–	–	–	–	–	–	–	–	–	–	–
	Footwork FA12-Porsche	–	–	–	–	25 R	29 DNQ	–	–	–	–	–	–	–	–	–	–
	Footwork FA12-Ford	–	–	–	–	–	–	30 DNQ	28 DNQ	–	–	–	–	–	–	–	–
Nicola Larini	Lambo 291	17 7	32 NPQ	33 NPQ	31 NPQ	32 NPQ	NT NPQ	32 NPQ	32 NPQ	24 R	24 16	28 DNQ	23 16	29 DNQ	28 DNQ	28 DNQ	19 R
J.J. Lehto	Dallara F191-Judd	10 R	19 R	16 3	13 11	17 R	16 R	26 R	11 13	20 R	12 R	14 R	20 R	18 R	15 8	12 R	11 12
Nigel Mansell	Williams FW14-Renault	4 R	3 R FL	4 R	5 2	2 6 FL	2 2 FL	4 1 FL	1 1 FL	1 1	3 2	3 R	2 1	4 DSQ	2 1	3 R	3 2
Pierluigi Martini	Minardi M191-Ferrari	15 9	20 R	9 4	14 12	18 7	15 R	12 9	23 9	10 R	18 R	9 12	10 R	8 4	19 13	7 R	10 R
Stefano Modena	Tyrrell 020-Honda	11 4	9 R	6 R	2 R	9 2	8 11	11 R	10 7	14 13	8 12	10 R	13 R	12 R	14 16	14 6	9 10
Gianni Morbidelli	Minardi M191-Ferrari	26 R	21 8	8 R	17 R	15 R	23 7	10 R	20 11	19 R	23 13	19 R	17 9	13 9	16 14	8 R	–
	Ferrari 643	–	–	–	–	–	–	–	–	–	–	–	–	–	–	–	8 6
Roberto Moreno	Benetton B190B-Ford	8 R	14 7	–	–	–	–	–	–	–	–	–	–	–	–	–	–
	Benetton B191-Ford	–	–	13 R	8 4	5 R	9 5	8 R	7 R	9 8	15 8	8 4 FL	–	–	–	–	–
	Jordan 191-Ford	–	–	–	–	–	–	–	–	–	–	–	–	9 R	16 10	–	–
	Minardi M191-Ferrari	–	–	–	–	–	–	–	–	–	–	–	–	–	–	–	18 16
Satoru Nakajima	Tyrrell 020-Honda	16 5	16 R	10 R	11 R	12 10	13 12	18 R	15 8	13 R	14 15	22 R	15 R	21 13	18 17	15 R	24 R
Riccardo Patrese	Williams FW14-Renault	3 R	2 2	2 R	3 R	1 3	1 1	1 5	3 R	4 2 FL	2 3	17 5	4 R	1 1 FL	3 3 FL	5 3	4 5
Nelson Piquet	Benetton B190B-Ford	5 3	7 5	–	–	–	–	–	–	–	–	–	–	–	–	–	–
	Benetton B191-Ford	–	–	14 R	4 R	8 1	6 R	7 8	8 5	8 R	11 R	6 3	8 6	11 5	10 11	10 7	5 4

DRIVER PERFORMANCE CONTINUED

DRIVER	CAR–ENGINE	USA	BR	RSM	MC	CDN	MEX	F	GB	D	H	B	I	P	E	J	AUS
Emanuele Pirro	Dallara F191-Judd	9 R	12 11	31 NPQ	12 6	10 9	33 NPQ	31 NPQ	18 10	18 10	7 R	25 8	16 10	17 R	9 15	16 R	13 7
Alain Prost	Ferrari 642	2 2	6 4	3 DNS	7 5 FL	4 4	7 R	–	–	–	–	–	–	–	–	–	–
	Ferrari 643	–	–	–	–	–	–	2 2	5 3	5 R	4 R	2 R	5 3	5 R	6 2	4 4	–
Michael Schumacher	Jordan 191-Ford	–	–	–	–	–	–	–	–	–	7 R	–	–	–	–	–	–
	Benetton B191-Ford	–	–	–	–	–	–	–	–	–	–	7 5	10 6	5 6	9 R	6 R	
Ayrton Senna	McLaren MP4/6-Honda	1 1	1 1	1 1	1 1	3 R	3 3	3 3	2 4	2 7	1 1	1 1	2 2 FL	3 2	3 5	2 2 FL	1 1
Aguri Suzuki	Lola L91-Ford	21 6	17 DNS	20 R	19 R	22 R	19 R	22 R	22 R	22 R	22 R	27 DNQ	30 DNQ	25 R	27 DNQ	25 R	27 DNQ
Gabriele Tarquini	AGS JH25-Ford	22 8	24 R	27 DNQ	20 R	28 DNQ	28 DNQ	–	–	–	–	–	–	–	–	–	–
	AGS JH25B-Ford	–	–	–	–	–	29 DNQ	30 DNQ	29 DNQ	31 NPQ	32 NPQ	–	–	–	–	–	
	AGS JH27-Ford	–	–	–	–	–	–	–	–	–	–	–	32 NPQ	28 DNQ	–	–	–
	Fomet F1-Ford	–	–	–	–	–	–	–	–	–	–	–	–	–	22 12	24 11	31 NPQ
Eric van de Poele	Lambo 291	34 NPQ	31 NPQ	21 9	32 NPQ	33 NPQ	31 NPQ	33 NPQ	33 NPQ	30 DNQ	29 DNQ	30 DNQ	29 DNQ	30 DNQ	30 DNQ	29 DNQ	29 DNQ
Karl Wendlinger	Leyton House CG911-Ilmor	–	–	–	–	–	–	–	–	–	–	–	–	–	–	22 R	26 20
Alex Zanardi	Jordan 191-Ford	–	–	–	–	–	–	–	–	–	–	–	–	20 9	13 R	16 9	

FORMULA 1 RACE WINNERS

ROUND	RACE (CIRCUIT)	DATE	WINNER
1	Iceberg United States Grand Prix (Phoenix)	Mar 10	Ayrton Senna (McLaren MP4/6-Honda)
2	Grande Prêmio do Brasil (Interlagos)	Mar 24	Ayrton Senna (McLaren MP4/6-Honda)
3	Gran Premio di San Marino (Imola)	Apr 28	Ayrton Senna (McLaren MP4/6-Honda)
4	Grand Prix de Monaco (Monte Carlo)	May 12	Ayrton Senna (McLaren MP4/6-Honda)
5	Grand Prix Molson du Canada (Montréal)	Jun 2	Nelson Piquet (Benetton B191-Ford)
6	Gran Premio de México (México City)	Jun 16	Riccardo Patrese (Williams FW14-Renault)
7	Rhône-Poulenc Grand Prix de France (Magny-Cours)	Jul 7	Nigel Mansell (Williams FW14-Renault)
8	British Grand Prix (Silverstone)	Jul 14	Nigel Mansell (Williams FW14-Renault)
9	Grosser Mobil 1 Preis von Deutschland (Hockenheim)	Jul 28	Nigel Mansell (Williams FW14-Renault)
10	Magyar Nagydíj (Hungaroring)	Aug 11	Ayrton Senna (McLaren MP4/6-Honda)
11	Grand Prix de Belgique (Spa-Francorchamps)	Aug 25	Ayrton Senna (McLaren MP4/6-Honda)
12	Coca Cola Gran Premio d'Italia (Monza)	Sep 8	Nigel Mansell (Williams FW14-Renault)
13	Grande Premio de Portugal (Estoril)	Sep 22	Riccardo Patrese (Williams FW14-Renault)
14	Gran Premio Tio Pepe de España (Catalunya)	Sep 29	Nigel Mansell (Williams FW14-Renault)
15	Fuji Television Japanese Grand Prix (Suzuka)	Oct 20	Gerhard Berger (McLaren MP4/6-Honda)
16	Foster's Australian Grand Prix (Adelaide)	Nov 3	Ayrton Senna (McLaren MP4/6-Honda)

DRIVERS' CHAMPIONSHIP

	DRIVERS	POINTS
1	Ayrton Senna	96
2	Nigel Mansell	72
3	Riccardo Patrese	53
4	Gerhard Berger	43
5	Alain Prost	34
6	Nelson Piquet	26.5
7	Jean Alesi	21
8	Stefano Modena	10
9	Andrea de Cesaris	9
10	Roberto Moreno	8
11	Pierluigi Martini	6
12=	Bertrand Gachot	4
	J.J. Lehto	4
	Michael Schumacher	4
15=	Martin Brundle	2
	Mika Häkkinen	2
	Satoru Nakajima	2
18=	Julian Bailey	1
	Éric Bernard	1
	Mark Blundell	1
	Ivan Capelli	1
	Emanuele Pirro	1
	Aguri Suzuki	1
24	Gianni Morbidelli	0.5

CONSTRUCTORS' CHAMPIONSHIP

	CONSTRUCTORS	POINTS
1	McLaren-Honda	139
2	Williams-Renault	125
3	Ferrari	55.5
4	Benetton-Ford	38.5
5	Jordan-Ford	13
6	Tyrrell-Honda	12
7	Minardi-Ferrari	6
8	Dallara-Judd	5
9=	Lotus-Judd	3
	Brabham-Yamaha	3
11	Lola-Ford	2
12	Leyon House-Ilmor	1

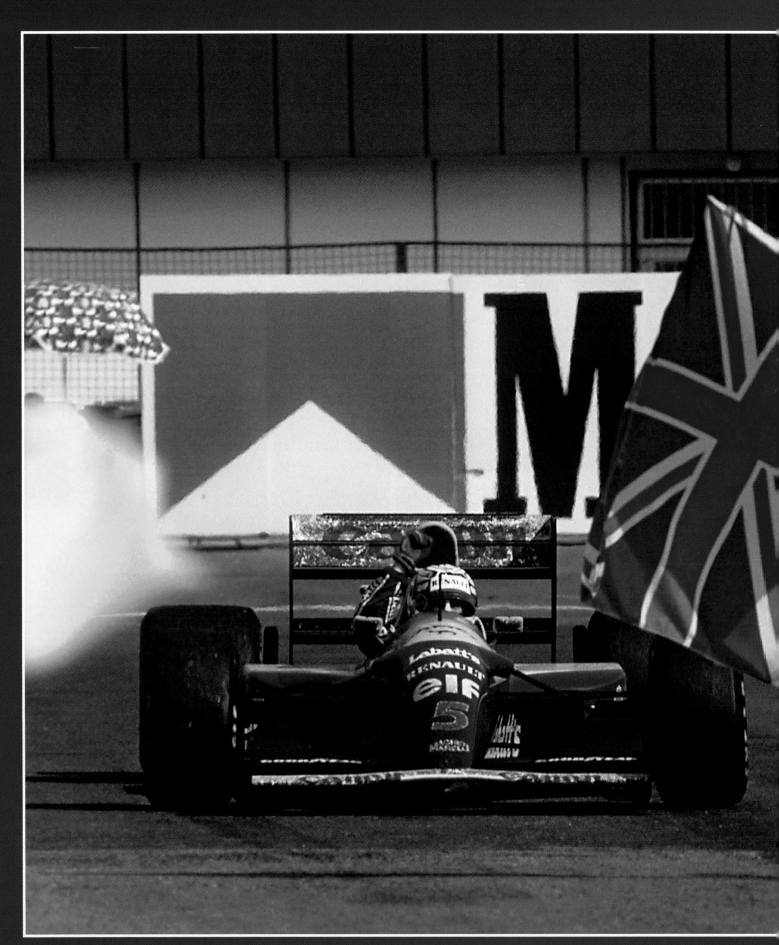

Nigel Mansell clinched the World Championship by finishing second in Hungary

1992
MANSELL AND WILLIAMS FW14B DOMINATE

Ayrton Senna held off Nigel Mansell in Monaco to score his first victory of 1992

There was a crowd invasion after Nigel Mansell's Silverstone win

After 12 years of drama and heroics, Nigel Mansell finally won the World Championship in 1992, and promptly quit F1. His Williams FW14B was the most sophisticated car seen to date and the Renault V10 now outgunned Honda's V12, so the Englishman enjoyed a season of rare domination.

For the first time in history, the World Championship visited all six inhabited continents with Kyalami hosting the first South African GP since 1985. The impressive new Nippon Autopolis was to have held the Asian GP on 5 April but the race was cancelled amid financial problems. The European GP was scheduled at Jerez (4 October) although that too was cancelled when the calendar was limited to 16 races as preferred by the teams. There was no United States GP although Tony George announced in July that Indianapolis wanted to attract both F1 and NASCAR to the Brickyard.

TAG Heuer superseded Longines as F1's official timekeeper. Peter Warr replaced Jan Corsmit as F1's permanent steward for this season only and chief scrutineer Charlie Whiting was named as the championship's technical delegate. English replaced French as the official language of F1 rules and regulations. Special fuels boosted hydrocarbons and increased power but the Fédération Internationale du Sport Automobile suddenly issued a clarification ten days before the Hungarian

Michael Schumacher sparks his way to his first victory in Belgium

GP, imposing commercial pump fuel with immediate effect. It was a controversial move that prompted legal action from Renault and Elf that rumbled on until a compromise was finally agreed for 1993.

The recession started to bite and mechanics were laid off at some teams during the winter of 1991/92. Andrea Moda (née Coloni), Brabham, Fondmetal (Osella) and March all started a GP for the last time in 1992. John Barnard worked as a consultant for Toyota's development arm TOM's (Tachi Oiwa Motorsports) but no F1 programme was sanctioned. Reynard tested a scale model of its F1 design in Imperial College's wind tunnel during 1991 before the project was shelved when a deal with Yamaha fell through and a suitable alternative could not be found. Giuseppe Cipriani's ambitious Il Barone Rampante F3000 team planned to graduate. Enrique Scalabroni began designing a chassis in August 1991 and Flavio Briatore brokered a deal to take over Jordan's Ford HB contract. Without the facilities to build the car in time, there was talk of buying Tyrrell or Fondmetal but those deals foundered.

Goodyear supplied the whole field following Pirelli's withdrawal so qualifying tyres were not required. Any tyre manufacturer wanting to enter the category in the future had to supply at least 25 per cent of the field.

Gerhard Berger shares the Australian podium with Michael Schumacher

CANON WILLIAMS TEAM

Williams updated its 1991 design with traction control and 'reactive' suspension (Lotus registered the term 'active suspension' in the 1980s), the computer-controlled ride-height system now reliable after 7,000 winter testing miles. An automatic clutch was tried before Christmas but only raced after both 1992 titles had been secured in Belgium. The FW14B was so dominant that its replacement (FW15) was not risked after completion in September.

Continuity also extended to the cockpit as Nigel Mansell and Riccardo Patrese were confirmed on 13 August 1991 with Damon Hill as test driver once more. Patrese's contract extension was a surprise to Ayrton Senna, who had spoken to Williams. Al Unser Jr, the 1990 Indycar champion, tested for Williams at Estoril during the week of 18–23 November 1991 but the American's much-anticipated F1 switch never happened.

Dominant in winter testing, Mansell won the opening five races (a record) from pole position with Patrese second at Kyalami, México City, Interlagos and Imola. Williams-Renault led every lap of those five races and only Patrese's crash in Spain prevented a fifth 1–2. The Italian then suffered whiplash and a bruised shoulder when he crashed heavily during the following week's Imola test after a tyre punctured at Tamburello.

Williams's winning run ended in Monaco when, believing he had a puncture, Mansell changed tyres with seven laps remaining. He caught new leader Senna but could not find a way past the 'wide' McLaren-Honda and lost by 0.214sec with the oversteering Patrese third. Senna beat the Williams-Renaults to pole in Canada and led

Mansell until lap 15. The Englishman lunged for the inside line at the chicane before the pits and lost control on the 'marbles' with his Williams-Renault launched over the kerb and out of the race. Mansell confronted McLaren's Ron Dennis and complained to the stewards but the consensus was that it had been his mistake. 'A more championship-minded driver would have weighed the odds,' David Tremayne wrote in *Motor Sport*, 'considered waiting a little longer to see how things developed and in any case wouldn't have tried down the inside of an area known to be slippery.' Patrese was second when his gearbox broke.

Canada was a blip as Mansell led Williams 1–2s in qualifying and race at Magny-Cours and Silverstone, where his home victory prompted an unruly track invasion. Normally overshadowed by Mansell, Patrese made the better start and restart in France, where he ostentatiously waved Mansell through in front of the pits. Unsettled since the spring by talk of Alain Prost joining Williams in 1993, Mansell then converted a third successive pole position into another victory at Hockenheim to stand on the cusp of the World Championship. Patrese spun away a podium finish while trying to take second from Senna on the last lap.

Mansell raced the new RS04 version of Renault's V10 engine for the first time in Hungary. Smaller than the RS03C and with new block, cylinder heads and crankshaft, it had improved torque and better fuel consumption. With the McLaren-Honda suited to the sinuous Hungaroring, Mansell qualified second, ran fourth after the start, changed tyres following a puncture and climbed from sixth to second to clinch the title with five races to spare. Patrese started

Nigel Mansell, Williams FW14B-Renault (Australian GP)

Riccardo Patrese, Williams FW14B-Renault (Monaco GP)

from pole and had a 30sec lead when he spun down to sixth place, after which his engine failed, a fault that may have been connected with FISA's insistence that commercial fuel be used from that race.

Williams was confirmed as constructors' champion after finishing second and third in Belgium, despite more engine troubles. Both drivers led in Italy only for hydraulic failures to eliminate Mansell and leave Patrese stuck in gear as he limped home fifth. Unhappy at Prost's imminent arrival and having announced his decision to defect to Indycars in 1993, Mansell scored his then-record ninth victory of 1992 at Estoril. Patrese was lucky to escape injury when he hit Gerhard Berger as the McLaren-Honda darted for the pits, his Williams-Renault launched into an end-over-end roll. In Japan, Patrese scored his sixth career victory after Mansell handed him the lead prior to an engine blow-up.

A triumphant campaign ended in more controversy when Senna crashed into Mansell as they disputed the lead in Adelaide. 'Senna has no place on the track,' the champion raged. 'He has a screw loose in his head.' New leader Patrese lost fuel pressure but was confirmed as championship runner-up when Michael Schumacher did not win the race.

HONDA MARLBORO McLAREN

McLaren-Honda needed extensive in-season engine development in 1991 to retain both World Championships for the fourth successive

season and so work on the 1992 version of Honda's V12 was delayed. The new RA122E had a revised vee angle (from 60 to 75 degrees), variable-length trumpets and pneumatic valves. Some increased internal frictional losses initially reduced power while both performance and tyre wear were compromised by the heavy fuel load required for the 12-cylinder unit.

There were vague rumblings of offers for Ayrton Senna's services from both Ferrari and Benetton before he re-signed with McLaren on 17 September 1991 while Gerhard Berger remained in the final year of his deal. Benetton's Giorgio Ascanelli was poached as Senna's race engineer while Berger continued to work with Steve Hallam. Dropped by Brabham, Mark Blundell joined Allan McNish as test driver. McLaren took over Ferrari's Guildford Technical Office to produce its iconic new road car.

For the first three races McLaren decided to use an updated MP4/6B with a longer nose and redesigned front wings. Stunned by Williams-Renault's speed and reliability in testing, Ron Dennis accelerated development of the new McLaren MP4/7A-Honda by a month. Having lost the opening race at Kyalami by 34.675sec, third-placed Senna told the press: 'There is no way I can fight the Williams. I can play a little, like today with Riccardo [Patrese], but no more than that.' His Mexican GP was a disaster for he wrote off his race chassis on Friday, badly bruising his legs, only qualified sixth and retired from third due to transmission failure. After Berger's fuel-saving fifth in South Africa, he had his own accidents during

Ayrton Senna, McLaren MP4/6B-Honda (Mexican GP)

Gerhard Berger, McLaren MP4/6B-Honda (South African GP)

Mexican practice and finished fourth as McLaren lagged behind both Williams and Benetton.

McNish conducted the MP4/7A's shakedown at Silverstone on the day after the South African GP before Blundell took over. Neil Oatley's design team (Henri Durand, David North, David Neilson and Matthew Jeffreys) eschewed McLaren's preferred evolutionary approach as every part was reassessed. TAG Electronics developed the new automatic transverse six-speed gearbox and electro-hydraulic clutch, which was operated by buttons on the steering wheel with back-up paddle shift if needed. The fly-by-wire throttle allowed the driver to change gear without lifting and traction control was introduced in Hungary. Conventional push-rod suspension via unequal wishbones was standard while the active MP4/7B was tried in Italy but not raced, its computer-controlled suspension developed in conjunction with Showa. New production methods were employed for the narrow carbon-fibre monocoque, the high and slim sidepods housed repositioned radiators and a raised nose was adopted for the first time.

Senna drove the MP4/7A at Silverstone on 11–12 March and three new chassis were sent to Interlagos in addition to the three MP4/6Bs used in Mexico. With 81 team members at the race, this unprecedented show of technical commitment and financial might was not a success. Both MP4/7As started from the second row of the grid but retired by lap 18, Senna after criticism by the Benetton drivers for blocking. With the MP4/7As proving to be unstable in high-speed corners and having to carry up to 60lb more fuel at the start, the cars continued to disappoint as Berger managed fourth place in Spain and Senna third at Imola, where Berger walked away from a big accident

Gerhard Berger, McLaren MP4/7A-Honda (Australian GP)

Ayrton Senna, McLaren MP4/7A-Honda (Portuguese GP)

while testing and retired after contact with Jean Alesi's Ferrari.

In Monaco, Senna crucially forced his way past Riccardo Patrese at the start and took the lead when Mansell pitted. He then defended brilliantly to hold off a quicker car on new tyres to score an unexpected fifth victory in the Principality, with Berger sidelined by gearbox failure. More competitive in Canada, Senna started from pole but collided with Mansell as they disputed the lead and retired due to an electronic glitch. Berger, having passed Patrese in the aftermath of the Mansell/Senna fracas, went on to win despite having to use the paddle-shift back-up after the gearbox buttons stopped working, and surviving a post-race scrutineering issue with his rear wing.

Senna was hit by Michael Schumacher on the opening lap in France and a CV joint failed moments after taking third in Britain. Berger blew his engine at Magny-Cours and as he crossed the line in fifth at Silverstone. Six days after the British GP, Japanese newspaper *Asashi Shimbun* reported that Honda was pulling out of F1, which was finally confirmed at the Italian GP. That left McLaren without an engine partner and Senna considering his future. 'If I do not get a competitive situation I am not going to drive next year,' he told reporters at Silverstone. 'I would prefer to stay in Brazil preparing myself for another year… To race for second or third is not worth it.'

Senna withstood Patrese's pressure to finish second in Germany and Mansell's to win in Hungary, where Berger finished third. In Belgium, the field had to take avoiding action when Berger's clutch failed at the start. Reckoning an alternative strategy was his only hope of victory, Senna stayed on slick tyres too long when it rained, eventually changing to wets to claim fifth. Senna won the Italian GP after the Williams-Renaults had problems and Berger passed the hamstrung Patrese for fourth on the last lap.

Berger was second in Portugal despite back pain and being hit by Patrese as he pitted; Senna was third after three stops and a late slow puncture. With his relationship with McLaren at an all-time low, Senna had engine failure on the second lap in Japan and crashed into Mansell while challenging for the lead in Australia. Second at Suzuka, Berger signed off his McLaren career by beating Schumacher to victory in that Adelaide finale.

This had not been a happy season although McLaren-Honda won five times and finished as runners-up in their last season together (until 2015). Berger scored just a point less than Senna in his best season with McLaren. However, fourth and fifth in the drivers' standings were slim pickings by recent McLaren standards.

CAMEL BENETTON FORD

The 1991 restructure meant that Benetton effectively had two team principals, with Tom Walkinshaw responsible for team and technical, and Flavio Briatore for commercial affairs. Having raced sports cars for Walkinshaw since 1985, Martin Brundle signed as Michael Schumacher's team-mate on 10 October 1991 and Alex Zanardi joined as test driver before the start of the season. Gordon Message

Michael Schumacher, Benetton B191B-Ford (Mexican GP)

Martin Brundle, Benetton B191B-Ford (Brazilian GP)

was team manager once more with Joan Villadelprat now factory-based. Pat Fry engineered Brundle's car with Pat Symonds early in his long and fruitful relationship with Schumacher. Reliability was excellent and Benetton-Ford scored points at every race to take third in the constructors' standings.

At the 1991 Canadian GP, Ford announced a new V12 engine for Benetton's exclusive use but it never materialised, so the latest-specification Ford HBs were used. The move into the new 85,000sq ft Whiteways Technical Centre at Enstone in the Oxfordshire countryside was completed in October 1992, with those previously based at John Barnard's Godalming offshoot also relocated.

An updated Benetton B191B and Series VI V8s were used at the opening three races, where Schumacher finished 4–3–3. In contrast, Brundle retired on all three occasions: his clutch failed after a first-lap incident at Kyalami, his engine overheated in Mexico and he hit Jean Alesi at Interlagos. Both drivers were critical of Ayrton Senna's robust defence of second place in Brazil, where the McLaren-Honda was clearly slower. 'I wouldn't have expected this kind of driving from a three-time World Champion,' Schumacher told the press afterwards.

Credited to Ross Brawn but with Rory Byrne's influence evident, the Benetton B192 ran at Silverstone on 7 April with the nose further raised and front wing supports now straight. There was no time to build active suspension or semi-automatic gearbox so conventional push-rod/twin-damper suspension and transverse six-speed gearbox were retained. The sidepods contained radiators for water and oil in the right but water only in the left. The new rear diffuser resembled Byrne's B190 with six vertical plates. Brundle tested at Silverstone

Michael Schumacher, Benetton B192-Ford (Spanish GP)

and Pembrey while Schumacher spent two days at Magny-Cours as teething problems were sorted.

Three B192s were sent to the Spanish GP, where Schumacher recovered from a heavy accident on Friday to qualify and finish second, while Brundle lost his clutch and spun out after four laps in the rain. They qualified on row three at Imola, where Brundle finally hit form despite back pain following a practice incident with Alesi. He held off Schumacher in the early stages and finished fourth; second best for once, Schumacher spun out of the race.

Both drivers scored in points in Monaco, Schumacher fourth and Brundle fifth after changing his nosecone. A new Series VII engine with pneumatic valves and revised internals and management system was tried in qualifying in Canada but not raced until Germany. The quicker Benetton driver in Canada, Brundle passed his team-mate and lay second when transmission failure denied him the chance of victory, leaving Schumacher to inherited second place. Brundle then scored his first podium finishes with third places in France and Britain. Schumacher collided with Stefano Modena during both races but survived at Silverstone to take three points. His tetchy relationship with Senna was worsened by contact at Magny-Cours and boiled over during the Hockenheim test when they scuffled in the pits after Senna claimed to have been baulked.

Third (Schumacher) and fourth (Brundle) in Germany thanks to Riccardo Patrese's last-lap spin, they collided during the Hungarian GP with Brundle going on to finish fifth. Rain showers turned the Belgian GP into a lottery in which Schumacher, a year on from his F1 début, changed tyres at the right moments and survived running wide at Stavelot to score his breakthrough victory. Brundle passed Schumacher during that brief 'off' but only finished fourth after changing to slicks a lap later.

After learning that he would be replaced in 1993, Brundle led a Benetton 2–3 at Monza, Schumacher having changed his nosecone following contact with Thierry Boutsen at the start. Brundle finished fourth in Portugal, where Schumacher started from the back and was delayed after running over debris from the Berger/Patrese accident. Laid low in Japan by food poisoning, Brundle nonetheless qualified in the midfield after a crash and finished third, Schumacher having retired with gearbox failure when third behind the Williams-Renaults.

They reverted to the older engine in Australia and scored a double podium, Schumacher's second place clinching third spot in the drivers' championship behind the unbeatable Williams-Renaults. Brundle was a career-best sixth in the final standings, having been out-qualified by his phenomenal young team-mate at every race.

SCUDERIA FERRARI

Key to the *Scuderia*'s revival in the 1970s, and recently responsible for organising the Italia 90 World Cup, Luca di Montezemolo returned to Ferrari by replacing Piero Fusaro as president on 15 November 1991.

With Alain Prost out of favour and eventually fired, Ferrari were looking for a new team-mate for Jean Alesi. Mario and Michael Andretti visited Maranello in September 1991, ostensibly to collect Mario's new F40 road car; a two-year offer for Michael's services was

Martin Brundle, Benetton B192-Ford (French GP)

reported although IndyCar's new champion remained with Newman-Haas Racing. Keke Rosberg lunched with Piero Ferrari on 7 November and there was talk of a substantial offer to lure Nigel Mansell back to the team. On the verge of signing for Scuderia Italia before Prost's dismissal, it was Ivan Capelli who signed on 22 November although the popular Italian's dream move soon turned sour. Nicola Larini replaced Andrea Montermini as test driver alongside Gianni Morbidelli.

A new technical director was a priority and Pierguido Castelli was reassigned within Fiat. Talks were held with Harvey Postlethwaite and John Barnard before the former's return was announced on 17 December. Steve Nichols and Jean-Claude Migeot initially reported to the Englishman but Nichols soon replaced Postlethwaite at Sauber. Paolo Massai and Amedeo Visconti continued to lead the engine and research departments respectively. Sante Ghedini was appointed as team manager, Claudio Lombardi remained general manager and di Montezemolo hired Niki Lauda as his personal adviser. 'It is an enormous challenge,' Lauda said. 'When it comes to winning it is all about strategy. That is where McLaren is so strong and we will try to work on it.' Francesco Longanesi returned to FISA and Marco Piccinini resigned, eventually becoming president of Italy's national motorsport body, the Commissione Sportiva Automobilistica Italiana, in May 1993. Both race engineers left in the winter so Luigi Urbinelli and Gianfranco Fantuzzi were responsible for Alesi and Capelli respectively.

The radical Ferrari F92A was introduced at Fiorano on 6 February with Nichols leading the design process. Distinctive sidepods drew

Jean Alesi, Ferrari F92A (Mexican GP)

Ivan Capelli, Ferrari F92A (Spanish GP)

comparison with an F15 fighter plane. Set apart from the chassis and raised by five inches, they channelled air to the twin diffusers at the rear. Migeot evolved his high-nose concept, which now featured a Benetton-inspired low-slung wing. Most unusual was the double-floor arrangement: the bottom flat as per the regulations, six inches below a sculpted aerodynamic arrangement. However, one side effect was that the rerouted exhaust system compromised airflow to the radiators. The F92A had traction control and push-rod suspension with a single front shock absorber, initially Bilstein but Penske from the Monaco GP. The revised engine was, according to Lombardi, 'the lightest and most compact V12 in Formula 1', but it was underpowered and unreliable. The longitudinal semi-automatic gearbox had six rather than seven speeds to save weight.

If 1991 had been disappointing, then 1992 was a complete disaster. The F92A lacked straight-line speed and grip while its high

centre of gravity resulted in poor handling. Alesi drove his heart out but his lack of testing acumen and Capelli's crumbling confidence did little to lift Ferrari out of this technical quagmire.

Alesi's engine failed during the opening two races and Capelli switched off at Kyalami before his blew up. They qualified behind the customer Dallara-Ferraris in Mexico where Capelli lined up 20th and crashed into Karl Wendlinger's March at the start. In search of reliability, they switched back to the 1991 engine to score points in Brazil – Alesi fourth, Capelli fifth – although Lombardi admitted that 'the car is a long way from being competitive'.

Capelli qualified fifth in Spain – his best starting position of 1992 – but lost a points finish when he spun with two laps to go. With the wet track masking the F92A's deficiencies, Alesi made a great start from eighth on the grid and spun twice before finishing third after a fine recovery drive. Alesi had a new undertray and transverse gearbox

Jean Alesi, Ferrari F92AT (Australian GP)

for the San Marino GP where both Ferraris crashed out of the race, the Frenchman having collided with Gerhard Berger's McLaren as he defended fourth. Alesi qualified fourth in Monaco and lay fifth when his gearbox electronics failed, while Capelli crashed. With speculation already growing about his future, Capelli crashed again in Canada, where Alesi reverted to the longitudinal gearbox to finish third after a race of attrition.

Unhurt in a heavy accident when something broke at Becketts during the Silverstone test in June, Alesi was denied another strong points score in the French GP when his engine failed late following a heroic drive on slicks in the wet. A new rear wing, undertray and rear suspension in Germany scarcely improved handling and Alesi finished a distant fifth. Only ninth at Silverstone, Capelli recovered from his own high-speed testing crash at Imola to finish sixth in Hungary only to be told he was being released.

There was yet more upheaval in the technical department in August as John Barnard returned on a five-year contract, reporting directly to di Montezemolo and based in England as before. The Guildford Technical Office had been sold to McLaren so Barnard found new premises to the south of Guildford. Lombardi now ran the engine department while Postlethwaite replaced him managing day-to-day team affairs and production.

Having become the last team to use a longitudinal gearbox, Ferrari introduced the F92AT with seven-speed transverse gearbox at August's Monza test. It had new rear suspension, revised aerodynamics with a shorter upper floor, a larger airbox and improved gearbox cooling. Alesi used the new car to qualify fifth at Spa-Francorchamps but collided with Nigel Mansell at La Source on lap eight. Capelli was sixth in the old F92A when his engine failed.

Ivan Capelli, Ferrari F92AT (Portuguese GP)

Both drivers had F92ATs for the Italian GP and qualified in the top seven, Alesi third after using a rapid development engine. They retired simultaneously on unlucky lap 13, Alesi's fuel pump having failed and Capelli stranded in the Parabolica sand trap. Neither finished at Estoril where it was Alesi's turn to spin on lap 13.

Larini had been testing all summer and had just driven a F92A fitted with new active suspension that had been developed in conjunction with Magneti Marelli. Ferrari decided to race it in Japan and Australia and chose Larini to replace Capelli as he had more experience of the system. Having stalled at the start of the Japanese GP and started from the back in Adelaide following a clutch issue on parade lap, Larini finished both races outside the top ten. Alesi completed an unsatisfactory year by finishing fifth in Japan and fourth in Australia. Nigel Roebuck was blunt in his assessment in *Autosport*: 'Ferrari's 1992 was abysmal, a pathetic embarrassment to a great name.'

Nicola Larini, Ferrari F92A (Australian GP)

Mika Häkkinen, Lotus 102D-Ford (Mexican GP)

Johnny Herbert, Lotus 102D-Ford (Spanish GP)

TEAM LOTUS

Lotus was one of the feel-good stories of 1992 as its resurgence continued under Peter Collins and Peter Wright, although that optimism eventually proved short-lived. Chris Murphy replaced technical director Enrique Scalabroni at the end of 1991; team manager Nigel Stepney formed a new F3000 outfit with Nelson Piquet so Benetton's Paul Bussey was hired; operations manager Greg Field joined Brabham. Having started 12 GPs for Lotus in 1969–70, John Miles returned as an engineer to work on the suspension. Renowned for his sponsorship-hunting skills during his own racing career, Guy Edwards arrived at the start of the season with responsibility for commercial affairs. Hitachi joined the growing list of sponsors in February and Castrol, which Edwards had previously taken to TWR Jaguar, became title partner before the British GP.

Lotus took over Jordan's supply of Ford HB Series V engines on a two-year deal, thus renewing its partnership with Ford and Cosworth 25 years after the début of the DFV-powered Lotus 49. Johnny Herbert and Mika Häkkinen were confirmed before Christmas. 'With the Ford HB engine, a young and promising driving team and a talented, highly motivated staff, we are confident,' Collins said. Lotus signed a new agreement with Frazer Nash to supply electronics and acquired another autoclave following the closure of Comtec (Composite Technics).

The old chassis was converted from Judd to Ford power as the Lotus 102D to serve while Murphy completed a new design. Despite the old machinery, Herbert was sixth in South Africa and Häkkinen sixth in Mexico, where Herbert recovered from spinning at the first corner to finish seventh. Inexplicably lacking grip in Brazil, Häkkinen finished

Johnny Herbert, Lotus 107-Ford (Monaco GP)

Mika Häkkinen, Lotus 107-Ford (Belgian GP)

tenth (when stuck in third gear) while Herbert was the innocent victim as the Ligiers crashed into each other.

Both 102Ds spun out of the wet Spanish GP on the day that the new Lotus 107 was launched. This had semi-active suspension at launch with springs and dampers (single at the front, twin to the rear) controlled from a computer in the right-hand sidepod. This could be switched to conventional passive suspension with ease and this was chosen for its début at Imola. The manual transverse gearbox with Xtrac internals and Lotus casing proved problematic. Aerodynamicist John Davis used Lotus's ex-Williams quarter-scale wind tunnel to design the attractive body shape. A fully active version, semi-automatic gearbox and traction control were all under development.

Teething problems ruined initial testing at Imola and Herbert's 107 was the first retirement from the San Marino GP through gearbox failure. Häkkinen did not qualify a 102D after two difficult days at Imola and had his own 107 for second qualifying in Monaco although neither Lotus finished that race or the next. Passive suspension was used in Canada where Herbert and Häkkinen started from a promising sixth and tenth respectively. They ran in the top seven only to retire at half distance. An excellent fourth (Häkkinen) and sixth (Herbert) in France, they again qualified in the top ten at Silverstone where Herbert stayed with the third-place battle before getting stuck in gear. Häkkinen missed the warm-up after being arrested for driving on the wrong side of the road at Whittlebury when trying to avoid the traffic and get into the circuit; he finished sixth.

Semi-active suspension was preferred at Hockenheim, where both engines failed after a difficult weekend. In Hungary, Herbert was eliminated by the warring Ligiers once more while Häkkinen passed Martin Brundle's Benetton around the outside to claim fourth despite a misfire-induced last-lap spin. Häkkinen enhanced his reputation as a future star with sixth in Belgium and fifth at Estoril, where the luckless Herbert, who did not score a point after Magny-Cours, was taken out by Jean Alesi's Ferrari at the start. Both Lotuses suffered engine failures at Monza and Suzuka, with both drivers denied the possibility of a podium finish at the latter. They were hit by rival cars during the early stages of the Australian GP so neither scored.

The Lotus 107 was a quick and simple car that often matched the works-supported Benettons despite having an older-specification engine. Fifth overall was a fine achievement.

TYRRELL RACING ORGANISATION

The loss of Honda engines and Braun sponsorship forced Tyrrell to regroup in the winter of 1991/92. Talks with F3000 team Il Barone Rampante (which had Ford HB engines for its planned graduation) broke down, Stefano Modena defected to Jordan and Satoru Nakajima retired – so Christmas approached with no drivers, title partner or engine. With time running out, a one-year deal was finally agreed in late December for Ilmor Engineering's 'small, light and powerful gem of a V10 engine' (*Autosport*).

Chief designer George Ryton started updating the disappointing 1991 chassis before departing in December and work on the 020B was completed by his replacement Mike Coughlan. The lighter, smaller engine lowered the centre of gravity although oversteer was an early problem. Tyrrell switched to Elf fuel and Goodyear tyres following Pirelli's withdrawal. Despite limited Japanese budget from Calbee and Club Angle, Coughlan and his team were able to introduce an active front ride-height system and traction control during the season. Additional budget was secured from Denim as a one-off for the Italian GP.

'We are talking to just about everybody,' admitted team manager Rupert Manwaring a week before the deadline for driver nominations. Olivier Grouillard signed at the 11th hour and Alex Zanardi was named when FISA published the official entry list on 10 February. However, a week later Tyrrell used one of its two permitted driver changes after Andrea de Cesaris secured sufficient budget. That late switch paid dividends for de Cesaris enjoyed another fine season and consistently out-performed Grouillard. Ex-Ferrari/Benetton Andy Le Fleming engineered de Cesaris's car while Coughlan worked with Grouillard.

Initial reliability was poor and de Cesaris's fifth place in Mexico (having driven through the field following an early spin) was Tyrrell's only finish from the first four races. Already under pressure to keep his drive, Grouillard was eighth at Imola but both Tyrrells retired

Andrea de Cesaris, Tyrrell 020B-Ilmor (Japanese GP)

Olivier Grouillard, Tyrrell 020B-Ilmor (Italian GP)

early in Monaco. The misfiring de Cesaris was a fine fifth in Canada where Grouillard almost ran leader Ayrton Senna off the road. The Frenchman secured his future by arranging a secondary sponsorship deal with Eurosport.

With Tyrrell less and less competitive as better-funded teams developed newer cars, Grouillard was 11th in France (despite three spins and a 10-second stop-go penalty for jumping the restart) and Britain but did not finish another race. Having spun at Magny-Cours and Silverstone and blown his engine during the German GP, de Cesaris scored five successive top-ten finishes, including a lucky sixth in Italy and an impressive fourth in Japan. Grouillard crashed into Pierluigi Martini's Dallara at the start of the Australian GP and de Cesaris lost another points score when his car caught fire.

Aguri Suzuki, Footwork FA13-Mugen (Italian GP)

FOOTWORK MUGEN HONDA

Following the expensive Porsche failure and with pre-qualifying looming, the design brief for the new Footwork FA13 was to keep it simple. Technical director Alan Jenkins penned a straightforward evolution of the FA12 around the Mugen (née Honda) MF-351H engine, supply of which was confirmed at the 1991 Japanese GP. Old and now heavy by contemporary standards, the 72-degree V10 was nonetheless powerful and reliable. The FA12's centrally supported front wing was ditched in favour of an anhedral device that followed Jordan lines. The undertray was totally new and twin shock absorbers were preferred at the front of the push-rod suspension. A new six-speed transverse gearbox was designed in conjunction with Xtrac, a company that Jenkins knew well from his time at Penske and Onyx; the gear-change was initially stiff but this was solved, then a sequential unit was introduced in Germany. Michele Alboreto remained for a third season while Aguri Suzuki, who had won the 1988 Japanese F3000 title for Footwork, signed in October. A new 40 per cent wind tunnel was opened at Footwork's factory in Milton Keynes.

The consistent Alboreto was a revelation and completely overshadowed his team-mate. Forced to pre-qualify for the first half of the season, the Italian veteran finished the first 11 races and only retired twice all year. Sixth in Brazil (where Paul Bowen replaced Bob Bell as his race engineer), Alboreto was fifth in the next two races, Barcelona and Imola, after non-stop runs. That Spanish success came at a cost as Footwork was fined $5,000 for changing to wet tyres on the grid after the five-minute board had been

Michele Alboreto, Footwork FA13-Mugen (Spanish GP)

shown. Seventh at the next four races, ninth in Germany, seventh on the grid and at the finish in Hungary (despite a spin), Alboreto's run of successive finishes was ended by gearbox failure at Spa-Francorchamps. He was seventh in Italy, sixth in Portugal and last in Japan. He qualified in the midfield once more for the Australian finale but was punted out of the race at the start.

Highly rated while at Larrousse, Suzuki lost his way during 1992 and had too many accidents. He initially struggled to fit in the Footwork and found its steering too low and heavy. A car was eventually built to his preferences and introduced at Silverstone but its repositioned steering column was too close to the brake pedal and caused him to spin out of the German GP so further modifications were made. Although he did not qualify in Mexico and Canada, he scored seven top-ten finishes but no points, seventh in Spain as close as he came to doing so.

Alboreto's efforts saw Footwork-Mugen share seventh in the constructors' standings. 'The turn-round… had been quite remarkable,' Alan Henry wrote in *Autocourse*. 'From having their backs to the wall, facing possible oblivion, the team had transformed itself into an effective midfield contender with clear aspirations to move further up the grid.'

LIGIER GITANES BLONDES

Without a top-six finish since the 1989 French GP, the well-funded Ligier team now had Renault V10 engines, albeit a step behind those used by Williams and prepared by Mecachrome in Bourges

rather than at the Viry-Châtillon works. Thierry Boutsen and Érik Comas remained under contract but some well-known names were interested in driving for the team. Nelson Piquet visited the factory on 25 November but proved too expensive. Alain Prost spent the winter in negotiations to drive with a view to eventually buying the team.

Boutsen tried an interim Ligier JS35R-Renault (with RS03 engine and new transverse six-speed Ligier/Xtrac gearbox) at Magny-Cours on 13 November and completed the shakedown of Frank Dernie's new JS37 at Magny-Cours on 16 January. This was a conventional design with high nose and anhedral front wing with skirts under the endplates. The fuel tank was low and wide while long sidepods housed the radiators as normal. Push-rod suspension had two Bilstein dampers at the front while low rear bodywork featured an unusual upswept diffuser with four vertical plates underneath. Steve Clark and Gérard Gerriet led active suspension and semi-automatic gearbox developments but both programmes were delayed. Ex-Ferrari race engineer Maurizio Nardon joined in January when Il Barone Rampante's F1 ambitions came to naught. Team manager since 1981, Jean-Pierre Paoli became managing director and was replaced by another long-time Ligier man, Dany Hindenoch.

After Boutsen drove for the first two days of testing at Circuit Paul Ricard, Prost unexpectedly took over on Sunday 19 January, wearing Comas's helmet. Reports of record pace during his second outing sent the French press into meltdown. That the car lacked grip, especially at slow speed and over bumps, was overshadowed by ongoing talks with Prost that rumbled on until they finally collapsed after the first race.

Érik Comas, Ligier JS37-Renault (French GP)

Comas remained idle all the while and first drove the JS37 in practice for the South African GP. Not race-fit as a consequence, he finished an impressive seventh after leading Boutsen throughout. The JS37s were a handful over the Mexican bumps and finished outside the points, but they were more competitive in Brazil only to collide during the race. That did not help the drivers' strained relationship, which deteriorated as the year passed. Neither finished in Spain and Boutsen lost points when his engine cut out at Imola while Comas spun on the way to ninth.

With a blame culture inside the team, a terrible weekend in Monaco saw the cars finish at the back. The threat of slipping into

Thierry Boutsen, Ligier JS37-Renault (Belgian GP)

pre-qualifying was only averted by Comas finishing fifth in France and sixth at Montréal. However, the Frenchman was fined $5,000 at Silverstone for causing Riccardo Patrese's practice crash and ignoring yellow flags. After another sixth place for Comas at Hockenheim, Ligier received updated RS03C engines in Hungary but the team's sparring drivers collided at the first corner, with two other cars eliminated in the resulting fracas.

Now in negotiations to sell, Guy Ligier reshuffled his technical staff in August with Dernie's contract not renewed and Gérard Ducarouge in charge. John Davis, Peter Wright's assistant in Lotus's research and development division, was poached to run Ligier's equivalent.

Comas missed Friday qualifying in Belgium when he crashed at Blanchimont so became a non-qualifier when it rained on Saturday. Boutsen started seventh but crashed in the wet two laps after changing to slick tyres. The Belgian ran in the top six at Monza before the electrics failed and Comas was eliminated in another accident. Boutsen finished eighth in Portugal despite a broken shock absorber and climbed from 22nd on the grid to claim fifth in Australia. Comas retired from the last three GPs of the season.

Equal seventh in the constructors' standings, Ligier was sold at the end of the season, with Guy Ligier retaining 20 per cent of the company. Although McLaren made a late bid for the team in the in the hope of securing Renault engines, a deal was finalised on 18 November with former AGS owner Cyril de Rouvre, who sold his various businesses to take a majority shareholding.

MARCH F1

In trouble since the arrest of Akira Akagi, this beleaguered team endured a race-by-race struggle for survival throughout 1992. Managing director Mike Smith resigned on 16 December 1991 and was replaced by Ken Marrable as managing director of holding company Leyton House Management while Vortex F3000 team owner Henny Vollenberg was responsible for team affairs in a management buy-out that was completed in January. The team name changed back from Leyton House to March.

A one-year extension for Ilmor V10 engines was delayed until the last possible moment. Karl Wendlinger and Paul Belmondo, son of famous French actor Jean-Paul, were entered for the World Championship having signed initial agreements for 14 and seven races respectively. More than half of the workforce was made redundant early in the year. Race engineer John Gentry returned to motorcycle racing with Marlboro Team Roberts and technical director Gustav Brunner left when his contract expired on 31 August. 'We have no money,' Marrable told *Autosport* in April. 'The team is up for sale. I've seen loads of people, but so far they've been time wasters.'

March did not have the money to build Brunner's new car so the old CG911 was dusted off and run at a chilly Silverstone before being sent to Kyalami, where Wendlinger was the star of qualifying in seventh place only to be involved in an accident at the start of the race. Also eliminated in a start-line shunt in Mexico, he qualified ninth in Brazil and Spain, then finished in a vital fourth place in Montréal. Already contracted to Sauber for 1993, Wendlinger suffered gearbox failures in France and Britain before qualifying tenth in Germany

Karl Wendlinger, March CG911-Ilmor (Monaco GP)

Paul Belmondo, March CG911-Ilmor (German GP)

Emanuele Naspetti, March CG911-Ilmor (Belgian GP)

Jan Lammers, March CG911-Ilmor (Japanese GP)

(where March was backed by Rial Wheels). Eliminated by Olivier Grouillard's Tyrrell after a messy weekend in Hungary, Wendlinger was tenth at Monza following a collision with his team-mate, then retired in Portugal. Wendlinger made a real impression, as team manager Charlie Moody told *Autocourse*: 'He is very special; bloody good. He formed an extremely good partnership with Gustav [Brunner] and kept him on his toes!'

Wendlinger was replaced at the last two races by Jan Lammers, who had not raced in F1 since 1982. 'Formula 1 is something I still find difficulty erasing from my mind,' Lammers said in 1991. 'I'm not stupid enough to say I could blow off Senna or whoever. But, if I'm honest, I really feel that what I've done in F1 does not represent my true potential.' Lammers demonstrated a CG911 at Zandvoort's F3 Masters, suffered gearbox failure in Japan and finished 12th in Australia.

Struggling in his first F1 season, Belmondo failed to qualify for the opening three races and finished last at Barcelona and Imola. Three DNQs in four races followed as he found enough money to extend his deal. He qualified ahead of Wendlinger in Hungary, his last appearance, and finished a career-best ninth.

Emanuele Naspetti used backing from Uliveto mineral water to replace Belmondo at the last five races. He was classified in Belgium, Portugal and Japan but crashed into Wendlinger at Monza and broke his gearbox in Australia.

Still needing to sell the team to safeguard its remaining workforce, Marrable negotiated its transfer to a Swiss investment company in the New Year and Lammers and Jean-Marc Gounon were announced as drivers for the 1993 World Championship. Two CG911s were updated to comply with 1993 rules and sent to Kyalami (minus engines) but no money changed hands and March withdrew from F1 after missing the first two races.

BMS SCUDERIA ITALIA (DALLARA)

Beppe Lucchini's BMS Scuderia Italia spent much of the summer of 1991 trying to take over from Minardi as Ferrari's engine client for the coming season and Lucchini had three meetings with Ferrari president Piero Fusaro. After the lapse at the end of July of the team's exclusive option on the compact Judd V10, a two-year agreement with Ferrari was announced in September. 'I hope that the technical co-operation with Ferrari will… help Scuderia Italia to develop further,' Lucchini said at launch. How disappointed he would be.

J.J. Lehto was retained but Emanuele Pirro was deemed surplus

J.J. Lehto, Dallara F192-Ferrari (Monaco GP)

Pierluigi Martini, Dallara F192-Ferrari (Monaco GP)

to requirements. Terms were agreed with Ivan Capelli before he attracted Ferrari's attention, so Minardi stalwart Pierluigi Martini signed at the end of November. Sporting director Pierpaolo Gardella moved to the 500cc motorcycle World Championship as race director at the start of 1992.

Unveiled at Madonna di Campiglio on 15 January, the evolutionary Dallara F192 had raised nose, mono-shock front suspension and a larger footwell to allow left-foot braking. Fuel capacity and radiators were enlarged to cater for the thirsty V12. There was initial optimism within the team and a couple of hopeful results but the F192 lacked grip in qualifying trim and wore its tyres at an unacceptable rate on Sundays. Handling was so inconsistent that Lehto told *Autosport* the car had 'as much rigidity as spaghetti'. They experimented with shock absorbers (Koni, Penske and Dynamic Suspension) and tinkered with the suspension, including the use of twin-shock front suspension at Hockenheim, but to no avail. A new undertray was introduced at the Italian GP where the drivers disagreed about whether or not it worked. Pirro's development skills were missed.

There were problems at the first race in South Africa, where they qualified and ran at the back before retiring. Stiffer front wings and revised front suspension helped in Mexico and both drivers qualified in the top ten, with Lehto finishing eighth. He was eighth again in Brazil despite a puncture while Martini started eighth and ran sixth before his clutch failed. Then Martini scored successive sixth-place finishes in the wet Spanish GP and at Imola. All this, however, proved to be a false dawn as the rest of the season did not bring any more points scores or top-ten grid slots.

Martini was taken out by Stefano Modena's Jordan on the opening lap in Monaco. The ill-handling F192s were reliable for the next five races without threatening to score. Come the Hungarian GP, Lehto did not qualify and Martini only scraped onto the grid, then served a stop-go penalty for baulking before his gearbox broke. Martini spun on the opening lap in Belgium while Lehto judged the changing conditions to take seventh, his best finish of 1992.

At Monza, Martini was eighth despite a spin and both were eliminated in Portugal by debris from the Patrese/Berger accident, a driveshaft from the Williams-Renault puncturing Lehto's monocoque. The Finn beat his team-mate into ninth after a race-long duel at

Suzuka and both retired in Australia, Martini having crashed into Olivier Grouillard's Tyrrell at the start.

The catalogue of disappointments took its toll. Scuderia Italia severed its ties with Dallara and announced a new partnership with Lola Cars at the Hungarian GP. 'We are delighted to be joining forces with BMS Scuderia Italia – a new power in F1,' Lola's Eric Broadley told the press. 'There is no doubt in my mind that we will become a top team.'

CENTRAL PARK VENTURI LARROUSSE

Gérard Larrousse announced yet more financial restructuring on 8 January after selling 65 per cent to GT manufacturer MVS Venturi, whose president Éric Guilloud assumed the same role for the renamed Central Park Venturi Larrousse. Unfortunately, the recession was biting and in August Venturi was forced to sell its shares in Larrousse to the Comstock Group, an association that was destined to be short-lived.

Lola ended its five-year alliance with Larrousse on 3 December 1991 so the French team turned to Robin Herd's design agency in Bicester (formerly Fomet 1) for its new car. A three-year contract was agreed with the company renamed Venturi Larrousse UK. The late agreement meant Tino Belli and Tim Holloway laid out a conventional raised-nose design with new carbon-fibre monocoque moulded at Advanced Composites in Derby and aerodynamics refined in Southampton University's wind tunnel. The Venturi (Larrousse) LC92 had push-rod front suspension with the rear pull-rod arrangement from the old Lola retained until Imola.

A year after losing Lamborghini engines, a new two-year deal was agreed with the Italian manufacturer for its V12 and transverse gearbox. The work of Mike Royce, a smaller and lighter version of the Lamborghini engine with over 700bhp at 13,800bhp was introduced at the Brazilian GP. Reigning Japanese F3000 champion Ukyo Katayama was in demand due to his backing from Cabin cigarettes and signed a three-year deal with Larrousse in the autumn. Bertrand Gachot and Andrea Montermini tested in the New Year before the former was confirmed at the launch in Paris on 3 February. Team manager Frédéric Dhainhaut moved to Andrea Moda in May and was replaced by Philippe Leloup. The team's 1991 points had been scored with a Lola so Larrousse was considered a new constructor and had to pre-qualify for the first half of 1992.

The LC92 impressed at times, especially on fast circuits, but it was sensitive to set-up changes and its reliability was the second-worst on the grid. Gachot was occasionally quick in qualifying but finished only four races. His undoubted highlight was sixth at Monaco to claim the team's only point and his best qualifying position was tenth at Monza. For Katayama, who struggled physically, the best finishes were ninth in Brazil and Italy, despite late transmission failure at Monza.

Katayama did not qualify in Spain when rain washed out the Saturday session and was eliminated in pre-qualifying at Monaco when he crashed at Tabac. Every point was crucial in the fight to escape pre-qualifying so Canada proved especially disappointing.

Bertrand Gachot, Larrousse LC92-Lamborghini (Japanese GP)

With co-founder Didier Calmels back with the team, the drivers collided at the hairpin and Gachot was later black-flagged when push-started after clashing with Olivier Grouillard's Tyrrell. Katayama qualified a season-best 11th in Montréal and was running fifth in the closing stages when he missed a gear and over-revved the engine, forcing him to retire. Those lost points meant Larrousse still needed to pre-qualify after the French GP, although the demise of rival teams eventually made that hour-long session redundant.

The team-mates collided again during the Japanese GP, where Gachot ran as high as sixth, and both drivers left at the end of an increasingly frustrating campaign. Another uncertain winter was assured when Comstock Group's Klaus Walz disappeared and was killed during a gun battle with the German police on 25 November.

Ukyo Katayama, Larrousse LC92-Lamborghini (Italian GP)

MINARDI TEAM

Minardi swapped one underwhelming Italian V12 for another when it lost its Ferrari deal to Scuderia Italia and announced a one-year agreement with Lamborghini Engineering at the 1991 Japanese GP. The team hoped Pierluigi Martini would stay for a fifth season but he followed the Ferrari engines to Beppe Lucchini's rival team. Gianni Morbidelli eventually re-signed and F3000 champion Christian Fittipaldi was confirmed in December, preferred to the likes of Andrea de Cesaris and Andrea Montermini. Budget was as limited as ever so testing was restricted.

A semi-automatic gearbox developed in conjunction with Gianni's father, Giancarlo Morbidelli, was tested but Lamborghini's transverse unit was raced throughout 1992. Morbidelli and test driver Marco Apicella drove a modified Minardi M191B-Lamborghini at Paul Ricard before Christmas and Morbidelli immediately beat any time recorded by a Minardi-Ferrari. 'The Lamborghini is supple, very useable and powerful,' he enthused to *Autosport*. After a year in which he had been shown his marching orders at both Ligier and Fondmetal, former Fittipaldi designer Richard Divila joined as Morbidelli's race engineer with Gabriele Tredozi on Fittipaldi's side of the garage.

Using the M191B for the first four races, both drivers qualified with relative ease but registered just one finish apiece – Morbidelli seventh in Brazil and Fittipaldi 11th in Spain. Morbidelli gave the Minardi M192 a brief shakedown during April's Imola test and it was taken to the Spanish GP although he raced the old car rather than risk the new one in the wet. Aldo Costa and René Hilhorst's

Gianni Morbidelli, Minardi M191B-Lamborghini (Brazilian GP)

Christian Fittipaldi, Minardi M191B-Lamborghini (Mexican GP)

M192 was conventional with push-rod suspension and raised nose, initially fitted with an anhedral front wing although a full-width alternative was also used. The monocoque was stiffened and, unusually, front shock absorbers were mounted externally for easy access. Unfortunately, a 15 per cent error in wind-tunnel data was only identified late in the season.

Both had M192s for the San Marino GP but suffered pronounced understeer and retired with transmission issues. They qualified in the midfield in Monaco where Morbidelli started late and had another transmission failure, but Fittipaldi finished eighth. Both were classified in Canada despite Fittipaldi's late gearbox fire and

Morbidelli was eighth at Magny-Cours, where Fittipaldi did not qualify after being punted off by Michele Alboreto's Footwork-Mugen. He climbed out of the wreck but had a fractured vertebra and had to miss three races.

Alex Zanardi stood in but did not qualify at Silverstone and retired after a lap in Germany. The team suffered a miserable time when it was finally able to test for three days at Hockenheim: only eight laps were completed as an upgraded engine proved unreliable and there were four gearbox breakages. Minardi's campaign reached its nadir when both failed to qualify in Hungary, Zanardi having his Saturday times deleted following a push start.

Gianni Morbidelli, Minardi M192-Lamborghini (Italian GP)

Alex Zanardi, Minardi M192-Lamborghini (German GP)

Christian Fittipaldi, Minardi M192-Lamborghini (Japanese GP)

Fittipaldi returned in Belgium but was a DNQ at that race and the next, finding the M192 to lack grip and now unsuited to his driving style. The experienced Gustav Brunner arrived as chief designer on 1 September and the M192 had a new nose (with the full-width wing increasingly preferred) and upgraded Lamborghini engine at Monza, where Morbidelli qualified a morale-boosting 12th. Both finished in Portugal following unscheduled tyre stops. Fittipaldi battled with Jean Alesi (Ferrari) and Stefano Modena (Jordan-Yamaha) at Suzuka, beating the Italian into an excellent sixth place to score his first championship point. They finished ninth (Fittipaldi) and tenth (Morbidelli after a spin) at the final race in Australia.

SASOL JORDAN YAMAHA

Although Jordan had been the most impressive newcomer for many a year, the team's second season was a bitter disappointment. Despite blue-chip sponsors in 1991, the cost of Ford HB engines had proved prohibitive, so the two-year deal with Ford and Cosworth was cancelled and instead free engines from Yamaha were negotiated after the Japanese company dropped Brabham. A four-year agreement for the 70-degree OX99 V12 was signed on 16 September with Yamaha's managing director Takehiro Hasegawa 'confident that the new partnership will allow Yamaha to seriously challenge for the World Championship in the near future'. Cosworth and its owners Vickers took legal action that was finally settled out of court on 16 October 1992.

Stefano Modena agreed to join on the Saturday of the 1991

Maurício Gugelmin, Jordan 192-Yamaha (Japanese GP)

Stefano Modena, Jordan 192-Yamaha (British GP)

Japanese GP and Jordan extended Alex Zanardi's option when it expired on 31 December. Zanardi first drove the Jordan 191Y-Yamaha test hack at Silverstone on 19 November and did much of the testing before Christmas so it was a surprise when Maurício Gugelmin was finally announced as Modena's team-mate in February.

Jordan moved into new premises across the Dadford Road from Silverstone circuit, where a predominantly green Jordan 192-Yamaha was unveiled on 22 January. This was an evolution of the 1991 car with wheelbase extended by an inch due to the longer V12 engine, which had been lightened by 12lb. The new seven-speed sequential gearbox was mounted transversely and the anhedral front wing raised by a couple of inches. The sidepods enclosed larger radiators and featured an optional air exit to the rear. The push-rod suspension was revised with a single shock absorber at the front.

Pepsi-Cola withdrew its 7Up sponsorship due to 'a change in business priorities' but Jordan announced Barclay cigarettes in December and signed a three-year deal with South African petrochemical giant Sasol as title partner in February, green replaced by two-tone blue as a consequence. Tragically, 32-year-old general manager Richard 'Bosco' Quinn was killed in a road accident on his way home on 18 December 1991.

Problems with the new gearbox limited testing miles, overheating was an issue until a faulty water pump was traced, and poor reliability led Yamaha to sacrifice performance. The South African GP was a chastening experience: Modena failed to qualify following engine problems while Gugelmin came from the penultimate row to finish 11th. Gugelmin qualified eighth in Mexico but did not last a lap, while gearbox failure ended Modena's race. Gearbox problems also accounted for both Jordan-Yamahas in Brazil. Mechanical issues in the only dry qualifying session in Spain meant another DNQ for Modena while Gugelmin crashed into the pit wall during the race.

Gugelmin was seventh at Imola, his best finish of the year. Modena's engine failed on the grid so he started from the pitlane in the spare, which expired with another gearbox failure. Both Jordans retired from the next four dispiriting races, which included crashes for Modena in Monaco and Gugelmin in France, the latter a collision with Andrea Chiesa's spinning Fondmetal.

Just as during 1991 with Tyrrell, Modena's motivation was questioned as the crisis continued and he did not qualify in Germany

or Italy. Gugelmin never gave up and at least had three consecutive finishes in Germany, Hungary and Belgium, the latter marking Jordan's only double finish. Gugelmin crashed in Japan and Australia, brake failure the cause in Adelaide. Modena was a fuel-saving seventh at Suzuka and finally scored the team's only point when sixth on the streets of Adelaide.

The unhappy marriage between Jordan and Yamaha was dissolved with an announcement made during the Japanese GP weekend.

MOTOR RACING DEVELOPMENTS (BRABHAM)

A month after being told that Yamaha would not supply engines in 1992, Brabham managing director Dennis Nursey announced a deal for the impressive Judd V10 in September. John Judd's engine team in Rugby was strengthened by the arrival of Mugen's Hiro Kaneda as head of design and development. Martin Brundle moved to Benetton and Mark Blundell was dropped in favour of monied drivers and Akihiko Nakaya and Eric van de Poele were announced in October 1991. Despite being a national F3 champion and Japanese F3000 race winner, Nakaya's super-licence application was rejected a week before driver nominations closed. Nakaya's appeal was unsuccessful so Nursey met with Giovanna Amati in Brussels on 4 February and she travelled to Milton Keynes to sign on the following day.

Sergio Rinland left the team that month and was replaced as chief designer by Tim Densham. Virtually all of the mechanics and staff were laid off at the end of November while the move to Milton Keynes was completed. That was initially in team owner Middlebridge's F3000 unit while Sherbourne House (on the estate that now houses Red Bull Racing) was ready after the South African GP. Race engineer Dave Morgan followed van de Poele to Brabham with Densham responsible for the other car on race weekends. F3000 team manager Ray Boulter was promoted to the F1 team while Greg Field arrived from Lotus as operations manager. The Middlebridge Group was renamed Alolique in January. Backing continued from Yamazen and Madras, and additional budget was secured from Landhurst Leasing using Brabham's name and equipment.

Such was Brabham's financial plight that it did not test during the winter and rumours of sale or closure were never far away. It was

Eric van de Poele, Brabham BT60B-Judd (South African GP)

Giovanna Amati, Brabham BT60B-Judd (Mexican GP)

little surprise that the Brabham BT60B-Judds were not competitive. Van de Poele scraped onto the South African GP grid by 0.092sec and finished last. He did not qualify again. Amati was a DNQ at the opening three races when slowest by some considerable margin before being replaced by Williams test driver Damon Hill for the next race in Spain.

Nursey managed to smooth over engine payments and find some funds for the Spanish GP. The team had no spare car that weekend because a transporter was impounded at the French border due to an unpaid bill. New Japanese backing was found from Yaesu and Sunimoto to prolong Brabham's participation through the summer

with John MacDonald briefly returning as Nursey desperately sought new owners. Brabham had a bright new identity from the French GP with traditional blue and white replaced by garish blue and purple.

Hill failed to qualify for six of his first seven races but made it into his home fixture at Silverstone, starting at the back and driving steadily to 16th place. Van de Poele quit before the Hungarian GP and took his LeasePlan money to Fondmetal. Julian Bailey was placed on standby but Brabham ran one car for Hill at the Hungaroring, where he started 25th after writing off a BT60B in practice and survived the race despite losing feeling in his legs to finish 11th and last. That proved to be this once-great team's final race for Landhurst Leasing collapsed at the end of the month. Brabham's assets were frozen and its holding company was wound up on 14 October.

Successful among the five bids for Brabham's name and assets was a consortium led by Englishman Alan Randall, who had recently failed to find backing to enter ex-works Jaguar XJR-14s in the 1992 World Sportscar Championship. Brabham's return in 1993 was announced with Banco Internacional sponsorship for 1991 Mexican F2 Champion Carlos Guerrero and Dave Prewitt's GP Motorsport running the cars. Indianapolis 500 winners Galmer were approached to build a new car, a base was found near Silverstone and Jordan's Tim Scott hired as team manager. Galmer's Alan Mertens and Andy Brown began design work but stopped at the end of December as no engine had been confirmed and payments were delayed. Brabham's entry was refused for the 1993 World Championship.

Damon Hill, Brabham BT60B-Judd (French GP)

Gabriele Tarquini, Fondmetal GR01-Ford (Monaco GP)

FONDMETAL

Rather than close his team after the difficult 1991 campaign, Gabriele Rumi expanded Fondmetal to a two-car line-up and made new arrangements for chassis and engine supply. Robin Herd Limited (formerly Fomet 1) chose to work for Larrousse in 1992 so Rumi signed a deal on 17 December with Sergio Rinland's new company (Astauto) to design the Fondmetal GR02. The Argentinian hired nine ex-colleagues from Brabham and set up premises in Tolworth, Surrey, over the Christmas break. Having ended negotiations with Lamborghini in September, Fondmetal replaced its out-of-date DFRs with Ford HB engines.

Formerly with Ferrari and Minardi, Tommaso Carletti joined in April as chief race engineer. While Gabriele Tarquini remained as lead driver, Gregor Foitek and Emanuele Naspetti held talks before F3000 race winner Andrea Chiesa signed a one-year deal in the New Year thanks to sponsorship from SgommaTutto household polish. Budget was limited so the team could only afford two days' testing during the season and the drivers had to conserve parts and machinery at all times. Using Brabham's old wind tunnel at Chessington, Rinland hired aerodynamist Max Sardou as a consultant and penned a conventional and compact car around the small Ford V8. It had a pencil-thin raised nose, anhedral front wing, Series V HB engine, six-speed transverse gearbox and push-rod suspension. Hitco discs and pads were originally fitted but Tarquini switched to SEP after a difficult practice in Canada.

While waiting for Rinland's new car, Tarquini and Chiesa drove the old Fomet 1 – renamed Fondmetal GR01 and using Series IV engines – for the first six races. During this period Tarquini always qualified

and always retired. Chiesa had not driven the car before he arrived in South Africa and failed to qualify for four of those six races, spinning out of the Mexican and Spanish GPs when he did make the field.

The first GR02 was completed at Palosco in June and was due at the Magny-Cours test but the transporter broke down in the Alps. It was towed back to the factory and Tarquini instead drove the GR02 at Fiorano on 5 June, completing 30 laps before it was freighted to Montréal, where teething trouble culminated in gearbox breakage at the start, with Chiesa's GR01 failing to qualify. In seven races with the new car, Tarquini only finished once, a clutchless 14th at Silverstone after a stall at his pitstop. However, the GR02 was fast enough for him to qualify 11th in Belgium and 12th in Hungary to embarrass some better-funded rivals.

Andrea Chiesa, Fondmetal GR01-Ford (South African GP)

Gabriele Tarquini, Fondmetal GR02-Ford (German GP)

Andrea Chiesa, Fondmetal GR02-Ford (French GP)

Eric van de Poele, Fondmetal GR02-Ford (Belgian GP)

Chiesa had his own GR02 by Magny-Cours and qualified last, then hit Maurício Gugelmin's Jordan on the opening lap and destroyed the car against a barrier in a high-speed impact from which he was lucky to emerge unscathed after being hit on the shoulder by a wheel. He failed to qualify a GR01 for the next two races before being dropped amid claim and counter-claim. Eric van de Poele replaced Chiesa from Hungary, where both Fondmetal GR02s were involved in the first-corner mêlée. Tarquini went out on the spot and van de Poele damaged his undertray as he ran wide and crashed out on lap three of an expensive afternoon. Van de Poele finished tenth in Belgium after a couple of spins and tyre stops, but his clutch failed at the start of the Italian GP.

Not prepared to spend any more money, Rumi withdrew from the Portuguese GP. Talks were held with prospective entrant Franz Konrad, F3000 driver Giuseppe Bugatti and a mysterious consortium from Luxembourg, but neither new investment nor a buyer were forthcoming so the team closed its doors.

ANDREA MODA FORMULA

Italian shoe magnate Andrea Sassetti acquired Coloni Racing's assets in September 1991, arranged a supply of Judd GV V10 engines and hired Banbury-based Simtek Research to build a new car, which was based on work carried out for BMW in 1990. Michel Costa (formerly of Coloni and AGS) arrived as technical director while Riccardo Rosa (Fiat, Fondmetal) and Paul Burgess (Coloni, Lotus) fitted Judd engines and transverse gearbox to a converted Coloni C4B that Alex Caffi tested in February, with Enrico Bertaggia chosen as team-mate. Frédéric

Roberto Moreno, Andrea Moda S192-Judd (Monaco GP)

Dhainhaut joined as team manager in May but left after the Canadian GP when recommendations were ignored and was replaced by Sergio Zargo from Cagiva's 500cc motorcycle team.

Caffi took part in the Thursday test session at Kyalami (Bertaggia's chassis was not completed) but Andrea Moda was excluded from the meeting for failing to deposit the bond required by new teams. Excused the fine for missing the race but not allowed to use the old Coloni, Simtek sped up production of the new Andrea Moda S192, two of which were part-completed before Mexico. Nick Wirth, who had set up Simtek with backing from Max Mosley in 1989, designed a conventional car with push-rod/double-wishbone suspension front and rear. The team only arrived in the Mexican paddock on Friday after delay in transit, by which time pre-qualifying had already been cancelled, so the mechanics spent the weekend completing the first chassis. Rosa left after the South African débâcle and both drivers quit after Mexico. Andrea Moda announced Roberto Moreno and Perry McCarthy as replacements.

Moreno failed on his first three attempts to pre-qualify before succeeding in Monaco, where he scraped onto the grid by 0.036sec and blew his engine after 11 laps at the back. Protesting truck drivers blockaded the French GP and Andrea Moda was the only team whose transporter did not make it to Magny-Cours. Moreno next pre-qualified in Hungary but was a predictable DNQ.

McCarthy did not run in Brazil following a mix-up regarding his super licence, which was finally issued following a fax vote on 14 April. Thereafter eight attempts to pre-qualify were all thwarted and he could not even run in Canada because his engine was withheld while the freight company waited for an outstanding bill to be settled. He was often kept in the pitlane in case Moreno needed a spare car and in Hungary he was only allowed out with less than a minute of the session to go and therefore without time to start a timed lap. That prompted the stewards to warn Andrea Moda to make a genuine attempt to pre-qualify both cars or face a ban.

Andrea Moda's hapless campaign, among the worst in F1 history, reached rock bottom at Spa-Francorchamps despite pre-qualifying being cancelled following Brabham's demise. Hours after his cars failed to qualify when slowest, Sassetti was arrested as bailiffs tried to impound equipment on behalf of creditors. Released on race morning, Sassetti and the team travelled to Monza only to be excluded from the championship for bringing the sport into disrepute.

Perry McCarthy, Andrea Moda S192-Judd (Monaco GP)

1992 RESULTS

DRIVER PERFORMANCE

DRIVER	CAR–ENGINE	ZA	MEX	BR	E	RSM	MC	CDN	F	GB	D	H	B	I	P	J	AUS
Michele Alboreto	Footwork FA13-Mugen	17 10	25 13	14 6	16 5	9 5	11 7	16 7	14 7	12 7	17 9	7 7	14 R	16 7	8 6	24 15	11 R
Jean Alesi	Ferrari F92A	5 R	10 R	6 4	8 3	7 R	4 R	8 3	6 R	8 R	5 5	9 R	–	–	–	–	–
	Ferrari F92AT	–	–	–	–	–	–	–	–	–	–	–	5 R	3 R	10 R	15 5	6 4
Giovanna Amati	Brabham BT60B-Judd	30 DNQ	30 DNQ	30 DNQ	–	–	–	–	–	–	–	–	–	–	–	–	–
Paul Belmondo	March CG911-Ilmor	27 DNQ	28 DNQ	28 DNQ	23 12	24 13	30 DNQ	20 14	27 DNQ	28 DNQ	22 13	17 9	–	–	–	–	–
Gerhard Berger	McLaren MP4/6B-Honda	3 5	5 4 FL	–	–	–	–	–	–	–	–	–	–	–	–	–	–
	McLaren MP4/7A-Honda	–	–	4 R	7 4	4 R	5 R	4 1 FL	4 R	5 5	4 R	5 3	6 R	5 4	4 2	4 2	4 1
Enrico Bertaggia	Coloni C4B-Judd	NT DNP	–	–	–	–	–	–	–	–	–	–	–	–	–	–	–
	Andrea Moda S192-Judd	–	NT DNP	–	–	–	–	–	–	–	–	–	–	–	–	–	–
Thierry Boutsen	Ligier JS37-Renault	14 R	22 10	10 R	14 R	10 R	22 12	21 10	9 R	13 10	8 7	8 R	7 R	8 R	11 8	10 R	22 5
Martin Brundle	Benetton B191B-Ford	8 R	4 R	7 R	–	–	–	–	–	–	–	–	–	–	–	–	–
	Benetton B192-Ford	–	–	–	6 R	6 4	7 5	7 R	7 3	6 3	9 4	6 5	9 4	9 2	6 4	13 3	8 3
Alex Caffi	Coloni C4B-Judd	NT DNP	–	–	–	–	–	–	–	–	–	–	–	–	–	–	–
	Andrea Moda S192-Judd	–	NT DNP	–	–	–	–	–	–	–	–	–	–	–	–	–	–
Ivan Capelli	Ferrari F92A	9 R	20 R	11 5	5 10	8 R	9 R	9 R	8 R	14 9	12 R	10 6	12 R	–	–	–	–
	Ferrari F92AT	–	–	–	–	–	–	–	–	–	–	–	–	7 R	16 R	–	–
Andrea Chiesa	Fondmetal GR01-Ford	28 DNQ	23 R	27 DNQ	20 R	28 DNQ	29 DNQ	29 DNQ	–	29 DNQ	29 DNQ	–	–	–	–	–	–
	Fondmetal GR02-Ford	–	–	–	–	–	–	–	–	–	–	26 R	–	–	–	–	–
Érik Comas	Ligier JS37-Renault	13 7	26 9	15 R	10 R	13 9	23 10	22 6	10 5	10 8	7 6	11 R	NT DNP	15 R	14 R	8 R	9 R
Andrea de Cesaris	Tyrrell 020B-Ilmor	10 R	11 5	13 R	11 R	14 14	10 R	14 5	19 R	18 R	20 R	19 8	13 8	21 6	12 9	9 4	7 R
Christian Fittipaldi	Minardi M191B-Lamborghini	20 R	17 R	20 R	22 11	–	–	–	–	–	–	–	–	–	–	–	–
	Minardi M192-Lamborghini	–	–	–	–	25 R	17 8	25 13	28 DNQ	–	–	–	27 DNQ	27 DNQ	26 12	12 6	17 9
Bertrand Gachot	Larrousse LC92-Lamborghini	22 R	13 11	18 R	24 R	19 R	15 6	19 DSQ	13 R	11 R	25 14	15 R	20 18	10 R	13 R	18 R	21 R
Olivier Grouillard	Tyrrell 020B-Ilmor	12 R	16 R	17 R	15 R	20 8	24 R	26 12	22 11	20 11	14 R	22 R	22 R	18 R	15 R	21 R	13 R
Maurício Gugelmin	Jordan 192-Yamaha	23 11	8 R	21 R	17 R	18 7	13 R	24 R	24 R	24 R	23 15	21 10	24 14	26 R	20 R	25 R	20 R
Mika Häkkinen	Lotus 102D-Ford	21 9	18 6	24 10	21 R	27 DNQ	–	–	–	–	–	–	–	–	–	–	–
	Lotus 107-Ford	–	–	–	–	–	14 R	10 R	11 4	9 6	13 R	16 4	8 6	11 R	7 5	7 R	10 7
Johnny Herbert	Lotus 102D-Ford	11 6	12 7	26 R	26 R	–	–	–	–	–	–	–	–	–	–	–	–
	Lotus 107-Ford	–	–	–	–	26 R	9 R	6 R	12 6	7 R	11 R	13 R	10 13	13 R	9 R	6 R	12 13
Damon Hill	Brabham BT60B-Judd	–	–	–	30 DNQ	29 DNQ	28 DNQ	30 DNQ	30 DNQ	26 16	30 DNQ	25 11	–	–	–	–	–
Ukyo Katayama	Larrousse LC92-Lamborghini	18 12	24 12	25 9	27 DNQ	17 R	31 NPQ	11 R	18 R	16 R	16 R	20 R	26 17	23 9	25 R	20 11	26 R
Jan Lammers	March CG911-Ilmor	–	–	–	–	–	–	–	–	–	–	–	–	–	–	23 R	25 12
Nicola Larini	Ferrari F92A	–	–	–	–	–	–	–	–	–	–	–	–	–	–	11 12	19 11
J.J. Lehto	Dallara F192-Ferrari	24 R	7 8	16 8	12 R	16 11	20 9	23 9	17 9	19 13	21 10	28 DNQ	16 7	14 11	19 R	22 9	24 R
Nigel Mansell	Williams FW14B-Renault	1 1 FL	1 1	1 1	1 1 FL	1 1	1 2 FL	3 R	1 1 FL	1 1 FL	1 1	2 2 FL	1 2	1 R FL	1 1	1 R FL	1 R
Pierluigi Martini	Dallara F192-Ferrari	25 R	9 R	8 R	13 6	15 6	18 R	15 8	25 10	22 15	18 11	26 R	19 R	22 8	21 R	19 10	14 R
Perry McCarthy	Andrea Moda S192-Judd	–	–	NT NPQ	NT NPQ	32 NPQ	NT NPQ	NT NPQ	NT DNP	32 NPQ	NT NPQ	NT NPQ	29 DNQ	–	–	–	–
Stefano Modena	Jordan 192-Yamaha	29 DNQ	15 R	12 R	29 DNQ	23 R	21 R	17 R	20 R	23 R	27 DNQ	24 R	17 15	28 DNQ	24 13	17 7	15 6
Gianni Morbidelli	Minardi M191B-Lamborghini	19 R	21 R	23 7	25 R	–	–	–	–	–	–	–	–	–	–	–	–
	Minardi M192-Lamborghini	–	–	–	–	21 R	12 R	13 11	16 R	25 R	26 12	27 DNQ	23 16	12 R	18 14	14 14	16 10
Roberto Moreno	Andrea Moda S192-Judd	–	–	31 NPQ	31 NPQ	31 NPQ	26 R	31 NPQ	NT DNP	31 NPQ	31 NPQ	30 DNQ	28 DNQ	–	–	–	–
Emanuele Naspetti	March CG911-Ilmor	–	–	–	–	–	–	–	–	–	–	–	21 12	24 R	23 11	26 13	23 R
Riccardo Patrese	Williams FW14B-Renault	4 2	2 2	2 2 FL	4 R	2 2 FL	2 3	2 R	2 2	2 2	2 8 FL	1 R	4 3	4 5	2 R	2 1	3 R
Michael Schumacher	Benetton B191B-Ford	6 4	3 3	5 3	–	–	–	–	–	–	–	–	–	–	–	–	–
	Benetton B192-Ford	–	–	–	2 2	5 R	6 4	5 2	5 R	4 4	6 3	4 R	3 1 FL	6 3	5 7	5 R	5 2 FL

DRIVER PERFORMANCE CONTINUED

DRIVER	CAR–ENGINE	ZA	MEX	BR	E	RSM	MC	CDN	F	GB	D	H	B	I	P	J	AUS
Ayrton Senna	McLaren MP4/6B-Honda	2 3	6 R	–	–	–	–	–	–	–	–	–	–	–	–	–	–
	McLaren MP4/7A-Honda	–	–	3 R	3 9	3 3	3 1	1 R	3 R	3 R	3 2	3 1	2 5	2 1	3 3 FL	3 R	2 R
Aguri Suzuki	Footwork FA13-Mugen	16 8	27 DNQ	22 R	19 7	11 10	19 11	27 DNQ	15 R	17 12	15 R	14 R	25 9	19 R	17 10	16 8	18 8
Gabriele Tarquini	Fondmetal GR01-Ford	15 R	14 R	19 R	18 R	22 R	25 R	–	–	–	–	–	–	–	–	–	–
	Fondmetal GR02-Ford	–	–	–	–	–	–	18 R	23 R	15 14	19 R	12 R	11 R	20 R	–	–	–
Eric van de Poele	Brabham BT60B-Judd	26 13	29 DNQ	29 DNQ	28 DNQ	30 DNQ	27 DNQ	28 DNQ	29 DNQ	30 DNQ	28 DNQ	–	–	–	–	–	–
	Fondmetal GR02-Ford	–	–	–	–	–	–	–	–	–	–	18 R	15 10	25 R	–	–	–
Karl Wendlinger	March CG911-Ilmor	7 R	19 R	9 R	9 8	12 12	16 R	12 4	21 R	21 R	10 16	23 R	18 11	17 10	22 R	–	–
Alex Zanardi	Minardi M192-Lamborghini	–	–	–	–	–	–	–	27 DNQ	24 R	29 DNQ	–	–	–	–	–	–

FORMULA 1 RACE WINNERS

ROUND	RACE (CIRCUIT)	DATE	WINNER
1	Yellow Pages South African Grand Prix (Kyalami)	Mar 1	Nigel Mansell (Williams FW14B-Renault)
2	Gran Premio de México (México City)	Mar 22	Nigel Mansell (Williams FW14B-Renault)
3	Grande Prêmio do Brasil (Interlagos)	Apr 5	Nigel Mansell (Williams FW14B-Renault)
4	Gran Premio Tio Pepe de España (Catalunya)	May 3	Nigel Mansell (Williams FW14B-Renault)
5	Gran Premio Iceberg di San Marino (Imola)	May 17	Nigel Mansell (Williams FW14B-Renault)
6	Grand Prix de Monaco (Monte Carlo)	May 31	Ayrton Senna (McLaren MP4/7A-Honda)
7	Grand Prix Molson du Canada (Montréal)	Jun 14	Gerhard Berger (McLaren MP4/7A-Honda)
8	Rhône-Poulenc Grand Prix de France (Magny-Cours)	Jul 5	Nigel Mansell (Williams FW14B-Renault)
9	British Grand Prix (Silverstone)	Jul 12	Nigel Mansell (Williams FW14B-Renault)
10	Grosser Mobil 1 Preis von Deutschland (Hockenheim)	Jul 26	Nigel Mansell (Williams FW14B-Renault)
11	Marlboro Magyar Nagydíj (Hungaroring)	Aug 16	Ayrton Senna (McLaren MP4/7A-Honda)
12	Grand Prix de Belgique (Spa-Francorchamps)	Aug 30	Michael Schumacher (Benetton B192-Ford)
13	Pioneer Gran Premio d'Italia (Monza)	Sep 13	Ayrton Senna (McLaren MP4/7A-Honda)
14	SG Gigante Grande Premio de Portugal (Estoril)	Sep 27	Nigel Mansell (Williams FW14B-Renault)
15	Fuji Television Japanese Grand Prix (Suzuka)	Oct 25	Riccardo Patrese (Williams FW14B-Renault)
16	Foster's Australian Grand Prix (Adelaide)	Nov 8	Gerhard Berger (McLaren MP4/7A-Honda)

CONSTRUCTORS' CHAMPIONSHIP

	CONSTRUCTORS	POINTS
1	Williams-Renault	164
2	McLaren-Honda	99
3	Benetton-Ford	91
4	Ferrari	21
5	Lotus-Ford	13
6	Tyrrell-Ilmor	8
7=	Footwork-Mugen	6
	Ligier-Renault	6
9	March-Ilmor	3
10	Dallara-Ferrari	2
11=	Larrousse-Lamborghini	1
	Minardi-Lamborghini	1
	Jordan-Yamaha	1

DRIVERS' CHAMPIONSHIP

	DRIVERS	POINTS
1	Nigel Mansell	108
2	Riccardo Patrese	56
3	Michael Schumacher	53
4	Ayrton Senna	50
5	Gerhard Berger	49
6	Martin Brundle	38
7	Jean Alesi	18
8	Mika Häkkinen	11
9	Andrea de Cesaris	8
10	Michele Alboreto	6
11	Érik Comas	4
12=	Ivan Capelli	3
	Karl Wendlinger	3
14=	Thierry Boutsen	2
	Johnny Herbert	2
	Pierluigi Martini	2
17=	Christian Fittipaldi	1
	Bertrand Gachot	1
	Stefano Modena	1

Alain Prost celebrates at Estoril after clinching his fourth World Championship

1993

PROST RETURNS TO CLAIM HIS FOURTH TITLE

The Fédération Internationale du Sport Automobile World Council confirmed new regulations for 1993 in the middle of the previous year. These included reducing tyre width from 18in to 15in, a change that sole supplier Goodyear reluctantly accepted. Henceforth, if another tyre company entered F1 each must be prepared to supply 60 per cent of the field or 40 per cent if there were three suppliers. Each car was allowed seven sets of tyres (plus an evaluation set) per race weekend.

An Indycar-style new safety car was first used in Brazil but plans for mandatory tyre stops were abandoned. When 45-minute practice and qualifying sessions proved too short at the opening race in South Africa, a new timetable was also introduced in Brazil with an hour and a half for practice from 9.30am and an hour for qualifying from 1pm on both Friday and Saturday. The maximum number of laps permitted was just 23 in the morning and 12 in the afternoon. Teams could not test at overseas GP circuits until after that year's race had been held. Driver agreements now had to be lodged with the new F1 Contract Recognition Board in Geneva. The first such case regarded Mika Häkkinen's wish to move from Lotus to McLaren and the board found in favour of the latter.

Jean-Marie Balestre resigned as Fédération Internationale de l'Automobile (FIA) president and Max Mosley was confirmed as his replacement on 10 June when Royal Automobile Club chairman Jeffrey Rose withdrew at the last moment. The FIA was reorganised at that time with FISA abolished and all sporting matters handled directly by the main organisation with effect from 1 October. The FIA held a gala dinner to award its championships for the first time with 700 dignitaries in attendance at Paris's Opéra in December.

Just 26 cars were entered for the World Championship and this should have meant that 24 drivers qualified. However, everyone was allowed to start in South Africa, one driver was eliminated at the next eight races, and all 26 started from Germany onwards.

Tobacco advertising was a major issue in 1993 with a ban discussed by the European Community. In France, the 'Loi Évin' — a law introduced by health minister Claude Évin — outlawed tobacco and alcohol advertising from 1 January 1993 and led initially to cancellation of the French GP, but Balestre, who remained president of the Fédération Française du Sport Automobile, gained government assurances that foreign tobacco-backed teams would not face sanction if they raced at Magny-Cours and the event was reinstated on 25 February.

Ayrton Senna on the podium after winning the Brazilian Grand Prix

The class of 1993 pose for the traditional end-of-term photograph

Mosley campaigned to have electronic driver aids banned in 1994 and F1 technical delegate Charlie Whiting declared at the Canadian GP that all cars with active suspension or traction control already contravened the 1993 rules. His report was forwarded to the World Council, which voted for an immediate ban on 15 July. Divided thus far, the teams eventually agreed a unified solution at the German GP with new rules accepted for 1994 on the proviso that those systems could be used for the rest of 1993.

The Asian GP at Autopolis was cancelled for a second successive year. A surprise one-off agreement was reached instead with Donington Park to hold the European GP at Easter. Having fulfilled circuit owner Tom Wheatcroft's dream of staging a GP for the first time since 1938, this was one of the wettest races in history and included a record 63 pitstops. The Mexican GP was dropped and would not return until 2015.

A wiring fault was blamed when the green light failed to come on at the start of the Spanish GP but everyone started when the red went out (to be replaced by a flashing orange) and no one protested. Furthermore, fax and phone numbers for the motorhomes in Spain became muddled and some communications went to the wrong teams.

Ferrari made one of its sporadic threats to quit in favour of Indycar racing or GTs in February while Honda engineers secretly built an 'after hours' F1 car that tested the same month but never raced. Trebron and Dome both promised Japan's first F1 car for 16 years but neither was built. Austrian sports car entrant Franz Konrad also planned a contender: Johannes Gruber designed a car at Graz university and talks were held with Lamborghini, but this project also never saw light of day.

A puncture denied Damon Hill his breakthrough victory in Germany

CANON WILLIAMS RENAULT

Williams-Renault had been so dominant in 1992 that three World Champions – Nigel Mansell, Alain Prost and Ayrton Senna – squabbled over the number one drive. An offer for Mansell had been on the table since May but terms could not be agreed. Negotiations at the Hungarian GP, the very weekend he clinched the 1992 title, were complicated by Prost having already signed and Senna's offer to drive for free. 'My only motivation is to win,' Senna told the press. 'The money is irrelevant. The reason I have told Frank I am available for free is to show my motivation.'

The impasse continued for a month before Mansell announced his F1 retirement at a tense press conference on 13 September, five days before signing for two-time Indycar champions Newman-Haas Racing. Prost's signature was confirmed at the Portuguese GP and Senna, who had refused Derek Warwick's inclusion in the 1986 Lotus line-up, accused him of 'being a coward' when vetoed as his team-mate. There was talk of buying Riccardo Patrese out of his recently signed Benetton deal, a two-year contract offer to Martin Brundle was withdrawn and hopes of attracting Mika Häkkinen were refused by Lotus. Williams test driver Damon Hill, with just two GP starts to his name, was eventually confirmed as Prost's team-mate for the coming season on 11 December 1992.

Number one was not used in 1993 as Mansell did not defend his title, so Hill wore zero on his car. Although Hill was not formally replaced as test driver, F3000 star David Coulthard impressed at Silverstone in May and during many subsequent sessions. Respected engineer Paddy Lowe moved to McLaren after a period on 'gardening leave' and two Mansell acolytes – commercial director Sheridan Thynne and team manager Peter Windsor – also left, replaced by Richard West and Ian Harrison respectively.

FISA wanted to ban electronic driver aids against the wishes of Williams and McLaren. When Williams was late entering the 1993 championship, the governing body flexed its muscles by omitting the reigning champions. Williams's participation was initially opposed by Benetton and Minardi but the team was eventually readmitted by the World Council on 25 February. Future questions about the legality of Williams's fuel and electronics formed the backdrop to a testy campaign as new rules were imposed for 1994.

Furthermore, Prost had offended the governing body while on sabbatical in an interview with French magazine *Auto Plus* and was refused a super licence. A long letter from FISA president Max Mosley to Frank Williams that questioned Prost's criticisms of F1 and its governing body became public as the row intensified. A month after finally being granted his licence, Prost was summoned to appear before the World Council on 18 March. 'It is best to forget this business,' Prost said when no further action was taken. 'Let's go to Brazil and talk about sport.'

Hill completed the Williams FW15-Renault's shakedown at Silverstone on 15 September 1992 and the unraced new car was updated for winter testing as the FW15B, with 1993-specification aerodynamics, including raised front-wing endplates, plus narrower front track and wheels. The definitive race car (FW15C) ran at Estoril

Alain Prost, Williams FW15C-Renault (Portuguese GP)

Damon Hill, Williams FW15C-Renault (Portuguese GP)

on 15 February 1993 with the latest version of Renault's V10 engine (RS05) now featuring pneumatic valves and new conrods. There was a lower rear wing that rose to the centre in a limited anhedral shape. A new fly-by-wire throttle was used from the Spanish GP and ABS braking was introduced in France. The FW15C was more nervous than the all-conquering FW14B but delivered both titles once more.

Prost was unhurt in a 150mph shunt at Estoril on 29 January and Williams-Renault remained title favourites when first and second at that final test. Prost emphasised the team's superiority by starting all 16 races from the front row, including 13 pole positions.

At Kyalami, Prost made a poor start but passed Senna and beat the McLaren-Ford by 19.824sec. Hill qualified fourth, spun at the first corner and was knocked out of the race by Alex Zanardi after 16 laps. Consummate wet-weather Senna victories followed at the next two races at Interlagos and Donington, with Hill second on both occasions. Prost crashed into Christian Fittipaldi in the mid-race Brazilian downpour and pitted seven times on the way to an unhappy third in the English race.

Criticised for those two performances, Prost retook the points lead by dominating the San Marino and Spanish GPs, while Hill outbraked himself at Tosa on lap 21 at Imola and blew his engine in Spain. Harshly given a 10sec stop-go penalty for jumping the start in Monaco, Prost lost a lap when his broken clutch caused him to stall as he tried to rejoin although he charged back to fourth by the flag. Hill survived contact with Gerhard Berger's Ferrari to finish second.

Prost led a Williams 1–3 in Montréal and a 1–2 at Magny-Cours.

Delayed in the pits in Canada, Hill started from pole position for the first time in France and was robbed of victory at both Silverstone and Hockenheim. His engine failed with 18 laps of his home race to go and his left rear tyre punctured on the penultimate lap in Germany, Prost the beneficiary on both occasions. That German victory was despite another stop-go penalty for missing the Ostkurve chicane as the Frenchman avoided Martin Brundle's spinning Ligier-Renault on the opening lap of the race.

Hill finally broke his duck when he led all the way in Hungary, becoming a GP winner on his 13th start. Prost started last after being left on the dummy grid but forced his way up to fourth before losing ten minutes while a broken rear wing support was fixed. Hill won the next two races at Spa-Francorchamps and Monza, despite contact with both Senna and Berger on the opening lap in Italy. After Prost finished third in Belgium, engine failure denied him the Italian victory he required to clinch the title.

Prost announced his retirement in Portugal on Saturday, the day after Senna told Ron Dennis he was leaving, and went on to finish second to confirm his fourth world title. Polesitter Hill stalled at the start of the parade lap and came from the back to claim third. Prost completed his F1 career by finishing second in Japan and Australia and was feted on the Adelaide podium by arch-rival Senna. Fourth at Suzuka following a puncture, Hill spun while challenging Prost in Australia but recovered to finish third in the race and final standings. Williams-Renault retained the constructors' title having scored double the points of its closest challenger.

MARLBORO McLAREN

Honda's withdrawal was confirmed at the 1992 Italian GP and left Ron Dennis looking for an alternative engine partner for 1993 and beyond. A deal to buy Ligier's Renault V10s was scuppered by conflicting Shell (McLaren) and Elf (Renault) fuel contracts so agreement with Cosworth for customer Ford HB V8s was finalised in December, with McLaren conducting its own development programme with subsidiary TAG Electronics. The team out-performed Benetton and the season was spent agitating for engine parity with Ford's contracted works partner.

With Gerhard Berger having signed for Ferrari and Ayrton Senna craving a move to Williams, Michael Andretti realised long-term ambitions when he joined on 3 September 1992. 'It is a multi-year agreement and it is for many millions of dollars,' Dennis told the press in New York. 'We don't hire drivers for a year.' Senna turned down Ferrari and admitted that it was '50-50 whether I race or take a sabbatical' in October. He kept McLaren waiting throughout the winter and even tested a Penske PC21-Chevrolet Indycar at Firebird Raceway on 20 December as he considered his options.

With Senna's intentions still unclear, Mika Häkkinen signed in January once the F1 Contract Recognition Board decided he was not obliged to stay with Lotus. Benetton engineer Pat Fry joined Giorgio Ascanelli in the active-suspension department while Williams's Paddy Lowe eventually arrived as head of research and development. McLaren acquired Lydden Hill rallycross circuit near Dover but plans to develop it as a test track and factory were not realised.

Rain and electrical issues plagued Andretti's Silverstone shakedown of the McLaren MP4/8-Ford on 15 February. Neil Oatley's design team had refined the aerodynamics with a lower nose, the underside of which arched to increase front-end downforce, and a rear diffuser with three channels. Revised active suspension, fly-by-wire throttle, traction control and data acquisition were activated by a single TAG 'black box'. The transverse gearbox could be programmed to be fully automatic over a complete lap and car-to-pits telemetry was introduced at the Brazilian GP.

Senna first drove the MP4/8 at Silverstone on 3 March and McLaren announced that he would partner Andretti in South Africa with Häkkinen consigned to the role of highly paid reserve. Outwardly, Senna continued on a race-by-race basis until finally agreeing in the early hours of 30 June to complete the season, although Alan Henry wrote in *Autocourse* that this 'was nothing more than a ruse agreed by Ron Dennis and Senna to romance additional money for Ayrton's fee out of the team's sponsors.'

Second at Kyalami despite an issue with the active suspension, Senna then delivered two of the best wet-weather performances in history. In Brazil he recovered from a stop-go penalty for overtaking under yellow flags to score McLaren's 100th GP victory. Even more memorably, he passed four cars on his opening lap at Donington, pitted five times (including setting a new lap record when he drove straight through the pits on lap 57), lapped the field at one stage and won the European GP by 1m 23.199s.

Andretti endured a torrid start to his F1 career. He stalled at the start in South Africa and then crashed into the back of Derek Warwick's Footwork-Mugen on lap five. A season-best fifth on the grid in Brazil, Andretti had a heavy accident with Gerhard Berger's Ferrari at the start. He crashed into Karl Wendlinger's Sauber on the opening lap at Donington and spun at Imola, where Senna's hydraulics failed when running second.

Racing at a circuit he knew for the first time, Andretti was fifth at Barcelona to score his first points with Senna second despite

Ayrton Senna, McLaren MP4/8-Ford (Monaco GP)

a tardy pitstop. In Monaco the Brazilian recovered from a heavy crash at Ste-Dévote on Thursday, qualified third and won the street race for a record sixth time after Michael Schumacher's Benetton retired. Eighth in Canada was the worst grid position of Senna's McLaren career and he retired from second as Williams-Renault rival Alain Prost retook the points lead. In France, Senna was fourth and Andretti passed Rubens Barrichello for sixth with two laps remaining.

McLaren had the latest pneumatic valve Ford HB Series VIII engine from the British GP. Senna drove a storming race and only lost third when he ran out of fuel on the last lap, classified fifth after coasting to a halt at Club Corner for the third year in a row. Andretti's miserable form continued with a spin into retirement at the first corner of the British GP and damaged suspension when clouted by Berger's Ferrari on lap five in Germany. Senna was edged off the road by Prost on the opening lap at Hockenheim then recovered from last but one to finish fourth.

Throttle issues accounted for both McLaren-Fords in Hungary while Senna was fourth and Andretti eighth in Belgium. Having dropped to tenth at Monza following another first-lap collision, Senna apologised when he eliminated himself and Martin Brundle at the Ascari chicane. Andretti spun on lap two but finished third after a fine recovery drive from the back of the field.

That was not only Andretti's best F1 performance but also his last, for he signed with Chip Ganassi's Indycar team for 1994 and was replaced by Häkkinen for the remaining three races. The Finn made an immediate impact by out-qualifying Senna at Estoril although he crashed heavily during the race when running fourth. Senna, who had informed McLaren of his decision to leave on Friday, made his customary great start to chase surprise leader Jean Alesi's Ferrari until his engine blew.

Michael Andretti, McLaren MP4/8-Ford (Italian GP)

Senna led a McLaren 1–3 in Japan, where his post-race altercation with Jordan débutant Eddie Irvine created the headlines. In the presence of journalist Adam Cooper in Jordan's hospitality area, Senna punched Irvine, for which he received a suspended two-race ban in December. In Australia, Senna converted his first pole position of 1993 into a dominant race win (McLaren's record 104th) on his final appearance for the team while Häkkinen duelled with Damon Hill for third before retiring. Despite inferior machinery, Senna won five times as he and McLaren-Ford both finished as runners-up.

For most of the year McLaren lacked an engine partner for 1994, so an MP4/8 was converted to Chrysler (née Lamborghini) V12 power in September. Senna and Häkkinen drove the plain white car at Silverstone and Estoril before a new alliance with Peugeot was announced on 8 October, angering the American corporation, which then decided against taking over the Lamborghini programme and funding a full F1 graduation.

Mika Häkkinen, McLaren MP4/8-Ford (Portuguese GP)

Michael Schumacher, Benetton B193-Ford (Brazilian GP)

CAMEL BENETTON FORD

Emerging superstar Michael Schumacher remained as Benetton team leader despite Sauber's claim of a prior agreement but Martin Brundle departed after a single season. Al Unser Jr was Benetton's guest at the 1992 British GP although a planned test never materialised. Riccardo Patrese signed a two-year deal with Benetton on 3 September 1992 after speaking to McLaren and Sauber. Allan McNish replaced Alex Zanardi as test driver with Andrea Montermini and Paul Belmondo taking lesser roles. There was change among the race engineers as well for Pat Symonds joined Rory Byrne's research and development department and Pat Fry was poached by McLaren. Ex-Lotus/Ligier technical director Frank Dernie replaced Symonds as Schumacher's engineer. R.J. Reynolds extended its backing for another year and Elf Minol joined as fuel partner.

Riccardo Patrese, Benetton B193-Ford (South African GP)

A two-year extension as Ford's works team was agreed and guaranteed exclusive use of the latest-specification Series VIII HB engine, which now featured pneumatic valves. After Ford-equipped McLaren won two of the opening three races, Ron Dennis lobbied for parity and achieved it mid-season, putting pressure on the under-performing Benetton team. Having enjoyed impressive reliability and results with a passive/manual car in 1992, Benetton technical director Ross Brawn launched development programmes for active suspension (under Symonds), traction control, semi-automatic gearbox and anti-lock braking.

Brawn had already realised that a totally new design was required to optimise the narrower tyres by the time Schumacher shook down the evolutionary B193 at Silverstone on 14 January. Also known as the B193A, this was based on the 1992 car with active suspension and semi-automatic gearbox added in time for the first Estoril test. The aerodynamic package had been reworked and the cooling system improved.

From third on the grid, Schumacher disputed the lead at Kyalami with Ayrton Senna and Alain Prost before an attempt to pass the Brazilian ended in the barriers. At Interlagos he recovered from a botched pitstop and stop-go penalty (for passing under yellow flags) to snatch third. Patrese retired from both races (after a spin in South Africa) in a disappointing start to his campaign.

Under construction before the B193A turned a wheel, the all-new Benetton B193B-Ford – with a higher nose and revised aerodynamics – ran at Silverstone in the week before Brazil and was raced from the European GP at Donington. A double rear wing was tried at the European GP and traction control introduced in Monaco. Four-wheel

Michael Schumacher, Benetton B193B-Ford (Italian GP)

steering was tested at Estoril in October despite already being banned from the start of the 1994 season.

In need of a positive weekend to ease McLaren's pressure, Schumacher qualified third at Donington as the fastest Ford only to crash on lap 22. Patrese ran a conservative race in the midfield to finish fifth. Schumacher out-qualified Senna's McLaren-Ford at Imola and scored a much-needed second place after the Brazilian's retirement. Facing calls in the media to retire, most notably from James Hunt, Patrese spun on the opening lap at Tosa and stalled.

Schumacher was third after a troubled run in Spain and lost the Monaco GP when the hydraulics failed. Despite a poor start in Montréal, he split the Williams-Renaults with second place after Damon Hill was delayed. Struggling for grip at Magny-Cours, Schumacher only started seventh but adopted a two-stop strategy and passed Senna for third with nine laps to go. Furthermore, he benefited from Hill's misfortunes to finish second at Silverstone and Hockenheim. Fourth despite a mysterious vibration in Barcelona, Patrese responded to three successive races without a point by coming third in Britain and fifth at Hockenheim, the latter his 250th GP start.

There were revised electronics and new aero in Hungary, where Schumacher spun twice before retiring with an engine problem. On the day he was released from his 1994 contract, Patrese recovered from his own spin to finish second. Schumacher's launch control malfunctioned in Belgium but he fought back from the resulting poor start to overtake Prost and finish second, with Patrese sixth after a spin as he left the pits. Schumacher ran second at Monza before engine failure while Patrese claimed fifth.

The Benetton-Fords lacked balance during Portuguese qualifying

and sixth-placed Schumacher took the spare B193B to the grid. He gained the lead after his only pitstop and held off Prost to win a GP for the second time. With seven laps to go, Patrese was battling with Derek Warwick over the final point when he crashed into the Footwork-Mugen in a rash manoeuvre. The four-wheel steering system was used for the only time in Japan but Schumacher hit the back of Hill's Williams-Renault at the chicane and Patrese spun on his own oil. Both suffered engine failures in Australia, Patrese on the last lap of the last GP of his career.

Schumacher and Patrese were fourth and fifth in the World Championship but there was a chasm between their scores and performances. Benetton-Ford finished third in the constructors' standings, 12 points behind McLaren in the race to be the top Ford-powered team of 1993.

Riccardo Patrese, Benetton B193B-Ford (Canadian GP)

SCUDERIA FERRARI

John Barnard insisted that there was no quick fix to Ferrari's problems when he accepted its five-year offer in August 1992. He established a new remote facility – Ferrari Design & Development – in Shalford to the south of Guildford, Surrey. Having worked for Barnard at Benetton and blamed for the failure of the Tyrrell 021-Yamaha, Mike Coughlan joined in August 1993.

George Ryton, who had previously worked for Barnard at Ferrari's Guildford Technical Office, rejoined in July 1992 as chief designer, although now based at Maranello. The plan was for Ryton's interim Ferrari F93A to be superseded by Barnard's Ferrari 645 but the ban on electronic driver aids from 1994 resulted in the F93A being used throughout 1993, compromising the whole season. Nigel Stepney joined as chief mechanic following the closure of the Piquet F3000 team after a single season and he soon became a key link between Italy and Shalford.

Revealed on 22 December 1992, the F93A abandoned the double-floor concept of the unsuccessful F92A, with Jean-Claude Migeot a casualty of that failure. With conventional monocoque and sidepods, the car was narrower and its centre of gravity lower. Semi-automatic gearbox, traction control and active suspension were *de rigueur*. The 65-degree V12 initially had five valves per cylinder before a simpler four-valve version was raced from the German GP due to the standard fuel now permitted in F1. There was agreement with erstwhile World Championship rivals Honda for an exchange of information. Telescopic trumpets were introduced on Berger's engine at Monaco and raced in Canada.

In the final year of his contract with McLaren, Gerhard Berger met Luca di Montezemolo in August 1992 and secured a healthy retainer to be Jean Alesi's new team-mate. It proved a frustrating campaign for both drivers and Berger's driving grew erratic as race-day incidents and operations on a painful elbow took their toll.

Initial testing of the F93A was delayed by inclement weather and then plagued by software shortcomings for the new suspension. It was a measure of how bad winter testing had been that the South African GP was viewed as a relative success: Alesi qualified fifth and Berger, whose car was undrivable on full tanks, was classified sixth despite late engine failure. Berger crashed heavily in Brazil on Friday when caught out by the active suspension and again at the start following a high-speed clash with Michael Andretti's McLaren. Two stop-go penalties for infractions behind the safety car restricted Alesi to an eighth-place finish.

Sidelined by the suspension hydraulics at Donington, the Ferraris ran in the points at Imola before another double DNF. Berger

Jean Alesi, Ferrari F93A (Monaco GP)

Gerhard Berger, Ferrari F93A (Canadian GP)

salvaged sixth from a chaotic weekend in Spain where Barnard, frustrated by lack of progress with the active suspension, decided a new system was required. Those deficiencies were masked by the confines of Monaco, where they qualified in the top seven. After bumping each other at the Loews hairpin on lap 61 as they disputed third, Berger took the place a couple of laps later only to go out after hitting second-placed Damon Hill, again at the hairpin, leaving Alesi to inherit third and score his first points of 1993. They qualified on row three in Canada where a holed radiator denied Alesi more points and fourth-placed Berger held off Martin Brundle's Ligier at the finish.

Keen to hire a new sporting director, di Montezemolo began talking to Peugeot's Jean Todt in the spring. Todt agreed to join after June's Le Mans 24 Hours, which Peugeot won for a second successive year, placing Harvey Postlethwaite's future in doubt.

Barnard's simplified new suspension with an actuator and coil springs was introduced at Mangy-Cours, where new front wings and rear diffuser were also fitted. However, the team struggled to sort the heavily revised cars at that race and the next. Using the four-valve engine for the first time in Germany, Berger finished sixth (after running into Michael Andretti's McLaren on lap five and later easing Mark Blundell's Ligier onto the grass) and Alesi seventh (after recovering from an unscheduled pitstop).

Berger was now handicapped by a painful elbow that a series of operations did not alleviate for the rest of the European season. He survived heavy contact with Brundle's Ligier to finish third in Hungary, where Alesi crashed head-on following contact with Christian Fittipaldi's Minardi. Alesi qualified fourth at Spa-Francorchamps but suffered suspension failure in the warm-up and had to park his dangerous car after just four laps of the race. Berger

had a miserable weekend and collided with Blundell's Ligier on the last lap when disputing tenth.

After encouraging tests, Alesi was best of the rest behind the Williams-Renaults at Monza and inherited second when Alain Prost retired with five laps to go. Berger qualified sixth but his active suspension failed during the race and he crashed heavily after the chequered flag when avoiding Alesi's slow-moving car. Alesi stormed from fifth on the grid in Portugal to lead until his first pitstop on lap 20 but eventually finished fourth, while Berger lost control as he rejoined following a pitstop and crashed head-on into the opposing barriers. After both retired in Japan, they achieved Ferrari's only double points score in Adelaide, a lapped fourth (Alesi) and fifth (Berger) running with double rear wings for the first time.

Ferrari failed to win a race for the third successive season and finished 1993 in a disappointing and distant fourth overall.

LIGIER GITANES BLONDES

It was all-change for new Ligier owner Cyril de Rouvre, who released Thierry Boutsen while Éric Comas tired of waiting so moved to Larrousse. Having signed McLaren test driver Mark Blundell before Christmas and held unsuccessful talks with Mika Häkkinen, Ligier angered the French press on 19 January by announcing another Englishman, Martin Brundle, as his team-mate. Éric Bernard was named as reserve driver but there was no French race driver for the first time in the team's history.

Technical director Gérard Ducarouge and aerodynamicist John Davis designed a conventional car, the JS39, around the Mecachrome-prepared Renault RS05 V10 engine, which drove through a 1992-specification Williams transverse semi-automatic gearbox.

Martin Brundle, Ligier JS39-Renault (Portuguese GP)

The car had traction control although passive push-rod suspension remained, with single shock absorber at the front. Unveiled in Monte Carlo due to France's new tobacco-advertising laws, the JS39 had its first shakedown at Paul Ricard on 29 January and Blundell enthused. Although hampered initially by low- and medium-speed understeer, a series of upgrades made it competitive by mid-season. Active suspension was tested in April but never raced as the programme was cancelled on 15 July when a ban seemed imminent and Ligier's resurgence waned when active suspension was permitted for the rest of 1993. De Rouvre restructured with long-standing employees Michel Beaujon and Jean-Pierre Paoli leaving during the season. Brundle's race engineer Maurizio Nardon was replaced by Steve Clark in July.

Mark Blundell, Ligier JS39-Renault (German GP)

With a sorted and normally reliable package from the outset, Blundell finished third at Kyalami – Ligier's first podium since 1986 – and fifth at Interlagos. Brundle spun out of sixth in South Africa, after an earlier delay with a *tête-a-que* and subsequent front-wing repairs, and collided with Fabrizio Barbazza's Minardi on the opening lap of Interlagos. Qualifying at Donington was a disaster and both crashed during the race. They started inside the top ten at Imola but Blundell's race quickly ended with a crash exiting Tamburello on lap one due to suspected rear suspension failure; Brundle finished an excellent third after much attrition.

Covered in oil from Alex Zanardi's blown engine, Blundell lost sixth in Spain to Gerhard Berger with two laps to go. A new Williams-style front wing introduced in Monaco seemed beneficial as Brundle scored a point despite illness and an unscheduled pitstop following contact with Comas. With revised undertrays, the Ligiers were again top-ten qualifiers in Canada, where Brundle finished fifth while Blundell spun out. Thanks to another aero upgrade and home advantage, they lined up third (Brundle) and fourth (Blundell) behind the Williams-Renaults at Magny-Cours. Blundell held off Ayrton Senna and Michael Schumacher for fourth place until he taken out by Andrea de Cesaris's Tyrrell while lapping it (his third successive retirement). Brundle made two tyre stops and was disappointed to only finish fifth (his third successive points score).

Blundell had a huge accident in the wet during practice at Silverstone and finished seventh despite a spin. Brundle qualified sixth and lost fourth when his gearbox failed six laps from the flag.

In Germany, they qualified on the third row and Blundell finished a fine third after battling an obdurate Berger; Brundle was fifth on the opening lap but spun at the Ostkurve and received a harsh stop-go penalty for missing the chicane as a consequence. That and a subsequent botched tyre stop ended his hopes of a podium that day.

Unsuited to the slow and bumpy Hungaroring, the Ligiers emerged from the midfield to finish fifth (Brundle) and seventh (Blundell). Disappointing pace at the last three European races was eventually traced to an issue with the front aerodynamics. In Belgium, Brundle understeered his way to seventh while Blundell was furious with Berger once more when they crashed at Stavelot on the last lap. Brundle was rammed by an apologetic Senna on lap nine of the Italian GP and Blundell crashed on the exit to the Parabolica. Brundle was sixth after stopping twice in Portugal, where Blundell lost an even better result after being hit by Karl Wendlinger's Sauber. During testing that followed at Magny-Cours, Brundle crashed and was shaken when hit on the helmet by a wheel.

In Japan, where Brundle's car had a radical Hugo Pratt-designed livery, both qualified poorly and ran in the top ten until Brundle tangled with seventh-placed J.J. Lehto at the last corner of the race with Blundell inheriting that position. With the cars out of sorts on the Adelaide bumps due to their passive suspension, Brundle finished sixth at the end of a mixed season for the team.

It had been a fairly reliable campaign, with seven points-scoring finishes for Brundle and three for Blundell amounting to fifth position for Ligier-Renault in the constructors' standings.

TEAM LOTUS

Managing director Peter Collins was sure of Johnny Herbert's importance when Lotus exercised its option on his services on 27 August 1992: 'Johnny brings a rare combination of raw speed, technical feedback and infectious humour to the team.' Lotus announced 11 days later that Mika Häkkinen would remain before blocking Williams's attempt to sign the highly rated Finn in December. Frustrated to be denied such an opportunity, Häkkinen began speaking to McLaren and Ligier. He chose Woking and the F1 Contract Recognition Board found in McLaren's favour on 25 January 1993. Benetton test driver Alex Zanardi was announced as Herbert's new team-mate on 5 February.

Herbert tried passive and active suspension at the pre-Christmas Paul Ricard test, where he was a promising fourth quickest despite two accidents on day three alone. The Lotus 107B-Ford was launched at Claridge's Hotel in London on 24 February with fully active suspension using hydraulic struts rather than springs and dampers, although this system proved unpredictable. A manual six-speed gearbox was retained with development of a semi-automatic abandoned. Traction control was not available until Hungary. Loctite joined Hitachi and title partner Castrol as major backers but money was tight. Jordan's Trevor Foster arrived as director of racing with team manager Paul Bussey leaving in May.

A successful winter raised expectations so the South African GP proved a rude awakening when the cars qualified towards the back and retired. Zanardi crashed into Damon Hill's delayed Williams-

Johnny Herbert, Lotus 107B-Ford (French GP)

Alex Zanardi, Lotus 107B-Ford (German GP)

Pedro Lamy, Lotus 107B-Ford (Italian GP)

Renault as he tried to pass while Herbert lost a points finish when fuel pressure fell. The rain at Interlagos and Donington masked the car's deficiencies and Herbert judged conditions perfectly to claim fourth on both occasions. Zanardi was sixth at Interlagos despite driving the last 20 laps virtually one-handed after being hit by a stone. At Imola both cars went out late in the race, the Italian due to crashing while challenging for fourth and Herbert when his engine blew with three laps to go while lying fifth.

Using a double rear wing for the first time, Zanardi was seventh in Monaco. Short of grip in Canada, both cars finished outside the points. Following a fraught French GP weekend, Lotus tested at Snetterton and identified a problem with the active software at high temperatures. The next race at Silverstone saw Herbert qualify an improved seventh and finish fourth, while Zanardi crashed at Copse during qualifying and spun out of the race.

Roberto Moreno was placed on standby when Zanardi broke bones in his left foot while cycling but the Italian raced on, retiring in Germany (spin) and Hungary (gearbox). Tenth at Hockenheim following an actuator problem, Herbert stalled at the Hungaroring when the data box worked loose and caused him to spin. Zanardi was then sidelined by a 150mph head-on accident at Eau Rouge during Friday practice for the Belgian GP. Herbert raised morale by qualifying tenth and finishing fifth in the sole-surviving Lotus-Ford.

Pedro Lamy replaced Zanardi for the next two races after testing at Silverstone and Monza. Herbert qualified seventh in Italy but

crashed at Parabolica when challenging Gerhard Berger for fifth, while Lamy was classified 11th on début despite late engine failure. Lamy was the centre of attention at his home race in Portugal, where both Lotuses handled badly and crashed. Now confirmed for the last two races of the season, Lamy crashed during the closing stages in Japan following an active failure (he was classified 13th) while Herbert endured a troubled weekend. In Australia the Lotuses qualified among the backmarkers for a second successive weekend and both were eliminated by lap ten, Lamy hit by Ukyo Katayama at the first corner and Herbert following hydraulics failure.

Lotus-Ford finished sixth equal in the constructors' standings but the financial strain was beginning to show despite Collins's protestations to the contrary. Momentum gained in 1992, both on and off the track, had stalled.

SAUBER

Amateur hillclimber Peter Sauber built his first car in his parents' basement in Hinwil, near Zürich, in 1970 a year before giving up competition to establish PP Sauber AG in the town. Sauber manufactured a series of 2-litre sports-racing cars and ran a team in the spectacular but short-lived BMW M1 Procar championship. Sauber built two Group 5 BMW M1s in 1981 and Hans-Joachim Stuck/Nelson Piquet won that year's curtailed Nürburgring 1,000Kms in one.

Sauber entered the World Endurance Championship in 1982 with the Sauber C6-Ford, 'C' standing for his wife Christiane. BMW engines followed before a deputation from Mercedes-Benz visited Hinwil in October 1984. Mercedes, which had not had a works team since the 1955 Le Mans disaster, sanctioned a private engine supply for 1985 via Heini Mader's independent tuning company. Leo Ress joined as Sauber chief designer and the programme eventually gained full works support in 1989. At the beginning of a five-year agreement between the companies, Sauber-Mercedes won the 1989 World Sports-Prototype Championship and Le Mans 24 Hours, and retained the WSPC title a year later.

With sports car racing in decline, Mercedes-Benz motorsport chief Jochen Neerpasch and the racing department began evaluating F1. Tyrrell technical director Harvey Postlethwaite joined Sauber on 1 August 1991 while Ilmor Engineering was commissioned to design and build a new V10 engine. However, Daimler-Benz CEO Professor Werner Niefer announced in a short statement on 26 November 1991 the board's decision not to support works participation, a decision that prompted Postlethwaite's return to Ferrari and Sauber to take over the naming rights of the new engine.

With the promise of financial and technical support from Mercedes if it entered F1, Sauber moved into purpose-built state-of-the-art facilities close to its old base in January 1992 and confirmed its intentions on 5 February. The announcement was made through Mercedes channels and named former junior drivers Karl Wendlinger and Michael Schumacher as drivers, their previous sports car contracts allowing Sauber to call on their services for F1. Benetton reacted angrily to Schumacher's inclusion and the German confirmed he was staying at Enstone. 'I think the best thing for him is to drive where he wants to drive,' a diplomatic Peter Sauber told *Autosport* at the time, 'and that is Benetton.'

For a team that had not even raced, there was considerable change of personnel during 1992. Steve Nichols replaced Postlethwaite as technical director but left at the turn of the year. Peugeot's André de Cortanze, who had F1 experience with Renault, eventually took his place for the last two races of 1993. Having relinquished duties at Untertürkheim, sporting director Neerpasch lasted until August although he was retained as a consultant. Luigi Mazzola, Alain Prost's former Ferrari race engineer, joined on 1 March but lasted only four months.

As team-mate to Wendlinger, Riccardo Patrese and Thierry Boutsen were considered before J.J. Lehto signed in September 1992. Carmen Ziegler became the first female team manager in F1. In addition to Mercedes-Benz, Sauber attracted backing from finance company Lighthouse, Joop! clothing and Liqui Moly lubricants.

Postlethwaite drew the initial concepts for the Sauber C12 and Nichols arrived late in the process, so long-time designer Ress was the constant in the design office, supported by Mike Gascoyne (aerodynamics), Reinhard Lechner (chassis and gearbox) and Ian Thompson (composites). Gascoyne used a wind tunnel at Emmen and David Price Composites of Bookham, Surrey began construction of the monocoque in May. The first car was ready for shakedown at Lurcy-Lévis in France at the start of September.

The C12 was initially powered by Ilmor's standard type 2175A V10 engine, which, unusually for 1993, was driven through a longitudinal six-speed semi-automatic gearbox. The passive push-rod suspension

J.J. Lehto, Sauber C12-Ilmor (Monaco GP)

Karl Wendlinger, Sauber C12-Ilmor (South African GP)

J.J. Lehto, Sauber C12 (Australian GP)

Karl Wendlinger, Sauber C12 (Japanese GP)

had a single damper at the front; an active programme led by former Mercedes engineer Thomas Becker was cancelled when such systems were banned for 1994. There were gearbox teething problems in pre-season testing so a new unit was designed and manufactured in three weeks, after which Wendlinger lapped under Barcelona's qualifying record in November. Two C12s arrived at the pre-Christmas Paul Ricard test with 'concept by Mercedes-Benz' on the engine cover, showing that the relationship with the German manufacturer was far from over, although a promising programme was punctuated by accidents at Misano (Lehto) and Estoril (Wendlinger).

The well-prepared newcomers impressed on début in South Africa, where Lehto qualified sixth and finished fifth despite stopping to free a stuck gear. Fourth when the electrics failed in Brazil, he was forced to start the European GP from the pitlane in the spare car that had been set up for the taller Wendlinger and proved undrivable. At Imola, Lehto inherited fourth when Wendlinger's engine let go and held on to that position despite his own last-lap failure. Wendlinger qualified for the first five races in the top ten – including fifth at Donington and Imola – but retired on each occasion, including being knocked off by Michael Andretti on the opening lap of the European GP.

The Sauber-Ilmors ran nose to tail at Monaco before they collided at the Loews hairpin as Lehto tried to take seventh on lap 24, both drivers blaming each other. Wendlinger finished sixth at Montréal to score his first point with Lehto seventh despite gearbox issues on both cars. Those problems continued in France, where they retired, and the C12s were just not quick enough in Britain. As Sauber suffered a mid-season slump, new front wings and diffuser failed to improve poor handling. Lehto broke his wrist when he crashed during testing at Magny-Cours but did not miss a race, while Wendlinger came from 17th on the grid to finish sixth in Hungary. Lehto damaged his tub during practice in Belgium and Wendlinger was concussed in a testing accident at Monza's first chicane.

The new 72-degree Sauber V10 (type 2175B) engine ran on the dyno in April and was track tested with a redesigned gearbox at Imola six weeks later. A problem with piston rings delayed its race début, especially as the supplier was closed for its summer break at the time, but the engine was ready for the Italian GP. The lightest and smallest contemporary F1 engine, Mario Ilien's short-stroke design further boosted the Sauber C12's already impressive straight-line speed. Having started from the back after stalling on the parade lap at Monza, Lehto hit Rubens Barrichello in the first corner pile-up but Wendlinger enjoyed a strong race into fourth position.

Wendlinger held off Martin Brundle for fifth in Portugal, where only Lehto's stop-go penalty for baulking Michael Schumacher's leading Benetton (thinking it was Riccardo Patrese who he was racing against) prevented a double score. Lehto lost seventh at Suzuka when hit by Martin Brundle at the final corner of the race. A season that had begun with such promise came to an underwhelming conclusion in the Australian midfield, where the drivers battled each other before crashing independently.

MINARDI TEAM

After two difficult seasons with heavy V12 engines, Minardi let an option with Lamborghini expire on 31 August 1992 and signed a two-year agreement with Grand Prix Engineering for ex-Fondmetal Ford HB V8s (with Magneti Marelli engine management) that dated back to Jaguar's 1991 sports car campaign. Constrained by the lowest budget in F1, the conventional M193 penned by Aldo Costa and Gustav Brunner initially lacked the electronic gizmos that were now commonplace, although a hydraulic system controlled the dampers and traction control was tried by mid-season. Reliability was excellent and the chassis proved nimble, especially at slower circuits. Inevitably, the lack of testing and power deficit meant performance tailed off at the faster venues visited after mid-season. At the M193's launch on 20 January Christian Fittipaldi and Fabrizio Barbazza were confirmed as drivers, the Italian with just an eight-race agreement, and there was new sponsorship from Beta tools, Valleverde shoes and Cocif doors.

Fittipaldi was particularly kind to his tyres and often ran non-stop when others had to pit, starting in South Africa. An impressive 12th on the grid, he spun on lap six when his footrest broke and drove steadily thereafter to finish fourth, while Barbazza's GP début ended when Aguri Suzuki rammed him. Both Minardi-Fords crashed in the Brazilian rain. With a revised hydraulic system, Barbazza kept it on the island in difficult conditions to finish sixth in the European and San Marino GPs, while Fittipaldi was outside the points in these races. The Brazilian's fifth place in Monaco put Minardi fifth equal in the championship with one more point than Ferrari – but the rest of

Jean-Marc Gounon, Minardi M193-Ford (Japanese GP)

Christian Fittipaldi, Minardi M193-Ford (Hungarian GP)

the season brought no more points. Fittipaldi was ninth in Canada and eighth at Magny-Cours (despite being hit by Riccardo Patrese's Benetton-Ford as they battled for position) while Barbazza retired on his last two races for the team.

Perennial Minardi favourite Pierluigi Martini tested at Fiorano and replaced Barbazza from the British GP, where he crashed during first practice and damaged his ribs, injuries that affected him for the next three races. Both drivers finished outside the top ten at Hockenheim, where the lack of power really showed. That was less of a handicap at the twisty Hungaroring, where Martini qualified seventh and lay sixth when he spun out on lap 60, while Fittipaldi was ninth when he hit Jean Alesi's Ferrari. The Minardis crashed simultaneously on lap 15 during the Belgian GP. At Monza they were disputing seventh as they accelerated towards the finish line on the last lap only for Fittipaldi to clip Martini's right rear wheel at 190mph and launch himself into

a 360-degree aerial loop before the car landed on its wheels and slewed across the line with positions unchanged.

After running non-stop in Portugal, they finished eighth (Martini) and ninth (Fittipaldi). The Brazilian was dropped for the last two races to make way for Jean-Marc Gounon's much-needed backing from the Ardeche region and the French government. Unfortunately, the F3000 graduate lacked the fitness or speed to exploit the opportunity. In Japan, he crashed into Andrea de Cesaris on the opening lap, lost five laps while the car was repaired and was withdrawn to avoid further damage. He had five spins in practice for the Australian GP and two in the race, the second of which ended his short Minardi foray. Martini finished tenth at Suzuka but went out with gearbox failure after five laps at Adelaide.

Minardi's early-season form was rewarded with eighth in the constructors' standings.

Fabrizio Barbazza, Minardi M193-Ford (Monaco GP)

Pierluigi Martini, Minardi M193-Ford (Belgian GP)

Aguri Suzuki, Footwork FA13B-Mugen (South African GP)

FOOTWORK MUGEN HONDA

Outperformed by Michele Alboreto during 1992, Aguri Suzuki benefited from commercial considerations when Footwork confirmed him for the coming season before that year's German GP. Derek Warwick had won the Le Mans 24 Hours and World Sportscar Championship since his last F1 race in 1990 and he tested at Silverstone before travelling to Japan on 19 October 1992 to sign as Suzuki's team-mate. Having worked with technical director Alan Jenkins at Penske, race engineer Andy Le Fleming was a brief arrival before he rejoined John Barnard at Ferrari.

Footwork used the updated FA13B for the first two races. It featured a manual sequential gearbox and revised aerodynamics that included a second rear wing and extended front endplates. The

1993 Mugen V10 was lighter and lower than before, although still heavier than any other engine. The new FA14 was completed on 8 March when Warwick had an eventful shakedown at Silverstone, enduring an end-over-end shunt at Club Corner when a driveshaft assembly failed; the car landed on its wheels with Warwick shaken but otherwise unhurt.

The FA13Bs were off the pace in South Africa and Brazil. Warwick almost stole an unlikely point at Kyalami: having pitted after being rammed by Michael Andretti, he could not hold off J.J. Lehto for sixth as they started their last lap and was classified seventh after spinning; meanwhile Suzuki crashed into Fabrizio Barbazza's Minardi. At Interlagos Warwick finished ninth and Suzuki crashed again, into the pitwall during the mid-race downpour.

Derek Warwick, Footwork FA13B-Mugen (South African GP)

Aguri Suzuki, Footwork FA14-Mugen (Canadian GP)

Derek Warwick, Footwork FA14-Mugen (San Marino GP)

The FA14 was pressed into service at Donington Park. Lighter than the FA13B, it had a new semi-automatic gearbox, traction control, passive push-rod suspension and a revised aero package that included the optional double rear wing that other teams copied. Both retired from the wet European GP following problems with the new gearbox, the slick-shod Warwick nine laps from a points-scoring finish when his failed. Suzuki was ninth at Imola after a stop-go penalty for blocking Karl Wendlinger and tenth in Barcelona. At Monaco, Warwick's throttle stuck open and Suzuki spun out.

The passive FA14 handled badly at slow speeds and active suspension developed in-house was still not ready. That programme was cancelled when Footwork agreed a two-year deal with TAG Electronics for the system used on the McLaren MP4/8. With handling particularly poor in Canada, TAG's active suspension made its début in France. It transformed the FA14's behaviour as soon as initial teething troubles were sorted, with qualifying times slashed by over a second. Both qualified in the top ten at Silverstone and Warwick finished sixth in front of his home crowd.

Warwick escaped serious injury in another huge accident during the warm-up at Hockenheim. Blinded by spray, he hit Luca Badoer's slow-moving Lola-Ferrari at full speed and was launched into a gravel trap, where his FA14 overturned and trapped him underneath. Undeterred by bruising to neck and fingers, and a headache, he took over the spare car only for a lengthy unscheduled stop to ruin his race. With both drivers again achieving top-ten start positions in Hungary, Warwick ran as high as third after not pitting for a second time and held off Martin Brundle to finish fourth.

The team's most competitive weekend came at Spa-Francorchamps, where Suzuki qualified a career-best sixth with Warwick starting seventh, and Suzuki ran fifth until hydraulic failure. The Footwork-Mugens collided at the start of the Italian GP and Warwick lost top-six finishes in Portugal and Japan, taken out by Riccardo Patrese and Eddie Irvine respectively. Fittipaldi was placed on standby when Warwick fell ill before the Australian GP but the exhausted Englishman recovered sufficiently to finish tenth on his final F1 appearance. After seven consecutive retirements, including spinning out of the British, Hungarian and Japanese GPs, Suzuki was seventh in Adelaide at the conclusion of an unsatisfactory campaign.

SASOL JORDAN

Jordan Grand Prix unearthed a new star driver and the technical package showed glimpses of real promise but 1993 was another largely frustrating campaign. The team ended its unhappy association with Yamaha after just one season and at the 1992 Australian GP announced an exclusive two-year agreement with Brian Hart. The small Harlow-based concern's new 72-degree V10, designated 1035, featured four valves per cylinder and Zytek engine management. The Hart engine ran on the dyno in January 1992 and at Silverstone on 17 November Maurício Gugelmin drove a modified Jordan 192B-Hart featuring a higher engine cover, traction control and new semi-automatic sequential gearbox.

Gugelmin and Stefano Modena departed and Jordan announced a two-year deal with 20-year-old Brazilian Rubens Barrichello on 26

Rubens Barrichello, Jordan 193-Hart (Belgian GP)

Ivan Capelli, Jordan 193-Hart (South African GP)

Thierry Boutsen, Jordan 193-Hart (Belgian GP)

November. Persistent winter rumours suggested Thierry Boutsen as his team-mate so Ferrari refugee Ivan Capelli was a surprise when announced on 28 January 1993, again on a two-year contract. Lotus-bound team manager/race engineer Trevor Foster was replaced by chief mechanic John Walton in the former role and by Peugeot's Tim Wright in the latter. Away from the sport since leaving Sauber, Steve Nichols joined Jordan as chief designer on 4 October 1992, reporting to technical director Gary Anderson. Sponsorship from Sasol, Barclay and Unipart continued, augmented by subsidiary new deals with Arisco and Uliveto.

Unveiled at Silverstone on 15 January, the Jordan 193-Hart retained the 1992 monocoque. The familiar anhedral front wing was replaced by a flat version attached to the raised nose by twin supports. The rear diffuser was larger than before and suspension was via push-rods with a single shock absorber at the front. Lucas electronics controlled the front ride height, traction control and transverse semi-automatic gearbox. The compact engine allowed Anderson to reduce wheelbase by 5in as he tried to eradicate the test car's understeer. Unfortunately, the 193 was overly nervous and rear tyre wear excessive until extending the wheelbase with three races to go transformed handling. A double rear wing was used from the third round at Donington.

A single car was sent to Estoril for the 15–19 February test where myriad electronic problems and Barrichello's high-speed loss of his rear wing hampered progress. Barrichello ran seventh at Kyalami but experienced gearbox issues during that race and the next. After Capelli crashed on the third lap of the South African GP and failed to qualify in Brazil, Boutsen replaced him.

Eddie Irvine, Jordan 193-Hart (Japanese GP)

Barrichello was in fine form at the wet European GP, where he started 12th and charged through to fourth by the end of the opening lap of Donington Park. He ran as high as second and was six laps from finishing third when the fuel-pressure light came on and the engine cut out. Boutsen used a manual gearbox for this race, where he struggled to fit in the car, and retired with a sticking throttle. Both pitted on the opening lap at Imola, Boutsen with terminal gearbox hydraulic trouble and Barrichello to change tyres following a puncture, but he spun out after 17 laps. They finished at the back in Spain and Barrichello, celebrating his 21st birthday, lost a points finish in Monaco when his tyres degraded.

An electronic clutch and revised suspension were introduced in France, where Barrichello qualified an improved eighth and ran sixth for much of the race before losing the place to Michael Andretti with two laps to go. Tenth at Silverstone, Barrichello retired from the next four races including crashing into Aguri Suzuki at the start in Hungary. Ninth in that race, Boutsen had a gearbox breakage on the opening lap of his home Belgian GP and announced his immediate retirement from F1 four days later.

Marco Apicella tested at Imola on 7 September and made his GP début on a one-off basis at Monza, where a succession of mishaps – including random activation of the traction control – ruined Jordan's weekend. J.J. Lehto nudged Barrichello into a spin at the first corner and Apicella was also eliminated in the resulting mêlée. With Apicella committed to Japanese F3000, test driver Emanuele Naspetti took over the second car in Portugal but retired after eight laps with the engine ablaze; Barrichello was delayed by a puncture and finished 13th.

Emanuele Naspetti, Jordan 193-Hart (Portuguese GP)

Marco Apicella, Jordan 193-Hart (Italian GP)

Barrichello had a fifth team-mate at the last two races in Japan and Australia when joined by Eddie Irvine. The long-wheelbase configuration introduced at Estoril was retained at Suzuka and helped deliver Jordan's best weekend of the year. In another wet/dry race, Barrichello recovered from a poor start to finish fifth, while Irvine, on a circuit he knew well, qualified an excellent eighth and finished sixth despite running into Derek Warwick's Footwork-Mugen in the closing stages. He even had the temerity to unlap himself from Ayrton Senna, a move that so angered the race leader that he lashed out during a post-race confrontation witnessed by journalist Adam Cooper. Australia was less satisfactory for Irvine crashed and Barrichello finished only 11th after being knocked into a spin at the start.

Jordan-Hart shared a disappointing tenth in the final standings with the troubled Larrousse concern.

LARROUSSE F1

Budget continued to be scarce at Larrousse following the ownership problems of 1992. It received a FF30 million (equivalent to £3.5 million at the time) government grant from the fund established in France to replace tobacco sponsorship and there was some investment from the Czech Republic. A subtle change in engine branding to Chrysler by Lamborghini reflected the parent company's increased interest in F1.

Érik Comas made an acrimonious exit from Ligier and spoke to Lotus and Jordan before signing for Larrousse on 25 January. Having

Philippe Alliot, Larrousse LH93-Lamborghini (European GP)

tested Philippe Alliot, who had raced Peugeot sports cars since 1991, and Paul Belmondo at Paul Ricard in December, Larrousse chose experience and single-lap pace over sponsorship funds when Alliot was announced in February.

Larrousse UK's Tino Belli and Tim Holloway evolved the existing design as the Larrousse LH93, which was launched on 3 March at the Paris showroom of French Lamborghini importer JB Automobiles. The monocoque was modified to comply with 1993 regulations with cars assembled at Larrousse's factory near Paul Ricard. The renamed Lamborghini LC01 (for Lamborghini-Chrysler) V12 engine was long but now 35lb lighter than before. A manual gearbox was retained

Érik Comas, Larrousse LH93-Lamborghini (Belgian GP)

while Larrousse's active-suspension programme was cancelled when FISA's intention to ban electronic driver aids became clear. So old-fashioned passive suspension was retained – push-rods at the front and pull-rods to the rear as before. The LH93 was difficult to set up and there was precious little development of either the chassis or engine during the season.

A promising 11th on the grid for the opening two races, Alliot finished seventh in Brazil while Comas was tenth despite a stop-go penalty for ignoring yellow flags and with his engine running on 11 cylinders. At the chaotic European GP, Alliot was up to seventh when taken out while lapping Andrea de Cesaris, and Comas finished ninth. They ran in tandem in the midfield at the San Marino and Spanish GPs with Alliot a career-best fifth at Imola. Comas was left disappointed as he faded from sixth to ninth in the closing stages at Barcelona with an oil-pump problem.

Out-qualified thus far, Comas started from an excellent tenth on the grid in Monaco and challenged for points before being rammed at Mirabeau by Martin Brundle's Ligier, then ran non-stop to finish eighth in Canada. Both drivers qualified in the top ten in France, where Alliot was ninth (despite a poor start and unscheduled pitstop) at the start of seven successive points-free finishes. In contrast, Comas's drive-shaft failure on the first lap at Silverstone was the beginning of four DNFs in a row that included another first-lap departure at Hockenheim. He ran non-stop to finish sixth at Monza but was restricted to 11th in Portugal by a couple of practice 'offs' and poor handling in the race.

Alliot stood down for Japan and Australia and was replaced by Japanese veteran Toshio Suzuki, who qualified and finished at the back in both races. Comas's engine failed during a frustrating Japanese GP and he came home 12th in Australia as Larrousse's cash-strapped campaign came to a suitably downbeat conclusion.

TYRRELL RACING ORGANISATION

Tyrrell had an exclusive manufacturer agreement and free engines for the first time in its 25-year history with its two-year deal with Yamaha announced on 2 November 1992. Furthermore, this was not the troublesome V12 that had previously frustrated Brabham and Jordan. Yamaha entered into partnership with John Judd's Rugby-based Engine Developments, which rebranded a new version of its promising V10 as the Yamaha OX10A. This had variable trumpets and pneumatic valves but engine developments throughout 1993 were masked by a disappointing chassis. Yamaha closed its Ypsilon Technology factory in Milton Keynes.

Ukyo Katayama ended his Larrousse contract early and took his Cabin cigarette money to Tyrrell. Andrea de Cesaris re-signed for a second season despite a clash with his normal backers Marlboro, the extension announced at the Auto Sports International show in Birmingham on 9 January. Unfortunately, Katayama spent too much time in the barriers and positives for de Cesaris were hard to find.

Engineers Tim Densham and Paul Burgess arrived in October 1992 from Brabham and Andrea Moda respectively while Andy Le Fleming moved to Footwork. Chief designer Mike Coughlan initially resisted

Toshio Suzuki, Larrousse LH93-Lamborghini (Japanese GP)

Andrea de Cesaris, Tyrrell 020C-Yamaha (Monaco GP)

Ukyo Katayama, Tyrrell 020C-Yamaha (Canadian GP)

Andrea de Cesaris, Tyrrell 021-Yamaha (Australian GP)

John Barnard's advances and redesigned the old Tyrrell 020 with its third different V10 engine in three years. He retained the anhedral front wing and active front suspension, fitted traction control and introduced new passive rear suspension, undertray and transverse manual gearbox. Katayama tried the revised Tyrrell 020C-Yamaha at a damp Silverstone on 8 February with de Cesaris taking over the following day. Electrical and gearbox issues hindered progress at the subsequent Estoril and Paul Ricard tests, and de Cesaris suffered a major rear suspension failure in France.

It was a chastening start to 1993 with the 020Cs slow and unreliable. The transmission failed on both cars before two laps of the South African GP were completed and it was Monaco before a Tyrrell finished, with de Cesaris tenth after knocking the handling askew against a barrier. He was black-flagged during the Spanish GP for a push by marshals following an engine problem.

The Tyrrell 021-Yamaha was finally ready to be launched on 27 May. Narrower and shorter than the old car, suspension was active at both ends but the unusual mono-shock rear was slow to react. Coughlan later told *Autosport*'s Adam Cooper that the 021's 'aerodynamics were wrong, and it was an ugly disaster that I don't want to remember. It was horrible!' Initial testing was so disappointing that the team retained the recalcitrant 020C for the next two races. Katayama was 17th and last in Canada (his first finish) after an early stop to repair his rear wing.

The new car was pressed into action at Silverstone but proved no quicker than the old. Katayama decided to race the spare 020C and finished 13th while de Cesaris stalled at the start and lost laps in the pits as his 021 was repaired after a clash with Luca Badoer's Lola. They retired in Germany but both finished for the first time in Hungary, after which Coughlan paid the price for the 021's failure and left on 25 August.

They ran at the back in Italy before Harvey Postlethwaite, still a shareholder in Tyrrell, was announced as managing director (engineering). However, Tyrrell's perilous situation was clear when 20 per cent of the workforce were laid off before the final European race at Estoril. Katayama retired from the last three races while de Cesaris was eliminated by Jean-Marc Gounon's Minardi on lap one in Japan and finished among the backmarkers at Estoril and Adelaide.

Tyrrell failed to score a championship point for the first time since its exclusion from the World Championship in 1984.

Ukyo Katayama, Tyrrell 021-Yamaha (Italian GP)

LOLA BMS SCUDERIA ITALIA

Having terminated its agreement with Larrousse at the end of 1991, Lola Cars of Huntingdon, Cambridgeshire planned to re-enter F1 in 1993. Former Kyalami circuit manager Brian Sims was appointed as commercial director but rather than go it alone as was originally intended, an agreement to supply BMS Scuderia Italia was announced at the 1992 Hungarian GP. Beppe Lucchini's team was in the second year of its Ferrari contract while veteran Michele Alboreto and F3000 champion Luca Badoer were announced as drivers in November.

The unpainted Lola T93/30-Ferrari first appeared on 18 February at the Estoril test, where gearbox niggles and Badoer's crash on the second day interrupted progress. This was a conventional design with none of the electronic driver aids required to be successful at the start of 1993, although traction control was available from the French GP. Having previously disappointed in Minardi and Dallara alike, the 65-degree Ferrari V12 engine lacked torque in slow and medium corners and the Lola had insufficient downforce everywhere. With the new alliance in disarray from the outset, Sergio Rinland returned to Scuderia Italia in April to liaise with Lola, although he soon switched to Dan Gurney's new All-American Racers Indycar programme. The only element that truly stood out was the garish colour scheme. Long-time backers Philip Morris chose to promote its Chesterfield brand with an orange, white and yellow livery.

The Lolas were the slowest cars at Kyalami before both retired and the last two finishers in Brazil, 11th (Alboreto) and 12th (Badoer). The new qualifying rule for the next seven races meant that the 26th (and last) car in qualifying would not start and in every case that was

Michele Alboreto, Lola T93/30-Ferrari (Brazilian GP)

a Lola, Badoer's at Donington and Monaco, Alboreto's elsewhere. As 26 cars were allowed to start from the German GP, at least both Lolas were guaranteed races thereafter, but they were always tail-enders with 21st the highest grid position, for Alboreto at Monza.

The year's best finish was Badoer's seventh place at Imola following a race of attrition while Alboreto never bettered his 11th in Brazil. The inevitable split between manufacturer and disgruntled team was announced before the Italian GP and Ferrari decided not to supply any customer engines in 1994. With Lucchini having sponsorship and Minardi able to build a chassis, talks between the two Italian concerns were concluded by the end of September and BMS Scuderia Italia made its final F1 appearance at Estoril before it withdrew from the last two GPs of the season.

Luca Badoer, Lola T93/30-Ferrari (Italian GP)

1993 RESULTS

DRIVER PERFORMANCE

DRIVER	CAR–ENGINE	ZA	BR	EU	RSM	E	MC	CDN	F	GB	D	H	B	I	P	J	AUS
Michele Alboreto	Lola T93/30-Ferrari	25 R	25 11	24 11	26 DNQ	26 DNQ	24 R	26 DNQ	26 DNQ	26 DNQ	26 16	25 R	25 14	21 R	25 R	–	–
Jean Alesi	Ferrari F93A	5 R	9 8	9 R	9 R	8 R	5 3	6 R	6 R	12 9	10 7	8 R	4 R	3 2	5 4	14 R	7 4
Philippe Alliot	Larrousse LH93-Lamborghini	11 R	11 7	15 R	14 5	13 R	15 12	15 R	10 9	24 11	23 12	19 8	18 12	16 9	20 10	–	–
Michael Andretti	McLaren MP4/8-Ford	9 R	5 R	6 R	6 R	7 5	9 8	12 14	16 6	11 R	12 R	11 R	14 8	9 3	–	–	
Marco Apicella	Jordan 193-Hart	–	–	–	–	–	–	–	–	–	–	–	–	23 R	–	–	–
Luca Badoer	Lola T93/30-Ferrari	26 R	21 12	26 DNQ	24 7	22 R	26 DNQ	25 15	22 R	25 R	25 R	26 R	24 13	25 10	26 14		
Fabrizio Barbazza	Minardi M193-Ford	24 R	24 R	20 6	25 6	25 R	25 11	23 R	24 R	–	–	–	–	–	–	–	–
Rubens Barrichello	Jordan 193-Hart	14 R	14 R	12 10	13 R	17 12	16 9	14 R	8 7	15 10	17 R	16 R	13 R	19 R	15 13	12 5	13 11
Gerhard Berger	Ferrari F93A	15 6	13 R	8 R	8 R	11 6	7 14	5 4	14 14	13 R	9 6	6 3	16 10	6 R	8 R	5 R	6 5
Mark Blundell	Ligier JS39-Renault	8 3	10 5	21 R	7 R	12 7	21 R	10 R	4 R	9 7	5 3	12 7	15 11	14 R	10 R	17 7	14 9
Thierry Boutsen	Jordan 193-Hart	–	–	19 R	19 R	21 11	23 R	24 12	20 11	23 R	24 13	24 9	20 R	–	–	–	–
Martin Brundle	Ligier JS39-Renault	12 R	16 R	22 R	10 3	18 R	13 6	7 5	3 5	6 14	6 8	13 5	11 7	12 R	11 6	15 9	8 6
Ivan Capelli	Jordan 193-Hart	18 R	26 DNQ	–	–	–	–	–	–	–	–	–	–	–	–	–	–
Érik Comas	Larrousse LH93-Lamborghini	19 R	17 10	17 9	17 R	14 9	10 R	13 8	9 16	17 R	16 R	18 R	19 R	20 6	22 11	21 R	21 12
Andrea de Cesaris	Tyrrell 020C-Yamaha	23 R	23 R	25 R	18 R	24 DSQ	19 10	19 R	25 15	–	–	–	–	–	–	–	–
	Tyrrell 021-Yamaha	–	–	–	–	–	–	–		21 NC	19 R	22 11	17 R	18 13	17 12	18 R	15 13
Christian Fittipaldi	Minardi M193-Ford	13 4	20 R	16 7	23 R	20 8	17 5	17 9	23 8	19 12	20 11	14 R	22 R	24 8	24 9	–	–
Jean-Marc Gounon	Minardi M193-Ford	–	–	–	–	–	–	–	–	–	–	–	–	–	–	24 R	22 R
Mika Häkkinen	McLaren MP4/8-Ford	–	–	–	–	–	–	–	–	–	–	–	–	–	3 R	3 3	5 R
Johnny Herbert	Lotus 107B-Ford	17 R	12 4	11 4	12 8	10 R	14 R	20 10	19 R	7 4	13 10	20 R	10 5	7 R	14 R	19 11	20 R
Damon Hill	Williams FW15C-Renault	4 R	2 2	2 2	2 R	2 R	4 2	2 3	1 2	2 R FL	2 15	2 1	2 1	2 1 FL	1 3 FL	6 4 FL	3 3
Eddie Irvine	Jordan 193-Hart	–	–	–	–	–	–	–	–	–	–	–	–	–	–	8 6	19 R
Ukyo Katayama	Tyrrell 020C-Yamaha	21 R	22 R	18 R	22 R	23 R	22 R	22 17	21 R	22 13	–	–	–	–	–	–	–
	Tyrrell 021-Yamaha	–	–	–	–	–	–	–	–	–	21 R	23 10	23 15	17 14	21 R	13 R	18 R
Pedro Lamy	Lotus 107B-Ford	–	–	–	–	–	–	–	–	–	–	–	–	26 11	18 R	20 13	23 R
J.J. Lehto	Sauber C12-Ilmor	6 5	7 R	7 R	16 4	9 R	11 R	11 7	18 R	16 8	18 R	15 R	9 9	–	–	–	–
	Sauber C12	–	–	–	–	–	–	–	–	–	–	–	–	13 R	12 7	11 8	12 R
Pierluigi Martini	Minardi M193-Ford	–	–	–	–	–	–	–	–	20 R	22 14	7 R	21 R	22 7	19 8	22 10	16 R
Emanuele Naspetti	Jordan 193-Hart	–	–	–	–	–	–	–	–	–	–	–	–	23 R	–	–	–
Riccardo Patrese	Benetton B193-Ford	7 R	6 R	–	–	–	–	–	–	–	–	–	–	–	–	–	–
	Benetton B193B-Ford	–	–	10 5	11 R	5 4	6 R	4 R	12 10	5 3	7 5	5 2	8 6	10 5	7 R	10 R	9 8
Alain Prost	Williams FW15C-Renault	1 1 FL	1 R	1 3	1 1 FL	1 1	1 4 FL	1 1	2 1	1 1	1 1	1 12 FL	1 3 FL	1 12	2 2	2 2 FL	2 2
Michael Schumacher	Benetton B193-Ford	3 R	4 3 FL	–	–	–	–	–	–	–	–	–	–	–	–	–	–
	Benetton B193B-Ford	–	–	3 R	3 2	4 3 FL	2 R	3 2 FL	7 3 FL	3 2	3 2 FL	3 R	3 2	5 R	6 1	4 R	4 R
Ayrton Senna	McLaren MP4/8-Ford	2 2	3 1	4 1 FL	4 R	3 2	3 1	8 R	5 4	4 5	4 4	4 R	5 4	4 R	4 R	2 1	1 1
Aguri Suzuki	Footwork FA13B-Mugen	20 R	19 R	–	–	–	–	–	–	–	–	–	–	–	–	–	–
	Footwork FA14-Mugen	–	–	23 R	21 9	19 10	18 R	16 13	13 12	10 R	8 R	10 R	6 R	8 R	16 R	9 R	10 7
Toshio Suzuki	Larrousse LH93-Lamborghini	–	–	–	–	–	–	–	–	–	–	–	–	–	–	23 12	24 14

DRIVER PERFORMANCE CONTINUED

DRIVER	CAR–ENGINE	ZA	BR	EU	RSM	E	MC	CDN	F	GB	D	H	B	I	P	J	AUS
Derek Warwick	Footwork FA13B-Mugen	22 7	18 9	–	–	–	–	–	–	–	–	–	–	–	–	–	–
	Footwork FA14-Mugen	–	–	14 R	15 R	16 13	12 R	18 16	15 13	8 6	11 17	9 4	7 R	11 R	9 R	7 14	17 10
Karl Wendlinger	Sauber C12-Ilmor	10 R	8 R	5 R	5 R	6 R	8 13	9 6	11 R	18 R	14 9	17 6	12 R	–	–	–	–
	Sauber C12	–	–	–	–	–	–	–	–	–	–	–	–	15 4	13 5	16 R	11 15
Alex Zanardi	Lotus 107B-Ford	16 R	15 6	13 8	20 R	15 R	20 7	21 11	17 R	14 R	15 R	21 R	NT DNP	–	–	–	–

FORMULA 1 RACE WINNERS

ROUND	RACE (CIRCUIT)	DATE	WINNER
1	Panasonic South African Grand Prix (Kyalami)	Mar 14	Alain Prost (Williams FW15C-Renault)
2	Grande Prêmio do Brasil (Interlagos)	Mar 28	Ayrton Senna (McLaren MP4/8-Ford)
3	Sega European Grand Prix (Donington Park)	Apr 11	Ayrton Senna (McLaren MP4/8-Ford)
4	Gran Premio di San Marino (Imola)	Apr 25	Alain Prost (Williams FW15C-Renault)
5	Gran Premio de España (Catalunya)	May 9	Alain Prost (Williams FW15C-Renault)
6	Grand Prix de Monaco (Monte Carlo)	May 23	Ayrton Senna (McLaren MP4/8-Ford)
7	Grand Prix Molson du Canada (Montréal)	Jun 13	Alain Prost (Williams FW15C-Renault)
8	Rhône-Poulenc Grand Prix de France (Magny-Cours)	Jul 4	Alain Prost (Williams FW15C-Renault)
9	British Grand Prix (Silverstone)	Jul 11	Alain Prost (Williams FW15C-Renault)
10	Grosser Mobil 1 Preis von Deutschland (Hockenheim)	Jul 25	Alain Prost (Williams FW15C-Renault)
11	Marlboro Magyar Nagydíj (Hungaroring)	Aug 15	Damon Hill (Williams FW15C-Renault)
12	Grand Prix de Belgique (Spa-Francorchamps)	Aug 29	Damon Hill (Williams FW15C-Renault)
13	Pioneer Gran Premio d'Italia (Monza)	Sep 12	Damon Hill (Williams FW15C-Renault)
14	Grande Premio de Portugal (Estoril)	Sep 26	Michael Schumacher (Benetton B193B-Ford)
15	Fuji Television Japanese Grand Prix (Suzuka)	Oct 24	Ayrton Senna (McLaren MP4/8-Ford)
16	Foster's Australian Grand Prix (Adelaide)	Nov 7	Ayrton Senna (McLaren MP4/8-Ford)

CONSTRUCTORS' CHAMPIONSHIP

	CONSTRUCTORS	POINTS
1	Williams-Renault	168
2	McLaren-Ford	84
3	Benetton-Ford	72
4	Ferrari	28
5	Ligier-Renault	23
6=	Lotus-Ford	12
	Sauber-Ilmor	12
8	Minardi-Ford	7
9	Footwork-Mugen	4
10=	Jordan-Hart	3
	Larrousse-Lamborghini	3

DRIVERS' CHAMPIONSHIP

	DRIVERS	POINTS
1	Alain Prost	99
2	Ayrton Senna	73
3	Damon Hill	69
4	Michael Schumacher	52
5	Riccardo Patrese	20
6	Jean Alesi	16
7	Martin Brundle	13
8	Gerhard Berger	12
9	Johnny Herbert	11
10	Mark Blundell	10
11=	Michael Andretti	7
	Karl Wendlinger	7
13=	Christian Fittipaldi	5
	J.J. Lehto	5
15=	Mika Häkkinen	4
	Derek Warwick	4
17=	Philippe Alliot	2
	Fabrizio Barbazza	2
	Rubens Barrichello	2
20=	Érik Comas	1
	Eddie Irvine	1
	Alex Zanardi	1

Ayrton Senna leads Michael Schumacher during the early laps of the San Marino Grand Prix

1994

SCHUMACHER INHERITS SENNA'S TRAGIC MANTLE

Michael Schumacher clinched the 1994 title in controversial circumstances

The 1994 Formula 1 season was a traumatic campaign that ended in suitably controversial circumstances. Roland Ratzenberger and Ayrton Senna were killed during the San Marino Grand Prix weekend, and injury also sidelined J.J. Lehto, Jean Alesi, Rubens Barrichello, Karl Wendlinger, Pedro Lamy and Andrea Montermini during a tragic and fraught season.

Devices that 'can control automatically any aspect of the

Roland Ratzenberger is presented to the press in Brazil

car's operation or in any way mitigate the effects of an error by the driver' were banned, including traction control, active suspension, fly-by-wire throttle (for one season only) and anti-lock brakes. Paddle-operated semi-automatic gearboxes, rather than fully automatic, were permitted in a compromise agreed among the teams during the 1993 German GP meeting. There was criticism that the wording was vague and scepticism as to how effectively the outlawing of 'electronic driver aids' could be policed. Cockpits had to be large enough to accommodate a 6ft 3in driver. Car-to-pit telemetry was retained but pit-to-car was not allowed.

The deaths of Senna and Ratzenberger triggered emergency new rules that prompted conflict between the FIA and concerned team bosses. The changes were eventually phased in at Monaco, Canada and Germany. Firstly, the front wing endplates were raised by 10mm and could not extend beyond the leading edge of the front wheel, and rear diffusers had to be shorter. Then, the cockpit sides were raised to improve lateral head protection, minimum weight raised to 515kg and lower front wishbones strengthened. Wholesale removal of the airbox (to reduce the ram effect) was replaced by holes drilled in positions agreed with the FIA's Charlie Whiting. Finally from Hockenheim, a 10mm wooden plank was fitted under the car to reduce downforce, with a maximum of 1mm wear permissible during a race, and the rear wing was lowered by 50mm. A pitlane speed limit

Damon Hill scored his first win of the season in Spain

of 80kph introduced at Monaco was deemed too slow for television and was later raised to 120kph.

Banned in 1983 on safety grounds, mid-race refuelling was reintroduced with FIA-supplied gravity-fed rigs that were manufactured by the French Intertechnique company. Williams's Patrick Head voiced the widespread concern: 'Can you have refuelling without incinerating people? You are going to get a fire at some point, the question is can you limit it?' Those fears were realised in Germany when Jos Verstappen's Benetton-Ford caught fire during his pitstop. Immediate calls to ban refuelling were resisted by Ferrari, whose thirsty V12 engine benefited by carrying less fuel during the race. A new system of light beams to detect jumped starts was introduced at the Portuguese GP and proved very sensitive.

In his third full season as a GP driver, Benetton-Ford's Michael Schumacher secured his first world title when he crashed into rival Damon Hill's Williams-Renault at Adelaide. Schumacher was undoubtedly the fastest driver in 1994 but the mid-season launch/traction-control row and conclusion inevitably tainted that success. He was disqualified from two races and banned from another three.

With Kyalami up for sale, the opening race in South Africa was originally replaced by a return to Argentina. A street circuit in Buenos Aires's Palermo district was initially preferred and supported by president Carlos Menem, before

it was switched to the Autodrómo Oscar Gálvez following local objections. After postponement until 16 October, the Argentinian GP was cancelled in June with the replacement European GP at Jerez announced for that date. Silverstone extended its contract until 2001 but a second British race at Donington in April was axed in favour of the Pacific GP at Japan's remote Tanaka International. This privately owned venue at Aida signed a five-year promotional contract with the Formula One Constructors' Association although the race was only held in 1994 and 1995. Various plans for a United States GP on the Eastern seaboard – a street circuit in Washington DC's West Potomac Park or new facilities in Baltimore, Maryland or Brandy Station, Virginia – never materialised in either 1994 or 1995.

The existing circuits were also modified as F1 came to terms with its tragic summer. Chicanes were installed at Barcelona (a temporary tyre-defined affair behind the paddock), in Montréal's old pitlane, at Spa-Francorchamps's Eau Rouge and where Martin Donnelly had crashed at Jerez. Silverstone's Copse, Stowe, Abbey and Priory were slowed and a hairpin section between Estoril's turns seven and eight was used. The Italian GP was threatened when alterations demanded by the reformed Grand Prix Drivers' Association were not forthcoming; work to tighten Curva Grande and second Lesmo was completed less than a month before the race with major works postponed to 1995.

Michael Schumacher, Benetton B194-Ford (Belgian GP)

MILD SEVEN BENETTON FORD

Michael Schumacher emerged as World Champion for the first time in 1994 after a tragic and at times controversial campaign. Despite an existing works contract with Ford, Benetton Formula managing director Flavio Briatore openly pursued Renault engines for 1994, with F1 ringmaster Bernie Ecclestone keen to facilitate. Renault Sport's Bernard Dudot and Patrick Faure insisted that they would not supply a third team and Briatore failed in attempts to buy Ligier's supply. So Benetton and Ford finally reconfirmed their partnership at the 1993 Australian GP. Title sponsor Camel withdrew and was replaced by a £28 million two-year deal with Japan Tobacco's Mild Seven brand.

Schumacher's status as F1's new superstar was illustrated by a lucrative approach from McLaren but he confirmed he was staying in October 1993. 'It is absolutely positive… that I will drive a Benetton next year, but Benetton has got to do something about my salary.' A new deal covering 1994 and 1995, with an option for 1996, was announced by Christmas.

Luca Badoer was considered as Schumacher's team-mate until he crashed three times while testing at Estoril in November. J.J. Lehto was faster and more consistent than Badoer, Éric Bernard or Andrea Montermini that week and was invited to Barcelona for a subsequent week-long comparison with Michele Alboreto. Having lapped 1.11sec quicker than the veteran, Lehto was announced as number two at the launch of the Benetton B194-Ford on 14 January. The highly rated Jos Verstappen turned down other race seats to sign as test driver. Gordon Message left at the end of 1993 to form an electronics

company and Joan Villadelprat was reappointed as team manager.

Ross Brawn's technical team committed to the early completion of the B194 so test mileage could be maximised. With active suspension banned, Benetton reverted to a double wishbone/push-rod configuration with inboard coil springs and dampers. The B194 had an elegant raised nose and high outer edge (or shoulder) to each sidepod. With the Ford HB engine now over four years old and the 'mythical' V12 project shelved, Cosworth Engineering developed a new 75-degree V8 for Benetton's exclusive use. While no match for the outright power of the Renault V10, the Zetec-R revved to an impressive 14,500rpm (1,000rpm more than the HB) and developed a handy 720bhp. The semi-automatic six-speed gearbox was retained and mounted transversely.

Lehto first tested the B194 at Silverstone a week after the launch. He crashed at Stowe corner and fractured his fifth vertebra, forcing him to miss the opening two races and compromising his golden opportunity. Sidelined for much of the winter following a knee operation, Schumacher lapped Barcelona and Imola at record pace but entered the campaign as the title outsider.

Overwhelmingly the favourite, Ayrton Senna beat Schumacher to pole position at the first two GPs but could not match the German in the races. Schumacher lapped the field in Brazil and led all the way at Aida with Senna a retirement on both occasions. Verstappen replaced Lehto for these two races and endured incident-filled weekends, crashing spectacularly on début when Eddie Irvine's Jordan-Hart swerved into his path and spinning all on his own at Aida.

Schumacher won the tragic San Marino GP by almost a minute and at Monaco converted a first pole position of 1994 into another crushing victory. The Spanish GP was only lost when his B194 stuck in fifth gear after his first pitstop. That Schumacher still made another stop and finished second without changing gear was a remarkable feat. Another pole position and lights-to-flag victory in Canada gave him a 33-point advantage in the standings.

Driving in a neck brace, Lehto qualified fifth on his return at Imola but stalled at the start and was hit by Pedro Lamy's Lotus-Mugen. With confidence shaken and particularly out of sorts on tight, bumpy tracks, Lehto struggled at Monaco and but lay third in Spain when his engine blew. He was 2.815sec slower than Schumacher in Canadian qualifying but inherited sixth when Christian Fittipaldi was disqualified after the race.

Lehto was rested from the French GP, where Schumacher was out-qualified by both Williams-Renaults for the first time but won nonetheless. A rapid start that saw him lead into the first corner sparked paddock suspicions that the B194 must have launch control, but there was no protest. Having won six out of seven races so far, Schumacher's season began to unravel at Silverstone. He was given a five second stop-go penalty for overtaking on the parade lap but it was ignored at his first pitstop. Subsequent black flags went unheeded until lap 27 and he finished second on the road before being summoned to appear in front of the FIA World Motor Sports Council on 26 July. The verdict was disqualification from the British GP for ignoring black flags and a two-race ban; Benetton was fined

J.J. Lehto, Benetton B194-Ford (Monaco GP)

$500,000 for not following the stewards' instructions.

The World Council also published analysis of the electronic boxes taken from the top three cars at the San Marino GP. Working for the FIA, Liverpool Data Research Associates concluded that a 'computer system containing a facility capable of breaching the regulations' was present. Benetton was fined another $100,000 for being slow in providing its access codes, but the presence of software that could activate 'launch control' went unpunished as there was 'an absence of any evidence that the device was used, and certain evidence that it was not.'

Schumacher raced under appeal and challenged for the lead at Hockenheim before his engine failed before half distance.

Jos Verstappen, Benetton B194-Ford (Belgian GP)

Verstappen was engulfed in flames when fuel leaked onto the hot exhausts during his pitstop with driver and seven mechanics treated for burns. Intertechnique's subsequent investigation for the FIA concluded that the fuel valve closed slowly due to 'a foreign body' that was 'believed to have reached the valve because a filter designed to eliminate the risk had been deliberately removed'. Acting for the team, QC George Carman cited mitigating circumstances when pleading guilty to the World Council on 7 September and Benetton received no further penalty.

Schumacher and Verstappen responded to their difficult German GP weekend by finishing 1–3 in Hungary before more controversy at Spa-Francorchamps. Schumacher took the lead on the opening lap, survived a spin on lap 19 and eased to another victory. However, his car was disqualified that evening after the mandatory 10mm wooden 'plank' was found to have worn beyond the acceptable tolerance level. Furthermore, the FIA upheld Schumacher's two-race ban on the following Tuesday so Lehto replaced the championship leader in Italy and Portugal without threatening to score points. Third in Belgium, Verstappen was eliminated on the first lap at Monza after contact with Alex Zanardi's Lotus-Mugen and finished fifth in Portugal. Schumacher returned to dominate the subsequent Estoril test, where Indycar star Paul Tracy completed a promising two days without ever pursuing F1 ambitions.

Now just a point ahead of Damon Hill, Schumacher qualified on pole and dominated the European GP at Jerez. After Verstappen made a bad start and spun into the gravel at the final corner of lap 16, Briatore chose experience for the last two races and selected Johnny Herbert as Schumacher's team-mate, having bought the Englishman out of his Lotus contract for a reported $1 million. Herbert crashed when third in Japan and retired in Australia.

Hill beat Schumacher on aggregate at Suzuka to close within a single point of the German before the Adelaide finale. Schumacher led Hill from the start but damaged his right-rear suspension against a wall on lap 36. Unaware of the damage but realising that Schumacher had run wide, Hill went to pass his rival in the next corner and they collided. Hill limped back to the pits but Schumacher was declared World Champion when neither could continue; Benetton-Ford finished as runners-up in the constructors' standings, 15 points behind Williams-Renault.

ROTHMANS WILLIAMS RENAULT

Two weeks after Alain Prost's surprise decision to retire from F1, Williams-Renault announced Ayrton Senna and Damon Hill as its drivers for the coming season on 11 October 1993. Senna had agreed a two-year contract in September and reported that 'this is a dream come true for me. Frank Williams was the man who gave me my first opportunity to drive an F1 car. It is ten years since that test, and now, finally, we've come together.' Camel and Canon both left F1 after a lucrative new title sponsorship deal was struck with Rothmans, again for two years.

Test driver David Coulthard gave the new Rothmans livery its début at Estoril on 17 January before Senna and Hill took over the passive Williams FW15D-Renault. The Brazilian spun three times but ended the week with the quickest time. Senna was at the wheel of the Williams FW16-Renault for its shakedown at Silverstone on 24 February with further tests at Paul Ricard and Imola. This was an evolution of the successful Patrick Head/Adrian Newey designs, with all-new carbon-fibre monocoque and heavily revised rear end. The upper rear wishbones were lowered to the centre of the upright, just above the drive shaft, and enclosed in an aerodynamic carbon-epoxy shroud. The rear bodywork was lowered to improve air to the inverted V-shaped anhedral bottom rear wing. The push-rod suspension had torsion bars at the front and coil springs to the rear. Renault's latest V10 was the most powerful engine on the grid even before it was upgraded at Hockenheim (RS06B) and Monza (RS06C). The semi-automatic transverse six-speed gearbox was retained.

Senna was overwhelmingly the pre-season favourite. Williams initially struggled to set up the conventional suspension with slow-speed understeer and insufficient rear grip, but Senna nonetheless qualified on pole position for the first three races. He was chasing Michael Schumacher's leading Benetton-Ford when he spun in Brazil and he was hit by Mika Häkkinen at the first corner of the Pacific GP. Hill one-stopped to finish second at Interlagos and his transmission failed when running second at Aida.

Having missed the Pacific GP, Newey reworked the FW16 before the San Marino GP with revised bodywork to reduce buffeting, marginally shorter wheelbase and raised front wing. Deeply affected by the death of Roland Ratzenberger during qualifying, Senna led the opening five laps before his high-speed accident at Tamburello.

Johnny Herbert, Benetton B194-Ford (Japanese GP)

Damon Hill, Williams FW16-Renault (Monaco GP)

Ayrton Senna, Williams FW16-Renault (Brazilian GP)

A piece of suspension pierced his helmet and F1's greatest star succumbed to severe head injuries later that afternoon in hospital in Bologna. Hill restarted the race and finished sixth after changing his damaged front wing.

With team and sport in mourning, Hill drove a singleton Williams-Renault at Monaco but crashed into Häkkinen at the start. Williams considered a move for Sauber's Heinz-Harald Frentzen and *The Sun* broke news that Williams and Renault wanted to entice Nigel Mansell back from Indycars. Six days after that exclusive, Coulthard made an impressive GP début on a one-off in Spain, running in the top six before the electrics failed. Hill benefited from Schumacher's gearbox problems that day to win and raise Williams morale. Hill finished second in Canada despite a poor start, while Coulthard, given a

second opportunity, qualified and finished fifth.

Mansell agreed a one-off deal (for a reputed £1 million) for the French GP at Magny-Cours once conflicting sponsorships were overcome. Hill rose to the challenge of having another former champion as his team-mate by outqualifying Mansell as Williams-Renaults locked out the front row. They were beaten off the line by the suspiciously fast-starting Schumacher who adopted a three-stop strategy to beat Hill by 12.642sec. Mansell was running third when his transmission failed.

Angry at press speculation about his future, Hill converted British GP pole position into victory in a race that his father never won, taking the decisive lead when Schumacher finally served his stop-go penalty. With Mansell at the Cleveland Indycar race, Coulthard

David Coulthard, Williams FW16-Renault (Canadian GP)

Nigel Mansell, Williams FW16-Renault (French GP)

Nigel Mansell, Williams FW16B-Renault (Japanese GP)

David Coulthard, Williams FW16B-Renault (Portuguese GP)

recovered from disappointing qualifying (seventh) and a stall on the grid to finish sixth despite a spin and being stuck in gear by the finish. It had been eventful.

The revised FW16B was tested at Paul Ricard with the stepped flat bottom required from the German GP. The sidepods were 12in shorter so larger bargeboards could be fitted as Newey recovered lost downforce. The top rear wishbones and bodywork were even lower and the diffuser was revised. Unwitting victims of a first-lap pile-up, they set the two fastest race laps but Hill could only finish eighth. Coulthard stalled at a pitstop after becoming stuck in sixth gear and retired a lap later.

The FW16B was much improved for Hungary and Hill was disappointed to only finish second, while Coulthard crashed while defending third position from Martin Brundle's McLaren. With Mansell confirmed for the last three GPs of the season and thought to have signed a deal for 1995, Hill inherited a crucial victory in Belgium when Schumacher's Benetton-Ford failed post-race scrutineering. Coulthard enjoyed another strong race at Spa-Francorchamps and led Hill for 19 laps before a precautionary pitstop to check his rear wing reversed those positions. The Scot then survived getting stuck in gear once more and hitting Mark Blundell's Tyrrell at La Source to finish in fourth position.

Hill's title hopes improved two days later when the FIA Court of Appeal upheld Schumacher's two-race ban for ignoring black flags during the British GP. Hill had requested that race engineers David Brown, who had worked with the previous two World Champions, and John Russell swapped cars after Senna's death and this finally

Damon Hill, Williams FW16B-Renault (Japanese GP)

Jean Alesi, Ferrari 412T1 (Brazilian GP)

happened at Monza. With Schumacher out of action, Hill won at Monza and Estoril, where he had rolled on Friday after hitting Eddie Irvine's spun car. Coulthard led the Italian GP before letting Hill pass but ran out of fuel within sight of the flag and coasted home sixth. He completed a Williams-Renault 1–2 in Portugal before making way for Mansell's return, having led his last three races of an impressive rookie season.

Hill went to Jerez just a point behind the returning Schumacher and finished second to him. Mansell made a slow start from third on the grid, changed his front wing following contact with Rubens Barrichello, and spun out on lap 48. The title went down to the wire when Hill beat Schumacher on aggregate at Suzuka after a superb drive in the heavy rain, while Mansell finished fourth.

Lap 36 of the Australian GP proved decisive in the 1994 World Championship. Hill was two seconds behind Schumacher when the German ran wide and glanced the Turn 3 wall. The Englishman went to take advantage and made a pass for the lead at the next corner but Schumacher turned in and they crashed. Hill made it back to the pits but had to retire, so his rival was confirmed as champion for the first time. Mansell, who had qualified on pole, inherited the lead and held off Gerhard Berger's Ferrari to score the 31st F1 victory of his career.

A winner six times during 1994, Hill finished as a dignified runner-up in the World Championship and was voted BBC Sports Personality of the Year. Williams took its seventh constructors' title.

SCUDERIA FERRARI

There was real anticipation regarding the Ferrari 412T1, John Barnard's first *pukka* design of his second stint with the famous old team. Starting with a clean sheet of paper, Barnard retained the high nose he favoured at Benetton and made it even higher, prompting the car to be dubbed the 'anteater'. Elegantly sculpted sidepods had large curved intakes and, to everyone's relief at Ferrari, the troublesome active suspension was now banned. Instead, the front push-rods were mounted high with innovative outboard 'knife-edge' pick-up points for the lower wishbones. Torsion bars were employed front and rear. The narrow transverse semi-automatic gearbox had a chrome-molybdenum casing for rigidity and to save weight. Neat rear packaging and trademark 'coke bottle' rear allowed a large adjustable diffuser. Unveiled on 2 February 1994 and described by historian David Hodges as a 'gorgeous-looking creation', the 412T1 initially proved difficult to drive and was no match for rivals from Didcot or Enstone until mid-season.

Ferrari was alone in persisting with a thirsty 12-cylinder engine although refuelling reduced the heavy fuel load at the start. The existing 65-degree V12 was updated before a new 75-degree version was used in practice at Imola and raced from Hockenheim. The increased vee-angle required the shapely engine cover to sprout less attractive bulges but any loss of aesthetics was compensated by an extra 25–40bhp, and Ferrari's first victory in three years.

Gerhard Berger remained under contract and Jean Alesi spoke to

Gerhard Berger, Ferrari 412T1 (Pacific GP)

Nicola Larini, Ferrari 412T1 (San Marino GP)

Williams before agreeing a two-year extension in June 1993, ending speculation that Ayrton Senna may join. 'I have decided to stay at Ferrari because the future seems to be strong with all the work going on for next year,' Alesi told *Autosport*. 'And I want to drive the real John Barnard car.'

Having worked for Ferrari since 1978, Paolo Martinelli transferred from the road-car division to replace Claudio Lombardi as head of the F1 engine programme and Osamu Goto (ex-Honda) was prised away from McLaren. The chassis department in Maranello was augmented by the return of Gustav Brunner from Minardi while Luigi Mazzola (ex-Sauber) came back as a race engineer. Team manager Sante Ghedini left to run the Mugello circuit and was replaced by Claudio Berri, while research and development director Amedeo Visconti transferred to the road-car division.

Five engine failures and understeer blighted the first major test at Barcelona and those issues remained at the opening race in Brazil. A spectacular third in qualifying but forced to race the spare due to an engine problem, Alesi ran second in the early laps and finished third. Mechanical gremlins restricted Berger to 17th on the grid and he suffered three engine failures on Sunday alone, in the warm-up, when the replacement was fired up and after five laps of the race.

A week later, Ferrari tried a new front wing and floor at Mugello but Alesi crashed at the 125mph Arrabiatta corner and was knocked out and suffered three crushed vertebrae. That ruled him out of the next two races so test driver Nicola Larini deputised. The cars were fitted with a variable rev limiter at the Pacific GP and Larini caused uproar when he told Italian journalists that he had turned off his

Gerhard Berger, Ferrari 412T1B (Australian GP)

traction control. The FIA issued a statement on Sunday: 'It came to the notice of the FIA technical delegate that during free practice sessions on Saturday car numbers 27 and 28 were fitted with a device which in certain circumstances limited the power of the engine. As the FIA technical delegate was not satisfied that the device complied in all respects with the sporting and technical regulations, Ferrari were advised not to use it. This advice was complied with.' Fifth and seventh on the grid, Berger finished second but Larini could not avoid Senna's spinning car at the first corner.

Berger was deeply affected by the tragedies at Imola and withdrew after leading the restarted race, while Larini finished second on his last Ferrari appearance. In Monaco, they qualified and finished third (a downbeat Berger) and fifth (Alesi on his return) with Ferrari's lightning straight-line speed compensating for continuing poor handling. The modifications required to comply with the post-Imola rule changes compromised airflow and cooling but Alesi finished fourth in Spain. In Canada, the Frenchman used Ferrari's power to qualify on the front row for the first time and finished third (despite late gearbox trouble) with Berger fourth.

With Barnard focused on 1995, Brunner overhauled the 412T1 to improve its cooling and balance. The 412T1B was introduced at Magny-Cours with revised weight distribution, new front wing and endplates, 'elaborate' two-piece barge boards ahead of shorter sidepods with straight inlets and angled radiators, new rear suspension and titanium gearbox casing. These revisions significantly lowered water and oil temperatures and Berger finished third although Alesi hit Rubens Barrichello's Jordan-Hart when recovering from a spin. With the new 75-degree engine used for qualifying, the Ferraris occupied the second row at Silverstone, where Berger briefly led before his old-specification V12 failed while the one-stopping Alesi inherited second place after Michael Schumacher's disqualification was confirmed.

The new engine was ready to race in Germany and its extra power helped annex the front row. Pole-winner Berger led throughout to end Ferrari's 58-race wait for victory but Alesi's electrics failed before reaching the first chicane. The 412T1B was 'hopeless' when downforce was required at the twisty Hungaroring and early engine failures eliminated both cars in Belgium, Alesi having run second after a great start. With power at a premium, Alesi led a Ferrari qualifying 1–2 at Monza (his first pole position) and dominated the early exchanges before gearbox failure at his first pitstop left him distraught and angry. Having survived a high-speed accident at the Roggia chicane in the warm-up, Berger led following his team-mate's demise only for a slow pitstop to demote him to second by the finish.

In Portugal, Berger qualified on pole and withstood David Coulthard's pressure for the first seven laps before the transmission failed, while Alesi was denied a podium after tripping over David Brabham's Simtek-Ford. Berger was fifth at Jerez and Alesi struggled home tenth. Alesi beat Nigel Mansell into third in Japan but Berger's electrics packed up after nine soggy laps behind the safety car. While Alesi was restricted to sixth in Australia following a couple of slow pitstops, the Austrian led after Michael Schumacher and Damon Hill collided only to lose out to Mansell when he ran wide – but second

Jean Alesi, Ferrari 412T1B (Japanese GP)

was enough to clinch third position in the World Championship.

There may have only been one victory but third-placed Ferrari had made progress, especially with the engine. Despite its mid-season revisions, the Ferrari 412T1 had not been an unqualified success. President Luca di Montezemolo later reflected that 'we reversed the downward trend… we won a race. It's not enough and I obviously want to win them all.'

MARLBORO McLAREN PEUGEOT

Peugeot, the reigning World Sportscar Champions, announced on 7 April 1993 that it was shelving plans to enter its own F1 team because independent commercial sponsorship could not be found. Sporting director Jean Todt left as soon as Peugeot successfully defended its Le Mans crown in June but Jean-Pierre Boudy's engine department continued to develop a new 72-degree V10 for F1, the vee-angle reduced by eight degrees from its sports-car cousin to optimise aerodynamic packaging.

McLaren converted an MP4/8 chassis to evaluate Chrysler-Lamborghini's V12 engine in September 1993 amid rumours that new Peugeot Talbot Sport boss Jean-Pierre Jabouille had agreed to supply old colleague Gérard Larrousse. Jabouille set a three-year target when Peugeot confirmed its F1 programme on 15 September: 'If we get close to podiums next year I will be very happy. I hope we can win grands prix in 1995 and fight for the World Championship in 1996.' He visited McLaren and Benetton prior to the announcement on 8 October of a four-year agreement with the Woking-based team, to the dismay of both Larrousse and Chrysler.

The prototype V10 (designated A4) featured five valves per cylinder when it was bench-tested in December with Boudy 'proud to have built this engine in 23 weeks'. The evolutionary McLaren MP4/9-Peugeot was launched at the McLaren factory on 28 January, with a more powerful four-valve (A6) engine preferred. There were just two pedals as the clutch was operated by paddles on the steering column, an arrangement that particularly suited Mika Häkkinen's preference for left-foot braking. Both undertray and sidepods were revised. Power steering was available from Monaco and preferred at slower tracks. 'We will win races in 1994,' Dennis predicted at launch – but the engine lacked power and the cooling system, finalised before

Mika Häkkinen, McLaren MP4/9-Peugeot (French GP)

it had run, was inadequate, an issue initially masked by the cooler temperatures at winter testing.

With Ayrton Senna departing after six seasons to join Williams-Renault, the close season was another in which Alain Prost claimed the headlines only not to race. The newly retired champion denied *Le Journal du Dimanche*'s story on 17 October 1993 that he was talking to McLaren but Dennis persisted. Despite complications regarding Prost's severance from Williams-Renault if he reversed his decision to retire, he completed a four-day test at Estoril in early March 'because I still love driving an F1 car, and I just wanted to see if that would be enough to compensate for all the other bad things in this sport.' Clearly it was not: Prost told French television on 15 March that he would not be returning.

While Häkkinen signed an extended three-year contract, McLaren assessed other drivers. Jordan and Lotus thwarted approaches for Rubens Barrichello and Johnny Herbert respectively. Peugeot sports-car drivers Philippe Alliot and Yannick Dalmas tested and emerging talents such as Jos Verstappen and Luca Badoer were also tried. Martin Brundle ran at Silverstone and Estoril in March. With the Prost possibility unresolved, Brundle and Alliot signed contracts without knowing if they would race, but eventually the Englishman was chosen to partner Häkkinen on a race-by-race basis. It was the first time in McLaren's history that the team began a season without a race winner in its line-up.

The Brazilian GP brought trouble with the MP4/9s' new cable-operated throttles (fitted in place of fly-by-wire only two weeks

Martin Brundle, McLaren MP4/9-Peugeot (Monaco GP)

Philippe Alliot, McLaren MP4/9-Peugeot (Hungarian GP)

before the race) and overheating throughout the weekend. Häkkinen was up to fifth when his electronics failed and Brundle was eliminated in the Verstappen/Irvine shunt. With modified radiators for the Pacific GP, the drivers qualified in the top six, Häkkinen fourth despite running wide at the final corner. Using the five-valve engine, the Finn ran second from the start before hydraulics failure and Brundle was denied a third-place finish when sidelined by overheating.

Both drivers complained of poor straight-line speed at the San Marino GP despite an engine upgrade worth another 20bhp. Third after a fine drive at Imola, Häkkinen qualified on the front row at Monaco only to collide with Damon Hill at the first corner. Brundle was second after first qualifying but dropped to eighth on the grid after hitting a wall on Saturday. He then benefited from an early first pitstop to finish second, equalling his best-ever F1 result.

Modifications introduced at Barcelona further improved cooling and Häkkinen qualified third, led for eight laps and was challenging for second when his engine failed. Brundle seemed on course for a podium when his clutch disintegrated on the main straight. Both suffered engine-related retirements in Canada and France, where Peugeot's higher-revving Evo2 V10 further boosted power. Brundle's engine burst into flames on the Silverstone grid and Häkkinen clashed with Barrichello at the final corner of the race. Not penalised when marshals pushed him out of the gravel trap, Häkkinen limped across the line and inherited third when Schumacher was disqualified.

Before the German GP, McLaren was buoyed when Häkkinen was fastest in Paul Ricard testing, but at Hockenheim he was blamed for the start-line accident and, under observation following Silverstone, was banned for one race. Brundle was delayed by contact on lap one and suffered yet another blown engine as the relationship between team and manufacturer grew ever more tense.

Peugeot had agitated for Alliot to replace Brundle, at least for the French GP, and the 40-year-old Frenchman took Häkkinen's place at the Hungaroring, where a new rear wing and floor were used. Alliot qualified in a disappointing 14th position and retired without making an impression while Brundle started sixth and lost third when the alternator failed on the last lap, leaving him classified fourth. Häkkinen returned to claim a fine second in Belgium after fifth-placed Brundle spun out of the race at Les Combes.

McLaren was given two days' notice to appear in front of the World Motor Sport Council on 7 September due to Häkkinen's gearbox having an automatic up-shift at Imola. The team argued its interpretation of the rules and was let off although the FIA stipulated that henceforth any such system had to be disabled. Using a low-downforce set-up to offset lack of power, McLaren-Peugeot scored double points finishes at Monza and Estoril, then the impressive Häkkinen took a third successive third place at Jerez.

Unhappy in the Japanese rain, Häkkinen threatened another podium (or better) in Australia only to be penalised for speeding in the pitlane and then crashing when his brakes failed. At Suzuka, Brundle aquaplaned off at the Degner Curves, narrowly missed a recovery vehicle tending to Gianni Morbidelli's stranded Footwork,

and hit a marshal and broke his leg. A week later, Brundle completed his McLaren career by finishing third in Australia.

It was no surprise when McLaren and Peugeot dissolved their unhappy alliance after the European GP and sought new partners for 1995. The single McLaren-Peugeot season failed to deliver Dennis's promised victory and was seen as an unmitigated failure at the time. But how McLaren would have celebrated eight podium finishes and fourth in the World Championship when Honda returned in 2015?

SASOL JORDAN

The 1993 Japanese GP had shown a glimpse of the potential of the Jordan-Hart partnership when Rubens Barrichello and Eddie Irvine both scored points. The highly rated Brazilian remained under contract and McLaren's advances were rebuffed. Irvine was confirmed as his team-mate in January and they delivered Jordan's best season so far, scoring 28 points and finishing fifth in the constructors' standings.

Kelvin Burt signed a four-year agreement and joined Vittorio Zoboli as test driver. Title sponsor Sasol was in the final year of its contract. Barclay cigarettes did not renew so Barrichello's long-time backers Arisco had increased prominence on the sidepods. New chief designer Steve Nichols augmented Gary Anderson's technical staff while race engineer Tim Wright moved to Sauber.

Barrichello shook down the 'very promising' Jordan 194-Hart at Silverstone on 10 January, a day before it was launched to the press. Another evolutionary design, it reverted to an anhedral front wing and had shortened sidepods. It was fast and reliable during pre-season testing although Irvine wrote off the prototype chassis in a 100mph accident at Magny-Cours in March.

While Barrichello finished fourth in Brazil, Irvine continued the controversial start to his F1 career when he was blamed for the accident that eliminated Jos Verstappen, Martin Brundle and Éric Bernard. Jordan appealed Irvine's one-race ban that had been imposed by the stewards only for the FIA to extend it to three races. Barrichello recovered from stalling at his pitstop to claim an excellent third at Aida, where Aguri Suzuki replaced Irvine but struggled before steering failure caused him to crash.

Aguri Suzuki, Jordan 194-Hart (Pacific GP)

Rubens Barrichello, Jordan 194-Hart (British GP)

The San Marino GP weekend began badly when Barrichello lost control at the Variante Bassa during Friday qualifying and was knocked unconscious when the car was launched into the fencing and rolled onto its side. Fortunate to escape with a bloody nose and facial lacerations, the young Brazilian took no further part in that tragic meeting and was understandably subdued at Monaco. Original Jordan driver Andrea de Cesaris drove the second car at Imola and Monaco. Having crashed during testing at Mugello and late in the San Marino GP, de Cesaris outqualified Barrichello in Monaco and finished fourth. 'Probably one of the best drives I have ever seen in a Jordan,' Eddie enthused.

Barrichello was back on form next time out in Spain where he qualified fifth and ran as high as second before engine failure

prevented another strong result. Irvine finished sixth on his return from suspension despite an unscheduled pitstop to replace his car's damaged nose. Both drivers started inside the top seven in Canada and France as Jordan confirmed its underlying pace although troublesome gearbox electronics (plus Jean Alesi's 'brain fade' at Magny-Cours) denied points.

Irvine's engine failed on the warm-up lap at Silverstone, where Barrichello made a great start and chased Mika Häkkinen until they collided at the final corner of the race. With suspension broken and unaware that it was the last lap due to a faulty radio, Barrichello pitted to retire but crossed the line and inherited fourth following Michael Schumacher's disqualification. Both Jordan-Harts were eliminated at the first corner of the opening lap in Germany and

Eddie Irvine, Jordan 194-Hart (Canadian GP)

Andrea de Cesaris, Jordan 194-Hart (San Marino GP)

at the second corner at the Hungaroring, with Irvine blaming Barrichello for the latter collision. Barrichello then judged the changing conditions in Belgium to snatch Jordan's first pole position and become the youngest pole-winner at that time. Irvine qualified fourth but neither finished.

F1's *enfant terrible*, Irvine received a suspended race ban for causing the start-line shunt that stopped the Italian GP, prompting Johnny Herbert to say: 'Irvine has done far too much damage this year and should be properly penalised. Formula 1 doesn't need drivers like this.' Barrichello finished fourth in Italy and Portugal (having led during the first pitstops) and Irvine took that position at Jerez. Barrichello qualified fifth at that latter race only for a puncture and fading brakes to ruin his race. On the anniversary of his F1 début, Irvine lined up sixth in Japan and survived the downpour to finish fifth on aggregate. They filled the third row in Australia, where Irvine spun at the end of the Dequetteville Straight and Barrichello finished sixth to conclude an excellent season for the team.

LIGIER GITANES BLONDES

Despite progress during 1993, Ligier's future looked uncertain when owner Cyril de Rouvre was arrested on 14 December in connection with fraud in a film-distribution company that he also owned. He spent two months in a Paris jail and when released on bail sought a buyer for Ligier. Having failed to take Ligier's prized Renault engines during the winter, Benetton managing director Flavio Briatore met de Rouvre and Ligier's sponsors in Paris on 6 April 1994. After seeing off Gérard Larrousse's rival bid, Briatore's acquisition of the team was announced at the Monaco GP, with Tony Dowe and Ian Reed (of Benetton director of engineering Tom Walkinshaw's American operations) installed to evaluate the team. Long-time team manager Dany Hindenoch resigned, Cesare Fiorio joined on a one-year contract as sporting director on 1 July, and Frank Dernie returned to replace Ducarouge as technical director.

Following Ligier's controversial all-British driver line-up in 1993, Éric Bernard, Olivier Panis and Emmanuel Collard tested at Magny-Cours and Paul Ricard before Christmas. Bernard was confirmed on a one-year contract in January and Panis agreed a race-by-race deal on the eve of the season after Martin Brundle's move to McLaren. With income frozen during the uncertain winter months, Ligier relied throughout 1994 on the reworked JS39B, which was heavy and lacked grip, but was reliable. Despite having the best engine on the grid, the Ligier-Renaults rarely qualified in the top dozen and half the season passed before they scored points.

They filled the tenth row in Brazil, where Bernard was caught up in the Eddie Irvine/Jos Verstappen accident. They were lapped five times at the back of the Pacific GP field and were the last two cars to complete the San Marino GP. Panis finished the first six races of his F1 career, including beating Bernard into seventh in Spain, and his only retirement came in France when he crashed into Gianni Morbidelli's Footwork. Speculation that the Benetton-contracted Verstappen would replace Panis following the takeover

Olivier Panis, Ligier JS39B-Renault (French GP)

Éric Bernard, Ligier JS39B-Renault (Hungarian GP)

Johnny Herbert, Ligier JS39B-Renault (European GP)

proved false and he signed a new two-year contract before the end of the European season.

Qualifying performance started to perk up mid-season and at Hockenheim, where the Ligiers lined up 12th (Panis) and 14th (Bernard), the drivers avoided the opening-lap shunts and used Renault power to score a shock double-podium result, Panis second and Bernard third. Panis then qualified a fine ninth in Hungary and escaped a penalty for jumping the start to claim sixth, just 0.168sec behind Mark Blundell's Tyrrell-Yamaha. The impressive newcomer lost another points finish when he stalled in the pits in Belgium and qualified a season-best sixth at Monza. Overshadowed by Panis thus far, Bernard stalled at the restart in Italy before driving through the field to finish seventh. Panis was disqualified from ninth in Portugal due to excessive wear on his wooden skid-block and with that Bernard inherited tenth.

On the Wednesday before the European GP, Bernard discovered that he had been dropped in favour of Lotus star Johnny Herbert, who found himself driving in that race for the man who had ended his original Benetton career. The Englishman qualified an impressive seventh and finished eighth with Panis ninth. Briatore then promoted Herbert to Benetton for the last two races so Panis had another new team-mate.

Having signed as test driver in September, F3000 runner-up Franck Lagorce spun out in Japan and finished 11th in Australia. Panis completed a consistent rookie campaign by finishing fifth in Adelaide – the 15th out of 16 possible finishes (his Portuguese disqualification included) – as Ligier-Renault shared sixth overall.

TYRRELL RACING ORGANISATION

New managing director (engineering) Harvey Postlethwaite wasted little time in reorganising the technical department. Within a month of him rejoining Tyrrell on 17 September 1993, a contract until the end of 1995 was signed with Casumaro-based Fondmetal Technologies, a new design studio with a 50 per cent wind tunnel established by former Tyrrell aerodynamicist Jean-Claude Migeot. Another 'old boy', Mike Gascoyne, was poached from Sauber in October. On the driving strength, Ukyo Katayama re-signed in November and Ligier's Mark Blundell was announced as team leader in the New Year. Japan Tobacco switched brands from Cabin to Mild Seven although budgets remained tight.

The Tyrrell 022-Yamaha was launched at London Olympia's *Evening Standard* Motor Racing Show on 24 February. Needing to reverse Tyrrell's decline, Postlethwaite 'tried to achieve something rather boring – a small, neat, reliable and aerodynamically perfect racing car that's easy to work with and develop.' Conventional by design, the 022 had push-rod suspension with inboard coil springs and dampers. The rear diffuser was shallower than others while John Judd made great strides in developing his Yamaha OX10A V10 engine. The lighter J1-specification version introduced at the Pacific GP featured revised intake design, altered oil and fuel pumps, and air compressor-operated pneumatic valves. Butterfly valves were fitted for the final European race at Jerez.

Although reliability proved a concern, Tyrrell firmly re-established itself in F1's midfield with Katayama a revelation. He started two of the opening three races from inside the top ten and

Franck Lagorce, Ligier JS39B-Renault (Australian GP)

Ukyo Katayama, Tyrrell 022-Yamaha (Monaco GP)

finished fifth at Interlagos and Imola, where he briefly held second. Running sixth in Brazil when he crashed heavily following front-wheel failure, Blundell was eliminated at the first corner of the Pacific GP and was ninth at Imola.

The cars sprouted rear winglets at Monaco that were widely copied and they challenged for points before retiring. Blundell then scored Tyrrell's first podium since 1991 by finishing third in Spain. Both spun during the Canadian GP and Katayama lost points in France due to a puncture. Sixth following Michael Schumacher's disqualification from the British GP, Katayama started the next two races in Germany and Hungary from career-best fifth on the grid. Blundell crashed on the opening lap of the German GP while Katayama initially ran third before his throttle stuck open. In Hungary, Katayama collided with both Jordan-Harts at the second corner of the race while Blundell withstood Olivier Panis's pressure to hold on to fifth at the finish. He repeated that result at Spa-Francorchamps despite contact with David Coulthard's ailing Williams-Renault at La Source.

Katayama made a superb start in Italy and ran with the leaders before both crashed due to brake disc failures, denying Katayama a fourth-place finish. In Portugal, Katayama qualified sixth but started from the pitlane and ground to a halt with gearbox failure. Katayama stalled at the start of the European GP before a storming drive into seventh when just 0.153sec from scoring an unlikely point. Neither finished in Japan (where Katayama crashed

into the pit wall) or Australia (where both crashed).

Tyrrell showed a marked improvement in 1994 and shared sixth overall with the far better-funded Ligier-Renault. Ken Tyrrell and his crew looked forward to 1995 with enthusiasm.

Mark Blundell, Tyrrell 022-Yamaha (Canadian GP)

SAUBER-MERCEDES

Having bankrolled Sauber's F1 graduation and financed Mario Ilien's promising new V10 engine in 1993, Mercedes-Benz officially re-entered grand prix racing in 1994. It acquired a 25 per cent stake in Ilmor Engineering and the Sauber V10 was rebadged with the three-pointed star on its cam covers.

Karl Wendlinger was retained to lead Sauber-Mercedes but J.J. Lehto announced he was leaving in the autumn. Heinz-Harald Frentzen, a former Mercedes junior driver like Wendlinger, tested behind closed doors at Mugello on 5 August 1993 and was confirmed for the coming season on 22 October. Aerodynamicist Mike Gascoyne resigned in October and was replaced by Ligier's Loïc Bigois, while Wendlinger's race engineer, Walter Naher, switched to the test team. Willi Rampf (ex-BMW) and Tim Wright (Jordan) were hired to engineer Wendlinger and Frentzen respectively. André de Cortanze remained as technical director while chief mechanic Beat Zehnder replaced team manager Carmen Heer (née Ziegler) when she left in July 1994.

Everything seemed set fair for Sauber to establish itself as a leading team. The problem, however, was money. A four-year deal with as-yet-unpublished *Broker* magazine as title sponsor was announced at the Geneva motor show on 8 March but it was terminated in June when payments were missed, leaving a reputed £10 million hole in Sauber's budget. Fearing imminent closure of the team, Mercedes covered that shortfall, much to the main board's

displeasure. Mercedes arranged branding for Tissot watches to be carried from the French GP through its association with holding company SHM, with a new polka-dot livery adopted at the German GP. Mercedes set Sauber a 30 September deadline to prove its future financial plans and Peter Sauber missed the Belgian GP as he tried to find new sponsorship. However, an alliance between McLaren and Mercedes was announced on 28 October 1994, leaving Sauber to seek a new partner for 1995.

Sauber was the first team to reveal its 1994 challenger when Wendlinger drove the Sauber C13-Mercedes at Barcelona on 13 December. This logical evolution of Sauber's original F1 challenger was designed around a 225-litre fuel tank from the outset before capacity was reduced when refuelling was announced. Gascoyne refined the C13's aerodynamics before he left and hours in the wind tunnel at Emmen resulted in a heavily revised rear diffuser. Uniquely for 1994, chief designer Leo Ress continued to mount the six-speed semi-automatic gearbox longitudinally. Passive push-rod suspension was retained with inboard coil springs and dampers. Revised suspension geometry was introduced in Germany (front) and Belgium (rear) with some success. Sauber installed an autoclave at the factory during 1994 and the final C13 monocoque was produced in-house rather than at David Price Composites in England.

Variable length trumpets were tested on the V10 engine in the winter and pneumatic valves were tried during practice for the San Marino GP, although their race début was delayed until Canada while air leakage was eradicated. Frentzen used an upgraded engine in Belgium but it was shelved when piston failures caused a double retirement at Monza.

Both Sauber-Mercedes cars qualified in the top seven in Brazil with Frentzen starting his début from an impressive fifth. The German spun out when sixth and it was Wendlinger who scored the final point. Having qualified poorly at Aida, Wendlinger was running sixth when eliminated by a rash Michele Alboreto manoeuvre. Frentzen finished fifth despite slowing in the closing stages as he feared an impending engine failure.

Fourth at Imola, Wendlinger crashed at the chicane during Thursday practice in Monaco. He suffered grave head injuries and remained in a coma for 19 days. Well enough to be a welcome guest of the team at the Italian GP, Wendlinger tested a Sauber C13-Mercedes at Paul Ricard after the final European race of the season and was announced for the final two races, although that comeback was delayed until 1995.

Sauber withdrew from the Monaco GP following Wendlinger's accident and ran a single car for Frentzen in Spain, where the impressive German climbed into the top five before the gearbox jammed in neutral. Sauber waited for Wendlinger's condition to improve before signing Andrea de Cesaris as Frentzen's team-mate from the Canadian GP. The Italian's car sported a special livery to commemorate his 200th GP start at that race – joining Riccardo Patrese and Nelson Piquet as the third driver to reach that landmark – but both cars retired. Frentzen was fourth at Magny-Cours with de Cesaris sixth as Sauber-Mercedes threatened to take fourth in the constructors' standings.

Andrea de Cesaris, Sauber C13-Mercedes (Hungarian GP)

Karl Wendlinger, Sauber C13-Mercedes (Pacific GP)

Heinz-Harald Frentzen, Sauber C13-Mercedes (Belgian GP)

Seventh at Silverstone after spinning on the last lap, Frentzen qualified in the top ten for all but one of the remaining races only for poor reliability and accidents to prevent significant results. Neither survived the chaotic opening lap in Germany. De Cesaris crashed at Spa-Francorchamps's 'Bus Stop' chicane when his throttle stuck open and spun out of the Hungarian and Portuguese GPs. Frentzen was fifth when he exited the Belgian GP at the new Eau Rouge chicane, and had gearbox failures at the Hungaroring and Estoril, while lying third in the latter.

With its Mercedes partnership under threat and Sauber admitting 'our situation is grave and there's no point in saying otherwise', Frentzen qualified an excellent fourth at Jerez and finished sixth to deliver Sauber's first point since France. De Cesaris had terrible weekend, crashing his race car and hire car on Saturday and retiring from his 208th and final GP on Sunday. He stood down to make way for Wendlinger's return only for the Austrian to postpone due to neck pains experienced following a test in Barcelona.

Chastened by a difficult campaign with Benetton, Lehto returned to Sauber-Mercedes for those last two races without having tested. His engine failed on the opening lap of Suzuka and he finished tenth in Australia following a puncture. One of the few positive stories of 1994, Frentzen excelled in Japan on a track he knew well. He qualified third only to run wide while attempting to pass Damon Hill's second-placed Williams-Renault on lap two. His car was virtually undrivable when the rain was at its heaviest but he took sixth from Mika Häkkinen as conditions improved. He was seventh in Australia as Sauber-Mercedes finished eighth in the constructors' championship.

J.J. Lehto, Sauber C13-Mercedes (Australian GP)

FOOTWORK FORD

Amid economic recession in Japan, Footwork shareholders insisted that Wataru Ohashi cease his involvement in F1 with the departure of Aguri Suzuki and Mugen engines a direct consequence. Lamborghini and old-specification Ilmors were considered before a deal for ex-McLaren Ford HB V8 power was agreed. Jackie Oliver and Alan Rees reacquired Ohashi's shares in Arrows Grand Prix International by the end of the year but the official car remained Footwork as to change would have forfeited FOCA travel money.

Derek Warwick was tired of uncompetitive machinery so there was an all-new driver line-up. Mark Blundell visited but moved to Tyrrell while Jos Verstappen, Paul Stewart (son of Jackie) and Christian Fittipaldi all tested at Estoril during 28–30 September

Gianni Morbidelli, Footwork FA15-Ford (Brazilian GP)

1993, Verstappen proving very quick before he crashed. The Dutch sensation signed for Benetton and Stewart retired from driving to concentrate on running Paul Stewart Racing. Fittipaldi signed on his 23rd birthday (18 January) and, having spent a year out of F1, 1992 Minardi team-mate Gianni Morbidelli was confirmed on 8 March.

The Footwork FA15-Ford, an evolution of the FA14, first turned a wheel at a foggy Silverstone on 17 February, two days late due to snow. The compact V8 engine allowed Alan Jenkins to pen a neat design with high needle-nose and sculpted front-wing endplates. Software for the six-speed Footwork/Xtrac transverse semi-automatic gearbox was written in-house after the association with TAG Electronics ended prematurely. Early engine vibration limited reliability and test mileage but the FA15 was quick out of the box only for the

post-Imola rule changes to compromise its aero package and render the car uncompetitive.

Morbidelli qualified an impressive sixth on his comeback in Brazil but both cars jumped out of gear from the start and retired. That promise was confirmed at Aida, where Fittipaldi converted ninth on the grid into fourth at the finish and Morbidelli shadowed his team-mate before spinning on his own oil when the engine failed. The Brazilian was denied further top-four finishes at Imola and Monaco (where he led an impressive Footwork 6–7 on the grid) by brake failure and a loose gearbox wire respectively. With front endplates emasculated by new regulations, Fittipaldi only qualified 21st for the Spanish GP and his Ford engine was one of those to blow up. He was sixth on the road in Canada but the car was underweight and so disqualified. Morbidelli crashed at the start in Monte Carlo, had the refuelling valve drop into the tank in Spain, had gearbox failure in Montréal while fourth, and crashed into Olivier Panis at Magny-Cours – all of which meant that he had retired from the first eight GPs.

Footwork's competitive nadir came in France and Britain but the team avoided Hockenheim's first-lap mayhem to finish fourth (Fittipaldi) and fifth (Morbidelli). That proved a false dawn for the FA15s lacked traction in the heat of Hungary at a circuit that was expected to mask the V8's lack of power. In Belgium Morbidelli received a suspended three-race ban and $10,000 fine for ignoring yellow flags during Friday qualifying but enjoyed a good race when he inherited a sixth-place finish following Michael Schumacher's disqualification. New triple-spring front suspension introduced at that race improved ride-height control and worked particularly well when

Christian Fittipaldi, Footwork FA15-Ford (Canadian GP)

a new floor and diffuser were fitted in Portugal.

Fittipaldi's engine failed during the Belgian and Italian GPs while Morbidelli was the unwitting victim of Alex Zanardi's Lotus on the opening lap at Monza. They scored top-ten finishes at Estoril before Morbidelli, having brought extra sponsorship to continue in the team, qualified eighth at Jerez. Hopes of a strong result in Japan were lost when Morbidelli's tyres degraded too much and he crashed heavily at Suzuka's Degner Curves in the deluge, leading to the race being red-flagged when Martin Brundle aquaplaned a lap later and hit a marshal who was moving Morbidelli's car. Fittipaldi finished eighth in Japan and Australia on his final GP starts before switching to Indycars.

MINARDI SCUDERIA ITALIA

Minardi entered 1994 in an improved financial position due to a new accord with Beppe Lucchini's BMS Scuderia Italia that was confirmed in January. Giancarlo Minardi and Lucchini each took a 40 per cent stake with Vittorio Palazzani (a long-time Lucchini associate), Dino Marniga and Enrico Gnutti all minority shareholders. Scuderia Italia managing director Paolo Stanzani was appointed as vice-president of the amalgamated outfit and shared team principal duties. One driver from each team was retained, Michele Alboreto joining Minardi stalwart Pierluigi Martini to form the most experienced pairing on the grid. Out of work since the demise of BMS Scuderia Italia as an independent outfit, Luca Badoer joined as test driver in September. Of the 67 employees at the start of the year, only four came from Scuderia Italia.

The two-year agreement for ex-TWR Ford engines was cancelled at

Michele Alboreto, Minardi M193B-Ford (Brazilian GP)

Pierluigi Martini, Minardi M193B-Ford (Monaco GP)

Pierluigi Martini, Minardi M194-Ford (Belgian GP)

Michele Alboreto, Minardi M194-Ford (European GP)

the end of 1993 in favour of a deal for old Series VII and VIII Ford HB V8s agreed direct with Cosworth. The revised Minardi M193B-Ford was revealed with its new livery on 7 March and began 1994 in the midfield as the ban on electronic gizmos initially levelled performance. A semi-automatic gearbox was introduced in Germany (for Alboreto) and proved reliable. New hydraulic suspension was less satisfactory and was eventually abandoned.

Martini was eighth in Brazil in his only finish from the first three GPs. Alboreto threatened to score points at Aida before crashing into Karl Wendlinger's Sauber-Mercedes and lost his right rear wheel at his second pitstop at Imola, the errant wheel injuring mechanics from Ferrari and Lotus. An impressive ninth on the grid in Monaco, Martini crashed with Gianni Morbidelli at the start and so it was sixth-placed Alboreto who delivered Minardi's first point of 1994. Using an M193B with the monocoque from the soon-to-be-completed new car, Martini confirmed the team's form with a competitive fifth place in Spain. However, the safety-induced rule changes were a hammer blow as Minardi lacked the budget and wind tunnel to react quickly.

Elements of the M194 had been introduced progressively at the previous three races and the completed new car was first used in Canada, where both finished outside the points. An evolution of the M193B, the M194 proved slippery in a straight line despite old V8 power but only scored points once – Martini's fifth place at Magny-Cours – as Minardi gradually slipped down the grid.

The British GP was compromised by not testing at the revised Silverstone and having an incorrect strategy. Both crashed on the opening lap at Hockenheim. They battled for position in Hungary until Martini spun on oil but Alboreto finished seventh, which could have been sixth had Minardi not been too late in protesting Olivier Panis's jumped start. Shorter sidepods were introduced at Spa-Francorchamps, where Minardi celebrated its 150th F1 start by finishing eighth (Martini) and ninth (Alboreto). They retired from a disappointing Italian GP and were uncompetitive finishers at Estoril – where Martini drove with broken ribs sustained in a football match – and Jerez.

Unsighted due to heavy rain at the rolling restart of the Japanese GP, Martini crashed into Franck Lagorce's Ligier-Renault and Alboreto spun to avoid the incident. Having announced he was swapping F1 for the German Touring Car Championship in 1995, Alboreto retired in Adelaide with rear suspension failure while Martini came ninth.

TOURTEL LARROUSSE F1

Gérard Larrousse was left disappointed when Peugeot chose to supply McLaren with engines in 1994. He had been in talks with Peugeot competition boss (and old friend) Jean-Pierre Jabouille since the summer and French rumours suggested that terms were agreed. 'I have worked on the Peugeot deal for many months,' Larrousse told *Autosport*. 'I am surprised, and disappointed for French motor racing. There will now not be a winning French team in the immediate future.' Furthermore, Chrysler negotiated to sell Lamborghini to the Indonesian Megatech company throughout the winter and Larrousse tired of waiting for confirmation of its continued F1 programme. So the team decided on 15 December 1993 to switch to Series VII Ford HB engines, leaving Lamborghini without a team – and Daniele Audetto's hope that the company would return did not happen.

Olivier Beretta tested at Barcelona before Christmas and Larrousse announced him as Érik Comas's team-mate on 4 January while confirming Kronenbourg brewery as title sponsor. Without the French government's anti-tobacco backing that had kept the wheels turning in 1993, the Larrousse-Fords were normally seen in the green, blue and yellow of low-alcohol Tourtel beer, although Kronenbourg's familiar red-and-white colours were adopted at the Pacific, San Marino and Monaco GPs. Despite such a high-profile brand as title sponsor, budgets remained tight as Larrousse's hand-to-mouth existence continued for a final season. Patrick Tambay

Olivier Beretta, Larrousse LH94-Ford (Monaco GP)

Philippe Alliot, Larrousse LH94-Ford (Belgian GP)

Érik Comas, Larrousse LH94-Ford (Monaco GP)

and Michel Golay's Fast Group were retained on the eve of the season to generate additional sponsorship. In keeping with other small teams, the emergency rules changes after the San Marino GP drained resources and rendered much-needed in-season testing and development impossible.

The late engine decision forced Robin Herd's Larrousse UK design agency to evolve the existing car once more, with the resulting Larrousse LH94-Ford completed in just 80 days. The monocoque was cut away at the back to fit the smaller engine and 220-litre fuel tank. At least Larrousse finally had a transverse semi-automatic gearbox after agreement was reached with Benetton to use its 1993 six-speed. The front suspension was unaltered although Penske replaced Bilstein in supplying shock absorbers. Low-speed grip and pronounced understeer were issues from the off, and Larrousse faded from the midfield towards the back of the grid as the months wore on.

Comas caused cautious optimism by finishing in the top ten at three of the first four races, including sixth place at Aida after a stop to change a damaged nose section at the end of lap one. The only exception was Imola, where he was inadvertently waved out of the pitlane after Ayrton Senna's accident and so witnessed trackside attempts to save the Brazilian at first hand and was too distraught to continue. He retired from the Spanish GP and the next three races as Larrousse suffered a spate of failures that prompted Cosworth to recall engines.

Little was expected of Beretta, who retired from the first three races without making an impression. Eighth in his home race

Yannick Dalmas, Larrousse LH94-Ford (Portuguese GP)

Hideki Noda, Larrousse LH94-Ford (Japanese GP)

Jean-Denis Délétraz, Larrousse LH94-Ford (Australian GP)

Johnny Herbert, Lotus 107C-Mugen (Brazilian GP)

(Monaco), he had engine failure on the parade lap in Spain and during the races at Montréal and Magny-Cours. Comas and Beretta avoided Hockenheim's first-lap accidents to finish sixth and seventh respectively having run in tandem throughout. They finished outside the points in Hungary, where Beretta was ninth on his last appearance before the money ran out.

Emmanuel Collard was close to arranging a GP début at Spa-Francorchamps but it was Philippe Alliot who made a one-off return. He outqualified Comas by 1.255sec and started 19th, the highest grid position for the increasingly uncompetitive LH94 during the second half of the season. Both drivers suffered engine failure in Belgium on another disastrous day for the strugglers.

Fabrizio Barbazza was tipped to partner Comas at the Italian GP but it was another former driver, Yannick Dalmas, who returned for two final F1 starts, spinning out at Monza and finishing 14th at Estoril. Comas used a one-stop strategy to finish eighth in Italy and was battling Pierluigi Martini at Estoril when they baulked David Coulthard as the inexperienced Scot lost the lead. Comas finished ninth in the Japanese monsoon on his last F1 appearance.

Larrousse continued to juggle as he eked out the finances with pay drivers. Hideki Noda replaced Dalmas for the last three races of the season, qualifying towards the back and retiring on all three occasions. Débutant Jean-Denis Délétraz hired Comas's car for the Australian GP and ran at the back before being penalised for speeding during his pitstop. He retired when he had a problem shifting down the gearbox. Larrousse-Ford finished 11th in the World Championship.

Gérard Larrousse went into another winter trying to secure his team's future. Talks with Jean-Paul Driot's DAMS F3000 team broke down on 8 February 1995 but an 11th-hour agreement was reached with Jean Messaoudi's and Laurent Barlesi's Junior Team, which was thought to have secured sponsorship from Malaysian oil company Petronas. Steve Nichols was hired to update the LH94s but the work required to comply with the new side-impact test made the modified cars overweight. Larrousse planned to make a delayed entrance at the San Marino GP with Éric Bernard and Christophe Bouchut named as drivers. However, the team withdrew from F1 on 18 April amid insurmountable debts and facing heavy fines for missing the opening two GPs.

TEAM LOTUS

The attempts of Peter Collins and Peter Wright to re-establish Lotus finally ended in 1994 and the famous old team closed its doors at the end of the campaign. Collins initially denied there were difficulties but title sponsor Castrol did not renew and deals with Miller beer, Mobil 1 oil and *The European* newspaper did not cover the shortfall. A restructure and redundancies occurred before the season and rumours of unpaid bills remained.

The Ford Cosworth engine contract expired so an exclusive two-year deal for Mugen's powerful if old V10s was agreed. Pedro Lamy, a late substitute in 1993, was retained and Johnny Herbert, who had driven for Collins since 1989 and was Lotus's greatest asset, was confirmed at the 1993 Japanese GP with the recovered Alex Zanardi as reserve driver. Nigel Stroud, who engineered Nigel Mansell's car in 1982, returned as chief race engineer with Jock Clear responsible for Herbert's car and Andy Tilley for Lamy's.

Technical director Chris Murphy updated his two-year-old design for the start of the season and Herbert gave the Lotus 107C-Mugen its shakedown at Silverstone in December. This had a new semi-automatic six-speed transverse gearbox and passive mono-shock suspension but lacked grip and was overweight. The cars were over five seconds off the pace during the pre-Christmas Barcelona test with cooling a critical issue. Wanted by McLaren and disenchanted by the situation, Herbert wrote a letter to Collins that was leaked in *The Mail on Sunday*: 'Allow me the chance to fulfil my ambition of becoming World Champion. Please have the strength and courage to let me go.' Financial worries overshadowed the summer with takeover talks denied and Lotus ordered to pay an outstanding £2.1 million to Cosworth for its 1993 engines.

The Lotuses qualified among the backmarkers at Interlagos and Aida but they finished, Herbert a reliable if slow seventh on both occasions, with Lamy tenth and eighth respectively. Lamy was uninjured when he crashed into J.J. Lehto's stalled Benetton-Ford at the start of the San Marino GP, showering debris across the track and launching a wheel into the grandstand, but he was not so lucky in testing at Silverstone on 24 May. He lost control at 200mph when his rear wing mounting failed on the straight after Abbey. He broke his right wrist and both legs as his 107C somersaulted over the fence and into the spectator tunnel under the bridge.

Pedro Lamy, Lotus 107C-Mugen (Monaco GP)

Alex Zanardi, Lotus 107C-Mugen (Spanish GP)

Zanardi completed the new Lotus 109-Mugen's shakedown test at Snetterton on 18 May although the rule changes meant that Murphy's original front endplates and rear diffuser were immediately compromised. This was a lightened evolution of the 107 with Mugen V10 engine, new composite monocoque, revised cockpit, shorter sidepods and reprofiled raised nose. Herbert spun the singleton 109 out of its début in Spain before finishing the next three races. He was seventh in France (just 0.65sec behind sixth-placed Andrea de Cesaris) but morale within the cash-strapped team was at its lowest ebb. Zanardi replaced Lamy from the Spanish GP and finished ninth in a 107C on his race return. The Italian had

his own 109 for the French GP but retired when it caught fire as he passed the pits.

Both drivers were involved in separate first-lap shunts at Hockenheim and did not figure in Hungary. Rumours of an imminent sale overshadowed the Belgian GP and prompted Lotus to issue another denial. 'A number of rumours in the Formula 1 paddock this weekend have linked the ICS Group, Peter Hall and Tom Walkinshaw with plans to acquire ownership and control of the team. No formal approach has been tabled with the board of Team Lotus.' Financial necessity meant that bespectacled Belgian Philippe Adams drove twice in place of Zanardi, enduring an incident-filled

Johnny Herbert, Lotus 109-Mugen (German GP)

Alex Zanardi, Lotus 109-Mugen (Italian GP)

Philippe Adams, Lotus 109-Mugen (Belgian GP)

Éric Bernard, Lotus 109-Mugen (European GP)

Mika Salo, Lotus 109-Mugen (Australian GP)

début weekend at his home race and finishing last in Portugal.

Promise of a new Mugen engine provided a glimmer of hope throughout an unhappy summer among the backmarkers. Developed by former Honda engineer Hiroshi Shirai with a variable camshaft, it was 35lb lighter and developed 740bhp with an improved power curve. It was tested at Silverstone in August and handed to Herbert for the Italian GP. With the 109's weight distribution dramatically improved, he qualified a remarkable fourth only to be eliminated by an out-of-control Eddie Irvine at the start. Forced into the spare (with old engine) for the restart, the chance of vital points was lost.

There were personnel changes in September with commercial director Guy Edwards informed on arrival at Monza that he was no longer required and director of racing Trevor Foster's contract not renewed. With creditors now circling, Lotus entered administration on the day after the Italian GP with chartered accountants Robson Rhodes appointed.

Estoril did not bring a repeat of Herbert's Monza qualifying performance, with the new engine less suited to this track and the 109 lacking rear traction. The Englishman qualified 20th and finished 11th on his final appearance for Lotus. Barely on speaking terms with Collins for much of the summer, Herbert met with the administrators and Lotus management in London on 11 October and his transfer to Ligier was announced on the next day in a swap with Éric Bernard for the European GP. The Frenchman finished 18th

on his one-off at Jerez despite an ill-fitting seat that caused him to lose feeling in his limbs.

Robson Rhodes's Neil Cooper admitted that the team's continued existence was 'hand-to-mouth' but the courts gave Lotus permission to complete the season. Mika Salo used backing from his Japanese F3000 sponsor 5-Zigen to partner Zanardi at Suzuka, initially as another one-off. Having not previously tried an F1 car or paddle-shift gearbox, the Finn qualified and was invited to remain for the Australian GP after passing Zanardi (whose mirrors had fallen off) during the race to finish tenth. Both cars retired in Adelaide as the story of the original Team Lotus came to an unhappy end. It was the first season since its arrival in F1 in 1958 that the famous team had failed to score a championship point.

Sale of Lotus to American enthusiast and former driver Sam Brown was apparently agreed before the Japanese GP but negotiations were inconclusive. David Hunt, former F3000 driver and brother of 1976 World Champion James Hunt, was announced as the new owner on 7 December. He formed Team Lotus Grand Prix Limited and set a deadline of February to resurrect the organisation. Mugen switched its supply to Ligier citing non-payment, the staff were temporarily laid off and build of the new Murphy-designed Lotus 112 suspended. The remaining 55 staff were made redundant on 17 January 1995 and a 'marriage of convenience' (in Autosport's words) with Pacific Grand Prix was announced when Lotus was not granted an entry for the 1995 World Championship.

David Brabham, Simtek S941-Ford (Belgian GP)

MTV SIMTEK FORD

Former Leyton House March aerodynamicist Nick Wirth formed Simtek (Simulation Technology) Research in August 1989 with investment from Max Mosley. A base was established in Banbury and Simtek helped install Ligier's wind tunnel at Magny-Cours. Wirth designed a car for BMW as it evaluated F1 in 1990 (which later formed the basis for the unsuccessful Andrea Moda S192). Mosley sold his shares in Simtek when he was elected as FIA president.

Jean-François Mosnier announced Escuderia Bravo F1 España in November 1989 with Adrián Campos as his assistant and commissioned Simtek to supply the chassis. Judd engines were agreed and David Price Composites began manufacturing the first monocoque. Bravo entered the 1993 F1 World Championship but the project was abandoned when 46-year-old Mosnier succumbed to a recurrence of cancer.

Undeterred, Wirth announced in May 1993 that Simtek was graduating in its own name. David Brabham signed as lead driver on 9 August with his father, three-time World Champion Sir Jack, acting as an adviser to the newcomers. Jean-Marc Gounon was listed as Brabham's team-mate when the official entry list was published in January 1994 but could not finalise his budget so Roland Ratzenberger signed a six-race deal in March. Long-time Eddie Jordan associate Fred Rodgers assisted with commercial matters and the MTV music channel became title sponsor on the eve of the season. There was additional backing from Korean Air in Japan and Australia but finance and

tragedy meant Brabham had five team-mates during 1994.

The Simtek S941 was revealed at the factory on 29 October 1993. Despite pre-publicity hinting at radical features and unusual cantilever front suspension, the car was largely conventional although the drooping nose was distinctive and the front wishbones were mounted high to optimise airflow to the half-length sidepods. It was powered by the Series V version of Ford's HB V8 engine mated to a transverse six-speed Xtrac gearbox; this was a manual sequential unit as the semi-automatic alternative was not perfected. Without experience as a race team, Simtek agreed a partnership with former DTM champions Schmidt Motor Sport. Ex-March team manager

Roland Ratzenberger, Simtek S941-Ford (Pacific GP)

Andrea Montermini, Simtek S941-Ford (Spanish GP)

Taki Inoue, Simtek S941-Ford (Japanese GP)

Jean-Marc Gounon, Simtek S941-Ford (Hungarian GP)

Domenico Schiattarella, Simtek S941-Ford (European GP)

Charlie Moody was hired and chief race engineer Paul Crooks (ex-Ligier and Benetton) arrived late in the season. Brabham gave the S941 its shakedown on 17 December 1993 although the winter programme was delayed when wheels did not arrive.

After failing to qualify in Brazil following trouble, Ratzenberger used prior knowledge of Aida to finish 11th on début before the fateful San Marino GP. During Saturday qualifying the popular Austrian crashed at over 170mph on the approach to Tosa, with front wing failure suspected, and was pronounced dead eight minutes after arriving at Bologna's Maggiore Hospital.

In difficult circumstances, Brabham had a solid season in the lead car, always qualifying and invariably quicker than his various team-mates. He started the San Marino GP despite the previous day's tragedy only to crash with steering failure blamed. At Monaco, where Simtek ran just one car, Brabham's rear suspension was broken in a clash with Jean Alesi's Ferrari at the chicane. Tenth in Spain proved to be the best of his season's six classified finishes. Brabham was lucky to escape with a bruised knee when he rolled at Stowe Corner during testing after the British GP. A ninth-place finish in Germany was denied when the clutch failed in the closing laps and he lost a wheel following his second pitstop at Spa-Francorchamps. Brabham had a lighter chassis at Estoril and outqualified both Larrousse-Fords before his quickest times were deleted when he missed the pitlane exit red light. He received a suspended race ban when he collided with Alesi once more while being lapped in Portugal.

After Ratzenberger's death, Andrea Montermini joined for Spain and Canada, but broke his heel and foot when he crashed during practice at Barcelona, forcing Simtek to slim down to a singleton entry in Montréal. Gounon signed an eight-race deal from the French GP and always qualified on the back row. Ninth on his F1 return despite two pitstops without an operational clutch, he finished half of his races before the money ran out. Domenico Schiattarella replaced Gounon at Jerez and finished last. Tom Kristensen was offered the last two races but the underqualified Taki Inoue bought the seat for Suzuka, where he started last and crashed after three laps at the back. Schiattarella returned in Adelaide only to retire with a gear selection issue.

PACIFIC GRAND PRIX

A championship-winning team owner in every category (Formula Ford 1600, FF2000, F3 and F3000) since forming Pacific Racing in 1984, Keith Wiggins confirmed F1 ambitions in June 1992 with Paul Brown (ex-Chevron, Zakspeed and March) named as technical director on 2 November. Established as a separate company, Pacific Grand Prix agreed an engine deal with Ilmor and signed Michael Bartels as lead driver for 1993. Reynard's Ian Dawson was appointed as team manager but promised monies did not materialise so Wiggins had to postpone graduation by a year.

The team took over Reynard's two-year-old stillborn F1 car and the resulting Pacific PR01-Ilmor was unveiled at the team's factory in

Thetford, Norfolk in a low-key press call on 15 October 1993, Brown having completed the design. As Rory Byrne had led the original Reynard project, it was unsurprising that the PR01 resembled a Benetton with high nose and low-slung front wing attached by twin supports, and there was pull-rod suspension with inboard coil springs and dampers. Reynard Composites was responsible for the carbon-fibre monocoque. When a low nose was introduced at the European GP, *Autosport* noted that the cars were 'no longer looking like Benettons as well as failing to go like them'.

Heini Mader prepared the old-specification Ilmor V10 engines, which lacked power. There was a spate of failures that the respected preparation expert blamed on an installation problem. The sequential six-speed gearbox was manual and mounted transversely with Reynard casing and Hewland internals.

Bertrand Gachot, who had won the 1985 British FF1600 and 1986 FF2000 titles with Pacific, invested in the project and was announced as lead driver for 1994. Paul Belmondo was preferred to Philippe Adams as Gachot's team-mate when the official F1 entry list was published on 21 January, the Frenchman in a position to commit his budget when it mattered. British F3 runner-up Oliver Gavin was named test driver in the New Year. Gearbox modifications delayed testing until 17 February, when all three drivers tried the PR01 at Snetterton. Money was in short supply and the £10 million budget target Wiggins had set was not reached. Without testing or development, the team began the season with just 18 staff.

The Pacific-Ilmors were the slowest cars of 1994 and regularly did not qualify, handicapped by aerodynamic drag and disappointing

Paul Belmondo, Pacific PR01-Ilmor (Spanish GP)

straight-line speed. The cars flexed at the rear end and attempts to eradicate this before the Canadian GP with strengthened engine mounts and gearbox casing did not succeed. Gachot qualified for five of the opening six races but retired on each occasion. He hit Olivier Beretta's Larrousse-Ford on lap two of the Brazilian GP and suffered mechanical failures thereafter. Belmondo only made the field in Monaco and Spain. He was lapped after eight laps in Monte Carlo and eventual withdrew when he lost feeling in his right leg. The Frenchman was last when he spun out of the Spanish GP on lap three. The Pacific-Ilmors were a double DNQ at the Pacific GP in April and neither qualified from the French GP on. Gachot celebrated after another qualifying failure in Australia. 'Today is a great day,' he told the press, 'because I will never have to drive the Pacific PR01 again!'

Bertrand Gachot, Pacific PR01-Ilmor (Pacific GP)

DRIVER PERFORMANCE

DRIVER	CAR–ENGINE	BR	PAC	RSM	MC	E	CDN	F	GB	D	H	B	I	P	EU	J	AUS
Philippe Adams	Lotus 109-Mugen	–	–	–	–	–	–	–	–	–	–	26 R	–	25 16	–	–	–
Michele Alboreto	Minardi M193B-Ford	22 R	15 R	15 R	12 6	14 R	–	–	–	–	–	–	–	–	–	–	–
	Minardi M194-Ford	–	–	–	–	–	18 11	21 R	16 R	23 R	20 7	18 9	22 R	19 13	20 14	21 R	16 R
Jean Alesi	Ferrari 412T1	3 3	–	–	5 5	6 4	2 3	–	–	–	–	–	–	–	–	–	–
	Ferrari 412T1B	–	–	–	–	–	–	4 R	4 2	2 R	13 R	5 R	1 R	5 R	16 10	7 3	8 6
Philippe Alliot	McLaren MP4/9-Peugeot	–	–	–	–	–	–	–	–	–	14 R	–	–	–	–	–	–
	Larrousse LH94-Ford	–	–	–	–	–	–	–	–	–	19 R	–	–	–	–	–	–
Rubens Barrichello	Jordan 194-Hart	14 4	8 3	NT DNP	15 R	5 R	6 7	7 R	6 4	10 R	10 R	1 R	16 4	8 4	5 12	10 R	5 4
Paul Belmondo	Pacific PR01-Ilmor	NT DNQ	28 DNQ	27 DNQ	24 R	26 R	27 DNQ	28 DNQ	28 DNQ	27 DNQ	28 DNQ	28 DNQ	28 DNQ	28 DNQ	28 DNQ	28 DNQ	27 DNQ
Olivier Beretta	Larrousse LH94-Ford	23 R	21 R	22 R	18 8	17 DNS	22 R	25 R	24 14	24 7	25 9	–	–	–	–	–	–
Gerhard Berger	Ferrari 412T1	17 R	5 2	3 R	3 3	7 R	3 4	–	–	–	–	–	–	–	–	–	–
	Ferrari 412T1B	–	–	–	–	–	–	5 3	3 R	1 1	4 12	11 R	2 2	1 R	6 5	11 R	11 2
Éric Bernard	Ligier JS39B-Renault	20 R	18 10	17 12	21 R	20 8	24 13	15 R	23 13	14 3	18 10	16 10	12 7	21 10	–	–	–
	Lotus 109-Mugen	–	–	–	–	–	–	–	–	–	–	–	–	22 18	–	–	–
Mark Blundell	Tyrrell 022-Yamaha	12 R	12 R	12 9	10 R	11 3	13 10	17 10	11 R	7 R	11 5	12 5	21 R	12 R	14 13	13 R	13 R
David Brabham	Simtek S941-Ford	26 12	25 R	24 R	22 R	24 10	25 14	24 R	25 15	25 R	23 11	21 R	26 R	24 R	23 R	24 12	24 R
Martin Brundle	McLaren MP4/9-Peugeot	18 R	6 R	13 8	8 2	8 R	12 R	12 R	9 R	13 R	6 4	13 R	15 5	7 6	15 R	9 R	9 3
Érik Comas	Larrousse LH94-Ford	13 9	16 6	18 R	13 10	16 R	21 R	20 R	22 R	22 6	21 8	22 R	24 8	22 R	24 R	22 9	–
David Coulthard	Williams FW16-Renault	–	–	–	–	9 R	5 5	–	7 5	–	–	–	–	–	–	–	–
	Williams FW16B-Renault	–	–	–	–	–	–	–	–	6 R FL	3 R	7 4	5 6	3 2 FL	–	–	–
Yannick Dalmas	Larrousse LH94-Ford	–	–	–	–	–	–	–	–	–	–	–	23 R	23 14	–	–	–
Andrea de Cesaris	Jordan 194-Hart	–	–	–	20 R	14 4	–	–	–	–	–	–	–	–	–	–	–
	Sauber C13-Mercedes-Benz	–	–	–	–	14 R	11 6	17 R	18 R	17 R	15 R	8 R	17 R	18 R	–	–	–
Jean-Denis Délétraz	Larrousse LH94-Ford	–	–	–	–	–	–	–	–	–	–	–	–	–	–	–	25 R
Christian Fittipaldi	Footwork FA15-Ford	11 R	9 4	16 R	6 R	21 R	16 DSQ	18 8	19 9	17 4	16 14	24 R	19 R	11 8	19 17	18 8	19 8
Heinz-Harald Frentzen	Sauber C13-Mercedes-Benz	5 R	11 5	7 7	NT DNP	12 R	10 R	10 4	20 7	9 R	8 R	9 R	11 R	9 R	4 6	3 6	10 7
Bertrand Gachot	Pacific PR01-Ilmor	25 R	27 DNQ	25 R	23 R	25 R	26 R	27 DNQ	27 DNQ	28 DNQ	27 DNQ	27 DNQ	27 DNQ	27 DNQ	27 DNQ	27 DNQ	28 DNQ
Jean-Marc Gounon	Simtek S941-Ford	–	–	–	–	–	–	26 9	26 16	26 R	26 R	25 11	25 R	26 15	–	–	–
Mika Häkkinen	McLaren MP4/9-Peugeot	8 R	4 R	8 3	2 R	3 R	8 R	9 R	5 3	8 R	–	8 2	7 3	4 3	9 3	8 7	4 12
Johnny Herbert	Lotus 107C-Mugen	21 7	23 7	19 10	16 R	–	–	–	–	–	–	–	–	–	–	–	–
	Lotus 109-Mugen	–	–	–	–	22 R	17 8	19 7	21 11	15 R	24 R	20 12	4 R	20 11	–	–	–
	Ligier JS39B-Renault	–	–	–	–	–	–	–	–	–	–	–	–	–	7 8	–	–
	Benetton B194-Ford	–	–	–	–	–	–	–	–	–	–	–	–	–	–	5 R	7 R
Damon Hill	Williams FW16-Renault	4 2	3 R	4 6 FL	4 R	2 1	4 2	2 1 FL	1 1 FL	–	–	–	–	–	–	–	–
	Williams FW16B-Renault	–	–	–	–	–	–	–	–	3 8	2 2	3 1 FL	3 1 FL	2 1	2 2	2 1 FL	3 R
Taki Inoue	Simtek S941-Ford	–	–	–	–	–	–	–	–	–	–	–	–	–	–	26 R	–
Eddie Irvine	Jordan 194-Hart	16 R	–	–	13 6	7 R	6 R	12 DNS	11 R	7 R	4 13	9 R	13 7	10 4	6 5	–	6 R
Ukyo Katayama	Tyrrell 022-Yamaha	10 5	14 R	9 5	11 R	10 R	9 R	14 R	8 6	5 R	5 R	23 R	14 R	6 R	13 7	14 R	15 R
Franck Lagorce	Ligier JS39B-Renault	–	–	–	–	–	–	–	–	–	–	–	–	–	–	20 R	20 11
Pedro Lamy	Lotus 107C-Mugen	24 10	24 8	21 R	19 11	–	–	–	–	–	–	–	–	–	–	–	–
Nicola Larini	Ferrari 412T1	–	7 R	6 2	–	–	–	–	–	–	–	–	–	–	–	–	–
JJ Lehto	Benetton B194-Ford	–	–	5 R	17 7	4 R	20 6	–	–	–	–	–	20 9	14 R	–	–	–
	Sauber C13-Mercedes-Benz	–	–	–	–	–	–	–	–	–	–	–	–	–	–	15 R	17 10
Nigel Mansell	Williams FW16-Renault	–	–	–	–	–	–	2 R	–	–	–	–	–	–	–	–	–
	Williams FW16B-Renault	–	–	–	–	–	–	–	–	–	–	–	–	–	3 R	4 4	1 1
Pierluigi Martini	Minardi M193B-Ford	15 8	17 R	14 R	9 R	18 5	–	–	–	–	–	–	–	–	–	–	–
	Minardi M194-Ford	–	–	–	–	–	15 9	16 5	13 10	20 R	15 R	10 8	18 R	18 12	17 15	16 R	18 9
Andrea Montermini	Simtek S941-Ford	–	–	–	–	27 DNQ	–	–	–	–	–	–	–	–	–	–	–

DRIVER PERFORMANCE CONTINUED

DRIVER	CAR–ENGINE	BR	PAC	RSM	MC	E	CDN	F	GB	D	H	B	I	P	EU	J	AUS
Gianni Morbidelli	Footwork FA15-Ford	6 R	13 R	11 R	7 R	15 R	11 R	22 R	15 R	16 5	19 R	14 6	17 R	16 9	8 11	12 R	21 R
Hideki Noda	Larrousse LH94-Ford	–	–	–	–	–	–	–	–	–	–	–	–	–	25 R	23 R	23 R
Olivier Panis	Ligier JS39B-Renault	19 11	22 9	23 11	20 9	19 7	19 12	13 R	14 12	12 2	9 6	17 7	6 10	15 DSQ	11 9	19 11	12 5
Roland Ratzenberger	Simtek S941-Ford	27 DNQ	26 11	26 DNS	–	–	–	–	–	–	–	–	–	–	–	–	–
Mika Salo	Lotus 109-Mugen	–	–	–	–	–	–	–	–	–	–	–	–	–	–	25 10	22 R
Domenico Schiattarella	Simtek S941-Ford	–	–	–	–	–	–	–	–	–	–	–	–	–	26 19	–	26 R
Michael Schumacher	Benetton B194-Ford	2 1 FL	2 1 FL	2 1	1 1 FL	1 2 FL	1 1 FL	3 1	2 DSQ	4 R	1 1 FL	2 DSQ	–	–	1 1 FL	1 2	2 R FL
Ayrton Senna	Williams FW16-Renault	1 R	1 R	1 R	–	–	–	–	–	–	–	–	–	–	–	–	–
Aguri Suzuki	Jordan 194-Hart	–	20 R	–	–	–	–	–	–	–	–	–	–	–	–	–	–
Jos Verstappen	Benetton B194-Ford	9 R	10 R	–	–	–	–	8 R	10 8	19 R	12 3	6 3	10 R	10 5	12 R	–	–
Karl Wendlinger	Sauber C13-Mercedes-Benz	7 6	19 R	10 4	NT DNP	–	–	–	–	–	–	–	–	–	–	–	–
Alex Zanardi	Lotus 107C-Mugen	–	–	–	–	23 9	23 R	–	–	–	–	–	–	–	–	–	–
	Lotus 109-Mugen	–	–	–	–	–	–	23 R	18 R	21 R	22 13	–	13 R	–	21 16	17 13	14 R

FORMULA 1 RACE WINNERS

ROUND	RACE (CIRCUIT)	DATE	WINNER
1	Grande Prêmio do Brasil (Interlagos)	Mar 27	Michael Schumacher (Benetton B194-Ford)
2	Pacific Grand Prix (Aida)	Apr 17	Michael Schumacher (Benetton B194-Ford)
3	Gran Premio di San Marino (Imola)	May 1	Michael Schumacher (Benetton B194-Ford)
4	Grand Prix de Monaco (Monte Carlo)	May 15	Michael Schumacher (Benetton B194-Ford)
5	Gran Premio Marlboro de España (Catalunya)	May 29	Damon Hill (Williams FW16-Renault)
6	Grand Prix Molson du Canada (Montréal)	Jun 12	Michael Schumacher (Benetton B194-Ford)
7	Grand Prix de France (Magny-Cours)	Jul 3	Michael Schumacher (Benetton B194-Ford)
8	British Grand Prix (Silverstone)	Jul 10	Damon Hill (Williams FW16-Renault)
9	Grosser Mobil 1 Preis von Deutschland (Hockenheim)	Jul 31	Gerhard Berger (Ferrari 412T1B)
10	Marlboro Magyar Nagydíj (Hungaroring)	Aug 14	Michael Schumacher (Benetton B194-Ford)
11	Grand Prix de Belgique (Spa-Francorchamps)	Aug 28	Damon Hill (Williams FW16B-Renault)
12	Pioneer Gran Premio d'Italia (Monza)	Sep 11	Damon Hill (Williams FW16B-Renault)
13	Grande Prêmio de Portugal (Estoril)	Sep 25	Damon Hill (Williams FW16B-Renault)
14	Grand Prix of Europe (Jerez)	Oct 16	Michael Schumacher (Benetton B194-Ford)
15	Fuji Television Japanese Grand Prix (Suzuka)	Nov 6	Damon Hill (Williams FW16B-Renault)
16	Australian Grand Prix (Adelaide)	Nov 13	Nigel Mansell (Williams FW16B-Renault)

CONSTRUCTORS' CHAMPIONSHIP

	CONSTRUCTORS	POINTS
1	Williams-Renault	118
2	Benetton-Ford	103
3	Ferrari	71
4	McLaren-Peugeot	42
5	Jordan-Hart	28
6=	Ligier-Renault	13
	Tyrrell-Yamaha	13
8	Sauber-Mercedes-Benz	12
9	Footwork-Ford	9
10	Minardi-Ford	5
11	Larrousse-Ford	2

DRIVERS' CHAMPIONSHIP

	DRIVERS	POINTS
1	Michael Schumacher	92
2	Damon Hill	91
3	Gerhard Berger	41
4	Mika Häkkinen	26
5	Jean Alesi	24
6	Rubens Barrichello	19
7	Martin Brundle	16
8	David Coulthard	14
9	Nigel Mansell	13
10	Jos Verstappen	10
11	Olivier Panis	9
12	Mark Blundell	8
13	Heinz-Harald Frentzen	7
14=	Christian Fittipaldi	6
	Eddie Irvine	6
	Nicola Larini	6
17	Ukyo Katayama	5
18=	Éric Bernard	4
	Andrea de Cesaris	4
	Pierluigi Martini	4
	Karl Wendlinger	4
22	Gianni Morbidelli	3
23	Érik Comas	2
24=	Michele Alboreto	1
	JJ Lehto	1

Michael Schumacher with the spoils of victory after retaining the World Championship

1995
MICHAEL SCHUMACHER IN A CLASS OF HIS OWN

Damon Hill and Michael Schumacher go wheel-to-wheel at Spa-Francorchamps

Johnny Herbert celebrates a popular victory at Silverstone

Acknowledged as the class of the field, Michael Schumacher successfully defended his world title by winning nine races as Benetton claimed its first constructors' title. Damon Hill again finished runner-up but their rivalry resulted in several incidents that led to a rebuke from Bernie Ecclestone and prompted the FIA to clarify (and reclarify) overtaking rules. The FIA prizegiving in Monte Carlo was postponed due to strikes and was eventually held at the Royal Automobile Club on London's Pall Mall on 19 January 1996.

The FIA sought to reduce power and downforce to slow down the cars and a return to 3-litre normally aspirated engines was ratified by the Motor Sport World Council on 2 June 1994. With pump fuel now mandatory, engine ram effect was to be reduced by exit vents in the airbox although this was abandoned after the first race. The air under the car was disturbed by a 50mm 'stepped flat bottom' and cornering speeds were further reduced by restricting the front wings and lowering the rear aerofoil. Cockpit dimensions were increased with increased lateral protection and side-impact crash tests were introduced. 'Fly-by-wire' throttles were relegalised as they were thought to be safer than conventional cables. The FIA demanded that teams provided their computer source codes and fuel samples before the season. The former prompted the teams to question the confidentiality of that information and the latter immediately caused controversy with the top two cars disqualified from the Brazilian GP. That decision was reversed two weeks later although neither Benetton nor Williams received constructors' points for that race. The majority wanted refuelling to be banned after Jos Verstappen's 1994 German GP pit fire but Ferrari resisted change. New sensors introduced to detect jumped starts caused a rash of 10sec stop-go penalties with the system's sensitivity called into question.

The new minimum weight limit of 595kg (1311.7lb) included car and driver. Cars were weighed at the opening race and Schumacher himself tipped the scales at 77kg (8kg heavier than in 1994), prompting suspicions that he was wearing ballast at the weigh-in.

A return to Argentina was to have been the opening race on 12 March but it was delayed by four weeks so renovations to the Autódromo Oscar Gálvez could be completed. Interlagos signed a new six-year deal although the mayor of São Paulo's suggestion that it should be restored to its original five-mile layout sadly did not happen. The Pacific GP at Aida was scheduled for 16 April but was postponed by six months when an earthquake devasted the surrounding area. Imola was originally omitted until a chicane was built at Tamburello. Spa-Francorchamps became a permanent facility when a new motorway was built in 1995 and the chicane that had emasculated Eau Rouge was removed. Hockenheim signed a new deal until 2000 and the European GP moved to the Nürburgring. The Italian GP remained in doubt while the

David Coulthard scored his first F1 victory in Portugal

need to fell 185 trees to extend the run-off at Monza's Curva Grande and first Lesmo was debated, so the reserve race in Hungary was confirmed as a championship round. Despite resistance from the teams, the calendar was stretched to 17 races for only the second time when the Italian GP was confirmed in July.

Jean and José Alesi return from the Canadian Grand Prix

Michael Schumacher, Benetton B195-Renault (Monaco GP)

MILD SEVEN BENETTON RENAULT

World Champion Michael Schumacher remained with Benetton for a final season but rumours in December that Nigel Mansell would be his team-mate were denied by Alessandro Benetton. Minority shareholder and still director of engineering at both teams, Tom Walkinshaw concentrated on running the sister Ligier operation as he pursued ambitions to own an F1 concern outright. Benetton's three-year engine contract with Renault Sport was confirmed on 23 August 1994.

Treviso was chosen to launch the Benetton B195-Renault on 30 January with Johnny Herbert finally announced as second driver. Jos Verstappen was loaned to Simtek and replaced as test driver by Emmanuel Collard. Ross Brawn and Rory Byrne evolved their championship-winning design, although the change of engine supplier and need to continue development throughout 1994 led to some compromises on the new car.

The rear bodywork was lowered and the RS07 engine's exhausts initially blew into the steeply angled central diffuser. These were modified for the German GP with exhausts repositioned to either side. The airbox was an ungainly 'stepped' affair at the start of the season due to the mandatory exit vents. Performance was affected more than for rivals when that rule was suddenly reversed before the Argentinian GP and a more shapely solution with enlarged inlet was introduced at the French GP. Benetton followed Williams's lead and enclosed the

upper rear wishbones, although the driveshafts remained exposed. A three-pedal layout was retained while the smaller fuel tank helped maintain weight distribution despite the longer engine, which had Magneti Marelli electronics.

Pat Symonds worked with Schumacher once more while Tim Wright arrived from Sauber as Herbert's race engineer. Nick Wirth joined in a research-and-development capacity when his Simtek concern closed down. Mild Seven extended its title sponsorship until the end of 1996.

Cold weather marred the Silverstone shakedown and problems with the gearbox's hydraulic pump restricted mileage at the first group test at Jerez. With handling initially a problem, Schumacher was out-qualified by Damon Hill at Interlagos following following a heavy crash on Friday when a steering pin failed at Ferradura. However, he took control of the race once Hill had retired and beat David Coulthard by 8.060sec only for both to be disqualified on a fuel technicality five hours after the race. They were reinstated two weeks later although neither Benetton nor Williams received constructors' points. Herbert started fourth in Brazil (after missing the first session while Schumacher's steering failure was investigated) and crashed into Aguri Suzuki's Ligier-Mugen to end a disappointing race.

Schumacher started and finished third in Argentina, where Herbert recovered from a poor qualifying performance to claim fourth. With improved handling following a test at Jerez, Schumacher took pole at

Imola although the weekend was otherwise a disaster. He crashed at the Variante Alta on Saturday and then led the early wet laps only to crash after changing to slicks. Starting on dry tyres, Herbert spun on his second lap and was lapped twice on the way to seventh at the finish.

With the team under pressure in the press and its lead driver criticised by FIA president Max Mosley, Schumacher converted another pole position into an emphatic lights-to-flag victory in Barcelona. After Hill experienced a gearbox problem on the last lap, Herbert inherited second to record his first F1 podium. The drivers surprised Williams by one-stopping in Monaco, Schumacher beating Hill by 35.447sec and Herbert finishing fourth.

Benetton brought a new front wing to Canada, where Schumacher was denied certain victory by a glitch in the gearbox electronics that required an unscheduled stop. For the French GP, the B195 had an upgraded RS07B engine, new airbox and vanes under the front wing. Having qualified second, Schumacher complained of being 'brake-tested' as he fought Hill for the lead, then eased to another clear victory after passing his rival in the first round of pitstops. Herbert jumped the start in both Canada and France only to be eliminated in both cases – by Mika Häkkinen on lap one in Montréal and by Jean Alesi at Magny-Cours – before he could serve his penalty.

The Schumacher/Hill rivalry was intensified by further controversy at Silverstone. Leading due to his one-stop strategy, Schumacher could not prevent the two-stopping Englishman from closing in as the race reached its critical phase. With victory seemingly his, Hill went for the lead at Priory on lap 48 but they touched and crashed out of the race. Amid rumours that Verstappen was about to replace him, Herbert inherited a popular home victory when Coulthard served a stop-go penalty. Denied pole by just 0.080sec at Hockenheim, Schumacher

took advantage of Hill's second-lap crash to win his first German GP and spark a track invasion, while Herbert finished fourth. Recently married to Corinna Betsch and announced by Ferrari for 1996, Schumacher was delayed by a refuelling issue in Hungary and lost second in the closing stages when his fuel pump failed. He could only qualify 16th in Belgium after crashing on Saturday, but he charged through the field to win, although his strong-arm driving tactics against Hill earned a one-race suspended ban. Fourth in Germany and Hungary, Herbert led the opening lap at Spa-Francorchamps but faded to seventh following a couple of spins.

Frustrated by being released for 1996, Herbert won the Italian GP after Schumacher and Hill clashed again and the Ferraris failed. Second in Portugal, Schumacher scored a superb victory at the Nürburgring to all but secure the title. He pitted three times in changeable conditions before charging back and snatching victory from Alesi with three laps to go. There had been more contact with Hill as they disputed third position on lap 18, without rebuke from rival or governing body this time. Herbert was fifth after changing his damaged nose assembly.

The rear suspension was revised for the Pacific GP, where Schumacher stopped three times in beating the Williams-Renaults to clinch the World Championship. Pole position at Suzuka was his first since Canada and he led a Benetton-Renault 1–3 to confirm the constructors' title. The season ended with Benetton's only double DNF following a troubled weekend in Adelaide, where Schumacher hit Alesi's Ferrari and Herbert suffered a late driveshaft failure that cost him second in the race and third in the standings.

The Benetton B195 was generally slower than the Williams FW17, certainly over a single lap, but it was more reliable and brilliance on the pit wall and in the cockpit eventually told.

Johnny Herbert, Benetton B195-Renault (Italian GP)

ROTHMANS WILLIAMS RENAULT

Williams extended its successful engine deal with Renault until the end of 1997 despite arch-rivals Benetton switching to the French manufacturer. There was much debate during the winter about Williams's driver line-up for 1995. The team exercised options on Damon Hill (on 19 September) and David Coulthard (15 November) while a big-money offer to retain Nigel Mansell was considered. Hill used his new status as a title contender to negotiate a pay rise and was confirmed before Christmas. Eager to continue his promising race career, Coulthard signed with McLaren only for the Contracts' Recognition Board to rule in Williams's favour on 14 December and he was confirmed in the New Year. Quick in tests at Paul Ricard and Estoril, F3000 champion Jean-Christophe Boullion was preferred to Emmanuel Collard as test driver. Team manager Ian Harrison moved to Williams's new British Touring Car Championship operation with chief mechanic Dickie Stanford his replacement.

Hill first tried the new 3-litre Renault V10 at Paul Ricard on 21 December and the Williams FW17 was launched at the team's conference centre on 21 February with technical director Patrick Head stressing that this was very much Adrian Newey's car. The most striking aspect of this evolution of the FW16 was the switch to a high nose as pioneered by John Barnard at Benetton, just as Barnard opted for a low nose on his Ferrari 412T2. The front wing was supported by two pillars and was slightly raised in the centre. The rear diffuser was larger than before while the anhedral lower rear wing was shallower and less pronounced. Push-rod suspension was retained with torsion bars at the front and coil springs to the rear. The shrouds at the back that enclosed the top wishbones and driveshafts, the transverse gearbox and the traditional three-pedal layout all remained. The reduced 30-gallon fuel tank meant the 76-degree V10 engine could be mounted forward with driving position further reclined. A third front damper was used from the German GP to control roll.

The shakedown at a cold Silverstone on 23 February was followed by warmer weeks at Estoril where the Williams drivers were half a second slower than Michael Schumacher and the new Benetton-Renault. Despite that, the FW17 was the class of the field at the Brazilian GP, where Hill and Coulthard qualified 1–3. Hill took the lead in the first pitstops only for a rear push-rod to fail. After Coulthard finished second on the road, he was disqualified on a fuel technicality but reinstated two weeks later, albeit without constructors' points. At a very wet Buenos Aires he claimed his maiden pole position but lost the lead when his engine faltered and then an electrical failure ended his challenge. Second on the grid, Hill passed Schumacher on lap 11 to score his first victory of 1995.

They only qualified on row two at Imola but Hill won again to take the points lead while Coulthard was fourth after a robust battle with Alesi and a 10sec stop-go penalty for speeding in the pitlane. With Schumacher dominant in Barcelona following a change of tyre construction, Hill lost second place (and the points lead) when his hydraulics failed on the last lap, and at Monaco he finished a distant second. Coulthard was running third in both races when his gearbox failed; he was using the spare car in Monte Carlo after being involved in the first-corner accident that stopped the race.

The Canadian GP was a disaster as Coulthard spun on lap two and Hill, who was slower in the race than Schumacher and both Ferraris, suffered another hydraulic failure. Upgraded engines and a new diffuser were fitted for Magny-Cours, where Hill qualified on pole for the third year in a row. However, he was again soundly beaten by Schumacher in the race and Coulthard, who was recovering from an operation due to tonsillitis, only just held onto third from Martin Brundle's Ligier-Mugen.

With the British GP pitstops completed, Hill was closing on the one-stopping Schumacher when he attempted to take the lead at Priory only for the rivals to collide yet again. Hill was roundly criticised for the incident in the British newspapers and within his team, although stories that Frank Williams called him 'a prat' were denied. Coulthard took the lead ahead of Johnny Herbert's Benetton-Renault but dropped to third when he served another stop-go penalty for speeding in the pitlane, his electronic speed limiter *hors de combat*.

Hill took pole in Germany only to crash at the first corner of lap two with a worn driveshaft joint a possible factor; Coulthard finished second. Hill bounced back in Hungary by leading a Williams-Renault 1–2 in both qualifying and the race. Having just been released for 1996, Coulthard charged from fifth on the grid in Belgium to take the lead on lap six and pull away at will. However, he had been hit from behind at the start and his gearbox lost oil. Only eighth on the grid after spinning at Stavelot during qualifying, Hill made five pitstops in the changeable conditions and was penalised for speeding in the pitlane before taking

Damon Hill, Williams FW17-Renault (Canadian GP)

David Coulthard, Williams FW17-Renault (German GP)

Damon Hill, Williams FW17B-Renault (Australian GP)

second from Brundle on the last lap at Les Combes.

Williams had protested Schumacher's tactics while defending the lead in Belgium and Hill crashed into the second-placed Schumacher at the Roggia chicane during the Italian GP. Coulthard qualified on pole only to spin at the Ascari chicane on the parade lap. A first-lap red flag meant the Scot took up his place on the grid and he led until a wheel bearing failed. Coulthard's FW17 finally held together at Estoril where he three-stopped to convert another pole into a resounding maiden F1 victory; Hill chose to stop twice and finished third as his title hopes faded.

Newey's upgraded FW17B was tested at Silverstone and Imola before being taken to Portugal. The rear end was modified with revised floor and narrower new gearbox to facilitate substantial revisions to the diffuser. The exhausts exited above the diffuser and the rear suspension shrouds were removed so that wide-angled upper wishbones and new suspension geometry could be fitted. Both cars were converted back to the normal specification for the race when a fault in the gearbox was found after qualifying.

Racing the FW17B for the rest of the year, Coulthard led a front-row lock-out at the Nürburgring but spun on his way to the grid. He took the spare car as a consequence and finished second. Following more contact with Schumacher, Hill had to change his front wing when he ran over a kerb as he disputed the lead with Alesi. Needing victory to maintain lingering title aspirations, Hill was closing on Coulthard when he crashed.

At Aida, Coulthard recorded his fourth successive pole position

and finished second after being delayed in traffic. Facing rumours that he would be replaced by Heinz-Harald Frentzen in 1996, Hill started the Pacific GP from the front row but could only finish third following a slow stop. They struggled for set-up at Suzuka and crashed out of the race on successive laps. 'Not one of our better days,' was Head's assessment. Coulthard out-dragged pole-winner Hill at the start of the Australian GP and led until he crashed in the pitlane as he made his first stop. Hill dominated the race thereafter and won by two full laps as rivals retired.

Hill and Coulthard were second and third in the drivers' World Championship. Williams-Renault finished as runners-up but it had been a disappointing campaign by the team's exacting standards.

David Coulthard, Williams FW17B-Renault (Australian GP)

Jean Alesi, Ferrari 412T2 (Italian GP)

SCUDERIA FERRARI

John Barnard and his 38 design staff at Shalford abandoned the high nose he had preferred since 1991 when the Ferrari 412T2 was launched at Maranello on 6 February. The clutch was operated by the left thumb so there were just two pedals. The front suspension 'knife-edge' joints for the lower wishbones were replaced by conventional uni-ball pick-up points as Barnard apparently bowed to internal politics. Torsion bars were fitted front and rear while carbon-fibre was used for the front push-rods and bellhousing. The shorter sidepods introduced on the 412T1B were retained to accommodate elaborate bargeboards that channelled airflow. The exhausts originally blew through the diffuser, although these were soon moved. While development of a new V10 began, the 3-litre iteration of Ferrari's 75-degree V12 drove through a six-speed transverse gearbox as before. Use of steel rather than cast iron for the block saved 20lb. As fuel capacity was reduced to 125 litres, the engine could sit 4in further forward. The best-looking car of 1995, the 412T2 had good grip, was easy to drive and had great handling.

Gerhard Berger contemplated retirement before agreeing a one-year extension in June 1994 to remain as Jean Alesi's team-mate. Benetton aerodynamicist Willem Toet joined and Giorgio Ascanelli, who had been Berger's race engineer at both Ferrari and McLaren, returned as senior race engineer.

There were early setbacks as Berger crashed on the 412T2's shakedown at Fiorano and again when the front suspension failed at Estoril. This was strengthened for the Brazilian GP, where Berger and Alesi qualified on the third row and diced before finishing a lapped third and fifth respectively. The Austrian celebrated victory five hours after the race when Michael Schumacher and David Coulthard were excluded on a fuel technicality although both were later reinstated. The engine had an improved power curve in Argentina but they only qualified sixth and eighth. Alesi spun at the start and called it a 'gift from God' when he saw the red flag. He took the spare car for the restart and drove a storming race to finish second; Berger was sixth after a poor start and delayed pitstop.

Both drivers had their company cars (a Ferrari 512 for Berger and F355 for Alesi) stolen from their hotels on the Friday night before the San Marino GP. On the track, Damon Hill broke *tifosi* hearts by beating Alesi and Berger into second and third respectively. The Austrian started from the front row, was first to change to dry tyres, set the fastest lap and led for 11 laps only to stall at his second pitstop. In Spain, Alesi qualified second and held that position until his engine failed. Berger started and finished third after excessive tyre wear forced him to switch to a three-stop strategy. Alesi was mighty in Monaco but left empty-handed. He was quickest in first qualifying, the warm-up and race, but hydraulic failure on Saturday restricted him to fifth on the grid. Running second, he was lapping Martin Brundle when the Ligier-Mugen spun at Tabac with both cars eliminated. Both Ferraris had been involved in the start-line accident and took spare cars for the restart; Berger finished third.

Montréal suited Ferrari's top-end power but the red cars still gave best to Renault-powered rivals. On his 31st birthday, Alesi started fifth and inherited the lead when Schumacher pitted with an electrical issue. The emotional Frenchman reeled off the remaining 12 laps to finally win a GP at the 91st attempt. Berger crashed into Brundle at the hairpin after an overly optimistic lunge.

That victory gave Ferrari the lead in the constructors' standings with fast circuits to come. A title challenge was expected but Renault took a major step forward at Magny-Cours. No match for Benetton or Williams thereafter, Alesi was fifth in France, despite knocking Johnny Herbert into a third-lap spin at the Adelaide hairpin, while a 53sec pitstop ended Berger's chances. Alesi made a storming start to run second at Silverstone although it took the Schumacher/Hill crash and David Coulthard's stop-go penalty for him to finish in that position. Having lost his front-left wheel after pitting in England, Berger was third in Germany (despite a stop-go for jumping the start) and Hungary (understeer). Alesi suffered whiplash in a huge qualifying shunt at the Hungaroring's Turn 10 and retired from both races with engine issues.

Berger beat the rain to lead a Ferrari qualifying 1–2 in Belgium, where neither car made it to half distance, Alesi's suspension having failed while in an early lead. There was further disappointment in the Italian GP: the Ferraris were on course for a 1–2 finish when Alesi's camera fell off and smashed Berger's front suspension and wing; after that, Alesi cruised onwards and was eight laps from the finish when mechanical failure (the right-rear wheel bearing this time) robbed him of victory at Monza for the

second year in a row. Sporting a special helmet design in Portugal that had been decided by a newspaper competition, Berger beat his team-mate into fourth by 0.550sec after adopting different strategies. Alesi refused team orders to let the three-stopping Berger past and was fined when he criticised Jean Todt in a post-race interview live on Italian television.

With both drivers leaving at the end of the season, another round of internal politics gripped Ferrari. Luca di Montezemolo's adviser since he returned to the *Scuderia*, Niki Lauda was fired and then reinstated, and Berger criticised press officer Giancarlo Baccini at the Nürburgring. Despite a damp track, Ferrari started the European GP on slick tyres and Alesi came within three laps of an unexpected victory. Having already forced Damon Hill onto the grass as he defended his lead, Alesi could not hold off Schumacher due to his worn tyres and the need to save fuel.

Lapped at Aida, the Ferraris were better suited to Suzuka, where Alesi qualified second only for both drivers to jump the start. Alesi charged back through the field after his stop-go penalty and a subsequent spin to run second before his transmission failed. Engine problems accounted for Berger at that race and the next, while Alesi was eliminated from the Australian GP when hit by Schumacher as they disputed second place.

At launch, Luca di Montezemolo had said 'I'd be happy with three wins' in 1995 so a single victory, and a lucky one at that, represented another underwhelming campaign. Third in the constructors' championship once more, there was major change for 1996, most notably in the cockpit.

Gerhard Berger, Ferrari 412T2 (German GP)

MARLBORO McLAREN MERCEDES

McLaren's fourth different engine partner in four seasons was confirmed when a five-year agreement with Mercedes-Benz was announced in Stuttgart on 28 October 1994. Rumours of a $20 million offer for former Mercedes junior Michael Schumacher had already been denied and Ron Dennis used the occasion to say 'there are four obvious candidates to join Mika [Häkkinen] next year – Heinz-Harald Frentzen, David Coulthard, Rubens Barrichello and Martin Brundle.' Coulthard signed for McLaren but the Contracts' Recognition Board ruled in Williams's favour on 14 December. Frentzen and Barrichello did not move and Brundle was allowed to join Ligier in January.

Overlooked by Williams, Nigel Mansell met Dennis and Mercedes representatives on 13 January and agreed a one-year agreement after lengthy negotiations. *Motor Sport* called it 'one of the sport's worst-kept secrets within living memory' when the former champion was confirmed at London's Hilton Hotel on 3 February. Steve Nichols returned as Head of Vehicle Engineering in July.

A fortnight after the driver announcement, the innovative if ugly McLaren MP4/10-Mercedes was revealed to the press at London's Science Museum. Chief designer Neil Oatley and aerodynamicist Henri Durand sought to regain some lost downforce with a Benetton-style raised nose, radical undertray and, most noticeably, additional wing mounted on the airbox. Carbon-fibre was used extensively in the push-rod suspension, which had inboard Bilstein dampers and springs, although Penske dampers were used from Canada. The central

wing was dropped from Canada apart from at high-downforce Hungaroring, Nürburgring and Aida. An aero upgrade in France included revised sidepods and central diffuser but nothing could save the MP4/10 from being an ungainly disappointment.

Urged by McLaren, Ilmor built an entirely new V10 engine rather than modify its existing 3.5-litre unit. The resulting Mercedes-Benz FO110 was narrow at the base and had a wider 75-degree vee-angle with hydraulic pump located between the cylinder banks. The twin-pedal and hand-clutch arrangement from the MP4/9 was retained, as was the transverse gearbox. McLaren ended its long-standing deal with Shell in favour of Mobil 1 as its new fuel partner.

The problems started at the first group test at Estoril when the drivers, particularly Mansell, struggled to fit in the cockpit. 'It's like doing the London Marathon in a pair of running shoes that are too small,' Häkkinen told *Autosport*. Mansell departed early as poor front-end traction and handling issues left Häkkinen two seconds off the pace. Initial power delivery was unsatisfactory, arriving 'all at once' rather than progressively.

Former test driver Mark Blundell signed a surprise deal on 15 March and McLaren announced two days later that he was replacing Mansell for the South American races. There was new rear suspension in Brazil, where both drivers qualified in the top ten and scored points. Häkkinen was a strong fourth despite a slow pitstop with Blundell sixth on the MP4/10's better-than-expected début. The rear wing was revised and front suspension tweaked for Argentina,

Mika Häkkinen, McLaren MP4/10-Mercedes (Brazilian GP)

Mika Häkkinen, McLaren MP4/10B-Mercedes (Hungarian GP)

Mark Blundell, McLaren MP4/10-Mercedes (Canadian GP)

Mark Blundell, McLaren MP4/10B-Mercedes (Japanese GP)

Nigel Mansell, McLaren MP4/10B-Mercedes (Spanish GP)

where both retired early, Häkkinen having chopped across Eddie Irvine's Jordan-Peugeot at the restart.

McLaren took just 33 days to redesign and build the MP4/10B with cockpit widened by a couple of inches to accommodate Mansell at the San Marino GP, where Häkkinen was 1.174sec quicker in qualifying. After both started on slicks, the Finn finished fifth despite a refuelling problem, but Mansell ran into Gianni Morbidelli and then Eddie Irvine, damaging the nose and puncturing a tyre respectively, and ended up two laps down in tenth place. After 18 laps of the Spanish GP, he parked his 'undriveable' car and walked away from the sport. This time there was no going back.

Blundell returned for the next two races and finished fifth in Monaco. Rumours that McLaren and Mercedes wanted Frentzen to replace him were denied and the Englishman continued for the rest of the season, albeit on a race-by-race basis. He battled Barrichello for fourth at Silverstone before they collided on the penultimate lap, Blundell puncturing a rear tyre and limping home in another fifth place. Häkkinen retired from seven out of eight mid-season races although his departure in Canada, where he used an upgraded engine, was due to an ill-fated first-lap overtaking attempt on Johnny Herbert rather than another mechanical gremlin. Silverstone saw another engine upgrade and the Finn ran fourth before it failed. Of some consolation was victory at Le Mans with an F1 GTR, which made McLaren the only constructor to win the F1 World Championship, Indianapolis 500 and the Le Mans 24 Hours.

McLaren challenged for podium finishes in Germany and Hungary but suffered engine failures at both races. New rear suspension with

pick-up points on a modified gearbox casing helped Häkkinen qualify third in Belgium only to spin at La Source on the second lap, while Blundell finished fifth despite four pitstops. Häkkinen led during the pitstops in Italy and benefited when five cars ahead of him retired to claim second, scoring his first points since Imola. At a time when Alain Prost returned in a test and development role to spark inevitable rumours of another comeback, the soon-to-be-married Blundell completed a double-points score by finishing fourth.

The cars were revised to MP4/10C guise for Estoril with an aero upgrade that included a vee-shaped diffuser, revised rear suspension, taller uprights and another new gearbox. Qualifying was a disaster so Häkkinen's car was converted back to B specification for the race. Blundell drove the spare with MP4/10B floor and C-specification

Jan Magnussen, McLaren MP4/10B-Mercedes (Pacific GP)

Mark Blundell, McLaren MP4/10C-Mercedes (European GP)

bodywork, although neither solution worked. The MP4/10C was used at the Nürburgring, where the drivers started on slicks despite the wet track; Blundell was passed by Jean-Denis Délétraz's Pacific-Ford before crashing and eighth-placed Häkkinen was lapped twice.

When Häkkinen missed the Pacific GP due to appendicitis, test driver Jan Magnussen, who had recovered from breaking his right leg in a scooter accident, did a solid job as stand-in. McLaren reverted to the MP4/10B for the rest of the season and finished ninth (Blundell) and tenth (Magnussen) at Aida. The MP4/10B was better suited to Suzuka's sweeping corners and the returning Häkkinen started third and finished second, while Blundell came home seventh after starting last following a 175mph qualifying accident at 130R. The year nearly ended in tragedy in Australia when Häkkinen broke his skull and required a trackside tracheotomy after crashing at 125mph on Friday. Blundell signed off his F1 career by finishing fourth but it had been a disappointing first season with Mercedes.

Mika Häkkinen, McLaren MP4/10C-Mercedes (European GP)

LIGIER GITANES BLONDES

The Flavio Briatore-controlled Ligier team reorganised with Benetton director of engineering Tom Walkinshaw as team principal and Bruno Michel general manager. Cesare Fiorio's contract as sporting director was not renewed after the French GP and Walkinshaw reappointed TWR USA faithfuls Tony Dowe (operations director) and Ian Reed (engineer). Frank Dernie agreed a new contract as technical director. Walkinshaw wanted to own an F1 team outright but plans to acquire Ligier would come to nothing.

With Renault engines diverted to Benetton, Ligier signed an exclusive two-year deal with Mugen on 30 November for its new 3-litre 72-degree V10 units. That prompted unsuccessful legal action from Minardi, which claimed to have a prior verbal agreement with the Japanese manufacturer. Olivier Panis remained under contract and a limited programme for Aguri Suzuki was part of the Mugen package. Walkinshaw favourite Martin Brundle agreed to share the number 25 Ligier-Mugen with Suzuki. Franck Lagorce continued as test and reserve driver. The lucrative deals with Gitanes, Elf and LOTO were all in their final year so 1995 was crucial to the team's future. There was valid concern in France that Walkinshaw wanted to relocate to England and former driver Jacques Laffite was hired in a PR role to reinforce Ligier's French identity.

The late engine deal meant round-the-clock work to complete the Ligier JS41-Mugen, which Brundle first drove at Magny-Cours on 2 March. 'Fabriqué en France' was emblazoned on the back of the rear wing at that test but many questioned whether it was just a blue Benetton, such was its similarity to the B195. The aero packages were very similar at launch and some components were shared, such as Benetton's six-speed transverse gearbox. Crucially, the FIA ruled that the Benetton and Ligier were different designs because, then as

Olivier Panis, Ligier JS41-Mugen (Monaco GP)

now, teams had to design and manufacture their their own cars. A driver-activated electronic handbrake was fitted after early-season jumped starts and a 'fly-by-wire' throttle was introduced. The JS41 handled well but oversteer prevailed when wet.

Ligier-Mugen were on the pace from the start of practice for the Brazilian GP so Panis was disappointed to only qualify tenth and crash at the start. He was seventh in Argentina (following a heavy shunt on Friday) and a gripless ninth at Imola after a poor start. Panis's team-mate thus far, Suzuki collided with an irate Mika Salo while being lapped in Argentina and finished outside the points at Interlagos and Imola.

Brundle replaced Suzuki for the Spanish GP, where the JS41 had revised front suspension and a new floor. The experienced Englishman immediately outqualified Panis only for a refuelling error to deny a top-six finish so it was Panis who scored Ligier's first point of 1995 by snatching sixth from Rubens Barrichello's ailing Jordan-

Peugeot on the last lap. Brundle was an excellent eighth on the grid in Monaco but hopes of another strong afternoon were dashed when both drivers were adjudged to have jumped the start. Brundle was recovering from his subsequent stop-go penalty when he spun in front of second-placed Jean Alesi at Tabac, causing the elimination of both cars and vocal criticism from the Ferrari star. Having crashed in Casino Square, Panis was the quicker Ligier driver in Canada and finished fourth, while Brundle lost fifth when Berger ran into him with eight laps to go.

Ligier celebrated its 300th GP start at its home circuit of Magny-Cours, where both qualified in the top ten. Sixth on the grid, Panis received another stop-go penalty for anticipating the lights and faded to ninth. Brundle used a three-stop strategy to harry David Coulthard's Williams-Renault to the line, finishing fourth just 0.467sec behind. The JS41 handled badly at Silverstone although Panis recovered from his third stop-go penalty in four races to claim

Aguri Suzuki, Ligier JS41-Mugen (Brazilian GP)

Martin Brundle, Ligier JS41-Mugen (Hungarian GP)

fourth. Using power steering for the first time, Brundle spun out of seventh at Luffield on lap 17.

Brundle stood down for the German GP and, in a foretaste of his future, worked for the BBC that weekend, six years after first sharing the commentary box with Murray Walker at the 1989 Belgian GP. In his first race since April, Suzuki crashed twice on Friday and recovered from a left-rear puncture to finish sixth. Panis was seventh and on course for a possible podium when sidelined by a water leak after 13 laps. The Ligier-Mugens were again quick in Hungary and qualified in the top ten. A late engine failure denied Brundle points and, as in Spain, Panis took sixth on the last lap from a hamstrung Barrichello.

Mugen introduced an engine upgrade at Spa-Francorchamps, where Panis qualified and finished ninth after being delayed in the pits. Brundle adopted a one-stop strategy and lay second on the last lap until, powerless to defend on worn tyres, Damon Hill passed him at Les Combes – but he still delivered Mugen's first podium. Neither finished in Italy and Panis was an early spinner at the last two European races. The Frenchman also managed to jump the start at both getaways in Portugal despite Ligier's electric handbrake. Brundle finished eighth in Portugal and seventh at the Nürburgring.

Back for the Japanese races, Suzuki spun out of the Pacific GP and broke a rib when he crashed at the Esses during qualifying at Suzuka, an injury that denied him a final GP start and the opportunity to announce his F1 retirement at his home race. Under pressure following a disappointing run of form, Panis qualified well at both circuits and finished fifth at Suzuka. Brundle crashed into Mark Blundell's McLaren-Mercedes during the Australian GP while Panis survived a race of attrition to finish second, his smoking engine somehow lasting the distance. That result was enough to vault Ligier-Mugen from seventh to fifth in the final constructors' standings.

TOTAL JORDAN PEUGEOT

In search of a works engine partner for 1995, Eddie Jordan met with Ford representatives before an exclusive three-year deal with Peugeot was announced in Paris on 25 October 1994. 'This is the single most important decision I have had to take in 25 years in motorsport,' EJ told the press. 'I believe this partnership offers us the best long-term possibility for success.' Total oil had long been associated with Peugeot and replaced Sasol as title partner alongside a patchwork of associate sponsors.

Rubens Barrichello remained under contract despite McLaren's overt interest and Eddie Irvine was confirmed in November in an unchanged line-up. Kelvin Burt and Laurent Aïello, who had just won the French *Supertourisme* title for Peugeot, were retained as test drivers but plans to operate a separate test team did not happen. Steve Nichols departed before Christmas while Tim Holloway left Robin Herd's design agency and joined as Barrichello's race engineer following the collapse of Larrousse.

A month to the day after the engine announcement, Irvine completed eight laps of Silverstone in the interim 3.5-litre Jordan 194-Peugeot test hack. The definitive Jordan 195-Peugeot was the first 1995 car to be revealed after it was completed in the early hours of 27 January. Designer Gary Anderson began work on a Hart-powered car and adapted the rear-end for a Ford unit even before the deal was struck with Peugeot. He was the latest to adopt a two-pedal layout to facilitate left-foot braking, with the clutch operated by paddles behind the steering wheel. Work in Southampton University's wind tunnel resulted in long sidepods with very narrow front inlets that wrapped above the stepped flat bottom. The throttle was 'fly-by-wire' and the new seven-speed hydraulic-electric sequential semi-automatic gearbox longitudinal. The push-rods were carbon-

Eddie Irvine, Jordan 195-Peugeot (Japanese GP)

fibre while Anderson used 'knife-edge' front pick-ups similar to those on the Ferrari 412T1. At the front, the upper wishbones were also carbon-fibre but steel was used at the bottom. The dampers were manufactured in-house for the first time and fuel capacity was reduced to 27 gallons. Peugeot's 3-litre V10 (designated A10E) had a new cylinder head, crankshaft and injectors.

Clutch problems at the Jerez group test were solved and only Michael Schumacher's Benetton-Renault was quicker than Irvine at Estoril. Although tricky to set up, the car regularly challenged for points only for questionable reliability to restrict Jordan-Peugeot to sixth overall in the constructors' standings.

The Brazilian GP was a 'weekend to forget' with gearbox hydraulics problematic all weekend and responsible for a double retirement. A handful over the bumps at Interlagos, the Jordan-Peugeots had modified gearbox actuators at Buenos Aires. Irvine outqualified Barrichello at the first six races and started the Argentinian GP from a promising fourth only for both to blow engines in the race. A complicated new diffuser with exhausts blowing under the centre was introduced at Imola. This generated downforce but at a cost to stability. Irvine finished eighth after an eventful race that included a front-wing change following contact with Nigel Mansell and stopping in the Ligier pit by mistake during another pitstop. Barrichello suffered more gearbox woes.

New bargeboards improved front-end traction in Spain, where the impressive Irvine qualified sixth and finished fifth. Barrichello was sixth as he entered the last lap but lost his throttle and was passed by Olivier Panis before the line. Both retired in Monaco – Irvine sixth when a wheel failed – but they enjoyed a welcome upturn in fortune in Montréal, where they qualified inside the top ten and survived a race of attrition and the need to save fuel to finish second (Barrichello) and third (Irvine).

Modification of Barrichello's pedals for the Canadian GP restored some confidence sapped by Irvine's pace and at Magny-Cours he outqualified his team-mate for the first time in 1995. The Brazilian started fifth, received a 10sec stop-go for jumping the start and finished sixth, while Irvine came home ninth after stalling at his pitstop. The Irishman retired early from the British GP, which brought *déjà vu* for Barrichello a year after colliding with Mika Häkkinen at the final corner. Following a fine recovery drive after another jumped-start penalty, he fought Mark Blundell's McLaren for fourth place in the closing stages only to collide, this time with two laps to go.

Jordan used the Evo2 Peugeot V10 to fill row three at Hockenheim although successive engine failures denied Barrichello possible podium finishes at that race and the next, his Hungarian heartbreak coming on the very last corner of the race when third. Irvine also lost strong results at both races when slowed by a throttle issue in Germany and stopped by a broken clutch at the Hungaroring.

Barrichello was sixth at Spa-Francorchamps following an unscheduled stop but Irvine, having duelled with Michael Schumacher in the early laps, was engulfed in flames when refuelling went wrong at his stop. Ligier and McLaren crews helped extinguish the fireball and thankfully no one was injured. With new wings and airbox to optimise straight-line speed, Barrichello qualified sixth at Monza

Rubens Barrichello, Jordan 195-Peugeot (Italian GP)

and led a lap during the pitstops only for both to retire on another afternoon of attrition. They lacked race pace in Portugal but both scored points in changeable conditions at the Nürburgring. While 'flu-ridden Barrichello finished fourth, Irvine – who followed the announcement of his move to Ferrari by splitting the red cars on the grid with fifth spot – had a messy race to sixth place: Johnny Herbert's Benetton-Renault hit him at the Veedol Chicane, then Irvine spun all on his own before being passed by Herbert with two laps to go.

Irvine qualified sixth at Aida only for his race to be ruined by a clout from Damon Hill and a puncture; Barrichello's engine failed. Irvine was fourth in the Japanese GP despite Barrichello crashing into him at the chicane and both retired from the final race in Adelaide, an understeering Barrichello having crashed behind the pits.

RED BULL SAUBER FORD

Just weeks after losing Mercedes-Benz engines, Sauber signed a two-year agreement with Cosworth and Ford for the latest Zetec-R. This marriage of convenience between jilted partners began badly but eventually showed some improvement. The highly rated Heinz-Harald Frentzen remained despite interest from McLaren while Christian Fittipaldi held talks before Karl Wendlinger's return from injury was confirmed on 18 January. That was following a successful pre-Christmas test at Barcelona where Kris Nissen, Pedro Lamy and new reserve driver Norberto Fontana also ran.

Frentzen gave the Sauber C14-Ford its shakedown at Paul Ricard on 6 February with the car finished in Ford blue. The latest offering from chief designer Leo Ress, with Heinz Zoellner responsible for the aerodynamics, had a drooping nose with shorter sidepods and initially Sauber was alone in blowing exhausts from above the central diffuser. The 75-degree Zetec-R V8 was mounted further forward due to the shorter 30-gallon fuel tank. The six-speed semi-automatic gearbox was now transverse, although the C14's weight distribution was compromised by its 2,999cc engine being larger and heavier

Heinz-Harald Frentzen, Sauber C14-Ford (Belgian GP)

than the previous 3.5-litre Mercedes. Expectations wavered during a challenging winter that included Frentzen writing off a monocoque at Estoril. As the car had fundamental flaws, a major redesign was introduced at the San Marino GP that included a raised nose, longer bargeboards and a weight-saving magnesium gearbox casing.

At least the precarious financial outlook that contributed to Mercedes's departure was eased by title sponsorship from Red Bull, which also took a shareholding in the team. Dietrich Mateschitz's energy drink brand was expanding distribution outside Austria and he declared his commitment was 'for much longer than two or three years'. The livery was unveiled at the Geneva motor show on 7 March and Petronas joined as secondary sponsor from the Monaco GP. André de Cortanze remained as technical director, Max Welti returned in May as a director and Minardi aerodynamicist René Hilhorst arrived in August.

Problems began from the moment the cars took to the track at Interlagos, where the bumps exposed the C14's lack of mechanical grip and excessive understeer, and both cars retired from the midfield. Frentzen scored points at the next two races, albeit lapped twice in Argentina and once at Imola. Wendlinger eliminated both Pacific-Fords and himself at the start in Argentina and hit Gerhard Berger's Ferrari at Imola before a wheel jammed during a pitstop. There was a new undertray and diffuser (with exhausts now blowing through it) for Spain but optimism expressed after the Imola test proved misplaced.

Struggling for confidence and massively outqualified by Frentzen thus far (by an average 2.840sec), Wendlinger was rested with Williams reserve Jean-Christophe Boullion his replacement. Monaco was a nightmare that began with worrying echoes of 1994 when the Frenchman crashed at the harbourside chicane on Thursday,

Karl Wendlinger, Sauber C14-Ford (Argentinian GP)

Jean-Christophe Boullion, Sauber C14-Ford (Monaco GP)

thankfully without injury. Frentzen slipped to 14th on the grid after crashing on Saturday morning, received a 10sec stop-go penalty for jumping the start and salvaged sixth despite ending the race stuck in fourth gear. Boullion was heading for eighth when Gianni Morbidelli ran into the back of him at Rascasse. They retired from the Canadian GP with Boullion stranded in the gravel. Frentzen was a distant tenth in France and sixth at Silverstone following a one-stop strategy. Boullion was nowhere in France and ninth at Silverstone after racing among the customer Minardi-Fords.

Cosworth introduced a high-revving engine for the German GP and progress was evident, the slow-starting Boullion finishing fifth to score his first points. Having recovered from illness, an exhausted Frentzen was also fifth in Hungary, just 0.513sec from a surprise podium. The German started the last seven races inside the top ten and finished fourth in Belgium (when he stayed on wet tyres and the rain returned) and third in Italy. Boullion came from the Monza pitlane to snatch sixth on the penultimate lap to secure Sauber-Ford's only double score of 1995.

Rapidly emerging as a future star, Frentzen qualified fifth in Portugal but stalled before the start. From the back, he charged through the field to claim sixth and another point. Both retired following incidents during the European GP and Boullion spun out of the Pacific GP on his last appearance. Wendlinger returned

for the last two races as Sauber assessed him for 1996 and at Suzuka he finished tenth after hitting Gianni Morbidelli on lap one. After crashing heavily at Adelaide's chicane during first practice, Wendlinger was sidelined on Saturday by a severe headache and withdrew from the race after eight laps – and with that his F1 career was over. Frentzen finished both Japanese races in the top ten and qualified an excellent sixth in Australia, where he ran as high as second only for the gearbox to fail.

FOOTWORK HART

Money was tight in Milton Keynes as the Arrows-run Footwork team contemplated another season in the F1 midfield. Ownership of the team had reverted to Jackie Oliver, who was very late in deciding drivers and engine. Ford and Peugeot agreed exclusive deals elsewhere so Oliver signed with Brian Hart on 30 January. The Harlow-based tuner had drawn a V10 before finalising a 72-degree V8 layout for his low-budget 3-litre engine. Rumours that it would be badged as a Daewoo proved false.

Gianni Morbidelli shook down the Footwork FA16-Hart at Silverstone on 14 March, less than a week before freight left for Brazil's opening race. Already announced by BMW for Italian *Superturismo*, he signed an initial eight-race contract to lead

Gianni Morbidelli, Footwork FA16-Hart (Pacific GP)

Taki Inoue, Footwork FA16-Hart (Portuguese GP)

Footwork's challenge in parallel. Oliver confirmed his team-mate at that time and was frank in telling *Autosport* why: 'I think Taki Inoue is willing to admit that he got the opportunity with us because he's going to help us with our budget.' Logos for the Japanese Unimat Group and Hype energy drink joined Sasol lubricants on the car although Footwork Arrows lacked the funds to develop car or engine sufficiently.

Regulation and engine change led Alan Jenkins to devise a totally new design, with Dominic Smith (ex-Ferrari Design and Development) responsible for the aerodynamics. There was a clear family resemblance with slender raised nose and twin pillars supporting the front wing. The triple-spring front suspension introduced during 1994 was replicated at the rear by season's end.

Jenkins switched to a longitudinal Xtrac gearbox that was mounted in front of the rear axle. This allowed the upper rear wishbones to be raised to improve exhaust-blowing to the central diffuser. An additional rear wing was fitted at high-downforce circuits. Team manager John Wickham left to run Audi's British Touring Car Championship team and Alan Harrison, his deputy and one of those to defect from Shadow when Arrows was formed in November 1977, was promoted in his place.

Despite just two days of pre-season testing, 1995 began with promise as Morbidelli challenged Jean Alesi's Ferrari for fifth in Brazil before retiring with dirt in the fuel-pressure valve. His electrics failed in Argentina and Morbidelli qualified 11th at Imola, the team's best grid position of the season, only to puncture a rear tyre when Nigel Mansell's McLaren-Mercedes hit him at the start. With his continued participation in doubt due to financial considerations, Morbidelli recorded four consecutive finishes that included sixth after a race of attrition in Canada.

Having easily outqualified Inoue at every race thus far, Morbidelli was replaced by test driver Max Papis from the British GP. Winner of the 1994 Barcelona F3000 race, Papis disappointed in his seven races for Footwork Arrows and was even outqualified twice by Inoue. He crashed in the pitlane during the British GP, spun on slick tyres at a wet Spa-Francorchamps, and was eliminated in the start-line shunt at Estoril. Papis finished only twice, seventh at Monza after Jean-Christophe Boullion's Sauber passed him with two laps to go, then 12th in the European GP despite a 10sec stop-go penalty for a grid infringement.

Max Papis, Footwork FA16-Hart (Portuguese GP)

Mika Salo, Tyrrell 023-Yamaha (Italian GP)

Papis flew to Japan for the Pacific GP and was frustrated to learn the day before practice that he was no longer required as Morbidelli was returning. Revisions to the FA16 for the last three races included modified uprights and front suspension, but a new floor and exhausts proved troublesome and were only fitted intermittently, including in Australia. Both cars suffered engine failures in Aida and Morbidelli was knocked off by Karl Wendlinger at the first corner of the Japanese GP. The Italian qualified an improved 13th in Adelaide and enjoyed 'the most fantastic day in my F1 career' to finish a shock third despite being lapped twice.

Little was expected of Inoue apart from his financial contribution, and his season is best remembered for two bizarre incidents with course cars. In Monaco he was being towed back to the pits on Saturday when Jean Ragnotti crashed the Renault Maxi Clio safety car into him in the Swimming Pool section; as the Footwork-Hart rolled, Inoue, having undone his seat belts, fell head-first onto the track. In Hungary, he was attending to a small fire on his FA16 when a course car ran him over. Thankfully, he was not badly harmed in either incident. The team was fined $20,000 in Argentina when Friday qualifying was red-flagged because Inoue's spun car was left in gear and could not be moved. Twelve retirements included another engine fire in Spain and accidents at Buenos Aires, Imola, Magny-Cours, Silverstone and Adelaide. He finished five times with a best result of eighth in Italy, just 2.501sec behind Papis.

NOKIA TYRRELL YAMAHA

Optimism prevailed following a promising 1994 campaign that included Mark Blundell's podium finish in Spain. A two-year extension was agreed with Yamaha and Ukyo Katayama re-signed for a third season. In need of a title partner, Mika Salo signed an option in January and Blundell was released, although confirmation of Salo was delayed by sponsorship negotiations and Lotus owner David Hunt's assertion that the Finn was committed to Lotus as part of his 1994 deal. Without an F1 entry, Hunt formed an alliance with Pacific Grand Prix and claimed that Salo should therefore drive for Pacific Team Lotus. The Contracts' Recognition Board eventually found in Tyrrell's favour.

Ukyo Katayama, Tyrrell 023-Yamaha (Belgian GP)

The Tyrrell 023-Yamaha was launched on 13 February at London's Design Museum, where Harvey Postlethwaite suggested that mechanical grip rather than aerodynamics was crucial now that downforce had been reduced. Key to that quest was innovative 'Hydrolink' suspension – a system of hydraulics rather than springs to control pitch and ride height – developed by Postlethwaite in conjunction with Jean-Claude Migeot's Fondmetal Technologies. This system was initially fitted just at the front but was added to the rear from Monaco, only to be discarded entirely after a back-to-back test before the German GP, the car having proved difficult to sort with lack of traction and excessive wheelspin. The transverse gearbox was retained and 'fly-by-wire' throttle tried in practice at Monza. There were initial engine problems with the air-pressure valve a weakness and 'all-or-nothing' power delivery.

Mike Gascoyne was deputy technical director and Nigel Beresford returned following two years engineering Paul Tracy's Penske Indycar. Having impressed in testing at Estoril, Salo eventually signed on 15 March after finalising sponsorship from Nokia mobile phones. British Touring Car Champion Gabriele Tarquini was retained as reserve. The predominantly blue livery at the first two races was replaced by a blue-and-white style at Imola. Rupert Manwaring switched to the commercial department and was replaced as team manager by his deputy, Steve Nielsen.

Tyrrell was another outfit to show initial pace only to fade. Salo completed his first full F1 season with reputation enhanced, despite visiting several circuits for the first time, but Katayama struggled. The Finn was running third in Brazil when cramp in his left arm caused him to spin, and he finished seventh driving virtually one-handed. With improved ergonomics, Salo qualified seventh in Argentina – Tyrrell's only top-ten start of 1995 – and would have finished fifth but for contact while lapping Aguri Suzuki; the drivers had to be restrained when they returned to the pits.

The Tyrrell 023's disappointing slow-speed traction was highlighted by Imola's third-gear chicanes and that weekend faulty camshafts caused four engine failures. Salo finished four of the next five races without scoring as Tyrrell struggled in the midfield. That included being awarded seventh in Canada after he lost that position on the last lap when he parked his car rather than run over spectators who had invaded the track. Following a sinus operation,

he was 15th in France (lapped three times) and came home eighth in changeable conditions at Spa-Francorchamps. At Monza, he recovered from a first-lap spin at the Ascari chicane and a slow fuel stop to claim fifth. That first points score was followed by further top-six finishes in Japan (sixth) and Australia (fifth). However, ninth in the constructors' standings did not match Tyrrell-Yamaha's pre-season expectations.

Katayama only finished four times as the promise of 1994 faded like a distant mirage. As Maurice Hamilton wrote in *Autocourse*, 'Ukyo disappointed even more than the car he was struggling to drive.' He was eighth in Buenos Aires, seventh of eight finishers at Hockenheim, last in Italy and 14th at Aida. There were too many incidents, most notably a start-line collision with Luca Badoer in Portugal that sent his Tyrrell-Yamaha somersaulting. As Katayama missed the next race, the Nürburgring, on doctor's orders, Tarquini stood in and came 14th as both Tyrrell-Yamahas finished outside the points.

MINARDI SCUDERIA ITALIA

Minardi Scuderia Italia faced an uncertain winter when an extended engine deal with Mugen was diverted to Ligier in November so its engine was listed as 'TBA' when the entry list was published on 27 January. A late agreement was reached to take over the Ford ED V8s, Magneto Marelli electronics and Xtrac gearboxes originally intended for the stillborn DAMS GD01. Cosworth's 1995 customer engine resembled the old HB with air valves, shorter stroke and revised internals. It was available at a reputed cost of £4 million a season.

The Minardi M195 was a nimble if underpowered machine. It had a raised nose and low front wing that originally curved downwards in the centre, to be replaced by a more conventional arrangement at the Spanish GP. Honeycomb was used for the side impact structures ahead of extremely short sidepods and tightly packaged 'coke-bottle' rear. The upper wishbones at the rear were mounted high to facilitate clean airflow to the diffuser. Fuel capacity was reduced to 24 gallons and wheelbase by 1½in. An additional high central wing was tried during practice in Brazil, attached to the rear aerofoil. Carbon-fibre shrouds for the upper front wishbones were introduced in Argentina with both top and bottom enclosed from Imola. New exhausts boosted power in Monaco with revised wings and bargeboards on the cars in Canada. There were changes in the design office during the season when technical director Aldo Costa joined Ferrari in July and aerodynamicist René Hilhorst moved to Sauber a month later.

Luca Badoer replaced DTM-bound Michele Alboreto as Pierluigi Martini's team-mate at the start of 1995 with Italian F3 Champion Giancarlo Fisichella now test driver. Gearbox issues restricted pre-season mileage and persisted throughout the campaign. Even worse, legal wrangles overshadowed the first half of the year due to fallout from the Ligier/Mugen deal and monies owed to Grand Prix Engineering for its 1993 engines. That came to a head at Magny-Cours when a court injunction prevented Minardi from running on Friday. The team raced with a bailiff in the pits and settlement was reached with Flavio Briatore, who controlled both Ligier and GPE, on the day after the race.

Both drivers suffered gearbox failures in Brazil (Martini on the

Gabriele Tarquini, Tyrrell 023-Yamaha (European GP)

Pierluigi Martini, Minardi M195-Ford (Monaco GP)

parade lap) and crashed in Argentina (Badoer at the original start). They were lapped four times but finished at Imola, where both drew criticism from the leaders for blocking. Badoer retired from the next two races, having lost seventh in Monaco when he tapped the barrier in Casino Square with ten laps to go, and finished eighth in Canada. Seventh in Monaco, Martini had a throttle-cable breakage in Canada after serving two stop-go penalties for jumping the start and holding up faster cars.

Retirees in France and Germany, both scored top-ten finishes at Silverstone with Martini seventh once more. Pedro Lamy had recovered from injuries sustained in 1994 and, unable to agree a deal with Footwork, brought much-needed funds to replace long-time

Minardi favourite Martini from the Hungarian GP.

Using the additional central wing at a track that masked Minardi's lack of horsepower, Badoer and Lamy finished eighth and ninth in Hungary. Badoer crashed out of the Belgian and Italian GPs and was involved in the Portuguese start-line shunt that sent Ukyo Katayama's Tyrrell-Yamaha cartwheeling. He took the spare for the restart and finished four consecutive races without troubling the scorers. An electronic problem on the grid sidelined him in Australia. Lamy outqualified his team-mate 5–3 and finished six of his eight races with Minardi. He delivered Minardi's only point of 1995 when sixth at the final race in Adelaide. That clinched tenth in the constructors' standings and vital FOCA travel money.

Luca Badoer, Minardi M195-Ford (German GP)

Pedro Lamy, Minardi M195-Ford (Belgian GP)

Giovanni Lavaggi, Pacific PR02-Ford (Italian GP)

Jean-Denis Délétraz, Pacific PR02-Ford (Portuguese GP)

PACIFIC TEAM LOTUS

Keith Wiggins's struggling team survived into its second season with the Norwegian beverage company Ursus remaining as major sponsor and Japanese businessman Ko Gotoh adding investment. Agreement was reached with new Team Lotus brand owner David Hunt so the cars carried the famous old badge although Hunt admitted 'we haven't contributed anything other than green paint'.

The renamed Pacific Team Lotus switched from Ilmor V10 engines to air-valve 3-litre Ford ED V8s. Chief designer Frank Coppuck began work early and the totally new Pacific PR02 passed its crash test at Cranfield on 9 January. However, the build process was slow because manufacture of 90 per cent of the parts was outsourced. It was six weeks before the completed PR02 was

launched at London's Strand Theatre and shakedown at Snetterton came only on 17 March. The eight laps completed that day was Pacific's only testing before Brazil.

This was a largely conventional car with push-rod suspension, semi-automatic transverse gearbox and a carbon-fibre monocoque from Advanced Composites. However, aerodynamicist Dave Watson opted for a distinctive 'platypus' nose following work in the wind tunnel at MIRA. The fuel capacity was less than 20 gallons so one-stop races were impossible. The PR02 was an improvement but reliability was wanting with gearbox hydraulics a recurring issue. At least Pacific normally beat newcomers Forti in the race to avoid being 1995's slowest team.

Shareholder Bertrand Gachot remained although he stepped

Andrea Montermini, Pacific PR02-Ford (Australian GP)

Bertrand Gachot, Pacific PR02-Ford (Argentinian GP)

aside for paying drivers in the second half of another cash-strapped campaign. Hunt claimed the services of Mika Salo through his ownership of Team Lotus but the Contracts' Recognition Board did not agree. Paul Belmondo, Pedro Lamy and Emmanuel Collard were considered for the second seat before Andrea Montermini was announced for the first half of the season.

The Italian finished ninth in Brazil despite a loose undertray to register Pacific's first F1 finish. Both cars were eliminated by Karl Wendlinger's Sauber-Ford on the opening lap in Argentina and by hydraulic leaks at Imola, where Montermini raced five days after keyhole surgery to remove his appendix. Gachot retired from the first seven GPs, in Spain due to a fire during his second refuelling stop. Montermini had another hydraulic problem on the parade lap that day and was disqualified at Monaco for not serving a jumped-start stop-go penalty within three laps.

New front suspension and aero upgrades arrived for Magny-Cours, where the drivers complained of understeer. Gachot finally recorded a finish when 12th and last at Silverstone before making way for tardy gentleman driver Giovanni Lavaggi, who signed a four-race contract despite questionable qualifications for a super licence. With Pacific now limiting engine mileage to save money, Lavaggi retired on each occasion, including early spins in Hungary and at Monza. Montermini was the last man still circulating at the finish in Germany and Hungary when eighth and 12th respectively. Former engine supplier Mader served an injunction before the

Belgian GP as Pacific's future appeared bleak.

Jean-Denis Délétraz's Swiss Francs replaced Lavaggi's Lire for the last two races of the European season. He withdrew with cramp after 16 laps in Portugal and was last at the Nürburgring when 3.157sec slower than his team-mate in qualifying. Montermini started from the pitlane in Portugal and raced among the slower Footworks and Minardis before another gearbox problem. A brief highlight – passing Mika Häkkinen's slick-shod McLaren-Peugeot on the wet second lap of the Nürburgring – turned sour during a botched pitstop: he departed before completion of refuelling, breaking refueller Paul Summerfield's leg and then running dry after three laps.

Little-known Japanese F3000 driver Katsumi Yamamoto tested at Silverstone on 11 October with a view to replacing Montermini from the Pacific GP but his licence application was denied. With Délétraz's tenure at an end, Gachot rejoined Montermini for the last three races but there had been yet more change planned for the final race in Adelaide. Former test driver Oliver Gavin was slated to make his début before a mix-up regarding the new British F3 Champion's licence application rendered his long journey in vain. Montermini retired as normal but Gachot ran at the back throughout to finish eighth in the team's final GP, matching its best result. With unpaid sponsorships and more stringent qualifying rules in 1996, Wiggins withdrew on 4 December, the fourth team to leave F1 within 12 months.

PARMALAT FORTI FORD

Guido Forti had been successful in the junior formulae since guiding Renzo Zorzi to victory in the 1975 Monaco F3 race. Based in Alessandria, Forti Corse won the Italian F3 title on four occasions in the period 1985–89. It had contested the FIA F3000 Championship since 1987, winning nine times thanks to Gianni Morbidelli, Emanuele Naspetti, Andrea Montermini and Olivier Beretta. Forti and business partner Carlo Gancia decided to graduate to F1 in the spring of 1994 and hired ex-Osella engineer Giorgio Stirano to design the Forti FG01. Sergio Rinland contributed on a freelance basis before joining as technical director at the start of the season. That arrangement proved short-lived as Rinland transferred to Keke Rosberg's DTM team after the San Marino GP.

Pedro Diniz, who was managed by Gancia and had driven for the F3000 team since 1993, brought substantial Brazilian sponsorship

Roberto Moreno, Forti FG01-Ford (Italian GP)

and signed a three-year contract. Talks with Andrea Montermini broke down and Roberto Moreno was confirmed on the eve of the season, initially for the opening two races although he remained with the newcomers throughout 1995.

Much of the manufacturing was outsourced, with Belco-Avia responsible for the monocoque, the first of which was completed on 18 January. Ford ED V8s supplied the power and Hewland the six-speed gearbox, the only manual in the field and the last to be used in F1. A semi-automatic unit was finally tried in practice for the Portuguese GP but was not raced. Aerodynamicist Hans Fouche used a wind tunnel in his native South Africa. The FG01 was launched on 31 January in Brazilian yellow, blue and green livery. Parmalat was confirmed as title partner with further sponsorship from Arisco, Sadia, Kaiser beer, Unibanco and Marlboro.

Diniz gave the FG01 its shakedown test at Varano on 20 February before heading to Paul Ricard later that week. Way off the testing pace, the heavy FG01s initially struggled to complete the distance required to be classified as finishers. Diniz was tenth (and last) on début in Brazil and again at Monaco. A new chassis for Diniz at Monaco was 9lb lighter but it was not raced there due to a gearbox issue. More weight was shed by switching to aluminium radiators in Canada and a higher nose was fitted to both cars in France, where Cosworth supplied an upgraded engine. Another new chassis for that race represented a virtual redesign but Diniz crashed into Pierluigi Martini on the opening lap, while Moreno finished 16th (and last). The wheelbase was extended and undertray revised following wind-tunnel testing in Turin and the FG01s outqualified the Pacific-Fords at Silverstone. Three successive double DNFs followed before they finished at the back in Belgium. Having been involved in the first-lap

Pedro Diniz, Forti FG01-Ford (Monaco GP)

shunt at Monza, Moreno could not restart and Diniz finished ninth in the spare car.

They were the last two runners in Portugal, with Moreno stuck in first gear. Diniz led both McLaren-Mercedes during the damp early laps of the European GP only to be lapped five times on the way to 13th. Moreno started that race two laps late due to a flat battery and retired with transmission failure. Former Forti F3000 driver Hideki Noda was refused a super licence so did not replace Moreno for the Japanese races as planned. Last again at Aida, they retired at Suzuka, Moreno stuck in fourth gear this time and Diniz a spinner at the Spoon Curve. Moreno crashed in Australia but Diniz beat Bertrand Gachot's Pacific-Ford to finish seventh.

MTV SIMTEK FORD

After enduring a traumatic début season, Nick Wirth's Simtek soon faced more of F1's harsh realities in 1995. David Brabham moved to the British Touring Car Championship with BMW and Flavio Briatore arranged a late deal for Benetton-contracted Jos Verstappen to gain race experience with Simtek. Domenico 'Mimmo' Schiattarella signed to drive the second car at the first five races with Hideki Noda due to take over from Canada. MTV remained as title sponsor and Noda brought backing from Tenoras.

The Simtek S951-Ford was only unveiled seven days before opening practice for the first race. Designed by Wirth and Paul Crooks, this was an evolution of the original Simtek with low nose, Ford ED engine, Benetton transverse gearbox and 28.5-gallon fuel tank (so one-stop strategies were an option). The elevated pick-up points for the upper front wishbones were replaced by a more conventional layout.

Neither car ran on Friday morning in Brazil for want of on-board fire extinguishers and the rest of the weekend was akin to a test session, both breaking down early in the race. Progress was made in Argentina, where Verstappen qualified 14th and led Gerhard Berger's Ferrari for ten laps, reaching an impressive sixth when the gearbox failed; Schiattarella finished ninth. They retired at Imola and finished outside the top ten in Spain after troubled races. With finance urgently required, Schiattarella was eliminated in the original start of the Monaco GP and further damage was caused when marshals dropped his car; yet another gearbox problem prevented Verstappen taking the restart.

Despite Wirth's entreaties during the Monaco weekend, promised sponsorship failed to materialise, sending Simtek Grand Prix and Simtek Research into administration and closure. The S951 had shown potential but it could not run on thin air.

Domenico Schiattarella, Simtek S951-Ford (Monaco GP)

Jos Verstappen, Simtek S951-Ford (Brazilian GP)

1995 RESULTS

DRIVER PERFORMANCE

DRIVER	CAR–ENGINE	BR	RA	RSM	E	MC	CDN	F	GB	D	H	B	I	P	EU	PAC	J	AUS
Jean Alesi	Ferrari 412T2	[6] 5	[6] **2**	[5] 2	[2] R	[5] R FL	[5] 1	[4] 5	[6] 2	[10] R	[6] R	[2] **R**	[5] **R**	[7] 5	[6] **2**	[4] 5	[2] R	[5] R
Luca Badoer	Minardi M195-Ford	[18] R	[13] R	[20] 14	[21] R	[16] R	[19] 8	[17] 13	[18] 10	[16] R	[12] 8	[19] R	[18] R	[18] 14	[18] 11	[16] 15	[18] 9	[15] DNS
Rubens Barrichello	Jordan 195-Peugeot	[16] R	[10] R	[10] R	[8] 7	[11] R	[9] 2	[5] 6	[9] 11	[5] R	[14] 7	[12] 6	[6] **R**	[8] 11	[11] 4	[11] R	[10] R	[7] R
Gerhard Berger	Ferrari 412T2	[5] 3	[8] 6	[2] 3 FL	[3] 3	[4] 3	[4] R	[7] 12	[4] R	[4] 3	[4] 3	[1] R	[3] **R** FL	[4] 4	[4] R	[5] 4	[5] R	[4] R
Mark Blundell	McLaren MP4/10-Mercedes-Benz	[9] 6	[17] R	—	—	—	—	—	—	—	—	—	—	—	—	—	—	—
	McLaren MP4/10B-Mercedes-Benz	—	—	—	—	[10] 5	[10] R	[13] 11	[10] 5	[8] R	[13] 6	[6] 5	[9] 4	—	—	[10] 9	[24] 7	[10] 4
	McLaren MP4/10B/C-Mercedes-Benz	—	—	—	—	—	—	—	—	—	—	—	[12] 9	—	—	—	—	—
	McLaren MP4/10C-Mercedes-Benz	—	—	—	—	—	—	—	—	—	—	—	—	—	[10] R	—	—	—
Jean-Christophe Boullion	Sauber C14-Ford	—	—	—	—	[19] 8	[18] R	[15] R	[16] 9	[14] 5	[19] 10	[14] 11	[14] 6	[14] 12	[13] R	[15] R	—	—
Martin Brundle	Ligier JS41-Mugen	—	—	—	[11] 9	[8] R	[14] R	[9] 4	[11] R	—	[8] R	[13] 3	[11] R	[9] 8	[12] 7	—	—	[11] R
David Coulthard	Williams FW17-Renault	[3] **2**	[1] **R**	[3] **4**	[4] R	[3] R	[3] R	[3] 3	[3] **3**	[3] **2**	[2] 2	[5] R FL	[1] **R**	[1] **1** FL	—	—	—	—
	Williams FW17B-Renault	—	—	—	—	—	—	—	—	—	—	—	—	—	[1] **3**	[1] **2**	[6] R	[2] **R**
Jean-Denis Délétraz	Pacific PR02-Ford	—	—	—	—	—	—	—	—	—	—	—	—	[24] R	[24] 15	—	—	—
Pedro Diniz	Forti FG01-Ford	[25] 10	[25] NC	[26] NC	[26] R	[22] 10	[24] R	[23] R	[20] R	[21] R	[23] R	[24] 13	[23] 9	[22] 16	[22] 13	[21] 17	[21] R	[21] 7
Heinz-Harald Frentzen	Sauber C14-Ford	[14] R	[9] 5	[14] 6	[12] 8	[14] 6	[12] R	[12] 10	[12] 6	[11] R	[11] 5	[10] 4	[10] 3	[5] 6	[8] R	[8] 7	[8] 8	[6] R
Bertrand Gachot	Pacific PR02-Ford	[20] R	[23] R	[22] R	[24] R	[21] R	[20] R	[22] R	[21] 12	—	—	—	—	—	—	[24] R	[23] R	[23] 8
Mika Häkkinen	McLaren MP4/10-Mercedes-Benz	[7] 4	[5] R	[6] 5	[9] R	—	—	—	—	—	—	—	—	—	—	—	—	—
	McLaren MP4/10B-Mercedes-Benz	—	—	—	—	[6] R	[7] R	[8] 7	[8] R	[7] R	[5] R	[3] R	[7] **2**	[13] R	—	—	[3] **2**	[24] DNS
	McLaren MP4/10C-Mercedes-Benz	—	—	—	—	—	—	—	—	—	—	—	—	[9] 8	—	—	—	—
Johnny Herbert	Benetton B195-Renault	[4] R	[11] 4	[8] 7	[7] 2	[7] 4	[6] R	[10] R	[5] **1**	[9] 4	[9] 4	[4] **7**	[8] **1**	[6] 7	[7] 5	[7] 6	[9] 3	[8] R
Damon Hill	Williams FW17-Renault	[1] **R**	[2] **1**	[4] **1**	[5] 4 FL	[1] **2**	[2] R	[1] **2**	[1] R FL	[1] **R**	[1] **1** FL	[8] **2**	[4] R	[2] **3**	—	—	—	—
	Williams FW17B-Renault	—	—	—	—	—	—	—	—	—	—	—	—	—	[2] R	[2] **3**	[4] **R**	[1] **1** FL
Taki Inoue	Footwork FA16-Hart	[21] R	[26] R	[19] R	[18] R	[26] R	[22] 9	[18] R	[19] R	[19] R	[18] R	[18] 12	[20] 8	[19] 15	[21] R	[20] R	[19] 12	[19] R
Eddie Irvine	Jordan 195-Peugeot	[8] R	[4] R	[7] 8	[6] 5	[9] R	[8] 3	[11] 9	[7] R	[6] 9	[7] 13	[7] R	[12] R	[10] 10	[5] 6	[6] 11	[7] 4	[9] R
Ukyo Katayama	Tyrrell 023-Yamaha	[11] R	[15] 8	[15] R	[17] R	[15] R	[16] R	[19] R	[14] R	[17] 7	[17] R	[15] R	[17] 10	[16] R	—	[17] 14	[14] R	[16] R
Pedro Lamy	Minardi M195-Ford	—	—	—	—	—	—	—	—	—	[15] 9	[17] 10	[19] R	[17] R	[16] 9	[14] 13	[17] 11	[17] 6
Giovanni Lavaggi	Pacific PR02-Ford	—	—	—	—	—	—	—	—	—	[24] R	[24] R	[23] R	[24] R	—	—	—	—
Jan Magnussen	McLaren MP4/10B-Mercedes-Benz	—	—	—	—	—	—	—	—	—	—	—	—	—	—	[12] 10	—	—
Nigel Mansell	McLaren MP4/10B-Mercedes-Benz	—	—	[9] 10	[10] R	—	—	—	—	—	—	—	—	—	—	—	—	—
Pierluigi Martini	Minardi M195-Ford	[17] DNS	[16] R	[18] 12	[19] 14	[18] 7	[17] R	[20] R	[15] 7	[20] R	—	—	—	—	—	—	—	—
Andrea Montermini	Pacific PR02-Ford	[22] 9	[22] R	[24] R	[23] DNS	[25] DSQ	[21] R	[21] NC	[24] R	[23] 8	[22] 12	[21] R	[21] R	[21] R	[20] R	[23] R	[20] R	[22] R
Gianni Morbidelli	Footwork FA16-Hart	[13] R	[12] R	[11] 13	[14] 11	[13] 9	[13] 6	[16] 14	—	—	—	—	—	—	—	[19] R	[15] R	[13] 3
Roberto Moreno	Forti FG01-Ford	[23] R	[24] NC	[25] NC	[25] R	[24] R	[23] R	[24] 16	[22] R	[22] R	[21] R	[22] 14	[22] R	[23] 17	[23] R	[22] 16	[22] R	[20] R
Olivier Panis	Ligier JS41-Mugen	[10] R	[18] 7	[12] 9	[15] 6	[12] R	[11] 4	[6] 8	[13] 4	[12] R	[10] 6	[9] 9	[13] R	[11] R	[14] R	[9] 8	[11] 5	[12] 2
Max Papis	Footwork FA16-Hart	—	—	—	—	—	—	—	[17] R	[15] R	[20] R	[20] R	[15] 7	[20] R	[17] 12	—	—	—
Mika Salo	Tyrrell 023-Yamaha	[12] 7	[7] R	[13] R	[13] 10	[17] R	[15] 7	[14] 15	[23] 8	[13] R	[16] R	[11] 8	[16] 5	[15] 13	[15] 10	[18] 12	[12] 6	[14] 5
Domenico Schiattarella	Simtek S951-Ford	[26] R	[20] 9	[23] R	[22] 15	[20] R	—	—	—	—	—	—	—	—	—	—	—	—
Michael Schumacher	Benetton B195-Renault	[2] **1** FL	[3] **3** FL	[1] **R**	[1] **1**	[2] **1**	[1] **5** FL	[2] **1** FL	[2] **R**	[2] **1** FL	[3] 11	[16] **1**	[2] R	[3] 2	[3] **1** FL	[3] **1** FL	[1] **1** FL	[3] **R**

DRIVER PERFORMANCE CONTINUED

DRIVER	CAR–ENGINE	BR	RA	RSM	E	MC	CDN	F	GB	D	H	B	I	P	EU	PAC	J	AUS
Aguri Suzuki	Ligier JS41-Mugen	15 8	19 R	16 11	–			–	–	18 6	–			–		13 R	13 DNS	–
Gabriele Tarquini	Tyrrell 023-Yamaha	–	–	–	–	–	–	–	–	–	–	–	–	19 14	–	–	–	–
Jos Verstappen	Simtek S951-Ford	24 R	14 R	17 R	16 12	23 R	–	–	–	–	–	–	–	–	–	–	–	–
Karl Wendlinger	Sauber C14-Ford	19 R	21 R	21 R	20 13	–	–	–	–	–	–	–	–	–	–	16 10	18 R	

FORMULA 1 RACE WINNERS

ROUND	RACE (CIRCUIT)	DATE	WINNER
1	Grande Prêmio do Brasil (Interlagos)	Mar 26	Michael Schumacher (Benetton B195-Renault)
2	Gran Premio Marlboro de Argentina (Buenos Aires)	Apr 9	Damon Hill (Williams FW17-Renault)
3	Gran Premio di San Marino (Imola)	Apr 30	Damon Hill (Williams FW17-Renault)
4	Gran Premio Marlboro de España (Catalunya)	May 14	Michael Schumacher (Benetton B195-Renault)
5	Grand Prix de Monaco (Monte Carlo)	May 28	Michael Schumacher (Benetton B195-Renault)
6	Grand Prix Molson du Canada (Montréal)	Jun 11	Jean Alesi (Ferrari 412T2)
7	Grand Prix de France (Magny-Cours)	Jul 2	Michael Schumacher (Benetton B195-Renault)
8	British Grand Prix (Silverstone)	Jul 16	Johnny Herbert (Benetton B195-Renault)
9	Grosser Mobil 1 Preis von Deutschland (Hockenheim)	Jul 30	Michael Schumacher (Benetton B195-Renault)
10	Marlboro Magyar Nagydíj (Hungaroring)	Aug 13	Damon Hill (Williams FW17-Renault)
11	Grand Prix de Belgique (Spa-Francorchamps)	Aug 27	Michael Schumacher (Benetton B195-Renault)
12	Pioneer Gran Premio d'Italia (Monza)	Sep 10	Johnny Herbert (Benetton B195-Renault)
13	Grande Premio de Portugal (Estoril)	Sep 24	David Coulthard (Williams FW17-Renault)
14	Grosser Preis von Europa (Nürburgring)	Oct 1	Michael Schumacher (Benetton B195-Renault)
15	Pacific Grand Prix (Aida)	Oct 22	Michael Schumacher (Benetton B195-Renault)
16	Fuji Television Japan Grand Prix (Suzuka)	Oct 29	Michael Schumacher (Benetton B195-Renault)
17	EDS Australian Grand Prix (Adelaide)	Nov 12	Damon Hill (Williams FW17B-Renault)

DRIVERS' CHAMPIONSHIP

	DRIVERS	POINTS
1	Michael Schumacher	102
2	Damon Hill	69
3	David Coulthard	49
4	Johnny Herbert	45
5	Jean Alesi	42
6	Gerhard Berger	31
7	Mika Häkkinen	17
8	Olivier Panis	16
9	Heinz-Harald Frentzen	15
10	Mark Blundell	13
11	Rubens Barrichello	11
12	Eddie Irvine	10
13	Martin Brundle	7
14=	Gianni Morbidelli	5
	Mika Salo	5
16	Jean-Christophe Boullion	3
17=	Pedro Lamy	1
	Aguri Suzuki	1

CONSTRUCTORS' CHAMPIONSHIP

	CONSTRUCTORS	POINTS
1	Benetton-Renault*	137
2	Williams-Renault*	112
3	Ferrari	73
4	McLaren-Mercedes-Benz	30
5	Ligier-Mugen	24
6	Jordan-Peugeot	21
7	Sauber-Ford	18
8=	Footwork-Hart	5
	Tyrrell-Yamaha	5
10	Minardi-Ford	1

*Williams and Benetton lost their manufacturers points from the Brazilian Grand Prix for fuel irregularities

Damon and Georgie Hill celebrate his World Championship success in Japan

1996

DAMON HILL EMULATES HIS FATHER AS CHAMPION

Michael Schumacher won in Spain after a masterful display in the wet

After two seasons as Michael Schumacher's closest challenger, Damon Hill took advantage of the German's highly paid switch to Ferrari to win the World Championship in his Williams FW18-Renault, the class of the field. The eventual champion was pushed to the final race by rookie team-mate Jacques Villeneuve but, even in his moment of glory, there was disappointment for Hill as he had already been dropped by his team for 1997.

New 3-litre engine regulations and slower circuits dictated that a V10 was the best configuration and even Ferrari and Ford (Cosworth) abandoned their preferred V12 and V8 alternatives. High cockpit surrounds and use of Euro 95 unleaded road car fuel were now mandatory, as was a rear-impact test. The cockpit rules caused controversy due to the interpretations of Williams and Jordan but a predicted row at the opening race did not materialise when the FIA declared those cars legal.

There were two developments designed to ensure a minimum quality among the whole field. Firstly, a driver had to qualify within 107 per cent of the pole time in order to start, although exceptions were made with mitigating circumstances. The field was limited to 12 two-car team franchises although this quota was not be filled until 2010. Ken Tyrrell's proposal to allow teams to run customer cars rather than build their own was rejected by the F1 Commission. Before each race, teams had to nominate a reserve driver who could substitute

if a regular was sidelined during the weekend.

The FIA responded to increasing live television coverage of qualifying by deciding grid positions during a single session on Saturday afternoon, with Friday and Saturday morning reserved for free practice. The numbering system was also revised with number one for the World Champion and his team-mate number two as before. The other teams were allocated numbers in order of the previous year's constructors' standings. A former submarine commander with no experience of international motor racing, Roger Lane-Nott, replaced John Corsmit as FIA race director, with Yamaha sporting boss Herbie Blash as his assistant. Roland Bruynseraede moved to the International Touring Car Series with FIA technical delegate Charlie Whiting now assuming responsibility for starting races as well. He oversaw a new procedure with five red lights illuminated at one second intervals. They went out after a pre-determined interval to signify the start. The race director could now start races in extreme wet weather behind the safety car and drivers were critical when this was not implemented at the Spanish GP. A new swipe-card system to control entry to the paddock was introduced at the opening race and Mercedes-Benz supplied the safety car for the first time. Testing was banned for a month after the 1996 season.

The Australian GP switched from Adelaide to Melbourne

Jacques Villeneuve started his F1 career from pole position in Australia

despite opposition from local residents and environmentalists of the 'Save Albert Park Group'. Originally scheduled to hold the Pacific GP on 21 April, Aida was omitted when the definitive calendar was published in December and Adelaide's request to take over that race was turned down. Sentul in Indonesia was slated to hold the final race on 3 November but this did not happen either so the season ended early at Suzuka. Michael Schumacher's popularity meant that the Nürburgring was preferred to Jerez as venue for the European GP. The organisers of the San Marino GP appeared in front of the FIA World Motor Sport Council on 11 June and were fined $1 million (75 per cent suspended for two years) for the track invasion at the end of the race.

F3000 championship winners Driot Arnoux Motor Sport (DAMS) finally abandoned its plans to enter F1 when sponsorship could not be found. The Claude Galopin/Rob Arnott designed DAMS GD01-Ford was launched in blue, yellow and white livery on 12 October 1995 but Jean-Paul Driot admitted that those ambitions were over at the 1996 Belgian GP. Tetzu Ikuzawa commissioned Enrique Scalabroni to design the Ikuzawa HW001 at the Essex headquarters of automotive consultancy Hawtal Whiting, with Peter Windsor involved at the start of the project. A scale model began wind-tunnel testing in July 1994 but the project was delayed and then cancelled.

Olivier Panis scored an unexpected victory in Monaco

Damon Hill, Williams FW18-Renault (Italian GP)

ROTHMANS WILLIAMS RENAULT

Williams-Renault had the fastest car/engine package in 1994 and 1995 but lost the drivers' title both years. Despite Damon Hill twice finishing runner-up and with 13 victories so far, Alan Henry posed the question in *Autosport*: 'Can Damon avoid fumbling the championship for the third successive season?' The Englishman signed a one-year contract extension although Heinz-Harald Frentzen's availability for 1997 was already a topic of conversation at both Williams's and Sauber's new-car launches.

With their famously critical assessment of drivers, Frank Williams and Patrick Head searched for the next superstar to rival Michael Schumacher as his Ferrari revolution gathered pace. Jacques Villeneuve, Gilles's son, won the Indianapolis 500 and Indycar title in 1995 and had F1 ambitions. His manager, Craig Pollock, visited the 1995 San Marino GP and spoke to Williams and others. Villeneuve flew to England after the 1995 Michigan 500, impressed when he tested an unbranded FW17 at Silverstone on 1 August, and signed a two-year contract to replace David Coulthard. Jean-Christophe Boullion remained as test driver.

Respected race engineer David Brown left after 14 years with Williams at the end of 1995 to join McLaren. James Robinson, a Williams employee in 1985–89 and most recently with McLaren's GT

operation, was appointed senior operations engineer in March 1996, co-ordinating engineers Jock Clear (for Villeneuve) and Tim Preston (Hill). The move from Didcot to a purpose-built new facility on a 28-acre site at Grove, Oxfordshire was completed in January.

Williams chose a low-key reveal for its Renault-powered FW18 at Estoril on 15 February. In this evolutionary design, Adrian Newey updated the transverse gearbox that had been introduced in the FW17B. The rear suspension and diffuser were revised, side winglets moved forward to comply with new regulations and sidepods marginally shortened. Newey incorporated controversial 'flick-ups' to lower the cockpit surround and improve airflow to the rear wing. Despite opposition from rival teams, the FIA's Charlie Whiting confirmed their legality at the first race. The hydraulic pump was relocated to improve reliability, an issue behind Hill's stymied challenge early in 1995. The latest RS08 iteration of Renault's 67-degree V10 engine revved up to 17,000rpm and produced 750bhp. Villeneuve preferred a two-pedal layout and hand clutch to facilitate left-foot braking. Hill continued to use a conventional three-pedal system, a choice that may explain Villeneuve's better race starts. There was a difference to their gearbox paddles as well: Hill had one either side of the steering wheel (right for upshifting, left for down) while Villeneuve had a single right-hand paddle that he pushed to select a higher gear and pulled to downshift. A hydraulic differential was tested in the spring and drag-reducing front wishbones were introduced at Monza. Williams-Renault won 12 of the 16 races and scored more than double the constructors' points of its nearest rival in 1996.

A self-assured Hill arrived in Australia as pre-season favourite but it was his team-mate who wrote the early headlines. Having covered over 9,000km during winter testing as he learned as many circuits as possible, Villeneuve became the third driver in F1 history to qualify on pole position for his début, matching Mario Andretti and Carlos Reutemann. He controlled the race and came within five laps of emulating Giancarlo Baghetti's feat of winning his first GP. With Hill in close attendance throughout, Villeneuve ran wide at Turn 1 on lap 34 and damaged an oil line as he ran over the kerb and onto the grass. The oil pressure sagged late in the race and Villeneuve was ordered to slow to avoid engine failure. With his car coated in Villeneuve's oil, Hill duly inherited victory in a dominant Williams-Renault 1–2.

Hill claimed pole for the next three races and coasted to victory in Brazil and Argentina (where 'God Save The Queen' was booed). Racing on unfamiliar circuits, Villeneuve started both races from third, although he damaged his nosecone during his final qualifying attempt in Brazil. He spun out at Interlagos while defending second from Jean Alesi's Benetton-Renault and recovered from a poor start to claim that position in Buenos Aires.

Villeneuve completed a Williams front-row lock-out for the European GP and, having made a better start than Hill, led from start to finish despite Schumacher's late pressure to win at his fourth attempt. Hill was fourth after being compromised by that bad start, a slow first pitstop to check his suspension and contact with Pedro Diniz. Williams-Renault's run of pole positions ended at Imola

where Hill beat Schumacher to victory by jumping his rival in the first pitstops. Delayed by a puncture when he banged wheels with Alesi at the start, Villeneuve recovered into the top six only for the suspension to fail late on.

Hill lost the Monaco GP when his engine failed and Villeneuve, who started tenth in his worst weekend of the season, was heading for fourth place when he hit Luca Badoer's lapped Forti-Ford at Mirabeau. A new central diffuser was used to dominate practice for the Spanish GP but pole-sitter Hill made another slow start and struggled in the torrential rain because he had not changed the car to full wet settings. There were a couple of early off-track excursions before he crashed into the pit wall. Villeneuve led in the early stages and finished third on a day when no one could live with Schumacher's wet-weather prowess.

Williams-Renault continued to dominate in Montréal with Hill and the one-stopping Villeneuve 1–2 in qualifying and the race. A major upgrade for the French GP included a new front wing, revised exhausts and more powerful RS08B engine. Schumacher beat Hill to pole position with Villeneuve only sixth on the grid following a 130mph crash in qualifying. However, Sunday belonged to Williams-Renault once more, for Schumacher's engine failed on the parade lap and Hill cruised to victory with Villeneuve second. Hill also led an all-Williams front row at Silverstone only to make another poor start and have his left-front wheel nut work loose at Copse on lap 27. Villeneuve took advantage of Hill's tardy getaway and eased to his second GP victory by 19.026sec.

Used to stories about his future, Hill arrived at Hockenheim with 'Frentzen Tipped for Williams Seat in '97: Has Hill been dumped?' emblazoned on the front cover of *Autosport*. The championship leader inherited victory in the German GP when Gerhard Berger's

Jacques Villeneuve, Williams FW18-Renault (German GP)

engine failed with three laps to go. Sixth on the grid after a couple of troubled days, Villeneuve passed Schumacher to take what became third on Berger's retirement. Hill made his customary poor start in Hungary and it was Villeneuve who led the Williams-Renault 1–2 that clinched the constructors' title and made sure the drivers' crown would be settled in-house.

Villeneuve claimed an excellent pole at Spa-Francorchamps after learning the track by playing a computer game and studying in-car footage of Ayrton Senna. He led from the start until losing out to Schumacher when he delayed pitting behind the safety car by a lap due to a problem with his radio, then went on to finish second. Hill, who had practised starts during a test at Barcelona, dropped from second to fourth off the line, then suffered when the team fumbled his pitstop instructions after deployment of the safety car, leaving Damon as low as 13th at one stage of the race, although he recovered to finish fifth.

With his departure at the end of the season confirmed before the Italian GP, Hill beat Villeneuve in qualifying only for a fast-starting Alesi to jump both off the line. It was a frantic first lap for Villeneuve straight-lined the first chicane and Hill passed the Benetton-Renault on the approach to Ascari despite Alesi fighting back on the entry to the corner. Hill pulled away only to crash at the first chicane four laps later. Villeneuve compounded a terrible day for Williams-Renault by damaging a steering arm when he clipped the tyres at the Roggia chicane on lap two, so he struggled home seventh.

At Estoril, Villeneuve recovered from his own poor start to pass Schumacher around the outside of the 140mph final corner, cleared Alesi at the first pitstops, and got ahead of Hill when they stopped

for the final time. His victory ensured that the championship went to final race in Japan, with Villeneuve needing to win again without Hill scoring. Villeneuve was slow away from pole position and the destiny of the title was confirmed when he lost his right-rear wheel following a pitstop. Hill led all the way to clinch the World Championship his father Graham had won in 1962 and 1968. The first son of a World Champion to also win the title, Damon Hill was named as BBC Sports Personality of the Year for a second time.

Hill was not the only key person to leave at the end of 1996 as Newey, who was contracted until July 1999, had been in dispute with Williams since the summer. He was placed on gardening leave in November and his move to McLaren was finally announced on 22 April 1997 after terms for his release had been agreed between the two British teams.

SCUDERIA FERRARI

The leading F1 drivers were all out of contract at the end of 1995 and Michael Schumacher set his price. In June, Ferrari president Luca di Montezemolo had told Agence France that '$26 million is totally crazy. Ferrari cannot pay as much money as that, even for Schumacher', but he openly wooed the World Champion. 'To win in Formula 1 you need three things,' he told La Stampa, 'a good organisation, a great car and a great driver… Schumacher is undoubtedly the number one driver and I have the duty to think of him.' Ferrari finally confirmed speculation when it announced Schumacher's two-year deal on 16 August 1995. 'If we don't win the World Championship with Michael, it will be our fault,' was

Michael Schumacher, Ferrari F310 (European GP)

Gianni Agnelli's straightforward assessment.

Ferrari wanted to retain Gerhard Berger but the Austrian was not enthusiastic to take a pay cut or team up with Schumacher. David Coulthard and Rubens Barrichello were thought to be leading candidates but the choice of second driver was a surprise. With Eddie Jordan stressing that 'continuity is important', he exercised his option on Eddie Irvine's services and announced an unchanged line-up at the 1995 Portuguese GP. Jordan and Irvine flew to Lugano on the following Monday to negotiate his immediate release with Irvine named as Schumacher's team-mate on Tuesday 26 September.

The *Scuderia* broke with tradition and replaced its 12-cylinder engine with a new V10 unit. 'I know all about Ferrari's history,' sporting director Jean Todt said at the 1995 French GP, 'but I suspect that we might have to forget about that in the interests of competitiveness.' The new engine had already been on the dyno for a month by then, and test driver Nicola Larini was entrusted with its track début at Fiorano on 4 October. Paulo Martinelli's engine department opted for a 75-degree four-valves-per-cylinder V10 with aluminium block and variable trumpets. A key contributor to the design process had been renowned ex-Honda/McLaren engineer Osamu Goto but he left Ferrari in June.

Schumacher and Irvine visited Maranello on 16 November and a couple of thousand locals watched as the double champion made his Ferrari début at Fiorano that day. There were platitudes about wanting to working together, but Schumacher did not agree with technical director John Barnard's preference not to attend races. Irvine's performances were compromised by limited testing as Schumacher gained as much mileage as possible.

Delayed by three weeks as Barnard finalised detail in British Aerospace's half-size wind tunnel near Bristol, the Ferrari F310 was revealed at Maranello on 15 February – the last 1996 challenger to appear – with Fiat's Gianni Agnelli in attendance and shown live on German and Italian television. The torsion bar/push-rod suspension from the 412T2 was revised with the 'knife-edge' mounting joints of the 412T1 preferred once more. A low nose was retained, albeit slightly higher than before, with a vee-shaped central support for the wings. Barnard interpreted the new cockpit regulations as literally as anyone and the result was an ungainly looking machine and disturbed airflow to the engine. The sidepods resembled the unsuccessful F92A's 'fighter jet' arrangement with a double floor between the bargeboards and radiators. The new transverse semi-automatic gearbox could be fitted with six or seven gears, and was cased in titanium to save weight, but proved temperamental. Ferrari was unusual in fitting power steering as standard. The bellhousing was carbon-fibre while the exhausts blew from above the rear diffuser. Shell replaced Agip as the team's fuel and oil partner. Architect Renzo Piano, at the time best-known for his work on the Pompidou Centre in Paris, designed a futuristic new wind tunnel ('Galleria del Vento') adjacent to Maranello's main entrance that opened on 15 April.

Initial testing was delayed while the carbon-fibre spacer between engine and gearbox was redesigned following oil leaks and subsequent running was curtailed by electrical and fuel-pump issues. The F310 was a handful in Australia with overly sensitive handling, locking rear brakes and disturbed airflow to the engine. Schumacher was outqualified by an F1 team-mate for just the

Eddie Irvine, Ferrari F310 (Canadian GP)

third time so far when Irvine lined up third in Melbourne, with the reigning champion fourth. Schumacher passed Irvine on lap two and ran third until his rear brakes failed; Irvine began his Ferrari career by finishing third behind the Williams-Renaults.

Cracks had been found in the gearbox casing after the race so Ferrari reverted to the 1995 gearbox, rear suspension and less sophisticated diffuser for South America. The car was very nervous in Brazil, where Schumacher was lapped on the way to third and Irvine finished a misfiring seventh. Schumacher was at his brilliant best to qualify second in Argentina and he maintained that position in the race until his rear wing was damaged by debris. Irvine struggled all weekend but withstood Jos Verstappen's last-lap challenge to claim fifth despite being stuck in sixth gear.

The F310 was refitted with its intended rear end, complete with reinforced gearbox casing, plus three-damper front suspension for the European GP at the Nürburgring. Schumacher qualified third and chased first-time winner Jacques Villeneuve to the finish, beaten by just 0.762sec after a mighty drive. As well as having a revised aero package, they had an upgraded engine for the San Marino GP (Friday and Saturday only) and Monaco (all weekend) where Schumacher claimed successive pole positions. With the car much-improved, he finished second at Imola despite fading brakes but crashed on the opening lap in Monte Carlo. Irvine recovered from a slow start to claim fourth at Imola and was classified seventh after an eventful race in Monaco. He ran as high as third before losing two laps in the pits when he stalled as his front wing was changed following contact with Olivier Panis. He then spun at the lower Mirabeau during the closing stages and was collected by Mikas Salo and Häkkinen, eliminating all three cars.

Schumacher had used the 1995 diffuser with 1996 gearbox/rear suspension in Monaco and both drivers adopted this configuration for the Spanish GP. No match for the Williams-Renaults in qualifying, the German dropped to sixth on the opening lap before delivering one of the greatest wet-weather drives in memory to pass Villeneuve and score his first victory for Ferrari; Irvine spun out of fifth position on lap two.

Schumacher's brilliance that day did not mask the inadequacies of the Ferrari F310 and, with a rift between di Montezemolo and Barnard denied, the team began to overhaul the recalcitrant machine. Maranello-based engineers Gustav Brunner and Willem Toet revised the aerodynamics with raised nose, new bargeboards and full-width front wing attached by angled supports. Schumacher tried the revised car at Imola on 7 June and it was introduced at the Canadian GP, where the drivers reported it was worth a tenth or two. They qualified in the top five after traffic had thwarted Schumacher's challenge for pole position but Sunday was a disaster. Schumacher started from the back when his engine refused to fire for the parade lap and Irvine was out by the end of lap two. Schumacher had climbed into the top ten when his driveshaft broke at his first pitstop.

France was even worse despite Schumacher's third pole position of the season. Irvine was disqualified from qualifying due to the height of his turning vanes and suffered early gearbox failure in the

race. Schumacher did not make it that far for a piston failed on the parade lap. Ferrari's mechanical carnage continued at Silverstone, where both cars failed by lap six for the second successive GP weekend, Schumacher racing despite a broken rib sustained while playing football with his mechanics.

Another upgrade for Hockenheim involved new rear suspension, uprights and diffuser, plus a low-downforce set-up with side winglets removed. The F310 was ill-balanced in practice but Schumacher qualified third and held off David Coulthard to finish fourth. On pole for the Hungarian GP, where the new aero worked better, Schumacher was denied a podium finish by a sticking throttle and a stall when he mistakenly selected neutral in the closing stages. Using a new seven-speed gearbox with steel casing for the first time, Schumacher crashed heavily at the Fagnes left-hander during Friday practice at Spa-Francorchamps. Having qualified third, Schumacher took the lead by pitting as soon as the safety car was deployed following Jos Verstappen's accident, and he held off Villeneuve to win again. He made a poor start at Monza but took advantage of Damon Hill's misfortune to challenge for the lead. He passed Jean Alesi in the pitstops thanks to a couple of trademark blistering laps to win in front of the delirious *tifosi*. Sidelined by gearbox problems in Germany, Hungary and Belgium, Irvine was third when he crashed at the first chicane on lap 24 of the Italian GP.

No one could touch the Williams-Renaults in Portugal, where Schumacher beat Alesi into third. Irvine ended a run of eight successive retirements by finishing fifth despite being knocked into a spin at the final corner of the race by Gerhard Berger, and he was furious with the Austrian when they collided again at Suzuka, an incident that launched his fourth-placed Ferrari into the air and caused his tenth retirement of 1996.

Schumacher's second place in Japan was enough for Ferrari to displace Benetton-Renault as runners-up in the constructors' standings. The campaign had been chaotic at times but Schumacher's three victories satisfied Ferrari's oft-stated pre-season ambitions.

MILD SEVEN BENETTON RENAULT
Although reigning World Champions, Benetton entered 1996 as underdogs such was the reputation of the driver it had lost. This was a fractious campaign with managing director Flavio Briatore criticising his drivers who in turn blamed the car for Benetton's first winless season since 1988. Even more damaging in the long term was to be the loss of key technical staff at the end of the year.

Briatore moved quickly when Michael Schumacher confirmed persistent rumours on 16 August 1995 and joined Ferrari. He agreed terms with Jean Alesi within days in what effectively became a driver swap. Jos Verstappen was released in September and Briatore mentioned Heinz-Harald Frentzen and Rubens Barrichello as possibilities before Gerhard Berger signed on 30 August, like Alesi having agreed a two-year contract.

Benetton chose Sicily's Third Century BC Teatro Antico di Taormina, with Mount Etna as a backdrop, for the most lavish F1 launch so far, on 5 February. Berger and Alesi drove the 1995 cars

Jean Alesi, Benetton B196-Renault (Italian GP)

through the ancient streets before unveiling the Benetton B196-Renault in front of an audience of 15,000 that included film star Gérard Depardieu. The B196 was a development of Benetton's title-winners with refined aerodynamics featuring short, reprofiled sidepods that fell away to the rear and without the raised outer 'shoulders' of the B195. The exhausts blew from over the central diffuser. The push-rod suspension originally had torsion bars but these proved troublesome and were replaced by coil springs after a three-day Silverstone test before the Spanish GP. The updated Renault RS08 V10 engine now drove through a seven-speed semi-automatic gearbox that was mounted longitudinally so that the undertray could be revised. An electronic differential tested before the British GP was heavier than the conventional alternative and did not offer an immediate performance advantage.

Mild Seven continued as title partner with Vijay Mallya's Kingfisher beer an associate sponsor. F3000 champion Vincenzo Sospiri was signed as test driver and Sergio Rinland arrived to lead the composites department. A three-year research and development contract was agreed with Jean-Claude Migeot's Fondmetal Technologies in Casumaro. The team officially changed its nationality from British to Italian while remaining based at Enstone in Oxfordshire.

Testing did not begin well as Berger, finding the existing B195 a handful, had hefty accidents during his first three outings before Christmas. His winter was further interrupted by a bout of pneumonia, the lingering effects of which lasted into the season. He was more comfortable in the new car but the reliability of the new gearbox and engine failures frustrated team and drivers alike.

Furthermore, the B196 was very nervous on corner entry and did not suit either driver's style.

In Melbourne's Albert Park the Benetton-Renaults were up to 20bhp down on power because airflow to their engines was disturbed by the drivers' helmets. Alesi crashed into Eddie Irvine's Ferrari in a rash early move while Berger finished fourth, 77.037sec adrift of the winner. The team then tested over 20 airbox configurations but the problem persisted and at Interlagos the cars were more than 10kph slower than the similarly powered Williams FW18s. Despite this, and an off-track excursion, Alesi used his wet-weather prowess to finish an excellent second, but Berger was anonymous. A new airbox design helped them to qualify in the top five in Argentina, where Berger was fortunate to avoid a large dog during practice. He lost third when his suspension broke on the severe bump in the fast Ascari corner, promoting Alesi, who was recovering after stalling at his pitstop, into third.

The Nürburgring was a disaster. Suffering understeer and after making terrible starts when their handbrakes locked on, Alesi crashed into Mika Salo on lap two and Berger finished ninth after stalling at his second pitstop. With tensions running high within the team and drivers under pressure, a three-hour meeting was held on the Thursday before the San Marino GP, where both scored points despite continuing understeer, Berger third and Alesi sixth after a messy race. He hit Jacques Villeneuve at the start, served a stop-go penalty for speeding in the pitlane, survived a spin and then ran wide before claiming the final point.

They qualified on the second row in Monte Carlo, where Alesi inherited a commanding lead when Damon Hill's Williams-Renault retired. He was cruising to a much-needed victory before a suspension spring broke with 15 laps to go. Berger retired early when third behind his team-mate. With the coil-spring suspension and aero upgrades at the next two races, Alesi finished second in the Spanish rain and third at Montréal; Berger spun on both occasions. Williams-Renault remained in a league of their own in France, where Alesi led a Benetton-Renault 3–4 in qualifying and the race as they also benefited from the upgraded engine.

The drivers were not optimistic before the British GP but Alesi made a great start to run second from the opening lap. One-stopping, he briefly led when Jacques Villeneuve made his first pitstop and remained on course to finish second until his right-rear brake failed on lap 44, leaving Berger, narrowly behind, to finish in that position. New wings and revised brakes at the German GP resulted in a temporary upturn in form. Berger qualified on the front row and they ran 1–2 for the first half of the race. Scheduled to stop once, Berger retook the lead when Hill refuelled for the second time but victory was denied when his engine expired with less than three laps to go. This time, it was Alesi who inherited second.

The Benetton-Renaults lacked grip and lagged behind both Williams-Renaults and Ferraris on the slow-speed Hungaroring. Alesi obeyed team orders to let Berger past but finished on the lower step of the podium when the Austrian's engine failed once again. Berger was the quicker driver at Spa-Francorchamps and should have been called into the pits before Alesi when the safety car was deployed following Verstappen's accident, a tactical error Berger

was sure cost him the chance of victory. Alesi finished fourth but Berger lost further ground when he spun before recovering to finish sixth after setting a succession of fastest laps.

Having just criticised the team in an interview with *Gazzetta dello Sport*, Alesi leaped from sixth on the grid to lead into the first corner of the Italian GP. He was demoted by Damon Hill on the opening lap following a mistake at the first Lesmo but reassumed the lead when the Englishman crashed. Although Schumacher passed him in the pitstops, he nonetheless finished a fine second. Berger lay fifth until his gearbox hydraulics failed on lap four. In Portugal, Alesi finished fourth and Berger sixth after they lost Ferrari battles with Schumacher and Eddie Irvine respectively, Irvine and Berger having clashed at the final corner.

Berger outqualified his team-mate for just the third time in 1996 at Suzuka. Alesi endured a torrid session and crashed on the opening corner of the race. Berger might have won but damaged his front wing on the kerbs at the chicane when he made an ill-judged attempt to pass Hill for the lead. He survived another collision with Irvine to finish fourth but Schumacher's second place demoted Benetton-Renault to third in the constructors' standings.

Despite rumours all year to the contrary, Briatore confirmed that both drivers would remain for 1997 although he had crucial vacancies elsewhere. Chief designer Rory Byrne announced that he was quitting to establish a diving school in Thailand. Technical director Ross Brawn moved to Ferrari in December and managed to persuade Byrne to follow him to Maranello.

Gerhard Berger, Benetton B196-Renault (Portuguese GP)

Mika Häkkinen, McLaren MP4/11-Mercedes (Japanese GP)

MARLBORO McLAREN MERCEDES

McLaren was under pressure to return to winning ways at the start
of 1996. Mercedes-Benz director Jürgen Hubbert had threatened
it would withdraw if it had another winless campaign and Philip
Morris was in the final year of its long-standing Marlboro sponsorship
contract. 'I haven't forgotten how to win,' Ron Dennis told the
Mercedes Stars and Cars gathering in December 1995. 'Maintain your
confidence in me… next year will be better.'

High-profile technical adviser Alain Prost decided not to come
out of retirement and David Coulthard was confirmed as Mika
Häkkinen's team-mate at the 1995 European GP after signing a
two-year contract. Mercedes DTM drivers Bernd Schneider and Dario
Franchitti both tested a McLaren MP4/10B-Mercedes at Jerez in
December. Häkkinen spent the winter recovering from the injuries
sustained in Australia and tested for the first time at Paul Ricard on 5
February. Respected Williams race engineer David Brown joined at the
beginning of the season and McLaren gave Michael Schumacher's
younger brother Ralf his first F1 test at Silverstone on 8 August as
they evaluated him as a possible reserve driver for 1997.

Coulthard's first test in an MP4/10B in December included a
couple of spins as he adjusted to McLaren's twin-pedal layout. The
elegant McLaren MP4/11-Mercedes was revealed in the Estoril pitlane
on 11 February with Prost conducting initial tests. This was a neat if
conventional car built around a new monocoque. Chief designer Neil
Oatley, with Henri Durand and Steve Nichols, retained the raised nose
but switched to a longitudinal gearbox. The curved cockpit protection

extended alongside the engine while the sidepods were lower. The
front wishbones were carbon-fibre with 'knife-edge' mountings
similar to the Ferrari 412T1 and Jordan 195. The exhausts blew from
the top on either side of the central diffuser that curved upwards
to the rear. Ilmor completely revised the 75-degree V10 Mercedes
engine to improve driveability. It matched rival engines for top-end
power and Coulthard set record straight-line speeds at fast circuits
such as Hockenheim and Monza. Häkkinen was quickest in the final
major test at Estoril although six engine failures limited Coulthard's
mileage and tempered expectations. Initially lacking front-end grip
and overly pitch-sensitive, the MP4/11 had a nervous rear end all year,
with disturbed air to the engine a further drawback.

While the Finn scored points in the opening two races, Coulthard
was involved in Martin Brundle's Australian accident and retired the
spare car in the restarted race when its throttle stuck open. The slick-
shod Coulthard then spun off in the rain in Brazil. The Scot qualified
in the top ten for the first time in Argentina, just two tenths behind
his team-mate. Fifth at the start and seemingly on course to finish in
that position after his final pitstop, Coulthard faded to seventh due to
a poor set of tyres, while Häkkinen retired with a throttle problem.

In need of an urgent fix, the test team went to Lurcy-Lévis with
reserve driver Jan Magnussen behind the wheel. A breakthrough at
the front end was made with L-shaped fences under the wing and
strengthened mounting points that eradicated flex and transformed
the handling. Coulthard outqualified Häkkinen for the first time at the
Nürburgring and scored a timely podium finish. Having jumped from

sixth to second at the start, Coulthard held off Damon Hill to claim third. This improved form continued at Imola, where the Scot qualified fourth and led the first 19 laps after another great start. However, a drop in hydraulic pressure caused him to stall at his second stop and he lost fourth when it failed altogether. Myriad problems restricted Häkkinen's qualifying efforts at both circuits and stop-go penalties ruined those races, twice for speeding in the pitlane during the European GP and for baulking Michael Schumacher at Imola.

McLaren remained at Imola to test what Dennis described as 'a short-circuit, high-direction-change specification' of MP4/11. A 2in wheelbase reduction adjusted weight distribution, the exhausts were straight, and the 'coke-bottle' rear end was reprofiled to improve cooling. This was used at Monaco, where the airbox-mounted additional wing also returned. Coulthard qualified fifth and, wearing a helmet borrowed from Schumacher due to his visor misting, finished second just 4.828sec behind Olivier Panis after a race of attrition. Having written off a chassis in the morning warm-up, Häkkinen challenged Mika Salo for fourth until they both hit Eddie Irvine's spun Ferrari at the lower Mirabeau with five laps to go.

They were over two seconds off the pace in qualifying for the Spanish GP, where the MP4/11s were returned to their standard configuration. Coulthard was unsighted by spray at the start and crashed; Häkkinen was the fifth of six finishers. There was an off-the-track development at that race for McLaren used its new £1.4-million motorhome – the biggest thus far seen in F1 – for the first time.

Despite lacking front-end grip once more, Coulthard and Häkkinen finished 4–5 in Canada, the Finn having spun while lapping Giancarlo Fisichella's Minardi. A stiffer front wing and revised rear suspension improved matters in France, where they qualified in the top seven and scored points behind the four Renault-powered cars. They reverted to

the short-wheelbase version (informally referred to as the MP4/11B) from Silverstone because it worked better with the new front wing/rear suspension in race trim. Häkkinen was delighted to qualify fourth and finish third. Struggling for rear-end grip, Coulthard recovered from a slow start to claim fifth.

In Germany, Coulthard broke the speed trap before the first chicane at 221.897mph in qualifying despite McLaren running more rear wing than its rivals. Having qualified fourth, Häkkinen made a bad start and retired early while Coulthard chased Schumacher's Ferrari home in fifth. With more corners than straights, Hungary proved troublesome but Häkkinen was fourth after quicker cars retired, while Coulthard's engine let go in front of the pits.

The high-speed nature of Spa-Francorchamps was better suited to the McLaren-Mercedes, which had a revised front end with a new wing and aerodynamic wishbones. Handling better than at any race so far, they lined up fourth and sixth, Coulthard ahead for the first time since Monaco, and following Jos Verstappen's accident they ran 1–2 behind the safety car. One-stopping, Häkkinen was denied a shot at victory by that full-course yellow but finished third nonetheless. Coulthard's second set of tyres wrecked his car's balance and he lost it at Stavelot, seven laps from finishing fifth.

Negotiations with Philip Morris continued throughout the summer with McLaren said to be talking to up to four tobacco companies at one stage. The end of a deal that dated back to 1974 was announced on 26 August with new sponsorship already agreed with Reemtsma for West to replace Marlboro as title partner in 1997.

Having qualified in the top five at Monza, where Coulthard hit 219mph on the straight, they experienced a different type of tyre trouble early in the race. Harried by Coulthard on lap two, fifth-placed Jacques Villeneuve dislodged some tyres that lined the

David Coulthard, McLaren MP4/11-Mercedes (Hungarian GP)

Roggia chicane and Coulthard hit them hard enough to break his steering. Jean Alesi did likewise next time around and Häkkinen damaged his front wing when he struck them. The Finn recovered from the subsequent pitstop to finish a fine third. Hopes for a strong result in Portugal ended when Häkkinen ran into the back of his team-mate at the hairpin as they disputed sixth. The front wing had to be strengthened while in Japan, where Häkkinen claimed another third place after his best drive of the year. Having forced the original start to be aborted when he stalled on the grid, Coulthard finished eighth after changing the nose assembly he had broken against the back of Pedro Diniz's Ligier-Mugen.

McLaren-Mercedes retained fourth in the constructors' World Championship but F1's perennial achievers had now not won for three full seasons (49 races).

BENSON & HEDGES TOTAL JORDAN PEUGEOT

Just days after being confirmed as part of an unchanged Jordan line-up for the coming season, Eddie Irvine signed for Ferrari on 26 September 1995. The day after this shock news, Eddie Jordan agreed terms with Martin Brundle, who had driven for his F3 team in 1983, to replace Irvine as Rubens Barrichello's team-mate for 1996. Although Irvine had outperformed Barrichello during 1995, he was seen as a destabilising influence so Brundle's calming work ethic was welcomed by the team. Gianni Morbidelli joined Fabrizio de Simone as test driver in March.

'We are going to win races,' Jordan enthused in *Autosport*. 'I've promised that to Peugeot and they deserve it. There'll be no excuses asked and none given.' Nothing less would do for, having tasted

success in rallying, sports cars and rally-raids, Peugeot president Jacques Calvert and his board were frustrated by the slow progress made thus far in F1. Peugeot competition boss Jean-Pierre Jabouille's contract was not renewed, with Vélizy factory supremo Pierre-Michel Fauconnier promoted in his place. Three years after moving to Lotus, Trevor Foster returned to Jordan as general manager and also assumed team managerial duties when John Walton joined Arrows in the summer.

For the second year running, Jordan was the first team to complete its new car and the 196 ran at a wet Silverstone on 13 January despite construction at the track limiting activity to a section between the pits and Becketts. Gary Anderson opted for a high-nose configuration he had last used in 1993 and switched to a longitudinal gearbox for the first time. His interpretation of the new head-protection rules led to a blended surround that was lower and less bulbous than most others. This was questioned by rivals but declared legal by the FIA's Charlie Whiting at the first race. The car's centre of gravity was lowered and Anderson reverted to a simplified rear diffuser, with exhausts blowing from the top. In order to improve airflow under the car, innovative sidepods had separate inlets for the water radiator to the front and alongside the driver's head for the oil cooler. The two-pedal layout was modified to allow Brundle to brake with his right foot and power steering was available from mid-season. The high-downforce set-up used at Buenos Aires, Monaco and the Hungaroring included an additional wing on the airbox. Peugeot used the winter to improve reliability and driveability of its 72-degree V10 while maintaining top-end power, which was said to be on a par with Renault and Ferrari.

Initial testing at Estoril and Barcelona was beset by hydraulic problems and unpredictable handling. Progress was made at Paul

Rubens Barrichello, Jordan 196-Peugeot (Spanish GP)

Martin Brundle, Jordan 196-Peugeot (Italian GP)

Ricard and prospects were boosted by a positive final Estoril test. Furthermore, new title sponsorship from Benson & Hedges was concluded on 27 February so the cars were hastily resprayed in the cigarette brand's yellow livery for the opening race. A new golden colour scheme was introduced for the Monaco GP.

Barrichello qualified in the top ten at all bar two races and ahead of Brundle for most of the year. There were issues with braking and turn-in, Brundle in particular struggling for rear grip and finding the car difficult to set up. The disappointments began in Australia, where Barrichello challenged for points until his engine failed while Brundle endured a terrible weekend. Starting from the back row after flat-spotting his tyres on his qualifying run, he was launched over the back of David Coulthard and Johnny Herbert on the opening lap when cars ahead of him concertinaed on the 180mph approach to Turn 3. The Jordan-Peugeot barrel-rolled into the gravel with engine and gearbox scattered, such was the force of the accident. Lucky to emerge unhurt, Brundle took the spare for the restart only to run into Pedro Diniz on lap two. Tim Holloway, Brundle's 45-year-old race engineer, had a heart attack before the Brazilian GP, so Anderson and then Paul White stood in while he recuperated.

Both Jordan-Peugeots started inside the top six in Brazil but failed to score. An excellent second on the grid for his home race, Barrichello was challenging Michael Schumacher for third when he spun and stalled at Subida do Lago with 11 laps to go. He converted sixth on the grid in Argentina into a fourth-place finish thanks to a one-stop strategy. Grieving the death of his father, Brundle continued

his character-building start to the season with two spins and a stalled pitstop in Brazil, and being rammed by Tarso Marques in Argentina.

With the diffuser modified to improve rear traction, Barrichello started and finished fifth at the Nürburgring with Brundle sixth to claim his first point of 1996. Fifth once more at Imola despite a couple of slow pitstops, Barrichello was hit at the first corner of the Monaco GP and spun at Rascasse before completing the opening lap. A botched fuel stop ruined Brundle's San Marino GP and he spun out of that race and the next. Both suffered transmission failures in Spain, Barrichello having run as high as second.

Brundle had another new engineer for the Canadian GP following the arrival of Andy Tilley, who had most recently worked for Minardi. This coincided with a much-needed upturn in form as Brundle qualified in the top ten at the next four races and finished on each occasion. He was sixth in Montréal (despite changing a damaged nosecone following contact with Pedro Lamy's Minardi-Ford) and Silverstone (after a puncture). They were disappointing also-rans in front of Peugeot's home crowd at Magny-Cours as pressure for results mounted. Barrichello finished fourth at Silverstone and scored back-to-back sixth places in Germany and Hungary.

Anderson missed the four races after the French GP, prompting speculation that he would be the fall guy after a largely disappointing year to date. With both drivers' futures also in doubt, they had their least competitive qualifying of the year in Hungary, where the cars oversteered on turn-in and understeered on exit. 'The more I try,' bemoaned an exasperated Barrichello, 'the slower I seem to go.'

They retired from the Belgian GP. With Anderson back at Monza in an overseeing capacity, Brundle and Barrichello ran in formation to finish fourth and fifth respectively after rival cars crashed. Neither looked like scoring in Portugal and Brundle, who outqualified Barrichello at four of the last five races, finished a strong fifth in Japan.

Jordan-Peugeot finished in a distant fifth overall, with just 22 points and no podiums – a far cry from the victories demanded by team and engine supplier alike. Both drivers departed, with Brundle, who drove a Ford Escort RS Cosworth on the following month's RAC Rally, accepting an offer to join ITV's new commentary team for 1997.

LIGIER GAULOISES BLONDES

Tom Walkinshaw's ambitions to buy Ligier remained at the start of 1996. He intented to leave the race team at Magny-Cours but relocate the design and test departments to TWR's new facility at Leafield in Oxfordshire. Indeed, Silverstone rather than Magny-Cours was nominated as Ligier's test track before the season. However, Walkinshaw met with concerted resistance from the French government and Guy Ligier (15 per cent shareholder) to keep the team French. Tired of manoeuvres to oust him, Walkinshaw resigned after the Australian GP and acquired Arrows instead. Satisfied that the team he founded would remain in France, Guy Ligier finally sold his remaining interest to controlling shareholder Flavio Briatore in August.

Technical director Frank Dernie and operations director Tony Dowe followed Walkinshaw to Arrows. They were replaced by André de

Cortanze, who had arrived from Sauber during the winter, and Didier Perrin respectively. Cesare Fiorio rejoined as sporting director in May.

Previously among the best-funded teams on the grid, Ligier announced a new two-year agreement with Société d'Exploitation Industrielle des Tabacs et Alumettes (SEITA) on 13 September 1995, albeit at a much-reduced rate. The now privatised tobacco company decided to promote Gauloises cigarettes rather than the Gitanes brand that had been associated with Ligier since the beginning. Elf and LOTO did not renew and there were 37 redundancies in December as a consequence of a restructure.

Attempts to buy Indycar Rookie of the Year Gil de Ferran out of his contract were turned down by Hall-VDS Racing. Vincenzo Sospiri, Emmanuel Collard and Jérémie Dufour all tested at Mugello in the first week of November but the 40 per cent budget shortfall was offset in part by Ligier's choice of team-mate for Olivier Panis. Rather than remain with Forti, Pedro Diniz transferred his Parmalat money to Ligier but endured a difficult first test at Barcelona before Christmas, spinning on his first lap out of the pits and crashing on his second. Kenny Bräck and Kelvin Burt were named as test drivers although the Englishman, who drove a TWR Volvo in the British Touring Car Championship, also left with Walkinshaw.

The Ligier JS43-Mugen was presented to the press in Monte Carlo on 29 January with Walkinshaw warning of a difficult year ahead. Dernie retained the front end from the Benetton-clone JS41, albeit with torsion-bar front suspension and revised sidepods. Paul Crooks was responsible for the chassis and Loïc Bigois the aerodynamics. The

Olivier Panis, Ligier JS43-Mugen (Monaco GP)

engine contract with Mugen was renewed for another year and the latest V10 (the raucous MF-301HA) was lower and lighter, with more power and improved reliability. The reduced dimensions allowed the rear packaging to be improved around the Benetton transverse semi-automatic gearbox. Three-damper suspension was tried in Canada, where a new version of the Mugen was introduced in practice. Experiments with exhaust blowing from the top of the diffuser were abandoned while poor braking and nervous handling at fast circuits were particular weaknesses.

Hampered by the JS43's inadequate qualifying pace and a tendency to lock its rear wheels under braking, Panis had several altercations on the first or second lap during 1996, including at Barcelona, Spa-Francorchamps and Monza, but he did enjoy one unexpected heady day in the limelight. Top-ten finishes in the opening three races included sixth at Interlagos despite a sticking throttle. He crashed into Eddie Irvine's Ferrari during the early laps at the Nürburgring and was lacklustre at Imola.

In Monaco, where he was only 14th on the grid, Panis made the most of the retirements by passing four cars on a circuit where overtaking was virtually impossible. He survived a spin and judged the changing weather conditions perfectly to score a shock victory. It was Ligier's ninth and final GP win.

That stand-out achievement was followed by Panis's best qualifying performance of the season, eighth in Spain. Both Ligiers suffered engine failures within a lap of each other in Canada and Panis lost a points score at Magny-Cours due to a problem with the refuelling rig. The JS43 lacked grip and balance at Silverstone where Panis crashed on Friday (a big shunt at Bridge corner) and Saturday. He eventually parked his ill-handling car after 40 laps of the race to end a weekend to forget. Seventh in Germany after an unscheduled stop to change flat-spotted tyres, Panis recovered from a poor start to claim fifth after another race of attrition in Hungary. Ligier were off the pace at Estoril and he just failed to add to his three points scores when seventh in Japan.

Diniz only outqualified his team-mate once, when Panis endured a troubled Saturday in Germany. After finishing an understeering eighth in Brazil, his Ligier-Mugen became engulfed in fire in Argentina just after its only fuel stop because the fuel valve had not closed. Delayed during the European GP when he collided with Damon Hill's recovering Williams-Renault, Diniz finished with back pain due to gravel that had been thrown into the cockpit in the incident. He was seventh at Imola despite a 10sec stop-go penalty for baulking Michael Schumacher and his transmission failed on lap six of the Monaco GP. Sixth and last in Spain, he retired from the next six GPs, having challenged for a point in France when ahead of his team-mate for once. Those DNFs came to an end at Monza where, a day after Jacques Villeneuve had called him an 'idiot' for driving him off the road on the approach to the Parabolica, Diniz used the prodigious Mugen power to finish a creditable sixth. He spun out at Estoril (having collided with Ricardo Rosset) and Suzuka, the latter incident his fourth accident of a long weekend.

Despite its first victory in 15 years, Ligier was only sixth overall due to poor reliability and accidents amid a turbulent campaign that ended with resurfacing rumours of Alain Prost's takeover.

RED BULL SAUBER FORD

Ford decided to follow the prevailing trend and build a new V10 engine even before the 1995 World Championship had begun. Martin Walters and his team at Cosworth settled on a 72-degree vee-angle and the prototype was on the dyno by the autumn. It was more compact and lighter than its V8 predecessor despite the additional cylinders. Already informed that newcomers Stewart Grand Prix would be Ford's works partner in 1997, Sauber spent much of 1996 solving engine teething troubles and searching for horsepower.

Heinz-Harald Frentzen was in the final year of his contract and no one triggered his $2 million buy-out clause. Twice a winner for Benetton, Johnny Herbert was preferred to Mark Blundell as Frentzen's team-mate. Norberto Fontana remained as test driver. Martin Whitaker replaced Peter Gillitzer as Ford's director of European motorsport in the spring.

The Sauber C15-Ford first turned a wheel at Paul Ricard on the evening of 15 January. This was a conventional chassis with a slender new semi-automatic six-speed mounted longitudinally in a magnesium casing. Leo Ress and aerodynamicist René Hilhorst retained the raised nose introduced at the 1995 San Marino GP and opted for a Williams-like anhedral lower tier to the rear wing. The sidepods were high and narrow while the push-rod suspension had three shock absorbers. 'Fly-by-wire' throttle and hand clutch/two-pedal layout were early developments. The original side-blown exhausts were replaced from round two by a new layout exiting over the central diffuser. A lower seat position was introduced in Canada when it was discovered that the tall Frentzen was disrupting airflow to the engine. The C15 and its drivers were officially presented at a 'showbiz' launch in Baden on 8 February to the sound of a Swiss rock opera entitled 'Space Dream'. Red Bull was contracted as title sponsor for the rest of the decade and the prominence of 'technical partner' Petronas was increased.

Pedro Diniz, Ligier JS43-Mugen (San Marino GP)

Heinz-Harald Frentzen, Sauber C15-Ford (British GP)

Sauber did not take part in that winter's major group tests so the C15's potential was unclear ahead of the Australian GP and it was initially plagued by a disappointing engine and handling that snapped from understeer to oversteer. Despite six different upgrades, the engine stubbornly remained 100bhp shy of its leading rivals. Frentzen qualified and finished in the top ten at Melbourne and challenged for points in Brazil before an engine issue halted proceedings, the first of four successive retirements that included spins in Argentina and at the Nürburgring. Herbert was involved in Martin Brundle's Australian accident and did not take the restart. Halted by electrical failure at Interlagos, Herbert was a near-brakeless ninth after an uncompetitive weekend in Argentina and seventh at the Nürburgring.

Both retired at Imola and were classified at the end of the chaotic Monaco GP. Frentzen could have won but had to change his front wing when he ran into the back of Eddie Irvine at Ste-Dévote. They ran third and fourth to the flag with Herbert scoring the team's second-only podium finish. Frentzen stopped in the pits after being shown the chequered flag a lap early but retained fourth as no other cars were running. Frentzen was fourth again in Spain where Herbert, who had outqualified his team-mate for the first time, aquaplaned off the circuit in the downpour.

Seventh in Canada, Herbert was disqualified from the French GP when his C15's bargeboards were found to be too high. Both finished without scoring at Silverstone and Frentzen understeered (the C15's persistent handling trait) to a distant eighth in Germany. Herbert used an upgraded engine with improved mid-range power to qualify eighth and run sixth in Hungary before both drivers'

engines failed. Having collided at the first corner in Belgium, Frentzen crashed at the Roggia chicane on lap eight of the Italian GP and Herbert lost seventh when his engine let go on the last lap.

Another lacklustre campaign for the Swiss outfit concluded with double finishes in Portugal and Japan. Frentzen made a bad start at Estoril but beat Herbert into seventh and signed off his Sauber career by finishing sixth at Suzuka. Sauber-Ford scored just 11 points – seven of which came in Monte Carlo – for an underachieving seventh in the constructors' standings.

Johnny Herbert, Sauber C15-Ford (French GP)

Mika Salo, Tyrrell 024-Yamaha (Japanese GP)

TYRRELL YAMAHA

Ken Tyrrell confirmed that Mika Salo had re-signed in the week following his fifth place at the 1995 Italian GP. Johnny Herbert, Ricardo Rosset and Vincenzo Sospiri were all mentioned as possible team-mates but the loss of title sponsor Nokia before Christmas placed increased importance on the money Ukyo Katayama could bring. He was confirmed for a fourth successive season on 12 January.

Tyrrell continued its exclusive partnership with Yamaha, which introduced a brand-new 72-degree V10 engine that was the smallest and lightest on the 1996 grid. More power, higher revs and better packaging were promised when the engine was revealed but the design was overly ambitious for Yamaha's limited budget so the OX11A proved a severe disappointment.

Ukyo Katayama, Tyrrell 024-Yamaha (Monaco GP)

The association with Fondmetal Technologies ended – running an underfunded team in Surrey with wind tunnel and technical facilities in northern Italy had proved far from ideal – although Gabriele Rumi's parent company still provided some backing. Katayama's presence ensured further sponsorship from Mild Seven while Korean Air and Morse computers bolstered Tyrrell's meagre budget.

The new engine, gearbox and rear suspension were tested in a modified 023B a week before the conventional Tyrrell 024-Yamaha was launched on 30 January. Harvey Postlethwaite and deputy technical director Mike Gascoyne aimed to improve aerodynamics, low-speed turn-in and reliability, while concentrating on engineering quality throughout the manufacturing process. They switched to a longitudinal semi-automatic aluminium gearbox and reverted to a raised nose, with twin supports for the full-width front wing. The conventional push-rod suspension had three shock absorbers as was now fashionable. Reserve driver Emmanuel Collard tested the previously discarded 'Hydrolink' suspension but it was not reintroduced as originally planned. The relatively simple rear diffuser was replaced as part of a revised aero package introduced at the Nürburgring. A novel solution to reducing drag was tried during German GP qualifying when smaller front tyres were fitted at the rear as well. The 024 had no particular vices but the engine was woefully unreliable and lacked horsepower. The car handled well from the outset but restricted mileage prevented drivers and engineers from optimising set-up.

Salo gave the new car its shakedown at Brands Hatch before Tyrrell travelled to Estoril, where the Finn raised hopes by lapping quicker than reigning champions Benetton-Renault. He was sixth at the subsequent group test at the Portuguese venue and scored points at the opening two races when sixth in Australia and fifth in Brazil. Too small for comfort until the cockpit was modified, the 5ft 5in Katayama finished outside the points at both races. He was ninth in Brazil after an eventful race: he was hit in the eye by debris at the start after leaving his visor open to prevent misting, spun around by Pedro Lamy's Minardi-Ford on lap two, then waved through the pitlane as the team waited for Salo. In Argentina, Salo's fifth place on Friday provided false hope as oversteer ruined qualifying and both cars retired without figuring.

The upgrade introduced at the European GP included aerodynamic carbon-fibre shrouds over the rear wishbones. Salo had a new chassis that was lighter and stiffer but both cars were disqualified after finishing tenth and 12th on the road. Salo survived being rammed by Jean Alesi's Benetton-Renault on lap two but was found to be 1.5kg underweight. Katayama stalled at the start and was excluded for the resulting push-start.

Salo started from a season-best eighth at Imola and made a great start to run fourth in the early stages. He resumed in that position after his first pitstop only for the engine to fail next time around. Katayama was sixth when his transmission failed. Both drivers crashed in Monaco, Salo while lying fourth when he hit Eddie Irvine's spun Ferrari with just five laps to go; with only four cars still circulating, Salo still earned two points on distance covered.

The top wishbones at the front were enclosed in a triangle of carbon-fibre at the Spanish GP to reduce drag. The FIA ruled that this did not constitute an illegal moveable aerodynamic device but drag-reducing suspension was limited for 1997. Salo's engine refused to fire before the start of the parade lap and he was black-flagged for switching to the spare car after the race had begun. Slowed by falling oil pressure at Magny-Cours, his engine blew in Canada and Italy as Tyrrell's relationship with Yamaha deteriorated. He finished seventh after a one-stop strategy at Silverstone and ninth in Germany as Tyrrell slipped down the order as richer teams developed their machinery. Eliminated on the opening lap of the Hungaroring, Salo beat Katayama into seventh in Belgium and 11th at Estoril on rare double finishes for the team.

Katayama retired from seven successive races that included engine problems in Spain (when running last), France and Britain. He received a suspended race ban for causing a collision with Ricardo Rosset in Canada and crashed at Hockenheim's first chicane during the German GP. Seventh in Hungary, despite a damaged radiator and rising water temperature, was the best of his six finishes. Tyrrell's season, and its partnership with Yamaha, came to an appropriate conclusion at Suzuka, where engine trouble forced both drivers to retire.

FOOTWORK HART

Arrows co-founder Jackie Oliver admitted that he only had 'a survival budget' on the eve of the new season and talks with Tom Walkinshaw were held after the 1996 Australian GP. Having planned to buy Ligier by the end of TWR's contract with the French team in July,

Jos Verstappen, Footwork FA17-Hart (Argentinian GP)

Walkinshaw grew tired of negotiations with Guy Ligier, who was still a minority shareholder and was reluctant to sell for fear of relocation to England. Walkinshaw visited Arrows on 15 March and his takeover was announced on the Saturday of the Brazilian GP.

Footwork Arrows's drivers for 1996 had good reputations but both endured difficult campaigns as the team stagnated. A month after being released by Benetton, Jos Verstappen tested a Footwork FA16-Hart at Silverstone on 10 October 1995 although mechanical gremlins prevented worthwhile mileage. Having impressed technical director Alan Jenkins during an Estoril test in September 1993, the Dutchman was quick again when he drove the FA16 at the same circuit in December 1995. Oliver confirmed Verstappen and F3000 runner-up Ricardo Rosset as his drivers and Verstappen gave the Footwork FA17-Hart its shakedown on Silverstone's National Circuit on 15 February. Kenny Bräck joined as test driver but left in August after just two outings with neither party happy.

Jenkins's last Footwork Arrows before he moved to newcomers Stewart Grand Prix was another neat design with high nose and pronounced lateral head protection, but it had inherent understeer and an underpowered V8 engine. The side winglets were mounted adjacent to the engine, three-damper suspension was retained front and rear, and the six-speed longitudinal semi-automatic gearbox revised. Chief engineer Alan McDonald had arrived from Paul Stewart Racing in August 1995 and Jordan team manager John Walton joined 12 months later.

Two white, blue and red FA17s were sent to Melbourne for the opening race of the season, sporting Philips Car Systems and Hype

Ricardo Rosset, Footwork FA17-Hart (German GP)

(energy drink) sponsorship. Sasol withdrew from F1 to concentrate on the South African market. There was no spare car and the team could only afford four engines. A star of Australian practice when he regularly featured in the top ten, Verstappen was disappointed to only qualify 12th following oversteer and a spin. His engine failed after 15 laps in the midfield.

With takeover agreed before the Brazilian GP, the cars had TWR motifs on the endplates at Interlagos and Power Horse (another Austrian energy drink) replaced Hype. New chairman Walkinshaw acquired 51 per cent of the team. Minority shareholder Oliver remained as sporting director and Daniele Audetto was appointed managing director. A planned move into TWR's new facility in the former British Telecom training centre at Leafield was delayed until final payments were made in July. The Arrows wind tunnel (40 per cent scale) in Milton Keynes was retained.

Seventh when an engine valve spring failed in Brazil, Verstappen's excellent seventh on the grid in Buenos Aires confirmed the promise of driver and chassis alike. He made a last-lap attempt to snatch fifth from Eddie Irvine's hamstrung Ferrari only to run wide and finish sixth. That proved to be Footwork-Hart's only points score of 1996.

The cars sported new red-and-blue colours at the Nürburgring, where Ligier's Frank Dernie and Tony Dowe attended their first race as new technical and operations director respectively. Verstappen could not repeat Friday's top-ten pace when it mattered in the European GP and had another refuelling mishap at Imola. He was waved on his way before David Lowe had disengaged the hose and the refueller dislocated his shoulder when he was sent flying by Verstappen's right-rear tyre. When Verstappen crashed head-on at the first corner of the Monaco GP, it was his third accident of an

expensive weekend as a frustrated Walkinshaw demanded he sign a 1997 contract or face being replaced by a pay driver.

Newly married to karting star Sophie Kumpen, Verstappen retired early in Canada and crashed when steering-arm failure ended an uncompetitive weekend in France. He tried Hart's new air-valve engine in qualifying but there was no budget to develop it. More and more frustrated as he slid down the grid, Verstappen finished tenth at Silverstone and crashed out of the next three races, including a 130mph shunt during the Belgian GP when a front hub failed at Stavelot. After eighth place in Italy, his engine failed in Portugal and 11th in Japan represented a downbeat conclusion to an increasingly disappointing campaign.

Rosset was the only driver to be outqualified by his team-mate at every race. Ninth on his début in Australia, Rosset crashed at Interlagos's 150mph final corner during his home race and was prevented from refuelling at Imola by Verstappen's problem. He completed a miserable Monaco weekend for the team by crashing at Rascasse on lap four. In Canada, he was outqualified by a Forti and crashed with Ukyo Katayama on the seventh lap of the race. Eleventh in the European, French and German GPs, he finished a career-best eighth despite an 'off' at the Hungaroring and passed Pedro Lamy to claim ninth in Belgium.

Arrows was contracted to Bridgestone when the Japanese tyre manufacturer confirmed that it was entering F1 in 1997. Testing began in June with an ex-works Ligier JS41-Mugen stationed at Suzuka (with Aguri Suzuki involved) and Footwork Arrows staying on after each GP. Understandably, Goodyear refused to supply tyres for 1996 testing so competitiveness waned. Verstappen's promising early showings were a distant memory by the end of the year.

Pedro Lamy, Minardi M195B-Ford (Japanese GP)

MINARDI TEAM

Minardi test driver Giancarlo Fisichella impressed during the winter but money was as tight as ever so a driver with a budget was preferred. Luca Badoer and Tarso Marques also tested before Taki Inoue was chosen as Pedro Lamy's team-mate in February. The little-known Esteban Tuero signed a long-term development contract that tied him to Minardi to the end of the millennium. The departures of Aldo Costa and René Hilhorst left technical co-ordinator Gabriele Tredozi as the senior engineer in a depleted department. Frédéric Dhainhaut returned to F1 as sporting director following a couple of years working in driver management.

Minardi's request to use old-specification Yamaha V10 engines was refused so it continued with Cosworth's Ford ED V8 and Magneti Marelli electronics, although the increased revs of the new ED2 engine caused an issue with its air valves. These were revised when Cosworth reworked the bottom of the engine in the ED3, which Minardi used from the Spanish GP. With revised electronics, the ED3 revved to 14,500rpm and a five per cent power increase was claimed. Restricted budget prevented a new car design and the lightly updated Minardi M195B-Ford (with mandatory raised cockpit surround) ran at Estoril on 14 February. The additional centre wing seen at high-downforce circuits in 1995 was used in Argentina.

Inoue promised a large proportion of Minardi's budget but his sponsor pulled out a week before the Australian GP so Minardi handed F1 débuts to Fisichella in Melbourne and Marques at both South American races. Each time they outqualified the more experienced Lamy but retired: Fisichella was impressive before his clutch failed while Marques was a first-lap spinner in Brazil and rammed Martin Brundle's Jordan-Peugeot in Argentina. Lamy

registered Minardi's only finish during that time when tenth in Brazil despite hitting Ukyo Katayama's Tyrrell-Yamaha on the second lap.

Marques could not secure enough sponsorship to continue so Fisichella returned at the Nürburgring, where the Minardi-Fords finished at the back. Racing with revised front suspension at Imola, Lamy outqualified a team-mate for the first time in 1996 and finished ninth following a 10sec stop-go penalty for speeding in the pitlane. When they squandered Minardi's best opportunity to score points by crashing into each other at Ste-Dévote on the opening lap of the Monaco GP, Giancarlo Minardi was furious: 'In 12 years of Formula 1, I have never seen anything like this… it's annoying to see

Giancarlo Fisichella, Minardi M195B-Ford (San Marino GP)

everything wasted by two unbelievable mistakes by our two drivers.' They managed to repeat the feat two weeks later in Spain, where heavy rain and zero visibility at least provided some excuse.

In Canada, Fisichella was eighth (and last) after a lonely race while Lamy was eliminated when he was hit while Brundle lapped him. They were last in France (Lamy) and England (Fisichella) before another driver change. The impressive Fisichella had outqualified Lamy on all bar two occasions but financial imperative led to 38-year-old journeyman Giovanni Lavaggi replacing him for six races from the German GP. A non-qualifier at three, Lavaggi was tenth after a spin in Hungary, blew his engine in Italy and was the penultimate finisher in Portugal.

Having circulated at the back in Germany when hampered by a slipping clutch and lack of horsepower, Lamy hit Pedro Diniz's spun Ligier-Mugen on the opening lap in Hungary but continued before retiring with damaged suspension at his first pitstop. Tenth and last following a refuelling problem in Belgium and sidelined by engine failure at Monza, Lamy lost two laps when he stalled at the start of the Portuguese GP so finished behind his tardy team-mate. He tried the prototype 1997 ED4 engine at the following week's Estoril test and reported improvements. Shaken by a 145mph testing shunt at Estoril's Turn 2, Lamy beat Ricardo Rosset's Footwork-Hart in qualifying for the Japanese GP (with the ED4) and in the race (having reverted to the ED3) as Minardi finished 1996 without scoring a point.

FORTI GRAND PRIX

Guido Forti's plans for 1996 received a double hit when the FIA passed the new 107 per cent qualifying rule and Pedro Diniz took his money to Ligier. Andrea Montermini had come close to signing in 1995 and represented the team at that year's Bologna motor show supersprint. He signed an eight-race contract in February and Luca Badoer was preferred to Gianni Morbidelli for the second seat. Forti hired Cesare Fiorio to review the team structure, although he left before his three-month contract was due to expire after the French GP. Former Ferrari designer George Ryton arrived and at the Spanish GP was confirmed as technical director for the rest of the season.

The cumbersome 1995 car was revised as the FG01B to comply with new regulations, with ex-Sauber Ford Zetec-R V8 engines replacing the EDs previously used. The Forti-Fords would have regularly non-qualified in 1995 if the 107 per cent rule had applied, so the drivers faced an uphill task before a new car was ready. As predicted, neither qualified in Australia or at the Nürburgring for round four, but both made it onto the grid at the intervening races – which, given pre-season scepticism in the press, was an achievement. The cars were fitted with the rear diffuser from the new car in Brazil, where Montermini started from the pitlane and spun twice on the same lap before parking his FG01B, while Badoer finished last (11th). Montermini was last (tenth) in Argentina but Badoer collided with Diniz while being

Tarso Marques, Minardi M195B-Ford (Brazilian GP)

Luca Badoer, Forti FG01B-Ford (Argentinian GP)

Giovanni Lavaggi, Minardi M195B-Ford (Italian GP)

Andrea Montermini, Forti FG01B-Ford (Brazilian GP)

lapped and rolled, the Italian able to crawl out unaided.

Having been unveiled in the paddock at the Nürburgring, the Forti FG03-Ford was lighter than its predecessor and featured a distinctive raised nose and lower sidepods. Chris Radage, who had worked for Sergio Rinland's Astauto design studio in Tolworth, began the design and Riccardo de Marco completed it. Ryton found the FG03 had an inherent aerodynamic problem with poor rear-end grip, although it was a step forward from the FG01B.

A single FG03 was ready for Badoer's use at the San Marino GP and after qualifying with ease he served two stop-go penalties for speeding in the pitlane and finished last (tenth). Montermini was given seven qualifying laps in the FG03 but did not make the cut and Forti's application for him to start in the old car was refused. Both drivers had their own FG03 at Monaco, where they qualified at the back and crashed. Montermini did not start after wrecking his car in the morning warm-up and Badoer received a $5,000 fine and a two-race suspended ban after colliding with Jacques Villeneuve while being lapped for the seventh time.

Forti arrived in Barcelona sporting the green, white and red colours of the mysterious Shannon Racing Team, which ran two cars in F3000 and sponsored 13 F3 cars across Europe. As part of the deal, the Finfirst Group that owned Shannon acquired a majority shareholding in Forti. The new alliance got off to a bad start for both failed to qualify once more. They retired in Canada, Montermini due to loose ballast in his cockpit, and in France –

Luca Badoer, Forti FG03-Ford (French GP)

but now there were new problems. The relationship with Finfirst was unravelling and Cosworth refused to supply engines for the British GP until outstanding bills were settled. Limited to just three qualifying laps apiece at Silverstone, neither driver qualified. To make matters worse, the transporter crashed into a car in a service station on its return journey to base.

The cars were sent to Hockenheim but spent the weekend in the garage as Guido Forti argued that Finfirst had forfeited ownership of the team as promised monies had not materialised. He insisted throughout the summer that the cars would return but Forti Grand Prix was not seen again.

Andrea Montermini, Forti FG03-Ford (French GP)

1996 RESULTS

DRIVER PERFORMANCE

DRIVER	CAR–ENGINE	AUS	BR	RA	EU	RSM	MC	E	CDN	F	GB	D	H	B	I	P	J
Jean Alesi	Benetton B196-Renault	6 R	5 2	4 3 FL	4 R	5 6	3 R FL	4 2	4 3	3 3	5 R	5 2	5 3	7 4	6 2	3 4	9 R
Luca Badoer	Forti FG01B-Ford	21 DNQ	19 11	21 R	22 DNQ	–	–	–	–	–	–	–	–	–	–	–	–
	Forti FG03-Ford	–	–	–	–	21 10	21 R	21 DNQ	20 R	20 R	22 DNQ	NT DNP	–	–	–	–	–
Rubens Barrichello	Jordan 196-Peugeot	8 R	2 R	6 4	5 5	9 5	6 R	7 R	8 R	10 9	6 4	9 6	13 6	10 R	10 5	9 R	11 9
Gerhard Berger	Benetton B196-Renault	7 4	8 R	5 R	8 9	7 3	4 R	5 R	7 R	4 4	7 2	2 **13**	6 R	5 6 FL	8 R	5 6	4 4
Martin Brundle	Jordan 196-Peugeot	19 R	6 12	15 R	11 6	12 R	16 R	15 R	9 6	8 8	8 6	10 10	12 R	8 R	9 4	10 9	10 5
David Coulthard	McLaren MP4/11-Mercedes-Benz	13 R	14 R	9 7	6 3	4 **R**	5 2	14 R	10 4	7 6	9 5	7 5	9 R	4 **R**	5 R	8 13	8 8
Pedro Diniz	Ligier JS43-Mugen	20 10	22 8	18 R	17 10	17 7	17 R	17 6	18 R	11 R	17 R	11 R	15 R	15 R	14 6	18 R	16 R
Giancarlo Fisichella	Minardi M195B-Ford	16 R	–	–	18 13	19 R	18 R	19 R	16 8	17 R	18 11	–	–	–	–	–	–
Heinz-Harald Frentzen	Sauber C15-Ford	9 8	9 R	11 R	10 R	10 R	9 4	11 4	12 R	12 R	11 8	13 8	10 R	11 R	13 R	11 7	7 6
Mika Häkkinen	McLaren MP4/11-Mercedes-Benz	5 5	7 4	8 R	9 8	11 8	8 6	10 5	6 5	5 5	4 3	4 R	7 4	6 **3**	4 3	7 R	5 3
Johnny Herbert	Sauber C15-Ford	14 R	12 R	17 9	12 7	15 R	13 3	9 R	15 7	16 DSQ	13 9	14 R	8 R	12 R	12 9	12 8	13 10
Damon Hill	Williams FW18-Renault	2 **1** FL	1 1 FL	1 1	4 1 FL	2 1 FL	2 R	1 R	1 1	2 1	1 R	1 1 FL	2 2 FL	2 5	1 **R**	1 2	2 1
Eddie Irvine	Ferrari F310	3 3	10 7	10 5	7 R	6 4	7 7	6 R	5 R	22 R	10 R	8 R	4 R	9 R	7 R	6 5	6 R
Ukyo Katayama	Tyrrell 024-Yamaha	15 11	16 9	13 R	16 DSQ	16 R	15 R	16 R	17 R	14 R	12 R	16 R	14 7	17 8	16 10	14 12	14 R
Pedro Lamy	Minardi M195B-Ford	17 R	18 10	19 R	19 12	18 9	19 R	18 R	19 R	18 12	19 R	18 12	19 R	19 10	18 R	19 16	18 12
Giovanni Lavaggi	Minardi M195B-Ford	–	–	–	–	–	–	–	–	–	–	20 DNQ	20 10	20 DNQ	20 R	20 15	20 DNQ
Tarso Marques	Minardi M195B-Ford	–	21 R	14 R	–	–	–	–	–	–	–	–	–	–	–	–	–
Andrea Montermini	Forti FG01B-Ford	22 DNQ	20 R	22 10	21 DNQ	–	–	–	–	–	–	–	–	–	–	–	–
	Forti FG03-Ford	–	–	–	–	22 DNQ	22 DNS	22 DNQ	22 R	21 R	21 DNQ	NT DNP	–	–	–	–	–
Olivier Panis	Ligier JS43-Mugen	11 7	15 6	12 8	15 R	13 R	14 **1**	8 R	11 R	9 7	16 R	12 7	11 5	14 R	11 R	15 10	12 7
Ricardo Rosset	Footwork FA17-Hart	18 9	17 R	20 R	20 11	20 R	20 R	20 R	21 R	19 11	20 R	19 11	18 8	18 9	19 R	17 14	19 13
Mika Salo	Tyrrell 024-Yamaha	10 6	11 5	16 R	14 DSQ	8 R	11 5	12 DSQ	14 R	13 10	14 7	15 9	16 R	13 7	17 R	13 11	15 R
Michael Schumacher	Ferrari F310	4 R	4 3	2 R	3 2	1 2	1 R	3 1 FL	3 R	1 DNS	3 R	3 4	1 **9**	3 1	3 1 FL	4 3	3 2
Jos Verstappen	Footwork FA17-Hart	12 R	13 R	7 6	13 R	14 R	12 R	13 R	13 R	15 R	15 10	17 R	17 R	16 R	15 8	16 R	17 11
Jacques Villeneuve	Williams FW18-Renault	1 **2** FL	3 R	3 2	2 **1**	3 11	10 R	2 **3**	2 2 FL	6 2 FL	2 **1** FL	6 3	3 **1**	1 2	2 7	2 **1** FL	1 R FL

FORMULA 1 RACE WINNERS

ROUND	RACE (CIRCUIT)	DATE	WINNER
1	Transurban Australian Grand Prix (Albert Park)	Mar 10	Damon Hill (Williams FW18-Renault)
2	Grande Prêmio do Brasil (Interlagos)	Mar 31	Damon Hill (Williams FW18-Renault)
3	Gran Premio Marlboro de Argentina (Buenos Aires)	Apr 7	Damon Hill (Williams FW18-Renault)
4	Grosser Preis von Europa (Nürburgring)	Apr 28	Jacques Villeneuve (Williams FW18-Renault)
5	Gran Premio di San Marino (Imola)	May 5	Damon Hill (Williams FW18-Renault)
6	Grand Prix de Monaco (Monte Carlo)	May 19	Olivier Panis (Ligier JS43-Mugen)
7	Gran Premio Marlboro de España (Catalunya)	Jun 2	Michael Schumacher (Ferrari F310)
8	Grand Prix Molson du Canada (Montréal)	Jun 16	Damon Hill (Williams FW18-Renault)
9	Grand Prix de France (Magny-Cours)	Jun 30	Damon Hill (Williams FW18-Renault)
10	British Grand Prix (Silverstone)	Jul 14	Jacques Villeneuve (Williams FW18-Renault)
11	Grosser Mobil 1 Preis von Deutschland (Hockenheim)	Jul 28	Damon Hill (Williams FW18-Renault)
12	Marlboro Magyar Nagydíj (Hungaroring)	Aug 11	Jacques Villeneuve (Williams FW18-Renault)
13	Grand Prix de Belgique (Spa-Francorchamps)	Aug 25	Michael Schumacher (Ferrari F310)
14	Pioneer Gran Premio d'Italia (Monza)	Sep 8	Michael Schumacher (Ferrari F310)
15	Grande Premio de Portugal (Estoril)	Sep 22	Jacques Villeneuve (Williams FW18-Renault)
16	Fuji Television Japanese Grand Prix (Suzuka)	Oct 13	Damon Hill (Williams FW18-Renault)

DRIVERS' CHAMPIONSHIP

	DRIVERS	POINTS
1	Damon Hill	97
2	Jacques Villeneuve	78
3	Michael Schumacher	59
4	Jean Alesi	47
5	Mika Häkkinen	31
6	Gerhard Berger	21
7	David Coulthard	18
8	Rubens Barrichello	14
9	Olivier Panis	13
10	Eddie Irvine	11
11	Martin Brundle	8
12	Heinz-Harald Frentzen	7
13	Mika Salo	5
14	Johnny Herbert	4
15	Pedro Diniz	2
16	Jos Verstappen	1

The Australian Grand Prix moved to Melbourne in 1996

CONSTRUCTORS' CHAMPIONSHIP

	CONSTRUCTORS	POINTS
1	Williams-Renault	175
2	Ferrari	70
3	Benetton-Renault	68
4	McLaren-Mercedes-Benz	49
5	Jordan-Peugeot	22
6	Ligier-Mugen	15
7	Sauber-Ford	11
8	Tyrrell-Yamaha	5
9	Footwork-Hart	1

Michael Schumacher and Jacques Villeneuve collide during the title decider at Jerez

1997

JACQUES DENIES MICHAEL AS RENAULT BOWS OUT

The Schumacher brothers crashed into each other at the Nürburgring, denting Michael's hopes

Jacques Villeneuve
FIA
Formula 1
World
Champion

Jacques Villeneuve celebrates with race engineer Jock Clear

Constructors' champions since 1992, Renault shocked its client teams by announcing its withdrawal at the end of 1997. That year's World Championship was a two-way battle between Williams-Renault's Jacques Villeneuve and Ferrari superstar Michael Schumacher that reached an unsatisfactory conclusion at Jerez. Schumacher was disqualified from the 1997 standings for driving into his rival but many believed he escaped lightly. Schumacher had already angered his colleagues at the pre-Italian GP test when he completed another four laps of Monza after the session had been red-flagged.

Villeneuve also had his run-in with the governing body. Already censured for criticising the 1998 rules, he received a one-race ban (suspended for one race) for a safety-car infringement at Silverstone. He was then handed another one-race ban (suspended until the 1998 San Marino GP) for ignoring yellow flags during the warm-up at Monza. He faced another ban when he did not heed waved yellows during practice for the Japanese GP, his third such offence of the year, but raced under appeal.

Bridgestone's entry into F1 precipitated a tyre war with Goodyear. The FIA moved quickly to prevent a return to qualifying tyres by stipulating that a driver must use the same compound of dry rubber in qualifying and the race.

Max Mosley was unopposed in securing a third term as president of the Fédération Internationale de l'Automobile. Charlie Whiting replaced Roger Lane-Nott as FIA race director after a single season, with Jo Bauer assuming the role of technical delegate. Aircraft-style data recorders ('black boxes') developed by Delco Electronics were mandatory so that accidents could be analysed and lessons learned. The length-to-width ratio of drag-reducing suspension was limited and the height of the winglets in front of the rear wheels reduced by 10cm. The Belgian GP was started behind the safety car due to the flooded track, a first for F1. Radical proposals to reduce GPs to two-day meetings were dropped.

The Concorde Agreement had expired but Williams, McLaren and Tyrrell did not sign the new document so the row regarding F1 governance for 1997–2001 rumbled on all season. A standard pitlane speed limit – 80kph during practice and qualifying, 120kph during the race – was introduced at all circuits. Testing was now only allowed at Barcelona, Magny-Cours, Silverstone and Monza plus F1-approved circuits that did not have a scheduled GP, with an FIA inspector and medical staff present.

Paul Ricard, Magny-Cours and Le Mans all bid to hold the French GP and the Fédération Française du Sport Automobile originally approved Ricard's application. However, a three-year contract extension with Magny-Cours was announced just six weeks later. Even then, a row with national television stations threatened the event and was only resolved

in April. The Austrian GP returned to the calendar on a revised version of the Österreichring, which was renamed due to sponsorship from the A1 mobile phone network. The Nürburgring remained on the schedule with the race now named after nearby Luxembourg. The calendar was extended to 17 races with the final race originally to be held in Portugal. However, that was replaced by the European GP at Jerez when work to update Estoril had not begun in May.

Prospective new challengers from Japan and Serbia failed to materialise. Minoru Hayashi's Dome company, 1994 Japanese F3000 champions with Marco Apicella, unveiled the Akiyoshi Oku-designed Dome F105-Mugen in Tokyo on 18 March 1996. This was a conventional F1 car with raised nose, all-in-one bodywork including the half-length sidepods and airbox, 1995-specification Mugen V10, Minardi six-speed gearbox and double-wishbone/push-rod suspension. A supply of old Goodyear tyres was agreed and the car first ran at Miné in April. An oil leak caused it to catch fire at Suzuka and the project was cancelled when budget could not be found before its self-imposed deadline of the 1996 Japanese GP. Sporadic testing continued for the rest of the decade but Dome never did enter F1. In Serbia, Zoran Stefanović announced a new team, Stefan Grand Prix, on 23 September 1996. George Ryton was approached to be technical director but this proved to be just the first of Stefanović's various unsuccessful attempts to enter F1.

David Coulthard won the Australian Grand Prix for McLaren-Mercedes

Jacques Villeneuve, Williams FW19-Renault (Japanese GP)

ROTHMANS WILLIAMS RENAULT

There was no sentiment in Williams's driver choice for 1997. Championship leader Damon Hill was released before the 1996 Italian GP with rumours that Sauber's Heinz-Harald Frentzen would be Jacques Villeneuve's team-mate finally confirmed. The German signed a two-year deal and began his Williams career by testing at Estoril on 22–24 October. That was in the FW18B test chassis with the 1997 engine and Villeneuve's preferred two-pedal set-up as Frentzen tried left-foot braking for the first time.

With chief designer Adrian Newey on gardening leave while his exit to McLaren was negotiated, the Williams FW19-Renault was launched on 31 January, a week later than originally scheduled. It immediately lapped Barcelona at record pace although the Benetton B197-Renault grabbed the single-lap headlines during the winter.

The FW19 was another evolution of the recent designs from Newey and technical director Patrick Head. The compact new six-speed transverse gearbox had already been tested at Jerez in another *muletta* – the FW18C – and power steering was an early addition. The nose was slightly lower, bargeboards longer and airbox reprofiled with teardrop-shaped inlet designed to reduce disturbance from the driver's helmet. The drag-reducing top-front wishbones introduced at the 1996 Italian GP remained within the new rules. Sculpted sidepods fell away ahead of the wheels and the rear bodywork that enclosed the suspension was lower than before. The deformable rear impact structure was integrated with the central wing support. Electronic brake bias was used for the first time at Monza and a longer-wheelbase version introduced in Austria.

Geoff Willis, who had worked with Newey at Leyton House March and Williams, was appointed chief aerodynamicist and Gavin Fisher became senior designer. In its final year before withdrawal, Renault reduced the height of its all-conquering V10 engine by widening the vee angle from 68 to 71 degrees. This RS09 version was nine per cent lighter than before, although Renault did not pursue the low-weight extremes of its rivals in order to maintain reliability.

Pre-season favourites once more, Williams-Renault dominated the Australian GP weekend only to leave Melbourne empty-handed. They locked-out the front row but pole winner Villeneuve was hit by Eddie Irvine's Ferrari at the first corner. Frentzen made the better start and had just set the fastest lap when he lost the lead due to a stubborn wheel nut at his second pitstop. He was second when his left brake disc shattered with two laps to go. Again slow away from pole position at Interlagos, Villeneuve ran off the road while trying to defend the outside line from Michael Schumacher. Relieved to see the red flag and beaten away again at the restart, he passed Schumacher on the opening lap and nursed a brake issue to win. Frentzen's Brazilian GP was a nightmare for he qualified only eighth and finished ninth having taken the spare car after an 'off' at the original start. They started from the front row in Argentina, where Villeneuve withstood illness, gear-selection difficulties and Irvine's pressure to win by 0.979sec, while Frentzen retired with clutch failure when second.

Frentzen's luck finally changed at Imola: he took the lead during the first pitstops and beat old sparring partner Schumacher by 1.237sec to score his maiden GP victory. On pole for the fourth successive race, Villeneuve retired when his gearbox randomly changed gear. Both drivers had received suspended race bans for failing to slow for waved yellows during qualifying.

In Monaco, which brought Frentzen's first pole position, Williams wrongly chose slick tyres for the start despite the wet track. An early change to intermediates dropped both drivers to the back and they crashed before making an impression. Villeneuve dominated the Spanish GP weekend where other Goodyear runners, including Frentzen, suffered blistering tyres.

Williams-Renault briefly lost its advantage to Ferrari, and more particularly Schumacher, in Canada and France, the German converting pole position into victory at Magny-Cours to open a 14-point lead in the drivers' standings. Erstwhile championship leader Villeneuve crashed into the 'Wall of Champions' on lap two of his home race. With hair freshly dyed blonde at Magny-Cours, he recovered from a heavy practice crash to finish fourth after spinning at the final corner of the race while trying to take third from Eddie Irvine. Fourth in Canada following a slow start and unscheduled stop to change blistered tyres, Frentzen qualified and finished second in France.

Williams-Renault was back on top at Silverstone, where Villeneuve qualified on pole but lost the lead due to a loose front wheel. Seventh after the first pitstops, he inherited Williams's 100th GP victory when Mika Häkkinen's engine failed with seven laps to go. Already criticised by Patrick Head in *Auto Motor und Sport* and relegated to the back of the grid after stalling at the original start, Frentzen crashed into Jos Verstappen at Becketts on the opening lap.

A lack of grip at Hockenheim restricted Frentzen and Villeneuve to fifth and ninth on the grid respectively. Worse was to come on Sunday for Frentzen hit Irvine at the first corner and Villeneuve spun while defending fifth from Jarno Trulli's Prost-Mugen. The Canadian nursed his tyres in Hungary to inherit a last-lap victory when Damon Hill's Arrows-Yamaha slowed. Frentzen correctly chose harder tyres but lost victory when part of his fuel valve broke, making refuelling impossible.

Starting the Belgian GP on wet tyres proved costly and the error was compounded when pole-winner Villeneuve switched to intermediates. He changed to slicks five laps later and stormed back to claim fifth (sixth on the road prior to Häkkinen's disqualification). Having scored points at just three of the 11 races so far, Frentzen survived contact with Rubens Barrichello and was promoted to third place – the first of five successive podium finishes. Frentzen was the quicker Williams driver at Monza when third once more; Villeneuve beat title rival Schumacher into fifth after a low-key afternoon. In Austria, Villeneuve drove an intelligent race after another slow start from pole and led a Williams-Renault 1–3 by the finish. That slashed Schumacher's championship lead to a single point and restored Williams-Renault to the top of the constructors' standings. They repeated that result at the Nürburgring, where Schumacher was hit by his brother at the start.

Villeneuve raced under appeal in Japan after ignoring yellow flags in practice, the third time he had been reprimanded for that offence during 1997. He started from another pole position but only finished fifth due to a poor pitstop. Frentzen's improved form continued at Suzuka where he passed Irvine for second place – and clinched Williams's record ninth constructors' title.

Disqualified from the Japanese GP when Williams dropped its appeal, Villeneuve went to the European GP at Jerez a point behind Schumacher. Improbably, the Ferrari driver and both Williams-Renaults recorded identical qualifying times (1m 21.072s), with Villeneuve handed pole as he was the first to post the time. Schumacher made the best start while wheelspin on the dirty side of the track saw Villeneuve also drop behind Frentzen. Up to second after the final pitstops, Villeneuve closed on Schumacher and attempted to take the lead at the Curva Dry Sack on lap 48, only for his rival to drive into him. The Ferrari went no further but Villeneuve's damaged car was able to continue. He slowed as a precaution and let both McLaren drivers pass as third place was enough to clinch the World Championship. Frentzen was sixth after stopping at the McLaren pit by mistake. He finished as championship runner-up when Schumacher was disqualified from the drivers' standings due to his actions at Jerez.

Heinz-Harald Frentzen, Williams FW19-Renault (German GP)

Michael Schumacher, Ferrari F310B (Italian GP)

SCUDERIA FERRARI MARLBORO

Enzo Ferrari had traditionally resisted commercial sponsorship despite Marlboro having paid driver salaries since 1984. Philip Morris ended its long association with McLaren and F1's most famous team was entered as Scuderia Ferrari Marlboro for the first time in 1997. Michael Schumacher signed a two-year contract extension (to the end of 1999) and Eddie Irvine was confirmed at the 1996 German GP. Gianni Morbidelli replaced Nicola Larini as test and reserve driver, a role he had fulfilled at the start of the decade.

The team also decided to relocate its entire technical department at Maranello. John Barnard, who insisted on working in England, left before his contract expired and took over Ferrari Design & Development in Shalford in April, renaming it B3 Technologies. Mike Coughlan stayed with Barnard, for whom he had worked since 1993.

Having orchestrated Schumacher's Benetton titles, Ross Brawn was hired as technical director and arrived on 16 December 1996 once a prior claim from Tom Walkinshaw Racing was dismissed. Due to retire from F1, chief designer Rory Byrne also transferred from Enstone, starting work at Maranello on 17 February in a technical department that already included Aldo Costa, Gustav Brunner and Willem Toet.

Unveiled at Maranello on 7 January, Barnard's last Ferrari design, the conventional F310B, was reminiscent of the Williams FW18 in many respects. Its raised nose was longer than before and as high as was practical, with twin supports for the low-slung front wing. The driving position was reclined so the cockpit surround could be lower and a larger headrest moved the driver's helmet away from the airbox to improve airflow to the engine. The F310's split floor was abandoned and the sidepods were shorter, higher and wider.

An electronic brake-balance system was fitted. The torsion-bar front suspension also followed Williams lines with 'knife-edge' mounts retained. The diffuser, rear suspension and transverse gearbox, which was cooled by a pair of NACA ducts, remained largely unaltered. The F310B had a relatively high centre of gravity that affected its handling, with understeer a problem all season. Revised bargeboards were introduced before the season and Irvine raced an electronic differential for the first time in Japan.

Early testing at Jerez was marred by three engine failures of the new type 046/2 iteration, so Ferrari began the year with the old-specification V10. 'We started from a poor base and I was very worried,' Schumacher said at the following Estoril test. 'We made a big step forward… and we are making progress.'

The German qualified third in Australia and finished second despite needing a late splash-and-dash following an earlier refuelling glitch. Irvine was branded an 'idiot' when he collided with Jacques Villeneuve and Johnny Herbert at the start. Low grip restricted Schumacher to fifth in Brazil and he clashed with Rubens Barrichello at the first corner in Buenos Aires. The new Evo 2 engine was used in qualifying at Imola, where Schumacher headed a Ferrari 2–3 finish. Always quick at Monaco and a master in the rain, Schumacher started on intermediate tyres and opened a 27sec lead in the first six laps alone. Dominant thereafter, he survived a moment at Ste-Dévote to win by 53.306sec. He took the championship lead that day, the first time since 1989 that a Ferrari driver had headed the standings.

Out of sorts all weekend in Brazil, Irvine crashed into Herbert (again) and Jan Magnussen at the original start, then for the restart took the spare car, which was set up for Schumacher, but found

Eddie Irvine, Ferrari F310B (European GP)

the seat belts too tight. Already under pressure in the Italian press, Irvine responded by scoring three podium finishes in a row, including second in Argentina when beaten by just 0.979sec.

Tyre blisters ruined Ferrari's Spanish GP, Schumacher finishing fourth and Irvine 12th after receiving a 10sec stop-go penalty for repeatedly baulking Olivier Panis. Schumacher used a revised aero package to qualify on pole in Canada and inherited victory after David Coulthard's slow final stop; only 12th on the grid, Irvine was the innocent victim of another first-corner contretemps. A new front wing improved balance at Magny-Cours, where the 046/2 engine was raced for the first time. Schumacher converted another pole position into a clear victory in the changeable conditions he so enjoyed. Irvine qualified fifth (his best Saturday performance since Australia) and finished third despite running across the gravel when challenged by Villeneuve at the last corner of the race.

Now 14 points ahead of Villeneuve, Schumacher was on course for victory at Silverstone when a wheel bearing failed and Irvine's driveshaft breakage when second completed a double DNF for the *Scuderia*. Schumacher was second in Germany despite loss of fifth gear and another refuelling problem, while Irvine suffered a race-ending puncture when he hit Heinz-Harald Frentzen on the opening lap. Using a stiffer, lighter new chassis with a larger fuel tank, Schumacher took pole in Hungary but was forced into the old-specification spare car after crashing in the warm-up and could only finish fourth due to excessive tyre wear, with Irvine knocked out of sixth by Shinji Nakano on the last lap.

Schumacher raced a lightweight chassis for the first time at Spa-Francorchamps and chose intermediate tyres from the start, which

was behind the safety car due to the wet track. Released after three laps, he took the lead and opened a minute's lead by the end of lap ten, cruising to victory thereafter. Irvine struggled throughout the weekend and, unsighted after losing a mirror, collided with Pedro Diniz while defending eighth on the last lap.

Only sixth in Italy and Austria (following a stop-go penalty for passing Frentzen under yellow flags), Schumacher's home race at the Nürburgring was a disaster. The Jordan-Peugeots collided at the first corner with Ralf Schumacher launched into his brother's Ferrari. Eighth in Italy, Irvine outqualified his illustrious team-mate for the first time this season at the A1-Ring but crashed into Jean Alesi at half distance.

Improved electronic throttle control and a new front wing that flexed at the extremities helped swing the title battle back in Ferrari's favour in Japan. Schumacher qualified second and led a scarlet 1–3 finish while Villeneuve was disqualified for ignoring yellow flags in practice. Now with a one-point lead in the championship standings, Schumacher and both Williams-Renaults officially set identical qualifying times for the deciding European GP at Jerez. He took the lead at the start but Villeneuve closed in after their second pitstops and attempted to overtake into Curva Dry Sack on lap 48. Schumacher closed the door and they collided, which left the Ferrari beached in the gravel. Villeneuve managed to finish despite damage to his car and claimed the drivers' title.

The FIA World Council summoned Schumacher to Paris on 11 November and disqualified him from the 1997 standings for deliberately driving into his rival. Ferrari kept the points he had won and finished as runners-up in the constructors' championship for the second successive season.

MILD SEVEN BENETTON RENAULT

Pat Symonds and Nick Wirth were promoted to technical director and chief designer respectively following Ross Brawn's and Rory Byrne's defection to Ferrari. Jean Alesi and Gerhard Berger remained to see out the second year of their contracts despite Flavio Briatore's open criticism during 1996. Alexander Wurz tested at Estoril in November and was announced as Benetton's test and reserve driver in the New Year.

For his last Benetton as chief designer, Byrne aimed to improve handling stability. The chassis was lowered and the cockpit surround was higher but less pronounced than its rivals. The raised nose was flat on top, curved underneath and marginally narrower than before, with twin vertical supports for the elaborate three-plane front wing. In a deviation from the B196, the short sidepods were noticeably waisted in front of the rear wheels between flat upper bodywork and the floor. The rear diffusers side channels had two vertical plates each. Push-rod suspension with torsion bars was retained while Benetton fluctuated between two and three dampers at the front.

Despite its impending withdrawal, Renault completely revised the V10 engine. The RS09 was now 24lb lighter with an increased vee angle (from 68 to 71 degrees) that lowered its centre of gravity. The new Benetton six-speed longitudinal gearbox optimised packaging and saved weight. Electronic brake bias and differential were fitted from the start of the season with power steering standard.

Berger gave the Benetton B197-Renault its shakedown at a foggy Silverstone on 19–20 December and lapped Jerez at record pace prior to the car's official launch on 23 January at an overcrowded function in London's Planet Hollywood. Benetton-Renault impressed during subsequent pre-season testing but struggled to generate heat in its Goodyear tyres for qualifying, especially at low-grip circuits, which restricted grid positions.

A set-up with insufficient ride height was blamed for lack of grip during practice for the Australian GP. The cars ran fifth and sixth until half-distance, then Alesi failed to heed instructions to pit and inevitably ran out of fuel four laps later, prompting an angry post-race outburst from Briatore. That farce elevated Berger, who just failed to catch Mika Häkkinen's third-placed McLaren-Mercedes by the finish. In Brazil, Berger qualified third and claimed a strong second place while Alesi started and finished sixth. Revised front suspension was introduced in Argentina to improve handling on the bumpy track, but the drivers struggled in qualifying at the next three races. Berger recovered from running wide to avoid the first-lap accident in Argentina to finish sixth, and Alesi was a lapped fifth at Imola. Neither scored in Monaco, where both qualified badly and had incidents during the race.

Jean Alesi, Benetton B197-Renault (Luxembourg GP)

Gerhard Berger, Benetton B197-Renault (German GP)

The high-grip nature of the Circuit de Catalunya near Barcelona helped mask the B197's shortcomings and both drivers lined up inside the top six. Two-stopping, Alesi managed his tyres to score a morale-boosting third place while blisters ruined Berger's race. Hopes were further buoyed when Alesi was quickest during a group test at Magny-Cours, although he wrote off a chassis when he crashed at the 100mph Estoril corner. That optimism was justified in Montréal, where Alesi finished second and Wurz made an impressive début as Berger suffered a recurrence of a sinus infection that had affected him since Imola. Denied points in Canada when the transmission failed, Wurz outqualified Alesi at both Magny-Cours and Silverstone. Alesi was fifth in France after knocking David Coulthard out of the way on the last lap and led Wurz home in a Benetton-Renault 2–3 at Silverstone.

Berger, whose father had just died in a light-aircraft accident, returned at Hockenheim and announced that he would leave Benetton at the end of the season. With revised front suspension and low-downforce set-up working well, he started from pole position and dominated the race to score Benetton's first GP victory since Schumacher's departure, while Alesi qualified and finished sixth. Among the Goodyear runners to struggle in Hungary, Alesi qualified on the front row at Spa-Francorchamps where Berger finished sixth. It was Alesi who benefited from the team's now excellent low-drag set-up to snatch pole for the Italian GP. He led until half-distance but was passed by Coulthard in the pitstops and finished second. The qualifying gremlins returned in Austria although Alesi was on course to score points before Eddie Irvine crashed into him.

Briatore's relationship with his drivers had deteriorated all year

and the colourful team boss seemingly fell out of favour with the Benetton family as well. His future was subject of paddock gossip for much of 1997 and Prodrive rally boss David Richards was appointed as the new chief executive before the Luxembourg GP at the Nürburgring, with plans to restructure the team, and Briatore soon quit. There was improvement in that race, especially in race trim, with Alesi finishing second and Berger fourth. Alesi was fifth in Japan and delayed at the European GP when he outbraked himself while trying to pass Jan Magnussen's Stewart-Ford. Berger announced his retirement from F1 in Vienna on 17 October and passed Irvine on the last lap at Jerez to claim fourth on his 210th and final GP start. As in 1996, Benetton-Renault was third in the constructors' standings.

Alexander Wurz, Benetton B197-Renault (Canadian GP)

WEST McLAREN MERCEDES

The McLaren MP4-12-Mercedes was completed at the team's factory in Albert Drive, Woking early on 14 January, with the new contender finished in McLaren's historic papaya orange for winter testing. There was a strong family resemblance to previous cars from the Neil Oatley-led design team. The cockpit surround was redesigned and driving position reclined to improve airflow to the engine. Its nose was lower than most rivals, with two curved supports for the full-width front wing. The aerodynamic wishbones introduced in 1996 were retained within the new limitations. The suspension was carbon-fibre except for the lower rear wishbones, which were steel due to heat from the exhausts. These blew into the top of the side diffusers, either side of a new central section. Used from mid-season, a secret second brake for one rear wheel (left or right depending on the circuit) applied a 'brake-steer' effect that controlled understeer and improved traction. Conceived by Steve Nichols, this was only revealed in Darren Heath's photographic exclusive in the November edition of *F1 Racing* magazine.

The Mercedes-Benz V10 engine was completely revised around a new block as Ilmor sought to add reliability to power. It was more compact than its predecessor and many ancillaries were repositioned, so the engine cover was slimmer and lower than before. The upgraded FO110F engine was used from the Spanish GP with vee angle reduced from 75 to 72 degrees. This had an improved power curve and was the most powerful engine in the field, although reliability issues remained, caused by cylinder-block weaknesses and air getting into the oil system.

David Coulthard was in the second year of his original deal and Mika Häkkinen signed a one-year extension in September 1996,

ending speculation that World Champion-elect Damon Hill would move to Woking. Pat Fry replaced David Owen as Coulthard's race engineer with Owen now responsible for McLaren's new young-driver programme. His first charge was German F3 star Nick Heidfeld, who first tested for the team at Silverstone on 17 March.

After a prolonged procedure to extricate 37-year-old Adrian Newey from his Williams contract, he was announced as McLaren's new technical director on 22 April but not allowed to start work until 1 August. The company was reorganised in the autumn with Ron Dennis now group chairman and Martin Whitmarsh managing director of the F1 team, McLaren International.

The MP4-12 was flown to Jerez straight after its launch, where Coulthard was entrusted with its shakedown on 15 January. Promising times were set at Estoril and Barcelona although limited tests alongside major rivals made pre-season form difficult to access. West McLaren Mercedes launched its race livery at a lavish function at London's Alexandra Palace on 13 February, with a striking return to the famed Mercedes 'Silver Arrows' of the 1930s and '50s; the 4,500 guests included 92-year-old pre-war Mercedes driver and 1937 Monaco GP winner Manfred von Brauchitsch and were entertained by music from Jamiroquai and the Spice Girls.

Coulthard and Häkkinen qualified fourth and sixth respectively in Australia and took advantage when the Williams-Renaults hit trouble, allowing Coulthard to score McLaren's first victory in 50 races with Häkkinen third. The Finn scored points at the next three races while Coulthard struggled with the MP4-12's rear-end instability. Häkkinen was fourth in Brazil, fifth in Argentina (using a one-stop strategy to recover from poor qualifying) and sixth in San Marino (despite an off-track excursion). A distant tenth at Interlagos, Coulthard lost a wheel

Mika Häkkinen, McLaren MP4-12-Mercedes (Spanish GP)

in the first lap mêlée in Buenos Aires and was denied a podium when his engine failed following a one-stop run at Imola. Coulthard started on intermediate tyres in Monaco but spun approaching the chicane for the second time, with his slick-shod team-mate also eliminated in the ensuing chaos.

As well as the engine upgrade at Barcelona, the MP4-12s had longer bargeboards to improve handling. Coulthard led a qualifying 3–5 and almost took the lead at the start. He was second during the middle phase of his three-stop race but blistered rear tyres slowed both cars. A race that had promised much ended in disappointment when Coulthard, struggling on badly worn rubber, made a mistake on the last lap and lost fifth to Johnny Herbert. The Scot continued as McLaren's on-form driver in Canada but lost victory due to an electronics glitch; Häkkinen was eliminated by Olivier Panis's Prost-Mugen at the first corner of the race.

Unsuited to Magny-Cours, where Coulthard lost points when hit by Jean Alesi on the last lap, the MP4-12s were transformed by the time of the British GP. Quickest in the pre-Silverstone test, Häkkinen qualified third and was set for a breakthrough victory when his engine failed with less than seven laps to go, while Coulthard finished fourth. It was a sign of the McLaren-Mercedes improvement that Häkkinen was disappointed with his third on the grid and in the race at Hockenheim, where Coulthard was an early retirement after an incident-filled lap and a half.

Neither finished the Hungarian GP and Spa-Francorchamps eventually proved to be another points-free weekend. Unhurt in a 200mph accident when his suspension failed on the Kemmel straight during morning practice, Häkkinen qualified fifth but raced under appeal due to an irregular fuel sample taken after that session. He started on intermediates and finished third after changing to slicks, only to be disqualified when the Court of Appeal upheld the stewards' original decision. Coulthard spun out at Stavelot having also changed to dry rubber.

The impressive power of the Mercedes V10 allowed McLaren to run with more downforce than its rivals at Monza, where they qualified on the third row. Coulthard made a good start and jumped his rivals in the pitstops to win again. Häkkinen, who had another high-speed crash during testing, led during the pitstops and set the fastest race lap only for a delaminated right-front tyre to ruin his victory hopes.

A new front wing was introduced at the Austrian GP. This was Newey's first upgrade since joining and it bore a strong resemblance to his Williams FW19. Häkkinen qualified on the front row and made the best start only for his engine to fail after a lap. Coulthard drove a strong race to split the Williams-Renaults in second. Revised bargeboards were fitted at the Nürburgring, where Häkkinen qualified on pole position for the first time. Coulthard made another great start from sixth and they ran 1–2 until engine failures after half-distance curtailed a dominant performance.

Fourth in Japan, Häkkinen's wretched luck finally turned at the last race of the season at Jerez. The McLaren men were promoted to second (Coulthard) and third (Häkkinen) when Michael Schumacher ran into Jacques Villeneuve on lap 48 and the Canadian slowed to protect his damaged car. With three laps to go, Coulthard let Häkkinen past, then Villeneuve waved both McLaren-Mercedes through on the last lap. So Häkkinen led a silver 1–2 and finally won a GP at the 96th attempt.

The fastest combination since mid-season, McLaren-Mercedes was fourth in the constructors' standings.

David Coulthard, McLaren MP4-12-Mercedes (Belgian GP)

Ralf Schumacher, Jordan 197-Peugeot (Canadian GP)

BENSON & HEDGES JORDAN PEUGEOT

Soon to be Formula Nippon champion, Ralf Schumacher signed a two-year contract with Jordan Grand Prix that was announced on the Friday of the 1996 Portuguese GP. Eddie Jordan originally wanted an experienced team leader and Damon Hill had seemed likely before he joined Arrows instead. Jean Alesi remained at Benetton and efforts to persuade Indycar star Alex Zanardi to return to F1 were rebuffed. Nigel Mansell tested a Jordan 196-Peugeot at Barcelona on 13 December 1996 but decided against another comeback four days later. That announcement coincided with Minardi's Giancarlo Fisichella having a two-day test at Jerez and the young Italian was confirmed as Schumacher's team-mate on 10 January. Jordan's new line-up began 1997 with just eight GP starts between them. F3000 star Ricardo Zonta impressed as test driver.

Rather than its traditional factory-based reveal, Jordan launched the Jordan 197-Peugeot at London's Hilton Hotel on 30 January. This was a development of the 196 although the sidepods were shorter and featured conventional single inlets rather than separate ducts for the water and oil radiators. The front suspension was wider and more streamlined than before while an oval airbox was designed to improve airflow to the engine. The rear diffuser had a tall central section, flanked by side channels with twin vertical elements. The lower rear wishbones were mounted above the diffuser. A raised nose and seven-speed longitudinal semi-automatic gearbox were retained. An active differential was tested in May and used at the French GP, although it was not a regular feature. Carbon-fibre front suspension was introduced in Japanese qualifying and raced at Jerez. Track testing of the latest Peugeot V10 (the A14), which was lower

and lighter than before, began in August 1996. Benson & Hedges entered its second season as title sponsor with a striking yellow 'snake' livery and Mastercard joined as an associate partner at the British GP.

Now in the final year of its Peugeot contract, and in the knowledge that the French manufacturer would be supplying Prost in 1998, Jordan was given until June to prove it was worthy of a secondary engine supply. The team expanded its workforce to over 100 people for the first time as its quest to break out of the midfield continued. The design department was doubled with technical director Gary Anderson taking a more hands-off managerial role. A new 40 per cent wind tunnel was opened in Brackley in the spring.

The Jordan 197-Peugeot was a quick package that excelled in fast corners and looked like a race winner on occasion. Often fast in testing and qualifying trim, Jordan achieved three podium finishes and its highest points tally to date, although fifth overall and no breakthrough victory tempered those achievements.

Teething troubles during testing at Estoril restricted mileage and both cars qualified in the midfield in Melbourne, unable to maintain Friday pace when it mattered. Furthermore, Schumacher had a driveshaft failure on lap two and Fisichella crashed while trying to pass Rubens Barrichello for ninth. Schumacher was quickest in the subsequent Silverstone test, where Fisichella cut his knee when he crashed heavily at Stowe. That improved pace continued in South America with qualification in the top ten at both races. Seventh on the grid at Interlagos despite yet another shunt, Fisichella was involved in the start-line accident that stopped the race, then took the spare to finish eighth, while Schumacher retired when his electronics played havoc with the fuel system. Eddie Jordan's prediction that there would

Giancarlo Fisichella, Jordan 197-Peugeot (European GP)

be fireworks between his two young chargers came true in Argentina, Jordan's 100th GP. Justifying pre-season claims that the 197 would be two seconds a lap faster than its predecessor, Schumacher qualified sixth and both challenged for a podium finish until the German collided with Fisichella when trying to take second place from him on lap 25. The furious Italian was unable to continue but Schumacher, who accepted blame, finished third on just his third F1 start.

They filled the third row at Imola, where Fisichella scored the first points of his F1 career by finishing a competitive fourth; Schumacher was running in that position when he suffered another driveshaft failure. Erratic all weekend in Monaco, Schumacher started on intermediate tyres and passed Fisichella into the Swimming Pool section on the opening lap to take third, but crashed in Casino Square on lap ten. The handling of Fisichella's car deteriorated when the rain was at its heaviest and he faded to sixth after changing to full wets. A longer and taller diffuser was introduced for the Spanish GP but high tyre wear forced a three-stop strategy and ruined their races. Only ninth that day despite setting the fastest race lap, Fisichella bounced back in Montréal by running second in the early stages and finishing third. Schumacher was fifth when he crashed heavily at the start of lap 15.

Schumacher qualified third in France, immediately behind his pole-winning brother in a German 1–2–3. He could not maintain that pace during the race and, delayed by a spin, he knocked David Coulthard out of the way at the final corner to claim sixth. At Silverstone Schumacher scored the first of three successive fifth places but Fisichella's chances of finishing second were lost after an 'off' at Copse and a consequent stop to change damaged tyres. The Italian's best race came at Hockenheim, where he qualified on the front row

and led during the pitstops. Fisichella retook the lead when Gerhard Berger made his final pitstop but he made a mistake at the second chicane that allowed the Benetton-Renault to pass as they entered the stadium. A strong second place was denied with just five laps to go by a puncture and subsequent damage.

The Jordan-Peugeots had an elaborate high-downforce rear wing in Hungary but struggled in qualifying. They were more competitive on hard race tyres although an overly impetuous Fisichella spun as he tried to pass Michael Schumacher for fifth. Ralf then battled his brother and finished fifth, beaten by just 0.214sec.

They had contrasting fortunes in Belgium, where it rained heavily before the start. Fourth on the grid, Fisichella finished an impressive second, but Schumacher lost control of his slick-shod car at Les Combes on the way to the grid and crashed the spare at the same place during the GP. Quickest in testing before the Italian GP, Fisichella qualified third for his home race and held off Jacques Villeneuve to finish fourth. Making too many mistakes as the season wore on, Schumacher made a slow start and drove into Johnny Herbert's Sauber-Petronas at high speed on the pit straight, an incident that drew Herbert's criticism after the race. A major aero upgrade at the A1-Ring included a new diffuser and sidepods but traffic and insufficient tyre temperatures ruined qualifying. It was a different story in the race as they used a one-stop strategy to climb through the field and finish fourth (Fisichella) and fifth (Schumacher, despite a slow pitstop). Their collision at the start of the Luxembourg GP sent Ralf's car into his brother's Ferrari, then a very disappointing Japanese GP brought finishes outside the points. The cars lacked grip at Jerez, where the team endured its worst qualifying (16th and 17th) and race of the season.

Olivier Panis, Prost JS45-Mugen (Monaco GP)

PROST GAULOISES BLONDES

Olivier Panis's 1996 Monaco GP success reawakened political pressure to form a competitive French national F1 team. In the summer of 1996 President Jacques Chirac urged Alain Prost, who had come close to buying Ligier in 1992, to become involved. Negotiations dragged on throughout the winter and were only concluded when Eddie Jordan became the final team owner to agree to a name change. The rebranded Prost Grand Prix and an engine deal with Peugeot for 1998–2000 were announced in Paris on 14 February.

Meanwhile, a one-year contract extension with Mugen was signed in July 1996 despite Tom Walkinshaw trying to divert the highly rated V10s to Arrows. Panis ignored interest from Jordan to re-sign a month later. Shinji Nakano tested a Ligier JS43-Mugen at Suzuka on 16 October 1996 with further European outings in the coming weeks. With the engine bill apparently reduced by $4 million if a Japanese driver was employed, Nakano was confirmed as Panis's team-mate in November. A tyre contract with Bridgestone was signed that month. Gauloises cigarettes remained as title sponsor and Prost's name helped attract additional support from Canal+, Alcatel, Bic and PlayStation.

With the takeover yet to be completed, Panis returned to the scene of his greatest triumph to help launch the Ligier JS45-Mugen on 21 January by driving it through the streets of Monte Carlo. André de Cortanze joined Toyota at the end of 1996 and was replaced as technical director by aerodynamicist Loïc Bigois. Former Ferrari engineer George Ryton arrived to run the research and development department. Cesare Fiorio remained as sporting director despite falling out with Prost during their time together at Ferrari in 1991. General

manager Bruno Michel quit in June following the arrival of ORECA boss Hugues de Chaunac.

Bigois led the development of the 1997 car around a new monocoque. He redistributed the weight further forward and reworked the aerodynamics to improve the car's sensitivity at high-speed tracks. It had a distinctive flat raised nose with full-width front wing, attached by two straight supports. A new six-speed transverse gearbox was built in-house to replace the Benetton unit that had been previously used. The sidepods had raised outer 'shoulders' above the inlets as had been seen on the Benettons of 1994 and 1995. While resisting the trend to build a small V10, Mugen moved the oil scavenge to lower the engine. A hand clutch was introduced on Panis's car in Canada. While the car would eventually be renamed a Prost, it retained Ligier's traditional designation style: 'JS' was in memory of Guy Ligier's lost friend Jo Schlesser, with odd numbers for racing cars and even ones for road cars (such as the JS2).

Panis set promising times during the winter but crashed head-on at Barcelona's final corner in February after front suspension failure. He was the fastest Bridgestone runner in Australia, where he qualified ninth and finished fifth. That promise was confirmed in Brazil when fifth on the grid and third at the finish after stopping once. Third fastest in qualifying for the Argentinian GP and planning to stop twice, Panis chased Jacques Villeneuve's three-stopping Williams-Renault during the early laps despite a bent steering arm following contact with Michael Schumacher at the start. He was seven seconds behind the leader and clear in second position when a hydraulic leak ended his day, denying a possible victory.

That qualifying pace continued at Imola, where he lined up fourth only for high tyre wear to ruin his race. Fourth in Monaco, he climbed through the field in Spain to finish second on a day when Bridgestone tyres proved superior to Goodyear rubber. Now third in the championship, Panis then suffered a high-speed accident during the Canadian GP. Having pitted for a new front wing after hitting Mika Häkkinen at the start, he had recovered to seventh when his suspension failed on lap 52 at the 150mph Turn 5. He glanced the inside barrier and crashed into the outside wall, breaking both legs.

Emmanuel Collard was expected to replace Panis but Minardi's Jarno Trulli proved 0.16sec quicker when they tested at Magny-Cours and was chosen. That faith faith was immediately justified when Trulli qualified sixth in France although a slow start and premature switch to intermediate tyres denied the chance of points on his début for the team. Hindered by braking issues during practice and tyres during the race at Silverstone, the inexperienced Italian finished an impressive fourth in Germany after pressuring title-challenger Villeneuve into a mistake. Uncompetitive in Belgium and Italy (where he was outqualified by Nakano), Trulli stunned the establishment in Austria by qualifying third and leading the opening 37 laps. He was passed by Villeneuve in the pitstops and lost a deserved second place when his engine failed with 13 laps to go.

Panis was fit enough to test at Magny-Cours, first in an F3 Dallara, then a week later in his Prost JS45-Mugen on 9 September. The impressive Trulli, rather than Mugen-backed Nakano, stood down for the last three races and Panis finished sixth at the Nürburgring on his return. A new evolution of the Mugen V10 engine proved unreliable at Suzuka and Panis finished a disappointed seventh in the European GP at Jerez.

Nakano began 1997 with a promising seventh place in Melbourne after a couple of wild moments. Despite losing a wheel before his pitstop, he finished 14th in Brazil, but then retired from five of the

Shinji Nakano, Prost JS45-Mugen (Australian GP)

next six races as he struggled to acclimatise to F1 without crucial testing miles. He was rammed by Damon Hill during the San Marino GP and crashed on the climb from Ste-Dévote in Monaco as rumours suggested that Collard or Gianni Morbidelli would replace him. However, Mugen refused to waive the reported engine subsidy so Nakano saw out the season, with the relationship between team owner and engine supplier strained.

The Japanese rookie survived contact with Jan Magnussen at the start in Canada and was sixth when the race was red-flagged. He spun in France before qualifying alongside Trulli at Silverstone, where he was denied sixth by engine failure on the penultimate lap. An unobtrusive seventh at Hockenheim, he scored the second point of his F1 career by conserving his tyres and passing Trulli in Hungary to claim sixth. He spun during the early laps of the Belgian GP and suffered mechanical failures in Austria, Luxembourg (Nürburgring) and Japan. Tenth at Jerez completed an underwhelming maiden season.

Prost-Mugen was sixth in the constructors' standings but 1997 would have delivered much more if Panis had not been injured.

Jarno Trulli, Prost JS45-Mugen (Italian GP)

Johnny Herbert, Sauber C16-Petronas (Luxembourg GP)

RED BULL SAUBER PETRONAS

Sauber spent 1996 looking for an alternative solution to the works Ford engine deal it had lost. Rumours of a deal with Ferrari were published in *Corriere dello Sport* in July 1996. Johnny Herbert held talks with Jordan and Stewart before signing a two-year contract extension in September. On 11 November, Sauber made two confusing announcements: firstly, it revealed a two-year deal for 1996-specification Ferrari V10s, rebadged with Petronas on the cam covers, only for this to be denied by the *Scuderia*; secondly, Red Bull owner Dietrich Mateschitz stated that Jos Verstappen would be Heinz-Harald Frentzen's replacement, but negotiations then fell through. In fact Sauber's use of Ferrari engines was confirmed a fortnight later and former Ferrari test driver Nicola Larini was duly named as Herbert's team-mate. Norberto Fontana was retained as test driver for a third year. Osamu Goto (ex-Honda, McLaren and Ferrari) joined on 1 November 1996 as head of Sauber Petronas Engineering, a new company formed to develop engines in-house. The original Petronas-inspired plan was to build a totally new engine for 1999, although that project was later shelved.

The late engine deal meant the Sauber C16-Petronas was the last car to be revealed when it was launched via the internet on 10 February. This was an evolution of Leo Ress's previous design with cockpit surround lowered, an improved aero package featuring a revised airbox and nose raised still further. Pre-season testing was limited to a two-day shakedown at Fiorano and five days in Barcelona. Additional small wings within the front suspension were used at the Monaco, Canadian, Hungarian and Austrian GPs. The

airbox was redesigned for the Spanish GP to reduce disturbance of the airflow from the driver's helmet. A new diffuser introduced at the Nürburgring had three (rather than four) outer channels with exhausts now blowing from above.

Despite pronounced understeer and difficult handling on bumpy tracks, Herbert used the Ferrari V10's extra power to qualify in the top ten at five of the opening six races, while regularly challenging for points. He was taken out by Eddie Irvine at the start in Australia, where Larini finished sixth on his return. Outside the points at Interlagos, Sauber-Petronas drivers had mixed fortunes in Buenos Aires, where Herbert withstood Mika Häkkinen's pressure and rode the kerbs to claim an excellent fourth despite a misfire, while Larini was delayed at his pitstop and crashed while trying to pass Jan Magnussen's Stewart-Ford.

Herbert started the next two races from eighth and but retired from both when well-placed: he lost a possible podium at Imola through electrical problems and in Monaco he crashed heavily at Ste-Dévote on lap ten while lying fifth, with Larini also crashing out on the approach to Casino Square after two earlier spins. Outqualified by his team-mate thus far and critical of Sauber in the Italian press, Larini was replaced by Ferrari test driver Gianni Morbidelli from the Spanish GP.

Herbert's fine form continued with fifth places in Spain and Canada, pressuring David Coulthard into a mistake on the last lap at Barcelona and despite a stop-go penalty for speeding at his only pitstop in Montréal. Morbidelli crashed as he left the pits during Friday practice at Barcelona and finished both GPs without

Nicola Larini, Sauber C16-Petronas (Brazilian GP)

threatening the top six. Morbidelli then missed the next three races after breaking his arm while testing before the French GP. Without recent time in the car, Fontana failed to impress as his stand-in: he wanted to quit during his début at Magny-Cours and spun when urged to continue; he took ninth places in Britain (having been sent to the back of the grid for missing the weighbridge) and Germany (despite another off-track excursion). Herbert was eighth in France while suffering 'flu, ran fifth at Silverstone after an excellent start until halted by another electrical issue, and retired in Germany when Pedro Diniz crashed into him.

Herbert was a well-judged third in Hungary, where Morbidelli was an early casualty on his return, hitting Magnussen at the start and blowing his engine on lap eight. The team was fined £15,000 when a fuel sample taken on Friday did not match that approved by the FIA. Talks with Benetton to place its test driver Alex Wurz in the second car were unsuccessful so Morbidelli continued. His race finishes at the next four events included ninth in the Belgian, Austrian and Luxembourg GPs, but he could not start in Japan when he broke his left wrist in a qualifying accident at the fast Dunlop Curve. Fontana returned for the European GP at Jerez and finished a distant 14th. Fourth in Belgium, Herbert was highly critical of Ralf Schumacher at the Italian GP after they collided on the main straight. He was eighth in Austria (despite blistered tyres) and Jerez, seventh at the Nürburgring and sixth in Japan.

Sauber-Petronas began 1997 with promise but limited in-season development compared with rivals and just a point scored from the second car restricted the team to seventh overall.

Gianni Morbidelli, Sauber C16-Petronas (Austrian GP)

Norberto Fontana, Sauber C16-Petronas (French GP)

Damon Hill, Arrows A18-Yamaha (Belgian GP)

DANKA ARROWS YAMAHA

Tom Walkinshaw had grand plans for Arrows following a frustrating transitional year in 1996. He signed a tyre contract with newcomers Bridgestone and chased a new team leader to replace Jos Verstappen. Talks were held with Rubens Barrichello before Damon Hill visited Leafield on 26 September 1996. The championship leader turned down Jordan, Stewart and Ligier to sign a one-year contract with TWR Arrows. Pedro Diniz was confirmed as Hill's team-mate at that year's Japanese GP with substantial backing from Parmalat as before. Among those to have tested Bridgestone tyres for the team during 1996, Jörg Müller was signed as reserve driver in the hope of securing a race seat in 1998.

In need of a competitive engine to turn around F1's perennial underachievers, Walkinshaw unsuccessfully attempted to divert Ligier's Mugen deal so a one-year agreement with Yamaha was announced on 7 October, despite its poor reliability during 1996. John Judd continued to prepare the lightest and most compact V10 in F1 and looked to address leaks in the engine blocks and breakages with more robust construction. An upgraded D-specification version with new cylinder heads, pneumatic valves and electronics was scheduled for Imola but was delayed by two months.

Walkinshaw's claim that Ferrari-bound Ross Brawn had previously

signed a contract with TWR was settled out of court. Without an F1 drive for the coming season, Martin Brundle was appointed as a non-executive director and tested a couple of times. Jackie Oliver remained as sporting director but did not attend all the races as his influenced waned. The cars and team had officially been known as Footwork since that company's withdrawal so that FOCA travel rights and prize money were not affected, but Walkinshaw now reverted to the original Arrows moniker.

New title sponsorship from Danka office machines was announced before Christmas. Autosport International at Birmingham's National Exhibition Centre was chosen for a very public launch of the Arrows A18-Yamaha on 9 January, sporting the number one that befitted the reigning World Champion. Frank Dernie said he had combined the best of his Ligier JS43 and the latest Footwork cars in finalising this largely conventional, high-nosed design. The main innovation was a load-bearing monocoque that extended beyond the engine to improve rigidity and reduce loads on the fragile Yamaha V10. However, the rear section was removed for the San Marino GP as it interrupted airflow to the engine. The small engine meant the longitudinal Arrows/Xtrac six-speed semi-automatic gearbox had to be redesigned. The A18 initially lacked grip, power and reliability, and the quality of some components was found to be sub-standard during a difficult start. However, progress was eventually made so that Hill became a factor during the second half of the season, especially where engine power was not at a premium.

Almost two weeks after the launch, Hill gave the A18 its shakedown at Silverstone late on 17 January. Subsequent tests were plagued by a catalogue of issues, both major and minor, during a shambolic winter. That said, not even the most pessimistic were ready for the team's disastrous Australian GP: Hill scraped onto the back of the grid and had a throttle actuator fail on the warm-up lap; Diniz, who was allowed to start despite qualifying outside 107 per cent of Jacques Villeneuve's pole time, hit Verstappen on the opening lap and finished last after changing his damaged front wing.

Having received the Order of the British Empire (OBE) on 18 March and following an improved test at Paul Ricard, Hill qualified a morale-boosting ninth at Interlagos. Tipped onto two wheels in the original start-line fracas, he ran as high as third before his engine caught fire with four laps to go, while Diniz spun out. Both retired from the next four races as Hill's torrid title defence worsened. They received suspended race bans at Imola – Hill for ramming Shinji Nakano's Prost-Mugen and Diniz for ignoring blue flags – and both drivers crashed in Monaco by the end of lap two.

With the team in disarray, John Barnard agreed a two-year deal and replaced Dernie as technical director on 1 May. He restructured the engineering department and sought to improve reliability. Both drivers finished in Canada, Diniz eighth and Hill a delayed ninth. With talk of an imminent switch to Prost denied, Hill was outqualified by his team-mate in France and finished last after both tangled with rivals. Openly criticised by Walkinshaw on the eve of the British GP meeting, Hill finally delivered the team's first point of 1997 by inheriting sixth with a lap to go when Nakano's engine failed. He was a lapped eighth at Hockenheim, where Diniz collided with Johnny Herbert's Sauber-Petronas.

When predicting a difficult year ahead in its season preview, *Autosport* had stated that 'miracles don't happen in motor racing' – but one nearly occurred at the Hungaroring. With engine power less important than normal and Bridgestone tyres superior in the heat, Hill started third after 'one of the best [qualifying laps] of my life' and held a 35sec lead at one stage. Arrows's first victory at its 299th attempt seemed certain, only for Hill's hydraulic pressure to drop on the penultimate lap. He was passed by Villeneuve with less than two miles to go and the number one Arrows-Yamaha limped across the line in second place after a heroic drive.

That improved form was maintained at Spa-Francorchamps despite this being a power circuit. Both Arrows-Yamahas qualified inside the top ten for once with eighth-placed Diniz marginally quicker. Hill struggled during the race after wrongly choosing full wet settings and making an early change to intermediates rather than slick tyres. Diniz drove a strong race before elbowing seventh-placed Eddie Irvine off the road on the last lap, rejoining to finish eighth on the road (seventh after the subsequent disqualification of Mika Häkkinen's McLaren-Mercedes).

The A18 lacked balanced at Monza, where Diniz's suspension failed after four laps and Hill's engine imploded when ninth in the closing stages. It was better suited to the stop/start nature of the A1-Ring, where Hill qualified seventh and was on course to finish sixth until Michael Schumacher's late pass. Quickest in Saturday free practice in Austria only for engine failures to compromise his weekend, Diniz withstood Olivier Panis's late pressure at the Nürburgring to finish fifth and score his only points of 1997. Hill lost his chance of scoring points when he stalled at his pitstop. Sadly off the pace at Suzuka despite Bridgestone's circuit knowledge, Arrows-Yamaha's fluctuating pace since mid-season was illustrated at Jerez as Hill challenged for pole position only to be baulked on his quickest lap. He qualified fourth nonetheless, just 0.058sec slower than the three Goodyear-shod drivers ahead. He made a slow start and lost another possible top-six finish when his gearbox failed. Diniz spun out of the last race of his mixed campaign.

Eighth in the constructors' standings after a largely frustrating year, Arrows and Yamaha split at the end of the season with the Japanese manufacturer leaving F1.

Pedro Diniz, Arrows A18-Yamaha (Luxembourg GP)

STEWART FORD

Paul Stewart Racing (PSR) had been a leading team in junior single-seaters since Jackie Stewart and his son founded it in 1988. Triple champions in British F3 (1992–94) and Formula Vauxhall (1993–95), it cancelled its order for F3000 cars on 11 December 1995 and confirmed the renamed Stewart Grand Prix's graduation to F1 at the 1996 Detroit motor show on 4 January. An exclusive five-year deal for works Ford engines was also announced. Jackie Stewart, a Ford ambassador for 31 years, was named as chairman with Paul as managing director.

Arrows designer Alan Jenkins joined on 1 March 1996 as technical director, Eghbal Hamidy (ex-Williams) was hired as chief aerodynamicist and Andy Le Fleming arrived from Ferrari as chief race engineer. Wind-tunnel testing began in the Swift Cars 50 per cent Sacramento facility in July 1996. Other key staff such as team manager David Stubbs stepped up from the F3000 outfit. The F3 and Formula Vauxhall teams continued to operate, so the existing factory in Milton Keynes was doubled in size while a new facility was established for 1998.

McLaren test driver Jan Magnussen dominated the 1994 British F3 Championship in a PSR Dallara F394-Mugen and he soon emerged as a prime candidate for the ambitious newcomers. He visited the factory on 30 September and signed a four-year contract three days later. Stewart had designs on Damon Hill as team leader but the son of JYS's original F1 team-mate joined Arrows instead. Rubens Barrichello was not retained by Jordan and a three-year deal with Stewart was announced in São Paulo on 22 October.

Title sponsorship from HSBC (Hongkong and Shanghai Banking Corporation) was announced in London on 17 September 1996 and blue-chip associate partnerships with Texaco Havoline, the Malaysian tourist board and Sanyo were added before the Stewart SF1-Ford was launched in London on 10 December 1996, with a bagpiper and tartan trim unmistakable nods to the Scottish roots. A tyre contract was finally agreed with Bridgestone despite Jackie Stewart's long-standing association with Goodyear.

This was a conventional design with the 72-degree Ford Zetec-R V10 engine driving through a Stewart/Xtrac longitudinal six-speed semi-automatic gearbox. Jenkins retained the fashionable raised nose he had settled on at Arrows, with the cockpit surround as low as was permitted. The push-rod suspension had three dampers front and rear, although a more traditional twin-spring layout was used when required. Initially there were two pedals (albeit configured differently for each driver) and a hand clutch to facilitate left-foot braking, although Magnussen reverted to a conventional layout from Argentina. The sidepods had raised inlets that were copied by some rival teams in 1998. New rear diffuser and exhausts were introduced in South America with bargeboards fitted amid the front suspension in Spain. The rear wing was revised for the San Marino GP and a high-downforce alternative used in Monte Carlo; the wing had a single plane at Hockenheim as the team chased straight-line speed despite the engine's lack of grunt.

Barrichello gave the SF1 its shakedown at Ford's Boreham test facility on 19 December 1996 with testing continuing after Christmas at Silverstone and Jerez. The team left Spain in optimistic mood despite gearbox oil leaks and Magnussen's loss of his left rear wheel on the final day. Vital mileage was lost in February when the Dane crashed heavily following a rear failure while negotiating Estoril's 150mph Turn 2; a wishbone pierced the carbon-fibre monocoque

Rubens Barrichello, Stewart SF1-Ford (European GP)

and he required six stiches to his left calf as a consequence.

The SF1 was well-balanced when it ran but poor reliability plagued Stewart-Ford's maiden F1 season. The Zetec-R lacked power despite numerous upgrades, from 'phase five' at the start of the year to 'phase nine' by the end. Engine blow-ups and mechanical failure caused the Stewart-Fords to DNF from over 60 per cent of their races. Barrichello normally qualified in the midfield but showed glimpses of the car's potential with three starts in the top six.

The first four races brought no finishes. Magnussen was a casualty of the first-corner incident in Brazil and Barrichello was tapped into a spin by Michael Schumacher in Buenos Aires, negating his fine fifth place in qualifying. Both cars needed new nose assemblies at the end of lap one in Argentina and suffered subsequent mechanical failures, although Magnussen covered enough distance to be classified tenth. The 'phase six' engine was tried in practice at Imola, where a ride-height change on the grid was blamed for Magnussen's second-lap crash at Acque Minerale. Barrichello raced with a badly sprained ankle following a training accident and had another engine fail.

The wet conditions and tight confines of Monaco masked the Zetec-R's inadequacies and provided Stewart's only double finish. Starting tenth, Barrichello drove an inspired opening stint and passed Ralf Schumacher for second at the chicane on lap six. Despite going straight over the chicane six laps later, he held that position to the finish, 53.306sec behind Michael Schumacher's dominant Ferrari. Magnussen's best result also came at Monaco when seventh after a couple of moments in the tricky conditions.

Following the promise of Monaco, Barcelona provided an embarrassing contrast as both cars were hopelessly slow in a straight line and were even outqualified by Mika Salo's Tyrrell with its inferior customer Ford V8. Then came double DNFs at the next five races, often because engine upgrades proved disappointing and temperamental. However, Barrichello qualified a shock third in Canada thanks to an extreme low-downforce set-up, only to fade during the race due to a poor start, limited straight-line speed and blistered tyres; Magnussen was knocked off the road on the opening lap by Shinji Nakano.

Having damaged his steering when he hit Gianni Morbidelli's Sauber-Petronas at the start in Hungary, Magnussen was warned that he had to improve if he was going to be retained for 1998. He ran as high as sixth in the Belgian chaos but finished 12th, while Barrichello broke a steering arm against Heinz-Harald Frentzen's Williams-Renault. With Barrichello only 13th at Monza and Magnussen showing improved form, the Stewart-Fords were altogether more competitive for the next races in Austria and at the Nürburgring. With Bridgestone rubber working well, they lined up on row three in Austria and ran in the top four – with Barrichello second for the opening 23 laps – before excessive tyre wear slowed them. Neither finished: Magnussen's engine failed and Barrichello crashed while defending seventh from Michael Schumacher with seven laps to go. Barrichello was running fourth at the Nürburgring, with second place a real possibility, when predictable gremlins denied a double points score for the Stewart-Fords.

Japan was a disaster as both drivers crashed by the end of lap six. Magnussen outqualified Barrichello for just the second time of the season at Jerez, where he finished ninth after being delayed in traffic; Barrichello retired for the 14th occasion in what had been a character-building year.

Jan Magnussen, Stewart SF1-Ford (Belgian GP)

TYRRELL RACING ORGANISATION

Having ended its four-year association with Yamaha, Tyrrell opted for reliability over power when it chose Cosworth Engineering's latest customer version of its 75-degree Ford V8 engine. The ED4 was used initially and plans to introduce the upgraded ED5 at the San Marino GP were delayed following problems on the dyno.

Tyrrell exercised its option on Mika Salo's services and Jos Verstappen was preferred to Emmanuel Collard as Minardi-bound Ukyo Katayama's replacement. Satoru Nakajima signed a three-year agreement to represent Tyrrell in Japan with fruits of that partnership immediately evident in 1997. Automotive supplier PIAA became Tyrrell's most prominent sponsor with Nakajima's protégé Toranosuke Takagi signed as test driver. Ricardo Rosset was added to the test roster in May following Lola's demise. McLaren aerodynamicist Ben Agathangelou joined Harvey Postlethwaite's technical team.

London's Capital Radio Café was the venue for the launch of the Tyrrell 025-Ford on 20 January. This was another evolutionary car with an elegant single strut now supporting the front wing. The steering column had to be modified for the second race because Verstappen was catching his feet between the pedals. Tyrrell remained loyal to Goodyear but struggled to generate sufficient tyre temperatures. The exhausts were modified in Canada to blow from above the diffuser. Unfortunately, poor traction, lack of power and limited development budget consigned Ken Tyrrell's famous old team to another season among the also-rans.

During the opening three laps in Australia, Verstappen crashed into Pedro Diniz, Katayama and then all on his own, while Salo was tenth when his electrics played up. They qualified on the back row in Brazil and remained among the backmarkers during a hugely

Jos Verstappen, Tyrrell 025-Ford (Spanish GP)

disappointing race. In search of extra downforce for the Argentinian GP, aerodynamicist Ben Wood suggested a novel if ungainly solution. As well as fins on either side of the raised nose, high 'x-wings' were mounted on either side of the cockpit and Verstappen ran as high as seventh before his engine failed. Top ten at that race and the next, Salo ran non-stop in the Monaco rain to finish fifth, eighth-placed Verstappen having protected him from attack by Giancarlo Fisichella during the closing laps.

Armed with the ED5 engine for the first time in Spain and with 'x-wings' removed, Salo qualified an improved 14th and ran in the top ten before his badly blistered left-rear tyre punctured. Verstappen finished 11th and both drivers retired from the next three races. They challenged for points on their strongest weekend so far in Montréal only to fail during the closing stages, then Verstappen crashed out of the French GP when his throttle stuck open. They suffered engine

Mika Salo, Tyrrell 025-Ford (Italian GP)

failures in practice and during the race at Silverstone. Verstappen was involved in the first-lap incident at Becketts that also eliminated Heinz-Harald Frentzen's Williams-Renault.

Slower than all bar the Minardi-Harts in Germany, the cars appeared in Hungary with 'x-wings' refitted and new front endplates. Tyrrell's travails continued on a circuit that should have masked the lack of horsepower due to the blistering tyres that affected Goodyear, and Salo finished last while Verstappen went out with gearbox trouble. Excellent in the changeable early conditions at Spa-Francorchamps, Verstappen climbed to eighth only to lose it at Malmédy, while Salo finished 11th.

With engine development frozen as Cosworth committed to V10s for its future customers, another double DNF followed in Italy. Now struggling to even beat the Minardi-Harts, Verstappen was last in Austria and Salo brought up the rear at the Nürburgring, the recent birth of his son Max giving Verstappen his only cause for celebration. They qualified on the last row in Japan and at Jerez as this disastrous campaign came to a close.

MINARDI TEAM

The 1996 season for F1's perennial low-budget outfit was dominated by takeover talks after Beppe Lucchini announced he wanted to reduce his stake in July. Flavio Briatore, who already ran Benetton and Ligier, brokered a deal for a consortium that included Fondmetal's Gabriele Rumi and former driver Alessandro Nannini to acquire a 70 per cent stake, announced on 27 November 1996. Giancarlo Minardi retained 14.5 per cent and remained in '360-degree control' of day-to-day matters. Rumi became the majority shareholder and

his involvement included access to the Fondmetal Technologies wind tunnel and consultancy in Casumaro, 85km to the northwest of Minardi's Faenza base.

An approach to Ferrari for engines was turned down by Luca di Montezemolo in June and Ford decided not to offer a customer version of its V10 unit. Reluctant to continue with the Ford V8s that had frustrated in 1996, Minardi concluded a deal with Brian Hart for his 72-degree air-valve V8 in November. With only limited in-season development, this also lacked power so Minardi were backmarkers once more.

Giancarlo Fisichella tried Bridgestone tyres at Imola on 18 November and a contract with the Japanese newcomers was announced later that month. There was an all-new driver line-up as Pedro Lamy quit F1 and Jordan Grand Prix chose Fisichella as part of its youthful team. After four years with Tyrrell, Ukyo Katayama signed before Christmas to bring experience and Mild Seven money. Long-term development driver Esteban Tuero finally drove a Minardi M195B-Ford at Misano on 28 October with that year's Italian F3 top two, Andrea Boldrini and João Barbosa, also tested. However, it was another F3 champion who completed Minardi's line-up for 1997: Jarno Trulli, Briatore's latest protégé, won the 1996 German title in his first full season racing cars and he signed on 13 January as part of the deal that took Fisichella to Jordan. Tarso Marques was retained as test and reserve driver.

Revealed on 4 February, the Minardi M197-Hart was a cautious development of the 1996 chassis under the direction of technical co-ordinator Gabriele Tredozi. The front wing endplates featured small outer winglets and the long bargeboards were shallower than normal. The top of the raised nose was flatter than before and the

Jarno Trulli, Minardi M197-Hart (Monaco GP)

cockpit surround lowered. Engine management by perennial Minardi supplier Magneti Marelli was preferred to Hart's previous partner, TAG Electronics, but proved complicated and took time to optimise. The longitudinal Minardi/Xtrac semi-automatic gearbox was retained. An upgrade for the San Marino GP included revised engine, rear bodywork, front suspension and wing, while a new diffuser was introduced in Canada. Three-damper suspension was tried in Italy and a modified system was fitted to both cars for the Austrian GP. However, the M197 tended to understeer, whatever changes were made. Katayama gave the new car its shakedown at Mugello before the Estoril group test saw the cars slowest of those present. Clutch problems limited further winter mileage.

Although fuel-feed problems caused misfires throughout the Australian GP weekend, Katayama's 15th on the grid proved to be Minardi's best starting position of the season. Already delayed after an incident with Jos Verstappen, his fuel system failed altogether after 32 laps. He was last in Brazil after stalling at the restart and spun out of the Argentinian GP. After finishing last at Imola and Monte Carlo, Katayama's DNFs at the next two races included a heavy crash when his throttle stuck open in Canada.

Katayama had been outpaced by Trulli thus far but fared better when his team-mate moved to Prost, to be replaced by Marques from the French GP. Katayama outqualified the Brazilian 8–2 in the ten remaining races, although any points scoring remained an impossible dream. Katayama finished 11th in France despite hurting his back

Ukyo Katayama, Minardi M197-Hart (Monaco GP)

Tarso Marques, Minardi M197-Hart (Hungarian GP)

when he straight-lined the chicane, then crashed into Silverstone's pit wall at the start of the British GP. He had another incident with Verstappen in Germany and ran out of fuel after his radio stopped working and could not see his pit board. Tenth in Hungary thanks to superior Bridgestone rubber, he had an electronics failure on the last lap of the Belgian GP. He crashed during practice, qualifying and the race at Monza and used a two-stop strategy to beat Verstappen into 11th in Austria. The Luxembourg GP was a disaster as both cars were eliminated by the end of lap two, Katayama a casualty of the first-corner mayhem. Faster than the Tyrrell-Fords at the last two races thanks to their tyres, both retired in Japan and finished outside the top ten at Jerez, Katayama last on his final F1 appearance before turning to mountaineering.

Trulli impressed by outqualifying Katayama from round two. He finished his first three GPs, including ninth in Australia and Argentina, and even had the temerity to overtake Eddie Irvine's Ferrari on the opening lap in Brazil. A broken hydraulic gearbox pump prevented him from starting at Imola and he crashed at Mirabeau during the early laps of the Monaco GP. He was last at Barcelona following a mid-race collision with Mika Salo's Tyrrell-Ford and a subsequent pitstop to change his damaged nose. His engine failed during the Canadian GP on his last appearance for Minardi before replacing the injured Olivier Panis at Ligier-Mugen.

Marques was drafted in for the French GP, where his engine failed after five laps. Last at Silverstone when troubled by tyre vibration and his brake pedal, Marques had transmission failure at the start of the German GP. Criticised for baulking faster cars, he was 12th in Hungary despite a painful shoulder sustained when he crashed following rear suspension failure during qualifying. He spun in Belgium and was last at Monza. Disqualified from qualifying in Austria due to an underweight car, Marques lined up 18th at the Nürburgring in his best showing of the year but retired from that race and the next. He was 15th in the European GP, the last race of another pointless season for Minardi.

MASTERCARD LOLA F1 TEAM

With the customer-car market in the junior categories changing, Lola founder Eric Broadley believed that entering a works F1 team for the first time was crucial to his company's future. However, this venture was an embarrassing failure that brought the famous old marque to the brink of extinction.

Undeterred by painful experiences with BMS Scuderia Italia and Ferrari in 1993, Lola built a new car in 1994 that was intended to be a mobile test bed throughout the following season. Julian Cooper (ex-Benetton) and aerodynamicist Chris Saunders (ex-Williams) designed the T95/30, which was completed before that Christmas. Allan McNish gave this conventional Ford-powered chassis its shakedown test on an English runway but the project was cancelled when sponsorship could not be found.

To confirm its 1997 F1 entry and start building a new car, Lola imposed a deadline of 31 August 1996 that came and went. Joint managing director Mike Blanchet, who had been a cornerstone of

Vincenzo Sospiri, Lola T97/30-Ford (Australian GP)

the company for 20 years, left in September, and the project was only given the go-ahead when title sponsorship from financial powerhouse MasterCard was announced on 5 November. This was a complicated deal with MasterCard's vast worldwide membership paying for exclusive access to an F1 club that would self-fund the sponsorship programme. The scheme was only due to be launched in February and, with little or no upfront payment, cashflow was always going to be an issue.

Tom Kristensen and Norberto Fontana were mentioned as possible drivers before former Super Nova F3000 team-mates Vincenzo Sospiri and Ricardo Rosset were confirmed at a function in São Paulo on 17 December. Following limited hours in the wind tunnel at Cranfield, the Lola T97/30-Ford was launched at the Hilton Hotel on London's Park Lane on 20 February with Broadley hoping to win races within the four years of the MasterCard deal. Broadley stressed that design of the T97/30 was a collective endeavour. It was a conventional machine with raised nose, in-house six-speed semi-automatic transverse gearbox, push-rod suspension with inboard springs and Bridgestone tyres. Al Melling's Rochdale-based MCD Consultants was commissioned to design and build a new Lola-branded V10 engine that was due for completion during 1997. In the meantime, a supply of leased old Ford Zetec-R 75-degree V8s was agreed as a stop-gap.

Pre-season testing was limited to a shakedown on the Santa Pod dragstrip (with an engine failure) and a couple of damp days at Silverstone where gearbox issues limited mileage to a handful of laps. With cars barely finished, the Australian GP was a disaster.

Gearbox software issues, evil handling and excessive drag saw the quickest Lola-Ford (Sospiri) 11.03sec off the pace, and over five seconds from qualifying under the 107 per cent rule. Sospiri thought 'the only consolation was that it can't get any worse' – but it did. The cars arrived at Interlagos but Lola withdrew from F1 on the Tuesday before the race, citing 'financial problems', and the team entered liquidation on 28 April.

Although the F1 team was a separate company, Lola Cars had lent it £3 million, which was not repaid. With the core Indycar market dwindling and one-make F3000 and Indy Lights contracts both low-margin, the parent company went into receivership in May. It was taken over by Irishman Martin Birrane, who restructured and concentrated on the customer-car market that had served it so well.

Ricardo Rosset, Lola T97/30-Ford (Australian GP)

1997 RESULTS

DRIVER	CAR–ENGINE	AUS	BR	RA	RSM	MC	E	CDN	F	GB	D	H	B	I	A	LUX	J	EU
Jean Alesi	Benetton B197-Renault	8 R	6 6	11 7	14 5	9 R	4 **3**	8 2	8 5	11 2	6 6	9 11	2 8	1 2	15 R	10 2	7 5	10 13
Rubens Barrichello	Stewart SF1-Ford	11 R	11 R	5 R	13 R	10 2	17 R	3 R	13 R	21 R	12 R	11 R	12 R	11 13	5 14	9 R	12 R	12 R
Gerhard Berger	Benetton B197-Renault	10 4	3 **2**	12 6 FL	11 R	17 9	6 10	—	—	—	1 **1** FL	7 8	15 6	7 7	18 10	7 4	5 8	8 4
David Coulthard	McLaren MP4-12-Mercedes-Benz	4 **1**	12 10	10 R	10 R	5 R	3 6	5 7 FL	9 7	6 4	8 R	8 R	10 R	6 **1**	10 2	6 **R**	11 10	6 2
Pedro Diniz	Arrows A18-Yamaha	22 10	16 R	22 R	17 R	16 R	21 R	16 8	16 R	16 R	16 R	19 R	8 7	17 R	17 13	15 5	16 12	13 R
Giancarlo Fisichella	Jordan 197-Peugeot	14 R	7 8	9 R	6 4	4 6	8 9 FL	6 3	11 9	10 7	2 **11**	13 R	4 2	3 4	14 4	4 R	9 7	17 11
Norberto Fontana	Sauber C16-Petronas	—	—	—	—	—	—	—	20 R	22 9	18 9	—	—	—	—	—	—	18 14
Heinz-Harald Frentzen	Williams FW19-Renault	2 8 FL	8 9	2 R	2 **1** FL	1 R	2 8	4 4	2 2	2 R	5 R	6 **R** FL	7 3	2 3	4 3	3 3 FL	6 2 FL	3 **6** FL
Mika Häkkinen	McLaren MP4-12-Mercedes-Benz	6 3	4 4	17 5	8 6	8 R	5 7	9 R	10 R	3 **R**	3 3	4 R	5 DSQ	5 9 FL	2 R	1 **R**	4 4	5 **1**
Johnny Herbert	Sauber C16-Petronas	7 R	13 7	8 4	7 R	7 R	10 5	13 5	14 8	9 R	14 R	10 3	11 4	12 R	12 8	16 7	8 6	14 8
Damon Hill	Arrows A18-Yamaha	20 DNS	9 17	13 R	15 R	13 R	15 R	15 9	17 12	12 6	13 8	3 2	9 13	14 R	7 7	13 8	17 11	4 R
Eddie Irvine	Ferrari F310B	5 R	14 16	7 **2**	9 3	15 3	11 12	12 R	5 3	7 R	10 R	5 9	17 10	10 8	8 R	14 R	3 **3**	7 5
Ukyo Katayama	Minardi M197-Hart	15 R	18 18	21 R	22 11	20 10	20 R	22 R	21 11	18 R	22 R	20 10	20 14	21 R	19 11	22 R	19 R	19 17
Nicola Larini	Sauber C16-Petronas	13 6	19 11	14 R	12 7	11 R	—	—	—	—	—	—	—	—	—	—	—	—
Jan Magnussen	Stewart SF1-Ford	19 R	20 R	15 10	16 R	19 7	22 13	21 R	15 R	15 R	15 R	17 R	18 12	13 R	6 R	12 R	14 R	11 9
Tarso Marques	Minardi M197-Hart	—	—	—	—	—	—	—	22 R	20 10	21 R	22 12	22 R	22 14	22 DNQ	18 R	20 R	20 15
Gianni Morbidelli	Sauber C16-Petronas	—	—	—	—	13 14	18 10	—	—	—	15 R	13 9	18 12	13 9	19 9	18 DNS	—	
Shinji Nakano	Prost JS45-Mugen	16 7	15 14	20 R	18 R	21 R	16 R	19 6	12 R	14 11	17 7	16 6	16 R	15 11	16 R	17 R	15 R	15 10
Olivier Panis	Prost JS45-Mugen	9 5	5 3	3 R	4 8	12 4	12 2	10 11	—	—	—	—	—	—	—	11 6	10 R	9 7
Ricardo Rosset	Lola T97/30-Ford	24 DNQ	NT DNP	—	—	—	—	—	—	—	—	—	—	—	—	—	—	—
Mika Salo	Tyrrell 025-Ford	18 R	22 13	19 8	19 9	14 5	14 R	17 R	19 R	17 R	19 R	21 13	19 11	19 R	21 R	20 10	22 R	21 12
Michael Schumacher	Ferrari F310B	3 2	2 5	4 R	3 **2**	2 1 FL	7 **4**	1 **1**	1 1 FL	4 **R** FL	4 2	1 **4**	3 **1**	9 **6**	9 **6**	5 R	2 **1**	2 **R**
Ralf Schumacher	Jordan 197-Peugeot	12 R	10 R	6 3	5 R	6 R	9 R	7 R	3 6	5 5	7 5	14 5	6 R	8 R	11 5	8 R	13 9	16 R
Vincenzo Sospiri	Lola T97/30-Ford	23 DNQ	NT DNP	—	—	—	—	—	—	—	—	—	—	—	—	—	—	—
Jarno Trulli	Minardi M197-Hart	17 9	17 12	18 9	20 DNS	18 R	18 15	20 R	—	—	—	—	—	—	—	—	—	—
	Prost JS45-Mugen	—	—	—	—	—	—	—	6 10	13 8	11 4	12 7	14 15	16 10	3 **R**	—	—	—
Jos Verstappen	Tyrrell 025-Ford	21 R	21 15	16 R	21 10	22 8	19 11	14 R	18 R	19 R	20 10	18 R	21 R	20 R	20 12	21 R	21 13	22 16
Jacques Villeneuve	Williams FW19-Renault	1 R	1 **1** FL	1 **1**	1 **R**	3 R	1 **1**	2 R	4 4	1 **1**	9 R	2 **1**	15 5 FL	4 5	1 **1** FL	2 **1**	1 DSQ	1 **3**
Alexander Wurz	Benetton B197-Renault	—	—	—	—	—	11 R	7 R	8 3	—	—	—	—	—	—	—	—	—

FORMULA 1 RACE WINNERS

ROUND	RACE (CIRCUIT)	DATE	WINNER
1	Qantas Australian Grand Prix (Albert Park)	Mar 9	David Coulthard (McLaren MP4-12-Mercedes-Benz)
2	Grande Prêmio do Brasil (Interlagos)	Mar 30	Jacques Villeneuve (Williams FW19-Renault)
3	Gran Premio Marlboro de Argentina (Buenos Aires)	Apr 13	Jacques Villeneuve (Williams FW19-Renault)
4	Gran Premio di San Marino (Imola)	Apr 27	Heinz-Harald Frentzen (Williams FW19-Renault)
5	Grand Prix de Monaco (Monte Carlo)	May 11	Michael Schumacher (Ferrari F310B)
6	Gran Premio Marlboro de España (Catalunya)	May 25	Jacques Villeneuve (Williams FW19-Renault)
7	Grand Prix Player's du Canada (Montréal)	Jun 15	Michael Schumacher (Ferrari F310B)
8	Grand Prix de France (Magny-Cours)	Jun 29	Michael Schumacher (Ferrari F310B)
9	RAC British Grand Prix (Silverstone)	Jul 13	Jacques Villeneuve (Williams FW19-Renault)
10	Grosser Mobil 1 Preis von Deutschland (Hockenheim)	Jul 27	Gerhard Berger (Benetton B197-Renault)
11	Marlboro Magyar Nagydíj (Hungaroring)	Aug 10	Jacques Villeneuve (Williams FW19-Renault)
12	Grand Prix de Belgique (Spa-Francorchamps)	Aug 24	Michael Schumacher (Ferrari F310B)
13	Gran Premio Campari d'Italia (Monza)	Sep 7	David Coulthard (McLaren MP4-12-Mercedes-Benz)
14	Grosser Preis von Österreich (Spielberg)	Sep 21	Jacques Villeneuve (Williams FW19-Renault)
15	Grosser Preis von Luxemburg (Nürburgring)	Sep 28	Jacques Villeneuve (Williams FW19-Renault)
16	Fuji Television Japanese Grand Prix (Suzuka)	Oct 12	Michael Schumacher (Ferrari F310B)
17	Grand Prix of Europe (Jerez)	Oct 26	Mika Häkkinen (McLaren MP4-12-Mercedes-Benz)

DRIVERS' CHAMPIONSHIP

	DRIVERS	POINTS
1	Jacques Villeneuve	81
2	Heinz-Harald Frentzen	42
3=	Jean Alesi	36
	David Coulthard	36
5=	Gerhard Berger	27
	Mika Häkkinen	27
7	Eddie Irvine	24
8	Giancarlo Fisichella	20
9	Olivier Panis	16
10	Johnny Herbert	15
11	Ralf Schumacher	13
12	Damon Hill	7
13	Rubens Barrichello	6
14	Alexander Wurz	4
15	Jarno Trulli	3
16=	Pedro Diniz	2
	Shinji Nakano	2
	Mika Salo	2
19	Nicola Larini	1

Michael Schumacher scored 78 points but was excluded from the championship for trying to drive into Jacques Villeneuve at the final race of the season. His drivers' points were taken away; the manufacturers' points and his race results remained unaffected.

CONSTRUCTORS' CHAMPIONSHIP

	CONSTRUCTORS	POINTS
1	Williams-Renault	123
2	Ferrari	102
3	Benetton-Renault	67
4	McLaren-Mercedes-Benz	63
5	Jordan-Peugeot	33
6	Prost-Mugen	21
7	Sauber-Petronas Ferrari	16
8	Arrows-Yamaha	9
9	Stewart-Ford	6
10	Tyrrell-Ford	2

The Belgian Grand Prix was the first race started behind the safety car

The McLaren-Mercedes MP4-13s of Mika Häkkinen and David Coulthard lapped the field in Australia

1998

McLAREN'S FIRST WORLD TITLE IN SEVEN YEARS

Mika Häkkinen celebrates clinching the title in Japan with David Coulthard

McLaren was the class of the field in 1998, seven years on from its most recent World Championship title. Mika Häkkinen qualified on pole position at nine races and won half of the 16 GPs to clinch the constructors' and drivers' titles. Their victory in the opening race in Australia, where David Coulthard respected a pre-race agreement and let his team-

Damon Hill led a Jordan 1–2 at Spa-Francorchamps

mate pass in the closing stages, led to confusion regarding team orders. The Fédération Internationale de l'Automobile initially banned 'any act prejudicial to the interests of any competition'. When Michael Schumacher later passed a slowing Eddie Irvine in Austria, the FIA World Council clarified that team orders were legal as long as they were in the interest of the World Championship.

The quest to slow F1 cars continued with downforce reduced by approximately 20 per cent. The cars were 20cm narrower and front suspension had to be mounted outside a 30cm cubed area around the pedals. The wheels were closer to the bodywork so controlling airflow in this area was vital. Stringent side-impact tests were introduced although some found ways to avoid the longer sidepods that were intended. Dry tyres had mandatory grooves to reduce contact with the road, despite both Goodyear and Bridgestone being against the change. Flexible front wings such as Ferrari introduced at the 1997 Japanese GP were banned, while 'x-wings' were outlawed from the Spanish GP. Requests for traction control to be legalised because it was too difficult to police were turned down by the FIA.

Drivers now had to be able to exit the cockpit and reattach the steering wheel within ten seconds and cars were all fitted with a camera on the engine cover. Lights in the cockpit supplemented marshals' yellow, red and blue warning flags

Michael Schumacher's challenge faded when he stalled before the Japanese GP parade lap

and were activated by transponders every 200m around the track. The effectiveness of gravel traps to slow a spinning car was investigated with tarmac run-offs suggested as a better solution in certain circumstances.

Central weight distribution and a low centre of gravity were key design priorities. Most cars were built under the weight limit so ballast could be used to vary the weight distribution for any given circuit. The tyre war was key with Bridgestone quicker and more consistent than Goodyear at the start of the year. Understandably, both companies developed rubber to suit their respective title challengers, McLaren and Ferrari, to the chagrin of some other clients. Despite persistent rumours that it would change its mind, Goodyear withdrew at the end of the season.

The French GP was originally omitted from the calendar due to a television dispute while a proposed tobacco-advertising ban threatened the Belgian GP, although both races were confirmed in the spring. The Portuguese GP was scheduled for 11 October but the race was cancelled when the government ruled out a grant to upgrade Estoril as required. An inaugural Chinese GP at the newly completed Zhuhai circuit and a return to Kyalami were listed as reserve events. However, no replacement race was held so there was a five-week gap between the last two GPs of the season.

Keen to avoid a repeat of Lola's short-lived F1 return, the

FIA demanded a $24 million deposit from any new team, which was to be paid back (with interest) throughout its first two seasons. Vickers sold Cosworth Engineering to Volkswagen in June in part of a wider deal for Rolls-Royce Motor Cars, but Ford acquired its long-term engine partner three months later.

Jacques Villeneuve endured a winless title defence

Mika Häkkinen, McLaren MP4-13-Mercedes (Austrian GP)

WEST McLAREN MERCEDES

Mika Häkkinen and David Coulthard were confirmed at the 1997 Belgian GP as McLaren's driver line-up for a third successive season, ending Damon Hill's hopes of joining. Ricardo Zonta combined his role as test driver with a title-winning race programme in the FIA GT Championship for Mercedes-Benz.

With Goodyear due to withdraw at the end of the season, McLaren ended its 13-year association with the American tyre company and switched to Bridgestone, which initially proved an advantage. McLaren was the last team to show its hand when the eagerly anticipated MP4-13 was launched on 5 February. For his first design as McLaren technical director, Adrian Newey went against prevailing trend and retained a relatively low nose, with the front wing attached by curved supports. The top of the monocoque was lowered, with small fins on either side and ahead of the driver to comply with the height regulations. The wheelbase was marginally longer, the bargeboards were larger and the tall sidepods had more pronounced curved winglets to the rear. The narrow airbox, which extended to the single support for the rear wing, had a triangular inlet and was further back to reduce air interference from the driver's helmet. The push-rod suspension was fitted with horizontal torsion bars at the front and inboard coil springs to the rear. The lower wishbones were mounted on the chassis at the front and

above the side diffuser channels to the rear. The steering arms were now located between the front wishbones. Ilmor Engineering concentrated on improved reliability for the latest Mercedes V10, the FO110G. Both engine and longitudinal six-speed semi-automatic gearbox were lighter and lower than before, while two exhausts exited adjacent to the central diffuser. The MP4-13 was fitted with the 'brake-steer' system, which caused the first protest of the season.

The McLaren MP4-13-Mercedes was the best package of 1998, with impressive aerodynamic grip and the most powerful engine in the field. It won nine of the 16 GPs and started from pole position 12 times. Reliability threatened to derail its championship charge and McLaren refused to impose team orders. As Dennis observed: 'By and large, the races Ferrari has won are the races that we have lost… they've been there to pick up the pieces.'

The MP4-13 stunned when it first ran at Barcelona on 11 February. On just his third flying lap, Häkkinen beat the fastest time achieved by any 1998-specification car so far and Coulthard subsequently went even quicker to confirm their status as pre-season favourites. There was a surprise at the Australian GP for McLaren announced it was building a two-seater F1 car – the McLaren MP4-98T-Mercedes. Passengers during 1998 included Max Mosley, Murray Walker, Michael Douglas and King Juan Carlos of Spain.

Häkkinen led Coulthard in a crushing 1–2 in Australian GP

qualifying and, fearing reliability issues, they agreed that whoever led into the first corner would win the race. The Finn made the better start but lost the lead on lap 36 when he drove through the pitlane following a radio communication error. He closed on Coulthard who respected their pre-race agreement and let him past with two laps to go, prompting the FIA to ban team orders. Further controversy followed in Brazil, where Ferrari and four other teams protested the 'brake-steer' systems as featured on the McLaren-Mercedes, Williams-Mecachrome and Jordan-Mugen. McLaren-Mercedes disabled it when the stewards upheld the complaint but the result was still the same – Häkkinen and Coulthard first and second in qualifying and on every lap of the race.

It was Coulthard who took pole in Argentina with Michael Schumacher using improved Goodyear rubber to split the silver cars. Coulthard had problems downshifting and Schumacher barged past on lap five. That spun the angry Scot down to sixth where he finished as the gearbox problems worsened and following a subsequent incident with Jacques Villeneuve. Häkkinen finished second on a day when McLaren's one-stop strategy proved slower. Coulthard beat his team-mate to pole at Imola by 0.102sec and led every lap, although he had to nurse rising temperatures in the closing stages; Häkkinen went out with a broken gearbox bearing.

Häkkinen led McLaren-Mercedes front-row lock-outs in Spain and Monaco and dominated both races. Coulthard was second at Barcelona but engine failure in Monaco's tunnel when second left him 17 points adrift in the championship. Coulthard took pole in Montréal but McLaren-Mercedes had a disastrous race: Häkkinen was stuck in gear at the start and race leader Coulthard lost power due to a throttle-linkage issue after 18 laps. Häkkinen was beaten

into third by the Ferraris in France and second at Silverstone, having started from pole and spun during both races. He damaged his front wing during a wild moment at Silverstone's Bridge corner and lost out to Schumacher when he then ran wide at Becketts. A faulty refuelling rig and four pitstops destroyed Coulthard's French GP, although he salvaged sixth and set the fastest lap. At Silverstone, he passed Schumacher for second position but spun his intermediate-shod MP4-13 at Abbey when the rain increased.

With Schumacher two points behind Häkkinen, McLaren-Mercedes enjoyed a strong test at Monza and returned to form in Austria. Team principal Ron Dennis threatened to protest Ferrari for illegal driver aids at that race but his cars dominated nonetheless. Häkkinen jumped from third on the grid to lead all but two laps. Only 14th on the grid after an off-track excursion when the drying track was at its best, Coulthard was hit on lap one, but stormed back from the subsequent pitstop to finish second. That form continued in Germany where they qualified on the front row and led every lap once more, Häkkinen heading the team's fifth 1–2 of the season as Coulthard, who hit 221.47mph in a straight line in qualifying, held station.

The qualifying domination continued in Hungary: Häkkinen led the opening stint from pole position before a loose anti-roll bar affected his car's handling and restricted him to sixth, while Coulthard finished second when beaten by Michael Schumacher. An eventful Belgian GP yielded only seventh place for Coulthard. Forced wide by Eddie Irvine's Ferrari as they exited La Source at the start, he spun into the opposite wall to trigger the 12-car pile-up that forced the race to be red-flagged. Come the restart, he spun on lap one after contact with Alexander Wurz's Benetton-Playlife and was about to be lapped when Schumacher's leading Ferrari hit the back of his McLaren-Mercedes at

David Coulthard, McLaren MP4-13-Mercedes (Luxembourg GP)

high speed. The German had already ended Häkkinen's race at the restart by tapping him into a spin that saw him collected by Johnny Herbert's Sauber-Petronas.

Schumacher won the Italian GP to draw level with Häkkinen on points. Coulthard's engine failed while comfortably in the lead and Häkkinen finished fourth despite a high-speed spin following front-brake failure. Only third on the grid for the Luxembourg GP, the Finn passed Irvine into the Nürburgring chicane on lap 14 and took a decisive lead from Schumacher in the pitstops after four race-winning laps; Coulthard finished third. With a four-point advantage before the final race in Japan, Häkkinen qualified second and led from start to finish, although he knew he was the new World Champion when Schumacher retired on lap 32. Coulthard finished third in the race and in the final standings, while McLaren secured its first constructors' title since 1991.

SCUDERIA FERRARI MARLBORO

Michael Schumacher remained under contract and Ferrari opted for stability when it exercised its option on Eddie Irvine's services on 31 July. Former Minardi driver Luca Badoer was announced as test driver in the New Year, initially on a one-year contract although he fulfilled the role for over a decade.

There was a different tone to Ferrari's pre-season rhetoric in 1998. Gone were the promises of transition and a title challenge in 12 months' time that had been commonplace throughout the 1990s. 'Ferrari is not content to merely do better,' sporting director Jean Todt said in December. 'It must challenge for the World Championship.' President Luca di Montezemolo reiterated that stance on 7 January as the Ferrari F300 was launched in Maranello. 'Today is the first day we can say with belief that Ferrari can win the World Championship. If we don't win it, it will mean we have failed.'

Chief designer Rory Byrne and his team penned an elegant new challenger, with raised nose that curved down at the front and had two straight supports for the wing. A slight bulge ahead of the cockpit diverted air around the driver's helmet and into the airbox, which had been moved further back. The rear bodywork was very low, with winglets placed at the back of the sidepods and the 'coke bottle' tightly packaged ahead of a complex rear diffuser. Torsion bars with 'knife-edge' mounts were retained in heavily revised front suspension, which featured three dampers. The lower front wishbones were fitted to the enlarged splitter that channelled air into the sidepods, which were smaller than normal for 1998 and passed the new lateral crash test because the driver was moved back. An all-new and very reliable version of the 75-degree V10 engine, the 047, was lighter and more compact than its predecessor to lower the centre of gravity and improve balance. It was designed to operate at hotter temperatures so smaller radiators could be fitted to reduce drag. Ferrari switched to a longitudinal gearbox, which was a narrow seven-speed semi-automatic design with titanium casing. The team remained loyal to Goodyear for the American company's final F1 season.

Gearbox electronics initially caused problems at Fiorano and a subsequent Jerez test was cut short when the exhausts overheated the rear suspension. The exhausts were temporarily repositioned to blow into the side diffuser and the electronics improved. The F300 appeared quick and consistent at Mugello although it had not tested alongside the new McLaren-Mercedes so there was a rude awakening in Melbourne where the silver cars annexed the front row and lapped the field. Schumacher qualified third despite a wild couple of days and suffered an early engine failure; Irvine finished fourth. The engine was upgraded for Brazil with revised valves and higher revs but Schumacher made a poor start and stalled at his second stop. He

Michael Schumacher, Ferrari F300 (Luxembourg GP)

Eddie Irvine, Ferrari F300 (Italian GP)

recovered to finish third, albeit a minute behind Mika Häkkinen.

In response to Bridgestone's strong start, Goodyear introduced a wider front tyre that was first used in Argentina. Schumacher split the two McLaren-Mercedes in qualifying and knocked pole-winner David Coulthard into a spin at the Entrada a los Mixtos hairpin on lap five. He eased to victory with Irvine completing a good day by finishing third. Soon-to-be-banned 'x-wings' were mounted on either side of the cockpit at Imola, where the Ferraris started from row two and finished second (Schumacher) and third (Irvine).

The compromise exhaust solution caused rear-end instability on deceleration, so a new 'periscope' arrangement was introduced for the Spanish GP whereby the exhausts exited through large oval holes in the rear bodywork adjacent to the airbox. Schumacher qualified and finished third despite a stop-go penalty for speeding in the pitlane. Irvine made a great start but crashed into Giancarlo Fisichella's Benetton-Playlife, with both drivers blaming each other and the Italian fined.

Now 12 points behind Häkkinen, Schumacher had a terrible Monaco GP weekend. He crashed in Casino Square on Thursday, broke a driveshaft on Saturday and only finished tenth. Already delayed by rear-suspension repairs following a wheel-banging incident with Alexander Wurz at Grand Hotel hairpin (formerly Station or Loews), Schumacher lost his front wing when he rammed Pedro Diniz on the last lap. Seventh on the grid following a qualifying crash at Rascasse, Irvine finished third.

After Schumacher's public criticism of Goodyear in previous weeks, his fortunes improved with three successive victories. In Canada, where both McLaren-Mercedes cars retired, he recovered from a stop-go penalty for driving Heinz-Harald Frentzen off the road, while Irvine staged a fine fightback from last place to finish third after puncturing a tyre in a clash with Jean Alesi. Schumacher led a Ferrari 1–2 in France before scoring another controversial victory at Silverstone that reduced Häkkinen's lead to just two points. Schumacher passed Wurz under yellow flags with 17 laps to go and was belatedly handed a 10sec stop-go penalty that he served on the last lap, crossing the finish line before reaching his pit and therefore declared the winner. Irvine made a slow start before climbing through the field to finish third once more.

McLaren protested Schumacher's Silverstone victory without success and lingering accusations that Ferrari was using untraceable electronic driver aids were refuted by team and FIA alike. Momentum swung back to McLaren at the next two GPs. In Austria, Ferrari denied implementing team orders, which had been banned after the controversial Australian GP. Schumacher challenged Häkkinen for the lead only to lose his front wing when he ran wide at the final corner on lap 18. Last after his unscheduled stop, he charged back through the field and passed third-placed Irvine, who had visibly slowed in the closing stages. The Ulsterman's sudden lack of pace was attributed to brake problems rather than anything nefarious. Only fifth at Hockenheim, Schumacher bounced back by winning the Hungarian GP thanks to a brilliant middle stint to his three-stop race. A slow pitstop ruined Irvine's German GP and his gearbox failed when running fourth in Hungary.

A long-wheelbase version of the F300, with a spacer between

Jacques Villeneuve, Williams FW20-Mecachrome (Hungarian GP)

engine and gearbox, had been tried during practice for the German GP and was introduced at Spa-Francorchamps. Irvine bruised his knee in the first-lap pile-up and took over Schumacher's spare for the restart. Revelling in the wet, Schumacher passed Damon Hill for the lead on lap eight and held a 37sec lead when he came to lap Coulthard after 25 laps. Unsighted and unaware that the Scot had slowed to let him through, Schumacher crashed into the back of the McLaren-Mercedes on the approach to Pouhon. That prompted an angry outburst in the pits with Schumacher having to be restrained. Irvine, who had already changed his front wing following an 'off' at Malmédy, spun out of sixth position.

Schumacher played down his hopes for the Italian GP but snatched pole for the first time in 1998. Fifth in the early laps after a poor start, he passed three cars, inherited the lead when Coulthard retired and eased to victory to draw level with Häkkinen in the standings. Irvine completed the perfect day for the locals by finishing second. Ferrari reverted to the short-wheelbase configuration for the Luxembourg GP and locked out the front row. They ran 1–2 from the start until Schumacher, with his hard tyres not generating enough grip, lost out to Häkkinen in the pitstops and was disappointed to finish second, while Irvine was fourth. Schumacher secured his third successive pole position for the title decider in Japan only to stall before the parade lap. Forced to start from the back, he was seventh after just five laps and third when his right-rear tyre punctured on the main straight, confirming Häkkinen as World Champion. Irvine finished second after stopping three times.

Schumacher and Irvine were second and fourth in the drivers' standings with Ferrari runners-up for the third year in a row.

WINFIELD WILLIAMS

Renault withdrew from F1 at the end of 1997 with its engine technology transferred to technical supplier Mecachrome in Aubigny-sur-Nère. Already negotiating a future partnership with BMW, Williams signed a two-year deal with Mecachrome on 29 January 1997 to lease the rebadged V10s in 1998 and 1999 at a reputed cost of £13 million per season. The Mecachrome GC37/01 lacked the development of Mercedes-Benz or Ferrari and the Williams FW20 proved too conservative a design, so the team endured its first winless campaign in a decade.

Williams exercised its option on Jacques Villeneuve in March 1997 despite rumours that he was central to Craig Pollock's ambitious new 'super team' for 1999. At the same time its agreement with Rothmans International was also extended for another year, although the tobacco company chose to promote its Winfield brand. Heinz-Harald Frentzen had disappointed for much of 1997 but remained under contract. Juan Pablo Montoya and Max Wilson were recruited as test drivers after outpacing Soheil Ayari and Nicolas Minassian in a two-day test at Barcelona in December 1997.

The Williams FW20-Mecachrome first turned a wheel at Silverstone on 28 January with a largely trouble-free test at Barcelona to follow. Senior designer Gavin Fisher evolved the 1997 car with higher nose, twin supports for the front wing, circular airbox intake and – to meet the new lateral impact test – long sidepods that curved upwards ahead of the rear wheels. It was the only 1998 car to retain a transverse gearbox. At the front, push-rods were swept back, lower wishbones mounted on the splitter, and torsion bars attached to the chassis under small humps in the bodywork. Coil springs were

Heinz-Harald Frentzen, Williams FW20-Mecachrome (Italian GP)

employed at the rear. Williams remained contracted to Goodyear.

In addition to Mecachrome's power deficit, the FW20 had inherent oversteer and a nervous rear end. Having locked out the Australian GP front row for the previous two years, Williams only started the 1998 race from the lower reaches of the top six. They adopted a one-stop strategy to finish third (Frentzen) and fifth (Villeneuve), albeit lapped by the dominant McLaren-Mercedes drivers. Frentzen started third and finished fifth in Brazil, where Villeneuve crashed on Saturday morning and struggled to find an adequate set-up. It was worse in Argentina as Goodyear's new front tyres suited the Ferraris but were of little discernible benefit to Williams. Villeneuve crashed with David Coulthard and Frentzen was ninth after stalling at a stop and serving a stop-go penalty for speeding in the pitlane.

The team travelled straight to Jerez as it tried to sort the recalcitrant FW20, with the rear suspension identified for particular development. Winfield arranged for reigning World Champions Mick Doohan (500cc motorcycle racing) and Tommi Mäkinen (rallying) to test a Williams FW19-Mecachrome at Barcelona on 23 April: Doohan spun on his first lap while Mäkinen missed a gearchange when travelling at 157mph and crashed.

At Imola, Villeneuve made a good start to run third in the early stages before finishing fourth despite problems with the fuel cap at both his pitstops; Frentzen was fifth. The woes deepened in Barcelona – where Williams had its worst qualifying since 1989 – and at Monaco, so Villeneuve's top-six finishes at both races were noteworthy. Frentzen qualified fifth in Monaco but was nudged into the barrier at the Grand Hotel hairpin as Eddie Irvine attempted to overtake on lap ten.

A revised FW20 was introduced at the Canadian GP with longer wheelbase to improve stability and rear-end grip. New rear suspension included repositioned lower wishbones that required the diffuser to be modified with the exhausts now exiting over the side channels. A longer engine cover improved airflow to the rear wing. Sixth and seventh after a troubled qualifying session, they challenged for a podium before Frentzen was forced onto the grass and out of the race as Michael Schumacher rejoined after his pitstop. That triggered a safety car and Villeneuve, having not pitted so far, tried to overtake Giancarlo Fisichella for the lead at the restart. He locked his brakes, ran wide and was hit by Esteban Tuero's Minardi-Ford as he got back up to speed. Williams unsuccessfully protested Schumacher's driving.

Shorter sidepods and revised bargeboards were introduced on the return to Europe and progress was confirmed by Villeneuve at the next five races. Fourth in France, he qualified third at Silverstone (where he sported purple hair) but only finished seventh after struggling in the rain. He rebounded from a poor qualifying and slow start to finish sixth in Austria. More competitive than at any time this season so far, Villeneuve qualified and finished third at Hockenheim and repeated that result in Hungary. In contrast, Frentzen was knocked unconscious in a testing accident at Magny-Cours and failed to score for four races in a row. He was classified in France despite having terminal suspension damage following a clash with Jean Alesi and he spun out of the British GP. Sixth when his engine failed at the A1-Ring, he was a lacklustre ninth at Hockenheim. Frentzen's poor run was ended by finishing fifth at the Hungaroring despite being ill.

Villeneuve's Belgian GP weekend began with a high-speed accident at Eau Rouge on Friday, his car hitting the barrier at Raidillon, and ended when he spun out of the race. Frentzen escaped running wide in the rain to finish fourth – his best result since Australia. Villeneuve was mighty in qualifying at Monza to line up second with an ultra-low-drag set-up that compensated for his lack of power. That made the car difficult to control and he was fourth when he spun into the gravel at the second Lesmo. Frentzen finished seventh despite running out of fuel before his pitstop and coasting to the pits. Villeneuve's Luxembourg GP was ruined by a faulty fuel rig and he finished sixth in Japan. Frentzen was fifth at the final two races of 1998 as Williams-Mecachrome held onto a distant third in the standings.

BENSON & HEDGES JORDAN MUGEN HONDA

Eddie Jordan announced in July 1997 that his eponymous team would use Mugen engines for the next two years in what was effectively an engine swap with Prost Grand Prix. A subsidiary of Honda, Mugen introduced a brand-new V10 with vee angle reduced to 70 degrees to allow chief engineer Tenji Sakai's team to reduce its size and weight. It was also designed to operate at hotter temperatures so drag could be reduced by fitting smaller radiators. Ralf Schumacher remained under contract but Jordan's attempts to prevent Giancarlo Fisichella's move to Benetton were unsuccessful. A year after turning down Jordan, Damon Hill signed a two-year contract with the Silverstone-based team on 16 September 1997, angering Alain Prost as he had also been negotiating with the former champion.

Arrows refused to release Hill early so it was new test driver Pedro de la Rosa who endured a troubled first run with the interim Jordan 197-Mugen at Silverstone in December. Problems with the electronics forced Jordan to abandon using this test hack and wait for the new Jordan 198-Mugen to be completed so chassis and engine development was compromised from the start. The 198 was launched at London's Royal Albert Hall on 19 January, complete with entertainment from the Cirque du Soleil. Technical director Gary Anderson chose suspension with unequal-length double wishbones as the best solution for the new grooved tyres. Understeer during the winter forced the front suspension to be redesigned but this did not fully eradicate the problem. The front endplates featured side winglets while the sidepods were squarer and unusually long. The twin-pedal arrangement meant that Hill used left-foot braking for the first time in his career. Jordan was among the first to introduce a long-wheelbase version to improve handling. Repsol became fuel partner as part of the deal that took de la Rosa to the team. Dino Toso and Sam Michael worked as race engineers for Hill and Schumacher respectively.

Positive initial tests proved deceptive for Hill was 2.66sec off the pace when they returned to Barcelona in February. That deficit was reduced to a second before the start of the season but Jordan-Mugen endured a miserable first half of the campaign thanks to a lack of mechanical grip and power. They started the opening race in Melbourne's Albert Park from row five and Hill finished eighth, then was disqualified from tenth for being underweight in Brazil. Schumacher crashed out of both GPs having completed a total of one racing lap. New Goodyear rubber and 'x-wings' improved

Ralf Schumacher, Jordan 198-Mugen (Brazilian GP)

Damon Hill, Jordan 198-Mugen (Italian GP)

qualifying pace for the Argentinian GP. Schumacher made a poor start from fifth on the grid, spun after 18 laps and crashed four laps later when the rear suspension failed. Ninth on the grid, Hill needed a new front wing after hitting Johnny Herbert's Sauber-Petronas and finished eighth again.

The long-wheelbase car was taken to Imola with revised front suspension, airbox and rear wing endplates. Having outqualified his team-mate for the first time when seventh, Hill ran into the back of Alexander Wurz's slow-moving Benetton-Playlife on the opening lap. He charged back from another wing change into seventh, only for his engine to fail with four laps to go. Schumacher inherited that position despite a problem with the fuel cap ruining his pitstops. They lacked straight-line speed in Spain, where Hill accused Heinz-Harald Frentzen of driving him off the road, and only qualified on the eighth row in Monaco. The sight of Shinji Nakano's Minardi-Ford harrying eighth-placed Hill in the closing stages emphasised Jordan-Mugen's current plight.

A two-hour crisis meeting was held after Monaco and Anderson missed the next two races to work in the wind tunnel. Tyrrell's Mike Gascoyne was hired as chief designer, reporting to Anderson. An engine upgrade helped in Canada and both cars lined up in the top ten with Schumacher fifth on the grid. His race was less successful for he stalled at the original start and spun at the restart to trigger another first-corner shunt. Hill ran second when

Michael Schumacher served his stop-go penalty and his robust defence sparked another war of words with his old rival, although mechanical failures denied Hill points in both Montréal and Magny-Cours. Sixth on the French GP grid thanks in part to improved Goodyear tyres, Schumacher damaged a steering arm when he collided with Alexander Wurz.

A new aero package at Silverstone featured shorter sidepods swept back at the front (requiring a new side-impact test) accompanied by larger bargeboards, with the rear diffuser and exhaust also revised. The British GP meeting began badly as Schumacher's best qualifying time was deleted for a yellow-flag infringement during practice and then he was relegated to the back of the grid for a scrutineering issue. The German made a great start (normally a weakness in 1998) and drove through the field to finish sixth and score Jordan-Mugen's first point of the season. Hill spun and stalled at Brooklands on lap 14.

With progress finally being made, Austria brought fifth (Schumacher following a wheel-to-wheel battle with his brother) and seventh (Hill). Both qualified in the top five at Hockenheim, where Schumacher chased the McLaren-Mercedes pair during the first stint of his two-stop strategy but then dropped behind his one-stopping team-mate and was disappointed to finish sixth, with Hill fourth. Hill qualified and finished fourth in Hungary as Jordan-Mugen's resurgence continued.

Hill qualified third in Belgium and narrowly avoided the lap-one carnage that stopped the original race. He took the lead at the restart as Michael Schumacher and Mika Häkkinen disputed the first corner before being passed by the Ferrari on lap eight. Ralf Schumacher benefitted from an early change of his intermediate tyres to full wets and was third behind his team-mate when his brother crashed into David Coulthard's McLaren-Mercedes. The Jordan-Mugens were suddenly first and second behind the safety car. Once released, Hill eased to victory despite a slow puncture incurred while lapping a Prost-Peugeot. Ordered not to challenge his team-mate and risk losing a famous 1–2 finish, Schumacher was visibly miffed post-race despite his best result to date.

Rumours of a disagreement between Eddie Jordan and his technical director regarding the need for a revised management structure circulated during the summer. Anderson, who had been with Jordan since it entered F1, resigned in September with Gascoyne now leading the technical department and Trevor Foster promoted to joint managing director.

An aero update in Italy included exaggerated 'flip-ups' ahead of the rear wheels and a new 'coke-bottle' rear end. Schumacher started sixth and passed Häkkinen for third with three laps to go, while Hill recovered from poor qualifying by adopting a two-stop strategy to finish sixth. The Nürburgring was Jordan's only race since mid-season without scoring: Schumacher's brakes failed when fifth and Hill was off-form due to illness. A year that had started bleakly then ended with Hill snatching fourth from Frentzen on the last corner of the Japanese GP, a result that displaced Benetton-Playlife from fourth in the constructors' standings and confirmed the Silverstone-based concern's best year to date.

MILD SEVEN BENETTON PLAYLIFE

Renault's impending withdrawal left Benetton Formula looking at its engine options for 1998. Renault handed its V10 engine programme to technical partner Mecachrome but the most popular theory was that Benetton would take over Ligier's Mugen deal. The Honda subsidiary finally partnered with Jordan so Benetton signed a one-year deal with Mecachrome, although confirmation was delayed as Benetton tried to find someone to pay the £13 million bill. No naming partner could be found so Benetton announced on the eve of the season that its engines would be rebadged as Playlife V10s to promote its new marketing philosophy and brand. Lacking the development budget of works rivals, the previously dominant engine gradually became less competitive.

Benetton-contracted Giancarlo Fisichella had impressed in 1997 while on loan at Jordan and to secure his services for 1998 the Enstone-based team had to go to the High Court on 15 September. Alexander Wurz had starred on three appearances and was confirmed as Fisichella's team-mate a week later. No reserve driver was named although 1994 reserve Jos Verstappen had positive tests at Silverstone and Jerez in the spring before joining Stewart Grand Prix. Title partner Mild Seven was in the final year of its contract.

Benetton was the first team to run a new car when Fisichella drove the B198 at Silverstone on 17–18 December. The first Benetton with Nick Wirth as chief designer, the B198 had a novel solution to the lateral safety requirements ahead of its short sidepods. Conventional bargeboards were replaced by small air deflectors that were incorporated with the low side-impact structures. It had a rounded, raised nose with twin supports for the front wing as before. The tapered rear end was more accentuated with a low

Alexander Wurz, Benetton B198-Playlife (Italian GP)

engine cover ahead of a single support for the rear wing. The single exhausts blew towards the square-shaped central diffuser with a single vertical divider in both side channels in a simplified arrangement. Carbon-fibre and titanium were used in the push-rod suspension, which again featured coil springs rather than torsion bars. Benetton switched to a hand clutch and two-pedal layout for the first time. Initial tests were on Goodyear rubber but a switch to Bridgestone was announced at the launch of the B198 on 15 January, angering some Goodyear-contracted rivals.

Fisichella set competitive times and enjoyed good reliability during winter testing at Barcelona before the new McLaren MP4-13-Mercedes went six tenths faster when it first ran. Fisichella qualified seventh in Australia and made a good start to run fourth, although his two-stop strategy proved an error. He had just made his final pitstop when the rear wing failed. Wurz spun during qualifying and could only finish seventh. The B198s were more competitive in South America with Wurz qualifying fifth in Brazil and scoring strong fourth places in both races. He set the fastest race lap in Argentina where he only lost third when he spun with seven laps to go. Outqualified by his team-mate on both occasions, a low-key Fisichella finished sixth and seventh respectively.

Fifth on the grid once more, Wurz's Benetton-Playlife stuck in gear on the opening lap of the San Marino GP and was rammed by Damon Hill. The steering wheel was changed and Wurz circulated behind Fisichella on the road but in last position until his engine broke. Fisichella challenged Heinz-Harald Frentzen for sixth until he crashed at the Villeneuve chicane, just before Wurz retired. Fisichella qualified fourth in Spain and was trying to take that position from Eddie Irvine in the race when they collided, with the Benetton driver fined $7,500. Fisichella was strong all weekend in Monaco and Montréal. Third on the grid in the Principality, he withstood Michael Schumacher's pressure until his pitstop and finished second despite spinning at Rascasse. He chose a one-stop strategy in Canada and led for 24 laps after Schumacher's first stop. Later slowed by a gear-selection issue, Fisichella finished second to repeat Benetton's best result of 1998.

Fourth in Spain, Wurz battled Schumacher for second in Monaco until the Ferrari barged past at the Grand Hotel hairpin. Wurz pitted five laps later and lost control in the tunnel next time around, possibly due to damage from the wheel-banging incident or pushing too hard on cold tyres. His B198 cannoned between the barriers before crashing head-on at the chicane. He barrel-rolled at the start of the Canadian GP after being launched over the back of Jean Alesi's Sauber-Petronas. In the spare for the restart, his contact pushed Jarno Trulli's Prost-Peugeot into Alesi to precipitate another accident, but Wurz continued to finish fourth once more.

One of the surprise packages of the season so far and third in the constructors' standings, Benetton-Playlife suffered as Bridgestone concentrated its development on McLaren-Mercedes's title challenge. The B198s only qualified on row five at Magny-Cours, where Wurz finished fifth and Fisichella ninth after a race that included a poor start, front-wing change (after hitting Alesi) and a spin. They lined up outside the top ten at a soggy Silverstone before

Giancarlo Fisichella, Benetton B198-Playlife (Monaco GP)

salvaging fourth (Wurz) and fifth (Fisichella). In Austria Fisichella exploited drying conditions to snatch a first F1 pole position. Third after a slow start, he was side-by-side with Alesi as he exited from his first pitstop, but neither was in the mood to give way on the approach to the Remus Kurve and they collided. They started from row four in Germany but finished outside the points.

Hungary saw a marginally longer version of the B198 with weight redistributed further forward to generate increased front-tyre temperature but the changes proved inconclusive as Fisichella finished eighth and Wurz's gearbox failed. Worse came at Spa-Francorchamps, where a front wing first tried at Hockenheim was back on the car. Wurz was involved in the original lap-one shunt so took the spare car for the restart and was eliminated when he tangled with David Coulthard's McLaren-Mercedes. Fisichella was fifth when he hit Shinji Nakano's Minardi-Ford at the Bus Stop chicane, his car catching fire as it came to rest.

The longer-wheelbase car was further revised for the Italian GP, with new front wing and rear diffuser, larger side winglets and lower engine cover. Wurz qualified seventh but broke another gearbox and Fisichella was eighth when delayed at his pitstop by a stubborn wheel nut. Fisichella qualified fourth at the Nürburgring and led Wurz home in sixth to score Benetton-Playlife's first point since the British GP. Frustrated in efforts to switch to Ford engines and at a perceived lack of support for his restructuring plans from the Benetton family, chief executive David Richards resigned before the final race and was replaced by 29-year-old Rocco Benetton. The cars qualified and finished in the top ten in Japan, where Fisichella lost seventh on the last lap. Damon Hill (Jordan-Mugen) finished fourth that day to demote Benetton-Playlife to fifth overall, which was something of a disappointment given the team's early form.

RED BULL SAUBER PETRONAS

Sauber's various second drivers had contributed a single championship point in 1997 so the Swiss team looked for an experienced team-mate for Johnny Herbert. Damon Hill visited Hinwil in the summer but negotiations were brief and it was Jean Alesi who signed a two-year deal after that year's Italian GP to form the most experienced line-up of 1998. Jörg Müller tested at Barcelona before Christmas and replaced Norberto Fontana as reserve driver. Team director Max Welti was released in January as Peter Sauber took a more hands-on management role. The technical department was expanded with aerodynamicist Seamus Mullarkey and new head of research and development Andy Tilley recruited from Jordan. Damon Hill's championship-winning race engineer in 1996, Tim Preston, arrived from Williams to run the test team.

The Sauber C17-Petronas was launched amid much pomp and ceremony at Vienna's Schönbrunn Palace on 21 January, with the specially composed 'Symphony of Luck' and actors in 18th century costume. Leo Ress, who had been promoted to technical director, penned a conventional car around a new carbon-fibre monocoque (due to new rules) that bore a strong resemblance to recent predecessors. Sauber began the year with an unmodified Petronas-badged 80-degree Ferrari V10 engine that lacked the power of newer rivals. A modified version was used in qualifying from Canada and raced at Monza for the first time. This was developed by Osamu Goto's in-house engine department with revised bore and stroke. A longitudinal six-speed semi-automatic gearbox was retained while the double wishbone/push-rod suspension had horizontal torsion bars mounted under small humps in the bodywork. Tall side wings (nicknamed the 'Petronas twin towers') were fitted from the second race in Brazil although these were banned after the San Marino GP.

Herbert gave the car its shakedown and Sauber endured a frustrating next two Barcelona tests. Alesi crashed backwards into the wall at Turn 9 (Campsa) on 2 February on his first run in the new car and reliability proved a problem later that month. Given Sauber's troubled winter programme, it was a surprise when Herbert qualified fifth after two uneventful days in Australia, 1.856sec quicker than his team-mate. In contention for points all race, Herbert finished sixth while Alesi was up to eighth when his engine failed. Alesi spent two days back at Ferrari's Fiorano test track trying to identify why he was slower than Herbert and they qualified alongside each other at the next three races, albeit in the midfield as would become customary. At first Alesi tended to over-drive during qualifying but generally prevailed over his team-mate once he adapted to the sensitive C17.

Herbert crashed head-on when the throttle stuck open in Brazilian practice and the resulting neck injury forced him to stop during the closing stages of the race (although he was still classified 11th). Ninth at Interlagos, Alesi crashed into Herbert on their first lap of Friday practice in Argentina although his weekend improved. Alesi scored

Jean Alesi, Sauber C17-Petronas (Monaco GP)

Johnny Herbert, Sauber C17-Petronas (British GP)

points in Argentina (fifth after a great start) and at Imola (sixth) while Herbert suffered race-ending punctures at both GPs.

Herbert qualified in the top ten in Spain and Monaco (despite excessive understeer) and finished seventh on both occasions. Alesi was set to finish fifth in Monte Carlo only for worsening gear-selection issues to prove terminal with five laps to go. They were both involved in the original first-corner accident in Canada but took the restart, Alesi in the spare. Take two, and Jarno Trulli crashed over Alesi's Sauber-Petronas while Herbert, who started from the pitlane, spun out of ninth after 18 laps.

Sauber introduced its long-wheelbase car at the Magny-Cours test and matched McLaren's times to raise expectations for the French GP. However, they lacked straight-line speed when it mattered so qualified in the midfield and only finished seventh and eighth, Alesi losing sixth to David Coulthard on the last lap. At Silverstone, they qualified in the top ten and challenged for points only to be disappointed. Alesi was fourth after another great start but emerged from his first pitstop behind his one-stopping team-mate. Herbert did not immediately move over when ordered to let Alesi past and soon spun out of the race at Luffield. Alesi was fourth when his electrics failed with seven laps to go and the atmosphere between the drivers was distinctly lukewarm after the race.

Austria provided one of Sauber's 1998 highlights but no points were scored once more. Excellent in changeable conditions, Alesi judged the drying track to qualify second. He made a poor start and was fifth when pole-winner Giancarlo Fisichella emerged from his pitstop. The young Italian attempted to pass into the Remus Kurve and hit the unyielding Alesi. The Sauber-Petronas was launched into

the air with both eliminated. Back in the midfield at the next two races, Alesi finished seventh in Hungary.

Wet weather again gave Alesi the chance to star in Belgium. Herbert was among half the field to be involved in the first-lap accident and hit Mika Häkkinen's spun McLaren-Mercedes at the restart. Alesi avoided those incidents and subsequent carnage to finish third behind the Jordan-Mugens. Without a points finish since the first race of the season, and already moving to Stewart for 1999, Herbert spun out of the Italian GP when a pair of pliers left in the cockpit by mistake became caught in his pedals! Alesi was on pole with ten minutes of the qualifying session to go but lined up only eighth due to traffic. Racing the revised engine for the first time, he finished fifth to complete a great day for the *tifosi*, who still considered him an honorary Ferrari driver.

Tenth at the Nürburgring, Alesi passed Fisichella on the last lap of the Japanese GP to snatch seventh place. Herbert, who had outqualified his team-mate for the first time since Monaco, stalled at the final restart and could only finish tenth on his last appearance for the team. Fixtures in F1's midfield, Sauber-Petronas climbed a single position in the constructors' standings to sixth despite its lowest points haul thus far.

DANKA ZEPTER ARROWS

Frustrated by the latest Yamaha engine and without a point scored so far, Tom Walkinshaw was looking for an alternative solution by the middle of 1997. He acquired Brian Hart's independent engine-preparation business that designed and built an all-new 72-degree

Mika Salo, Arrows A19 (French GP)

V10 engine. Walkinshaw wanted Yamaha's name on the new unit but the Japanese insisted its own engineers should be involved so agreement could not be reached. Pedro Diniz first drove the unpainted Arrows A19 at Silverstone on 31 January with details of the engine unconfirmed until its official launch at Leafield on 17 February. With no one to badge the engine, Arrows joined Ferrari as the only team to build its own car and engine in 1998.

Most notable among the innovations on John Barnard's compact but overcomplicated new car was the carbon-fibre longitudinal

Pedro Diniz, Arrows A19 (Hungarian GP)

gearbox. Most designers came up with similar solutions to the new rules but Barnard's attractive aero package was unconventional. The short sidepods had large exit vents immediately behind the radiators that channelled air over the tyres and away from the rear wing. The nose was even higher than on his last Ferrari with twin supports for the front wing, the endplates of which were moulded to deflect air outside the wheels. A bulge in front of the cockpit diverted air around the driver's helmet to the extremely low engine cover. The carbon-fibre suspension had torsion bars with the 'knife-edge' mountings he had pioneered at Ferrari. Bridgestone tyres were retained but the TAG Electronics system was new.

A day after Damon Hill agreed to join Jordan, Mika Salo signed as lead driver on 17 September 1997. The well-funded Diniz remained for a second season and Emmanuel Collard was confirmed as reserve driver at the launch. Testing was interrupted by gearbox overheating and hydraulic issues, and poor reliability persisted throughout another disheartening season.

Both cars were sidelined by mechanical failures at the first three races although Salo saw the A19's potential. 'With this car I could be in the top ten driving with one hand,' he told *Autosport* in Australia. It was nimble and well-balanced when it was running although it was often slowest in a straight line. An upgraded engine and new aero package were taken to Imola, where Salo finally finished: second in the warm-up, he was restricted to ninth (and last) after a problem with the fuel rig forced him to stop three times. Diniz outqualified Salo for the first time in Spain but lost a lap before the start due to a flat battery. They were running line astern when their engines failed simultaneously on the main straight.

Salo had finished fifth in Monaco for the last two years and its unique confines helped mask any inadequacies of the Arrows A19. The Finn qualified eighth and finished fourth, while Diniz completed a great day by claiming the final point despite being rammed by Michael Schumacher's Ferrari on the last lap. That form was short-lived for the A19s were back among the tailenders in Canada, where they triggered separate safety car periods. Salo crashed heavily when his steering failed and Diniz, who finished ninth, spread grass and mud across the track as he recovered from a spin. Slow but reliable in France, they both spun out in Silverstone's rain.

They had new C-specification engines in Austria, where Salo exploited the drying track to qualify sixth. Their race did not last long for they collided at the Remus Kurve on the opening lap, causing enough damage to have to retire. Rumours of a rift between Walkinshaw and Barnard, whose independent B3 Technologies concern had carried out suspension work for Prost Grand Prix, had circulated since April. Barnard left in the summer amid legal action while his assistant Mike Coughlan remained.

Unsuited to Hockenheim's flat-out demands, Arrows had better hopes for the Hungarian GP (which Hill had almost won in 1997) but Diniz's 11th place and Salo's engine failure presented further disappointment. Another (D-spec) engine upgrade was introduced at the Belgian GP although both blew-up in practice. It was an expensive weekend that ended with three damaged chassis and

welcome points. Salo had a 180mph accident at Eau Rouge during Saturday practice and required a brain scan before being cleared to qualify. Both were eliminated in the first corner pile-up but Diniz took the spare, which had been built up overnight, to finish fifth.

Arrows missed the subsequent Monza test as it repaired three cars for the Italian GP with the test chassis pressed into service although there was no reward for that hard work. The last three races yielded just one finish, Salo's distant 14th at the Nürburgring, as mechanical failures (plus Diniz's spins in Italy and Japan) brought another largely frustrating campaign to a downbeat conclusion.

STEWART FORD

Stewart Grand Prix endured a difficult second F1 season as poor reliability, especially with the radical carbon-fibre gearbox, and a move into new premises stymied progress. Despite being overly pitch-sensitive, the Stewart SF2-Ford showed some promise when it was on the track but that was not often enough. Rubens Barrichello and Jan Magnussen remained under contract and an unchanged line-up was confirmed at the 1997 Japanese GP. The FIA took the unusual step of requesting proof that the team had enough money to complete the season after the Malaysian tourist board withdrew its support. Sanyo also departed but new deals with Lear Corporation and MCI WorldCom were announced and the team was cleared to race.

Rubens Barrichello, Stewart SF2-Ford (Australian GP)

Jos Verstappen, Stewart SF2-Ford (German GP)

his team worked closely with Cosworth as they repackaged the Ford Zetec-R V10 engine with a narrow bottom end. 'Knife-edge' suspension pick-ups were employed with three shock absorbers and torsion bars all round, the front ones mounted on the chassis underneath bulges in the bodywork. Carbon-fibre was also used for the front wishbones and push-rods.

The new engine was only track-tested when fitted to a 1997 car in December and it caught fire at Barcelona during Magnussen's installation lap later that month. The SF2's shakedown at Santa Pod was delayed until 3 February due to gearbox-manufacturing delays so both car and engine were underdeveloped at the start of the season. Hydraulic leaks marred Barrichello's first experiences of the SF2 and Magnussen hardly made it out of the Silverstone pitlane when his engine failed on his first run. The first major test at Barcelona was curtailed when heat from the exhausts caused the rear wing to crack so a subsequent run at Silverstone was cancelled. This lack of testing made sorting the car near impossible with pronounced understeer a particular problem.

The issues continued in Australia with the fragile gearbox restricting mileage, to the point that Tora Takagi's customer Ford V10 outqualified both works Stewart-Fords. The race was a disaster. Barrichello could only complete one slow lap when stuck in third gear from the start and Magnussen crashed on Ralf Schumacher's gravel on lap two. The gearbox woes continued in South America although both drivers managed a tenth-place finish, Magnussen in Brazil and Barrichello at Buenos Aires.

The nadir came at Imola with senior Ford guests in attendance. Magnussen crashed into Barrichello at the first corner, dislodging

The slender Stewart SF2-Ford was unveiled at the Ford Research and Engineering Centre in Basildon, Essex on 13 January with the word 'risk' on the management's lips. While it bore a strong family resemblance to the SF1, there were notable departures in Alan Jenkins's latest design, most striking of which was the very narrow carbon-fibre gearbox. This six-speed semi-automatic unit was mounted longitudinally as before, which facilitated an accentuated 'coke-bottle' rear end. The tall, slim oil tank plus pump were moved ahead of the engine to concentrate weight at the centre of the car. Two water radiators were placed in the left-hand sidepod with another to the right, next to the smaller oil radiator. Jenkins and

Jan Magnussen, Stewart SF2-Ford (Monaco GP)

both front wings. Barrichello spun before completing the lap and Magnussen's gearbox failed seven laps after pitting for repairs. The suspension was revised for the Spanish GP, where Barrichello had a higher-revving Series 4 engine. With understeer improved, he qualified a morale-boosting ninth and finished fifth to score Stewart-Ford's first points since the previous year's Monaco shock. With his place in the team now under race-by-race review, Magnussen was troubled by his normal gremlins but completed a double finish when 12th at the chequered flag.

After rear-suspension failures on both cars in Monaco, Barrichello had a positive test at Silverstone before his SF2 appeared at the Canadian GP with a longer wheelbase and aero upgrade that improved straight-line speed. Barrichello finished fifth and Magnussen, who was using the old-specification car and had a big accident on Saturday morning, sixth. However, that first championship point was not enough to save Magnussen's drive. Jos Verstappen had negotiated with the team in April and he replaced the Dane despite being a second slower than Barrichello during a three-day test at Magny-Cours. Having caused the original French GP start to be aborted when he stalled, Verstappen took the restart and both SF2s finished, albeit outside the points.

The team had completed its move into a new factory in Tilbrook on the southern outskirts of Milton Keynes at the start of April and the 80,000sq ft facility was officially opened by HRH Princess Anne on 30 June, as Stewart's season further unravelled. Both cars retired from the next three races, although Barrichello exploited a drying track to qualify a surprise fifth in Austria. He ran fourth from the start but retired after just eight laps with brakes shot. Verstappen was a gripless 13th in Hungary, where rising gearbox temperatures sidelined Barrichello for a successive race.

At Spa-Francorchamps, Barrichello hurt his arm in the first-lap carnage and Verstappen blew his engine. Barrichello was tenth at Monza despite a slow pitstop and both cars were lapped twice and outside the top ten at the Nürburgring. Stewart's soul-destroying campaign concluded in a suitably low-key Japanese GP. Beset by handling issues, they qualified at the back of the midfield as normal and retired with mechanical failures.

GAULOISES PROST PEUGEOT

Alain Prost signed a three-year contract with engine supplier Peugeot on 14 February 1997 and believed close integration between the partners was crucial to future success. With that in mind he wanted to relocate the team from Magny-Cours to be near to Peugeot's factory in Paris. A former weapons research base in the western suburb of Guyancourt was acquired and the move was completed after the South American races.

Commercial arrangements demanded at least one French driver and the injured Olivier Panis agreed a contract extension in August 1997. Extended negotiations were held with Damon Hill so Prost was angry when his former team-mate instead joined Jordan. Alex Zanardi remained in Champ Cars so Jarno Trulli was re-signed in November. Prost Grand Prix doubled its staff to 150 and hired

Renault Sport's Bernard Dudot, who had worked with the owner in the early-1980s, as technical director with responsibility for all engineering matters. Loïc Bigois, who had filled that role in 1997, remained as chief designer and Tyrrell's Ben Wood arrived as head of aerodynamics. A new three-year contract was agreed with Gauloises owner SEITA as title partner and Bridgestone tyres were retained.

Bigois's Prost AP01-Peugeot was launched at the Circuit de Catalunya outside Barcelona on 20 January. This was an innovative design with distinctive sidepods that housed the radiators as close to the centre of the car as possible. The raised nose was long and had arched supports for the front wing, behind which was a shorter than normal splitter under the chassis. The elegant cockpit surround channelled air to the rear wing while the airbox was notably closer to the driver's helmet than most. Prost switched to a longitudinal six-speed semi-automatic gearbox for the first time but this proved heavy and unreliable. The clutch was repositioned at the back of the gearbox so the engine could be mounted lower. The push-rod suspension was fitted with torsion bars at the front, mounted on top of the chassis under bulges in the bodywork.

The AP01 was over the weight limit so ballast could not be used to optimise weight distribution, as was now the fashion, and the suspension proved a problem. Persistent gearbox overheating during Barcelona testing led Prost to concentrate the last month of its winter at Magny-Cours so that replacement parts could be manufactured and fitted quickly. Prost warned that 1998 would be a transitional year but it was a disaster with just a single point scored. The drivers only started from inside the top ten on five occasions between them, and reliability was poor.

Olivier Panis, Prost AP01-Peugeot (Brazilian GP)

Jarno Trulli, Prost AP01-Peugeot (French GP)

The AP01 only passed the mandatory side-impact test on the Thursday before the Australian GP, where the gearbox issues continued; 'x-wings' were fitted for qualifying but these were removed for the race as they interfered with the fuel nozzle. Trulli lay seventh, challenging for a point, when his gearbox broke. Relegated to the back row of the grid after the deletion of his best two lap times because he left his car in gear following a qualifying spin, Panis finished ninth and last.

Panis's ninth place on the Brazilian grid was a rare cause for optimism but he was lucky to walk away from a 130mph crash at Ferradura during the warm-up. Both cars retired in Brazil and Panis lost top-ten finishes at Buenos Aires, Imola and Barcelona due to late engine failures. Trulli was 11th in Argentina and ninth in Spain, but at Imola he had his throttle stick open at Rivazza. The cars ran at Imola with just the left-hand 'x-wing' attached due to the refuelling problem. They retired in Monaco and Canada: Trulli was involved in both start-line shunts in Montréal and came to rest on top of Jean Alesi's Sauber-Petronas at the restart.

Poor traction out of the corners and a nervous rear end had been particular problems thus far so new rear uprights and track rods were introduced in Canada with further upgrades at the French GP. With monocoque stiffened, the wheelbase was lengthened by 6½in although this made the cars even less driveable and was abandoned. John Barnard's B3 Technologies designed and manufactured stiffer new carbon-fibre rear suspension although the

AP01s appeared no quicker despite the changes. Panis was 11th in his home race while Trulli spun out there and in the next race. Panis started the British GP from the back following a scrutineering infringement and aquaplaned off the road at Priory, three laps after Trulli's own demise.

A year after leading the Austrian GP, Trulli ran as high as fifth at the A1-Ring before slowing with a broken shock absorber. Reliability had improved, especially with the recalcitrant gearbox, but the cars continued to frustrate despite reasonable power from the Peugeot V10. Much was hoped of the German GP so finishing outside the top ten was another crushing disappointment. Already penalised for a jumped start, the disenchanted Panis was further delayed by a puncture. The poor run continued in Hungary before the lottery of a wet Spa-Francorchamps finally delivered Prost-Peugeot's only point of 1998. Both drivers were involved in the first-lap pile-up but Trulli took the spare for the restart and stayed out of trouble to finish sixth, lapped twice.

Revised suspension geometry and aerodynamic tweaks, plus Peugeot power, helped Panis and Trulli qualify on the fifth row at Monza – their best combined qualifying performance of the season. However, Sunday only brought further heartache for a vibration forced Panis to retire and Trulli finished last following an unscheduled stop to reattach a loose wheel. Trulli's transmission failed during the early laps at the Nürburgring, where Panis finished 12th after being lapped twice.

A single, heavily revised Prost AP01B-Peugeot was taken to the final race at Suzuka after promising tests at Magny-Cours and Barcelona. This included the 1999-specification Peugeot A18 engine (which was 11lb lighter), a totally new, simplified semi-automatic six-speed gearbox and revised rear suspension. The drivers drew lots to decide who drove the new car with Trulli successful. Outqualified by Panis's standard machine, Trulli was forced to start in the old-specification spare when he crashed the AP01B head-on at Degner during the warm-up. Trulli started last after stalling at the original start and they ran at the back until the Italian's engine expired with two laps to go; Panis finished 11th. This had been a character-building start to the Prost-Peugeot partnership.

TYRRELL FORD

Now aged 73, Ken Tyrrell was finally ready to sell his team. Jacques Villeneuve's manager, Craig Pollock, was putting together an ambitious new outfit for 1999 with money from British American Tobacco. Rather than pay the $24 million deposit now demanded for newcomers, and keen to have the financial benefits afforded to members of the Formula One Constructors' Association, he began talks with Tyrrell and Minardi in the middle of 1996. Despite previous denials, the sale of Tyrrell to the Pollock-led consortium was completed on 25 November 1997.

The original intention was for the existing management team – Ken Tyrrell (chairman) and Harvey Postlethwaite (engineering managing director) – to continue to run day-to-day affairs from its base in Ockham for one final season. Test driver Toranosuke Takagi was promoted to the race team with commercial director Bob Tyrrell, Ken's son, believing 'he has the potential to become the best F1 driver Japan has produced.' They wanted to retain Jos Verstappen in the hope that the Tyrrell name would leave F1 with a final flourish. However, the new owners preferred to accept a pay driver and Ricardo Rosset was confirmed on 10 February. That decision angered Ken Tyrrell, who quit ten days later along with son.

The Tyrrell 026-Ford was completed by the end of January and Takagi was entrusted with its shakedown at Silverstone. Tyrrell re-signed with Cosworth for a customer supply of Ford Zetec-R V10 engines, two specifications behind those used exclusively by works partner Stewart Grand Prix. For the final F1 Tyrrell, Postlethwaite and deputy technical director Mike Gascoyne penned a conventional chassis with weight distributed towards the front to optimise their Goodyear tyres. The previously maligned V10 drove through Tyrrell's existing six-speed semi-automatic longitudinal gearbox. With the team being replaced by British American Racing in 1999, it was inevitable that staff looked to further their careers elsewhere. Gascoyne moved to Jordan in June while Postlethwaite worked on his own exit strategy with Honda.

Takagi was the quickest Goodyear-shod contender at one pre-season test and showed glimpses of single-lap pace but could not replicate that in race trim. Rosset struggled all season and failed to qualify on five occasions. It was a sad end to the Tyrrell story, without a point scored.

Takagi impressed in Australia by qualifying 13th (ahead of both

Ricardo Rosset, Tyrrell 026-Ford (Monaco GP)

Toranosuke Takagi, Tyrrell 026-Ford (San Marino GP)

troubled Stewart-Fords) but spun into Ralf Schumacher's Jordan-Mugen on lap two on gravel deposited on the track by the German. Both Tyrrell-Fords retired from the opening two races and finished outside the top ten in Argentina, where Takagi again lined up 13th as the quickest Ford. Air-compressor failures ended their San Marino GP and the under-pressure Rosset did not qualify for the next two races. He drew the World Champion's fury when he crashed into Jacques Villeneuve at the Swimming Pool during a fraught practice for the Monaco GP. Takagi finished 13th in Spain and 11th in Monaco, but retired from three of the next four races. The exception was Silverstone where he scored his best result of the year – ninth after an extra stop behind the safety car.

The upgraded 'phase 10' engine introduced in Canada had increased revs and was mounted lower to improve handling. Rosset finished eighth after a race of attrition. With points vital to safeguard FOCA privileges for BAR's first season, Pollock invited Tom Kristensen for tests at Monza and Magny-Cours. Poor weather rendered the former inconclusive and Rosset retained his seat when he proved quicker at the French venue, albeit using a newer version of the engine than the Dane. Rosset outqualified his team-mate for the first time when they returned for the French GP but both suffered engine failures in the race. That improvement was short-lived for he spun out of the British GP and was 12th (and last) in Austria after a last-lap puncture removed his rear wing. A wild spinner at the first corner of the Austrian GP, Takagi had his own accidents at Hockenheim's Turn 1 but finished 13th after running as high as eighth, followed by 14th on a lacklustre weekend in Hungary. Rosset did not qualify at Hockenheim (following a 110mph practice accident) or the Hungaroring.

Both drivers were involved in the first-lap pile-up at Spa-Francorchamps although Takagi took the spare for the restart and climbed into the top ten until he crashed at La Source and threw away possible points – it had been an expensive weekend. With his relationship with the team at a low, Rosset outqualified Takagi for a second time at Monza despite crashing at Parabolica on Friday. However, it was the Japanese rookie who was ahead when they

both finished, ninth once more after a two-stop strategy. Takagi was last at the Nürburgring, where Rosset blew another engine.

Winner of 23 GPs as a constructor, Tyrrell ended its long F1 involvement on a downbeat note at Suzuka. Rosset, who blamed Pollock for ruining his career, did not qualify and Takagi retired when Esteban Tuero's Minardi-Ford crashed over him at the chicane.

FONDMETAL MINARDI FORD

Flavio Briatore sold his minority shareholding in Minardi to Gabriele Rumi, who now owned 70 per cent of the company. Gustav Brunner returned from Ferrari as technical director on 1 February 1998 while Gabriele Tarquini was hired as a consultant. After its single season with Hart, Minardi returned to Cosworth for a customer supply of old-specification Zetec-R V10 engines. Brunner restructured an enlarged technical department and appointed George Ryton as chief designer, with Herbert Ehrlinspiel running an expanded composites department and race engineer Gianfranco Fantuzzi poached from Ferrari. The factory at Faenza was doubled in size.

Giancarlo Minardi had hoped that the improved financial terms of the new Concorde Agreement would mean that his team would no longer have to rely on paying drivers, but both choices for 1998 brought funding. Contracted to Minardi since 1996, Argentinian teenager Esteban Tuero was confirmed in the New Year, although he was not granted a super licence until he completed 1,200 miles in testing. His team-mate remained a mystery for much of the winter. Minardi exercised its option on Tarso Marques at the 1997 Luxembourg GP and he was quicker than Tom Kristensen, Laurent Redon and Oliver Martini – as well as Tuero – at Barcelona at the start of December. Kristensen was invited back before Christmas with former driver Luca Badoer also evaluated. However, it was Prost refugee Shinji Nakano who was named as second driver in February. Redon was confirmed as reserve at the launch of the Minardi M198-Ford, which Tuero had driven for three days at Mugello in January.

Limited finances forced technical co-ordinator Gabriele Tredozi to refettle the M197 with rear wing and some other parts that dated back to 1993, when Brunner was last with the team. The M198 was a simple design with the 72-degree V10 engine mated to Minardi's existing six-speed semi-automatic longitudinal gearbox and fitted with Magneti Marelli electronics. The push-rod/double-wishbone suspension had torsion bars front and rear while Bridgestone tyres were retained. The M198 was almost five seconds off the pace and all but undriveable at the first Barcelona group test so little was expected from F1's perennial minnows.

Two seconds a lap were found when Brunner fixed an initial anti-roll-bar problem. Further developments were introduced when budget allowed, with Jean-Claude Migeot's Fondmetal Technologies wind tunnel used to refine the aerodynamics during the season. The wheelbase was increased for the French GP with a 2in spacer between engine and gearbox while a new diffuser also helped improve grip and stability under braking. Another new diffuser was used at Spa-Francorchamps following a successful test at Mugello.

The winter testing times may have been poor but the M198 had

Shinji Nakano, Minardi M198-Ford (British GP)

been reliable and Nakano was classified at ten of the 16 races, including a run of three top-ten finishes in four mid-season GPs. Ninth when ahead of Michael Schumacher's Ferrari in Monaco, he was seventh in Canada and eighth at Silverstone. His Hungarian GP was ruined by a jammed fuel valve that caused his second pitstop to take nearly 40sec. Caught up in the La Source carnage at the start of the Belgian GP, Nakano took the spare for the restart and finished eighth despite repairs required when he collided with Giancarlo Fisichella's Benetton-Playlife. He made a spectacular exit from the Italian GP when his engine caught fire and was engulfed in plumes of smoke.

Tuero started the Australian GP from 17th position, Minardi's best Saturday performance of 1998, and he always qualified (unlike Tyrrell's Ricardo Rosset). His Australian GP was notable for 10sec stop-go penalties for jumping the start and then speeding in the pitlane when he served it, and he received another such penalty for baulking Heinz-Harald Frentzen in Spain. The best result in only four finishes during his single F1 season was eighth at Imola (of nine runners). He was unclassified at the Nürburgring after his mechanics spent ten laps repairing a driveshaft broken at the start. There were incidents aplenty, including in Argentina, Monaco (in Casino Square on the opening lap), Britain, Austria and Japan. He exited the championship finale when he crashed up and over Tora

Takagi's Tyrrell-Ford at Suzuka's chicane, injuring his neck.

Minardi's best race came in Montréal, where both drivers avoided the start-line accidents and figured in unfamiliar territory. Nakano ran as high as fifth but was ultimately unable to pass Jan Magnussen's Stewart-Ford to snatch sixth place. Tuero collided with Jacques Villeneuve's Williams-Mecachrome before suffering electrical failure, but that was only after holding off Alexander Wurz's Benetton-Playlife and Eddie Irvine's Ferrari for 23 laps before his pitstop. It was the third successive season that Minardi failed to score a point.

Esteban Tuero, Minardi M198-Ford (Brazilian GP)

DRIVER PERFORMANCE

DRIVER	CAR–ENGINE	AUS	BR	RA	RSM	E	MC	CDN	F	GB	A	D	H	B	I	LUX	J
Jean Alesi	Sauber C17-Petronas	12 R	15 9	11 5	12 6	14 10	11 12	9 R	11 7	8 R	2 R	11 10	11 7	10 3	8 5	11 10	12 7
Rubens Barrichello	Stewart SF2-Ford	14 R	13 R	14 10	17 R	9 5	14 R	13 5	14 10	18 R	5 R	13 R	14 R	14 R	13 10	12 11	16 R
David Coulthard	McLaren MP4-13-Mercedes-Benz	2 **2**	2 2	1 **6**	1 **1**	2 **2**	2 R	1 **R**	3 6 FL	4 R	14 **2** FL	2 **2** FL	2 2	2 7	4 **R**	5 3	3 3
Pedro Diniz	Arrows A19	20 R	22 R	18 R	18 R	15 R	12 6	19 9	17 14	13 R	13 R	18 R	12 11	16 5	20 R	17 R	18 R
Giancarlo Fisichella	Benetton B198-Playlife	7 R	7 6	10 7	10 R	4 R	3 2	4 2	9 9	11 5	1 R	8 7	8 8	7 R	11 8	4 6	10 8
Heinz-Harald Frentzen	Williams FW20-Mecachrome	6 3	3 5	6 9	8 5	13 8	5 R	7 R	8 15	6 R	7 R	10 9	7 5	9 4	12 7	7 5	5 5
Mika Häkkinen	McLaren MP4-13-Mercedes-Benz	1 **1** FL	1 **1** FL	3 **2**	2 R	1 **1** FL	1 **1** FL	2 R	1 **3**	1 **2**	3 **1**	1 **1**	1 **6**	1 R	3 **4** FL	3 **1** FL	2 **1**
Johnny Herbert	Sauber C17-Petronas	5 6	14 11	12 R	11 R	7 7	9 7	12 R	13 8	9 R	18 8	12 R	15 10	12 R	15 R	13 R	11 10
Damon Hill	Jordan 198-Mugen	10 8	11 DSQ	9 8	7 10	8 R	15 8	10 R	7 R	7 R	15 7	5 4	4 4	3 1	14 6	10 9	8 4
Eddie Irvine	Ferrari F300	8 4	6 8	4 3	4 3	6 R	7 3	8 3	4 **2**	5 3	8 4	6 8	5 R	5 R	5 2	2 4	4 2
Jan Magnussen	Stewart SF2-Ford	18 R	16 10	22 R	20 R	18 12	17 R	20 6	–	–	–	–	–	–	–	–	–
Shinji Nakano	Minardi M198-Ford	22 R	18 R	19 13	21 R	20 14	19 9	18 7	21 17	21 8	21 11	20 R	19 15	21 8	21 R	20 15	20 R
Olivier Panis	Prost AP01-Peugeot	21 9	9 R	15 15	13 11	12 16	18 R	15 R	16 11	16 R	10 R	16 15	20 12	15 R	9 R	15 12	13 11
Ricardo Rosset	Tyrrell 026-Ford	19 R	21 R	21 14	22 R	22 DNQ	22 DNQ	22 8	18 R	22 R	22 12	22 DNQ	22 DNQ	20 R	18 12	22 R	22 DNQ
Mika Salo	Arrows A19	16 R	20 R	17 R	14 9	17 R	8 4	17 R	19 13	14 R	6 R	17 14	13 R	18 R	16 R	16 14	15 R
Michael Schumacher	Ferrari F300	3 R	4 3	2 **1**	3 2 FL	3 3	4 10	3 **1** FL	2 **1**	2 **1** FL	4 3	9 5	3 **1** FL	4 **R** FL	1 **1**	1 **2**	1 **R** FL
Ralf Schumacher	Jordan 198-Mugen	9 R	8 R	5 R	9 7	11 11	16 R	5 R	6 16	10 6	9 5	4 6	10 9	8 2	6 3	6 R	7 R
Toranosuke Takagi	Tyrrell 026-Ford	13 R	17 R	13 12	15 R	21 13	20 11	16 R	20 R	19 9	20 R	15 13	18 14	19 R	19 9	19 16	17 R
Jarno Trulli	Prost AP01-Peugeot	15 R	12 R	16 11	16 R	16 9	10 R	14 R	12 R	15 R	16 10	14 12	16 R	13 6	10 13	14 R	14 12
Esteban Tuero	Minardi M198-Ford	17 R	19 R	20 R	19 8	19 15	21 R	21 R	22 R	20 R	19 R	21 16	21 R	22 R	22 11	21 NC	21 R
Jos Verstappen	Stewart SF2-Ford	–	–	–	–	–	–	–	15 12	17 R	12 R	19 R	17 13	17 R	17 R	18 13	19 R
Jacques Villeneuve	Williams FW20-Mecachrome	4 5	10 7	7 R	6 4	10 6	13 5	6 10	5 4	3 7	11 6	3 3	6 3	6 R	2 R	9 8	6 6
Alexander Wurz	Benetton B198-Playlife	11 7	5 4	8 4 FL	5 R	5 4	6 R	11 4	10 5	2 4	17 9	7 11	9 R	11 R	7 R	8 7	9 9

FORMULA 1 RACE WINNERS

ROUND	RACE (CIRCUIT)	DATE	WINNER
1	Qantas Australian Grand Prix (Albert Park)	Mar 8	Mika Häkkinen (McLaren MP4-13-Mercedes-Benz)
2	Grande Prêmio do Brasil (Interlagos)	Mar 29	Mika Häkkinen (McLaren MP4-13-Mercedes-Benz)
3	Gran Premio Marlboro de Argentina (Buenos Aires)	Apr 12	Michael Schumacher (Ferrari F300)
4	Gran Premio di San Marino (Imola)	Apr 26	David Coulthard (McLaren MP4-13-Mercedes-Benz)
5	Gran Premio Marlboro de España (Catalunya)	May 10	Mika Häkkinen (McLaren MP4-13-Mercedes-Benz)
6	Grand Prix de Monaco (Monte Carlo)	May 24	Mika Häkkinen (McLaren MP4-13-Mercedes-Benz)
7	Grand Prix Player's du Canada (Montréal)	Jun 7	Michael Schumacher (Ferrari F300)
8	Grand Prix Mobil 1 de France (Magny-Cours)	Jun 28	Michael Schumacher (Ferrari F300)
9	RAC British Grand Prix (Silverstone)	Jul 12	Michael Schumacher (Ferrari F300)
10	Grosser Preis von Österreich (Spielberg)	Jul 26	Mika Häkkinen (McLaren MP4-13-Mercedes-Benz)
11	Grosser Mobil 1 Preis von Deutschland (Hockenheim)	Aug 2	Mika Häkkinen (McLaren MP4-13-Mercedes-Benz)
12	Marlboro Magyar Nagydíj (Hungaroring)	Aug 16	Michael Schumacher (Ferrari F300)
13	Grand Prix Foster's de Belgique (Spa-Francorchamps)	Aug 30	Damon Hill (Jordan 198-Mugen)
14	Gran Premio Campari d'Italia (Monza)	Sep 13	Michael Schumacher (Ferrari F300)
15	Grosser Warsteiner Preis von Luxemburg (Nürburgring)	Sep 27	Mika Häkkinen (McLaren MP4-13-Mercedes-Benz)
16	Fuji Television Japanese Grand Prix (Suzuka)	Nov 1	Mika Häkkinen (McLaren MP4-13-Mercedes-Benz)

DRIVERS' CHAMPIONSHIP

	DRIVERS	POINTS
1	Mika Häkkinen	100
2	Michael Schumacher	86
3	David Coulthard	56
4	Eddie Irvine	47
5	Jacques Villeneuve	21
6	Damon Hill	20
7=	Heinz-Harald Frentzen	17
	Alexander Wurz	17
9	Giancarlo Fisichella	16
10	Ralf Schumacher	14
11	Jean Alesi	9
12	Rubens Barrichello	4
13=	Pedro Diniz	3
	Mika Salo	3
15=	Johnny Herbert	1
	Jan Magnussen	1
	Jarno Trulli	1

Dry tyres now had mandatory grooves to reduce cornering speeds

CONSTRUCTORS' CHAMPIONSHIP

	CONSTRUCTORS	POINTS
1	McLaren-Mercedes-Benz	156
2	Ferrari	133
3	Williams-Mecachrome	38
4	Jordan-Mugen	34
5	Benetton-Playlife	33
6	Sauber-Petronas Ferrari	10
7	Arrows	6
8	Stewart-Ford	5
9	Prost-Peugeot	1

The Hungarian Grand Prix was among Mika Häkkinen's five victories as he won the World Championship for the second successive year

1999
HÄKKINEN FINALLY RETAINS HIS CROWN

Michael Schumacher's challenge was derailed when he broke his leg at Silverstone

Reigning champions Mika Häkkinen and McLaren-Mercedes entered 1999 as overwhelming favourites but the championship went down to the wire. The Finn eventually prevailed by just two points after an inconsistent campaign while Ferrari won its first constructors' title since 1983. Michael Schumacher broke his leg on the opening lap at Silverstone, so it was Eddie Irvine who challenged for Ferrari's first drivers' title in 20 years. Both Jordan-Mugen and Stewart-Ford also won races during 1999.

Bridgestone, the only tyre supplier following Goodyear's withdrawal, introduced a harder compound. An extra mandatory groove was added to each tyre to further reduce

Eddie Irvine won in Germany to strengthen his title hopes

grip and cornering speeds. The Fédération Internationale de l'Automobile and Bridgestone wanted to restrict testing so a limit of 25 days of official group tests and another 25 free days was eventually agreed with the teams. Tethers were introduced to prevent loose wheels endangering spectators in the event of an accident.

A spate of rear-wing failures during pre-season testing was thought to be caused by teams trying to reduce drag by having supports that flexed by two to three degrees. A test was introduced at the Brazilian GP to prevent this and all the cars passed. Cars continued to be designed to be as light as possible and brought up to the 600kg (1,323lb) weight limit with ballast added to optimise centre of gravity and weight distribution. Ballast was even put in the underfloor plank until this practice was banned on safety grounds after the Spanish GP.

Following the incident involving Michael Schumacher and Heinz-Harald Frentzen at the 1998 Canadian GP, the FIA introduced a pit exit line that could not be crossed by cars leaving the pits. The FIA also acted to prevent a repeat of the 1998 British GP where Schumacher won the race in the pitlane after serving a stop-go penalty on the last lap: any such sanction in the last five laps would now result in 25 seconds being added to the driver's race time. A ten-second stop-go penalty was reinforced at the Monaco GP for backmarkers who ignored three or more blue-flag warnings after David Coulthard was held up at Imola.

F1 expanded into southern Asia with the Hermann Tilke-designed Sepang circuit holding the Malaysian GP. Harvey

Postlethwaite advised on a new South Korean track and leisure complex at Sepoong but it was not completed due to the region's financial crisis. Argentina was dropped on financial grounds and replaced by the inaugural Chinese GP on 21 March at Zhuhai, but the race did not happen because of logistical difficulties.

Honda investigated entering a works team in the F1 World Championship in 2000 with the 12th and final franchise reserved for the Japanese manufacturer. Honda Racing Development was set up in Bracknell, Berkshire with Postlethwaite as technical director. Fellow Tyrrell refugees included engineers Tim Densham, Chris Radage and David Brown; aerodynamicist Ben Agathangelou; team manager Steve Nielsen and director Rupert Manwaring. Dallara built the Mugen V10-powered test car that Jos Verstappen drove at Mugello and Jerez in January 1999. He was quicker than new cars from British American Racing, Stewart and Benetton at the Spanish venue, prompting the FIA to introduce scrutineering at testing for teams that were not competing in the World Championship. With Honda's main board debating the cost of setting up its own team, Postlethwaite suffered a fatal heart attack while in Barcelona on 15 April. The project was cancelled when Honda decided to supply works engines to BAR in 2000.

Heinz-Harald Frentzen scored two victories for Jordan, this one at Monza

Jackie and Paul Stewart celebrate Johnny Herbert's shock win at the Nürburgring

WEST McLAREN MERCEDES

McLaren and Mercedes-Benz extended their exclusive partnership to the end of 2002 and the MP4-14 was consistently the most competitive car during 1999, Mika Häkkinen's 11 pole positions in 16 races evidence of that outright pace. McLaren won seven GPs and could have doubled that tally but for mechanical failures or human error so its title battles with Ferrari went to the final race. An unchanged driver line-up of Häkkinen and David Coulthard was confirmed at the 1998 German GP, despite rumoured talks with Michael Schumacher and Jacques Villeneuve. Nick Heidfeld was retained as test and reserve driver.

Technical director Adrian Newey finalised the design of the very light McLaren MP4-14-Mercedes as late as possible, so it was 8 February before it broke cover at the Circuit de Catalunya. There was a strong resemblance to the MP4-13 although almost every component was redesigned. The wheelbase and drooping nose were extended by a couple of inches. The fins on top of the chassis to comply with height regulations were more pronounced so the monocoque could be lowered still further. There were small cooling inlets behind enlarged bargeboards. Hot air exited from the taller sidepods through the side winglets and was deflected around the rear tyres. The 'coke-bottle' rear end began further forward and packaging was even tighter than before. Twinned support for the rear wing replaced the MP4-13's single strut. The rear suspension was all new with torsion bars and dampers now preferred to coil springs. The oil tank was moved in front of the engine and a new six-speed gearbox was mounted longitudinally as before. The new

Mercedes-Benz FO110H 72-degree V10 engine was 15lb lighter and generated 785bhp at 16,700rpm. Severe vibrations initially caused hydraulic issues and the gearbox was temperamental, so McLaren could not match Ferrari's reliability.

The shakedown was halted when the alternator failed on Coulthard's first lap in front of the assembled press, although matters soon improved. Häkkinen, who did not drive for three months over the winter, and Coulthard were half a second quicker than Michael Schumacher's Ferrari F399 at the only test days they shared. McLaren-Mercedes did not indulge in headline-grabbing low-fuel runs, but its overall pace was impressive. Niggling issues prevented completion of a race simulation in testing so the team considered starting the season with its old car. However, three MP4-14s were despatched to Melbourne, where Häkkinen and Coulthard dominated qualifying, the Finn 1.319sec quicker than third-placed Schumacher. With Häkkinen racing the spare due to a misfire, they pulled away from the field with ease only to retire, Coulthard when stuck in sixth gear and Häkkinen with a faulty throttle linkage.

The five weeks before the next race were spent trying to negate vibrations and improve cooling. On pole once more in Brazil, Häkkinen slipped to third when he lost fifth gear. That temporary electronic glitch corrected itself and he passed Schumacher in the pitstops to win by 4.945sec. Second on the grid, Coulthard stalled at the start and it took three laps to get going from the pitlane, after which his gearbox failed at 22 laps. Häkkinen led another qualifying 1–2 at Imola but crashed out of the lead exiting the last corner. Coulthard seemed set for victory before being held up by

Mika Häkkinen, McLaren MP4-14-Mercedes (Japanese GP)

backmarkers as the two-stopping Schumacher delivered a blistering middle stint. While an irate Ron Dennis remonstrated with the Prost pit wall, Coulthard finally passed Olivier Panis only to run wide at Rivazza and Schumacher retained the lead when he pitted again. Second was a bitter disappointment.

Fuelled heavy for a one-stop strategy, Häkkinen was slow away from pole in Monaco and was beaten into Ste-Dévote by Schumacher. He was passed by Eddie Irvine and finished third because he went straight on at Mirabeau after hitting oil. Coulthard was fourth before a gearbox oil leak proved terminal. Now 12 points behind Schumacher in the standings, Häkkinen dominated in Spain with an oversteering Coulthard second. Häkkinen's run of pole positions ended in Canada when 0.029sec slower than Schumacher, but the German crashed out of the lead and another Häkkinen victory was assured when Coulthard hit second-placed Irvine at the restart. The Scot received a stop-go penalty for crossing the pit exit line after checking for damage and finished seventh.

Rain in France turned qualifying form on its head and McLaren sent its drivers out too late. Fourth on the grid and the fastest driver to set his time after the rain came down, Coulthard had just taken the lead and was pulling away on lap ten when his electrics failed. From 14th on the grid, Häkkinen stormed through the field and salvaged second place despite a spin to extend his points advantage. Back on pole at Silverstone, Häkkinen was dominating when his left-rear wheel was not tightened at his pitstop; despite pitting a lap later, the new wheel eventually fell off. Coulthard qualified third, took a decisive lead in the first pitstops and withstood Irvine's pressure to win his first race of 1999.

The cars were modified for the Austrian GP. In addition to revised rear suspension, both front wing and repositioned steering arms between the wishbones were reminiscent of the MP4-13. Häkkinen led away from another pole position only for Coulthard's attempted first-lap pass into the Remus Kurve to pitch him into a spin. Coulthard led the first half of the race but finished second after losing out to Irvine in the pitstops. Häkkinen was third after a fine recovery drive. With Schumacher sidelined, it was Irvine who now trailed the Finn by just two points.

Having recorded McLaren's 100th pole position, Häkkinen was denied victory in Germany by a faulty valve on his refuelling rig and resulting slow pitstop. That may have been immaterial in any case for he later suffered a high-speed rear puncture. Coulthard was fifth despite changing his front wing after he tagged Mika Salo, and a stop-go penalty for cutting a chicane. Häkkinen led every lap to score a vital win in Hungary after being quickest in qualifying once more. Coulthard made a slow start from third but took advantage when Irvine ran wide to complete another silver 1–2.

Despite retaking the points lead at Spa-Francorchamps, Häkkinen was angry after the race. He was slow away from pole position, a locked-up Coulthard passed him around the outside at La Source despite their cars rubbing wheels, and the Scot led the rest of the way to win by 10.469sec in his best performance of the season. In *parc fermé* there were no congratulations from Häkkinen, who was dismayed that Dennis had not imposed team orders. At Monza

David Coulthard, McLaren MP4-14-Mercedes (Malaysian GP)

Häkkinen secured his 11th pole position of the season, led from the start and established an 8sec advantage by lap 30 only to select the wrong gear at the first chicane and spin out of the race, prompting a very public display of emotion. Coulthard finished a distant fifth on a bad day for the team.

The bargeboards had Gurney flaps at the Nürburgring, where Coulthard qualified second and took the lead at half-distance. However, any lingering title hopes disappeared when he aquaplaned off the track and into the tyre barrier. Third on the grid, Häkkinen changed to full wets when it started to rain and lost a lap by changing back to dry tyres just four laps later. He recovered to finish fifth on a day when Ferrari did not score.

Schumacher returned to help Irvine's cause at the Malaysian GP and Ferrari locked-out the front row, ahead of Coulthard and Häkkinen. Coulthard passed Schumacher for second and harried Irvine only to lose fuel pressure. Third after being slowed by Schumacher's defensive tactics and a late fuel stop, Häkkinen appeared to have clinched the title when the Ferraris failed scrutineering due to their bargeboards. However, that decision was soon overturned on appeal and an incensed Dennis reacted with a war of words with FIA president Max Mosley.

Häkkinen and McLaren-Mercedes therefore entered the Japanese GP four points behind in the drivers' and constructors' standings. Second on the grid, Häkkinen beat pole winner Schumacher off the line and eased to victory to clinch his second world title by just two points. Coulthard passed Irvine in the first round of pitstops and slowed the Ulsterman by three or more seconds a lap as he replicated Ferrari's Malaysian tactics. With Irvine having stopped again, Coulthard crashed on the approach to Spoon on lap 34, pitted for a new front wing and retired with hydraulic failure five laps later.

First and fourth in the drivers' standings, McLaren-Mercedes finished runners-up to Ferrari in the constructors' title.

Eddie Irvine, Ferrari F399 (Italian GP)

SCUDERIA FERRARI MARLBORO

Michael Schumacher signed a lucrative new four-year contract in July 1998 and Eddie Irvine, who had spoken to Williams and Jordan, was confirmed later that month. Luca Badoer remained as test driver despite also racing for Minardi. Sporting director Jean Todt extended his contract and both Ross Brawn and Rory Byrne committed their futures to Ferrari until the end of 2001. Paolo Martinelli remained in charge of the engine department.

The evolutionary Ferrari F399 was revealed to the press on 30 January. A concerted effort to reduce weight produced a 45lb saving. The front wheels and suspension were moved forward to give an extended wheelbase, and a totally revised rear layout was introduced due to the four-groove tyres. Push-rod suspension was now all-carbon-fibre with 'knife-edge' mounting retained. The hump in the F300's monocoque ahead of the cockpit was removed. Electronic power steering was introduced while hours in Ferrari's two wind tunnels resulted in a revised airbox and 'flip-ups' on the sidepods. The periscope exhausts were smaller, while the radiators were angled so the sidepods swept inwards earlier. The 75-degree V10 engine now developed over 800bhp in qualifying trim. It was very reliable and Irvine suffered only one mechanical retirement and completed 98 per cent of the possible race laps, prolonging his unexpected title bid to the final race.

The new challengers from Maranello and Woking only tested together once at Barcelona and Ferrari's task was clear when Schumacher was four tenths slower. The Ferrari F399 was reliable,

handled well and was easy to drive, but it was not consistently fast enough over the full season.

The cars lacked grip in Australia, where Schumacher qualified third – 1.319sec off pole – and was forced to start from the back when left in neutral before the formation lap. He finished last after three unscheduled stops, successively for a new wing, replacement of a tyre punctured by running wide, and a different steering wheel. Irvine started sixth and took advantage of McLaren-Mercedes's failures to win his first GP. Enlarged bargeboards, modified 'flip-ups' (which doubled as air outlets) and a strengthened rear-wing support were introduced at Interlagos, where the qualifying deficit remained. Schumacher finished second while Irvine maintained his championship lead with fifth, despite an extra pitstop.

A new front wing at Imola helped close the gap. They qualified on the second row but won thanks to Schumacher's speed and Brawn's tactical acumen. Brawn switched to a two-stop strategy and Schumacher completed his middle stint at qualifying pace while erstwhile leader David Coulthard was held up when trying to lap Olivier Panis and the German retained his lead when he stopped again. Disappointed to be second on the grid in Monaco, Schumacher out-dragged Häkkinen into Ste-Dévote and led all the way to his 16th victory for Ferrari, surpassing Niki Lauda's previous record for the *Scuderia*. Third when his engine failed at Imola (his only DNF), Irvine took advantage of Häkkinen's error in Monaco to complete a Ferrari 1–2. Schumacher was bemused when Irvine outqualified him in Spain and neither could match the McLaren-Mercedes drivers in the race despite being closer than expected on a circuit that normally did not suit Ferrari. Irvine made a poor start from second and followed his team leader home, third and fourth, after an uneventful procession.

Schumacher recorded his first pole of the season in Canada using an updated 048B engine, which was 12lb lighter, had a lower centre of gravity and developed another 15bhp, but it was not raced until British GP. He was 4.2sec in the lead at Montréal when he lost control exiting the final chicane and crashed into the 'Wall of Champions'. Irvine spun on the restart when tagged by Coulthard and charged back into third by the finish, setting the fastest race lap. There was a major upgrade for the French GP with a rear aero package that owed much to the McLaren MP4-14. The 'coke-bottle' rear end was narrower to reduce drag, side winglets/outlets were revised and the engine cover lowered. They struggled in wet qualifying and endured troubled races into fifth (Schumacher) and sixth (Irvine).

Now eight points behind Häkkinen, Schumacher's challenge came to an abrupt halt at Silverstone. Slow away from second on the grid, he went to pass Irvine into Stowe only to suffer rear-brake failure due to a hydraulic leak. He crashed head-first into the barrier and broke his right leg in two places. With Ferrari hopes now on his shoulders, Irvine lost the chance of victory when he overshot his pit but finished second nonetheless. Mika Salo was preferred to Luca Badoer as Schumacher's stand-in, much to the Italian's *chagrin*.

Ten seconds behind Coulthard before the Austrian GP pitstops, Irvine extended his stint and used the overcut to win by 0.313sec. Salo's race was ruined by a front-wing change following his first-lap skirmish with Johnny Herbert, but he starred next time out in Germany. Fourth on the grid and quicker than his team-mate, Salo inherited the lead when Häkkinen stopped and waved Irvine through on the next lap. That unexpected Ferrari 1–2 gave Irvine the championship lead and cemented Ferrari's place on top of the constructors' standings.

McLaren-Mercedes regained the initiative in Hungary, where Irvine split the Silver Arrows in qualifying and finished third after running wide and being passed by Coulthard. He was fourth at Spa-Francorchamps as Ferrari struggled in high-speed configuration. In stark contrast to his performance at Hockenheim, Salo was painfully slow in Hungary and finished seventh in Belgium, where he held up Ralf Schumacher's Williams-Supertec to protect Irvine's position.

Monza accentuated Ferrari's woes and sixth-placed Irvine was relieved by McLaren's implosion. Salo outpaced his team-mate all weekend and finished third.

New bargeboards introduced at the European GP were an improvement although Ferrari left the Nürburgring empty-handed. Only ninth on the grid after he spun on his final qualifying attempt, Irvine had a shambolic 28.2sec pitstop after changing his mind and asking for dry tyres. A crucial points finish was lost when Häkkinen took advantage of his mistake at the chicane. Out of contention after changing his broken front wing, Salo spun out of his sixth and final race for Ferrari.

Four days after announcing that he would not race again in 1999, Schumacher made a U-turn on 8 October and went to Malaysia 'to help the team and to help Eddie'. Lauda, who had been Luca di Montezemolo's personal advisor before another clash with Todt, could not resist taking a swipe at his former rival over Ferrari's total focus on one driver. 'That has been Ferrari's biggest problem, and it was the mistake of my dear friend Jean Todt. Now they're paying the price. Ferrari is looking into emptiness even though Schumacher is coming back… Everything is standing still in Ferrari. Nothing works. It is red chaos.'

Armed with the latest 048C engine, Schumacher led a qualifying 1–2 at Sepang when almost a second quicker than Irvine. They led throughout with Schumacher holding up Häkkinen before handing victory to Irvine with four laps to go. However, both cars failed scrutineering because 'the upper parts of the deflector panels [bargeboards] do not lie on either the reference or step planes' so Häkkinen was provisionally declared World Champion. Six days later, Ferrari's lawyers successfully argued that the discrepancy was within an acceptable 5mm tolerance, so the decision was overturned by the FIA Court of Appeal.

Irvine took a four-point lead to the final race at Suzuka, where the bargeboards were modified rather than risk a repeat of Malaysia. Schumacher and Häkkinen were a class apart all weekend and the German qualified on pole with fifth-placed Irvine 1.505sec slower after a costly accident. Schumacher made a slow start and was no match for Häkkinen in the race, finishing second. Runner-up in the drivers' standings, Irvine finished a distant third as Ferrari clinched its first constructors' title for 16 years.

Michael Schumacher, Ferrari F399 (Malaysian GP)

Mika Salo, Ferrari F399 (Italian GP)

Damon Hill, Jordan 199-Mugen (Hungarian GP)

BENSON & HEDGES JORDAN MUGEN HONDA

Having finally won a GP for the first time, Jordan Grand Prix targeted third in the 1999 standings. Efforts in the High Court to prevent Ralf Schumacher from joining Williams proved in vain and Heinz-Harald Frentzen's one-year contract as team-mate to Damon Hill, the man he had replaced at Williams, was announced at the 1998 Italian GP. Shinji Nakano joined as test driver. Eddie Jordan sold 40 per cent of the team to private equity company Warburg, Pincus in the winter.

The Jordan 199-Mugen was launched at the London Palladium on 2 February, with live coverage on Jordan's website. With Gary Anderson not formally replaced as technical director, chief designer Mike Gascoyne and a team that included newly promoted chief

aerodynamicist John Iley chose evolution rather than revolution. They prioritised weight reduction, lowering the centre of gravity and optimising aerodynamics. A drooping high nose, sculpted sidepods and winglets in front of the rear wheels were features. Fins were fitted either side of a relatively low cockpit surround to conform to height regulations. The longitudinal six-speed gearbox was new and the oil tank was moved in front of the 72-degree Mugen V10 engine, which was marginally lighter, had a lower crankshaft and variable trumpets. There were contrasting fortunes on either side of the Jordan garage during 1999: Frentzen challenged for the world title while Hill could not adapt to the new tyres and grew increasingly dispirited during his farewell campaign.

With the new car well-balanced and reliable during winter testing, Frentzen was immediately a factor, second in Australia despite losing power and third in Brazil after running out of fuel on the last lap. Another podium was lost at Imola when he spun on Eddie Irvine's oil. Outpaced by his team-mate and already considering retirement, Hill was eliminated from three of the first four races in collisions with rival cars. Fourth in the San Marino GP was to be Hill's best result of 1999. He only qualified 17th in Monaco after a heavy crash at Rascasse on Saturday morning while Frentzen finished fourth.

Jordan was less competitive in Spain, where Frentzen lost more points when a transmission bearing failed and Hill snatched seventh from Rubens Barrichello on the penultimate lap. Both crashed out of the Canadian GP, Frentzen when a brake disc failed with three laps to go while lying second; he was airlifted to hospital and found to have escaped lightly with a hairline fracture to his right knee. Three days

Heinz-Harald Frentzen, Jordan 199-Mugen (Italian GP)

after being one of three former champions to crash on the exit of Montréal's final chicane, Hill announced his F1 retirement at the end of the season.

The contrast between Jordan drivers was never greater than at the French GP. Passed fit to race but walking with a limp, Frentzen qualified fifth on a very wet track and scored an unexpected victory, thanks in part to a member of the motorhome staff stationed two miles away to report the changing weather so that strategies could be adjusted. Frentzen stopped once and took the lead with seven laps to go after managing his fuel to the end. That was the first of seven successive top-four finishes that propelled him into the title race. Only 18th on the grid after a terrible session and delayed by a puncture, Hill was last at Magny-Cours when he retired due to a misfire. He considered quitting immediately with Jos Verstappen placed on stand-by, but continued after talks with Jordan.

An upgraded engine was raced at the British GP with a brand-new gearbox that was smaller and 20lb lighter than before. The rear bodywork was lowered and rear impact structure redesigned. The Jordan-Mugens started from the third row with Hill back on form. Both led laps due to their late final pitstops and scored points – Frentzen fourth, Hill fifth.

Frentzen was quickest in testing at Monza where a 2in longer wheelbase was tried. Hill preferred this configuration in Austria but spent much of the weekend off the track and only finished eighth. Fourth in qualifying and at the finish in Austria with the shorter car, Frentzen qualified second in Germany but made a slow start and only finished third. Hill endured a terrible German GP after changing to the same brake discs as Frentzen on race day. Disgruntled, he had had two offs by the time he parked the car on lap 14, saying it was too dangerous to continue and leaving before the finish.

Jordan-Mugen cemented its place among the top three teams of 1999 during the rest of the European campaign. Frentzen was fourth in Hungary and third at Spa-Francorchamps, where the cars started from the second row, and Hill finished a competitive sixth both times; in Hungary Jordan exploited a loophole to fit an additional wing on the airbox and Hill raced with this. A new rear wing was taken to Monza, where another engine upgrade was available for qualifying. Frentzen started second and won after McLaren-Mercedes self-destructed.

Now ten points behind the championship leaders with three races to go, Frentzen's prospects for snatching an unlikely title were strengthened by pole position at a drying Nürburgring. He led the opening 32 laps before coasting to a halt with an electrical problem that denied victory. Hill had an identical issue on the first lap that triggered a nasty accident and Pedro Diniz's roll. The Jordan 199-Mugen was not suited to Sepang but Frentzen salvaged sixth thanks to a one-stop strategy to secure third in the constructors' standings. He then clinched third in the drivers' championship by finishing fourth in Japan. Hill retired on the opening lap at Sepang due to Giancarlo Fisichella's over-exuberance and his F1 career came to a sad conclusion in Japan. Running last following repairs required after he ran wide at Spoon, he parked an operational car for the second time this season.

STEWART FORD

Rubens Barrichello failed to buy himself out of his contract to take up an offer from Williams so stayed with Stewart for a third and final season. Jos Verstappen's option was allowed to lapse and Johnny Herbert signed a two-year deal in September. Paul Stewart Racing juniors Mario Haberfeld and Luciano Burti also tested during 1999.

After a legal dispute with Arrows was settled, Gary Anderson joined as chief designer on 2 November 1998 to work alongside technical director Alan Jenkins. However, Jenkins left before Christmas following a meeting with Jackie and Paul Stewart. Aerodynamicist Eghbal Hamidy soon followed Jenkins out of the door to be replaced by Darren Davis, who had been working for the Arciero-Wells Champ Car team. Ford's head of advanced vehicle technology Neil Ressler was appointed to the boards of both Stewart Grand Prix and Cosworth Engineering. Ex-British Aerospace executive David Ring replaced Paul Stewart as managing director, with the co-founder now deputy chairman.

The Stewart SF3-Ford first ran before Christmas and was launched at Autosport International on 7 January. Jenkins drew inspiration from the McLaren MP4-13 for the last Stewart design under his direction. It had a new monocoque that was stiffer and lower, with fins on top to comply with height regulations. Large bargeboards were fitted between the front wheels and sidepods, which fell away to the rear and had relatively high intakes that slanted backwards from bottom to top. The seat was further reclined to lower the centre of gravity and pitch sensitivity improved by a new rear diffuser. The push-rod suspension featured torsion bars at the front and coil springs at the rear. Crucially, the carbon-fibre gearbox was dropped and replaced by a conventional six-speed semi-automatic longitudinal unit with magnesium casing. An all-new version of the 72-degree engine (the CR-1) was the smallest and lightest Cosworth V10 yet seen, over 60lb having been saved. Described by project leader Nick Hayes as 'radical', the engine followed the recent trend of being built to operate at hotter temperatures so that smaller radiators could be fitted to reduce drag.

The drivers were positive following the first warm-weather running at Jerez but engine failures cut short a subsequent test at Barcelona. A day after returning to the Circuit de Catalunya, on 20 February, Herbert suffered rear-wing failure when travelling at over

Johnny Herbert, Stewart SF3-Ford (Hungarian GP)

Rubens Barrichello, Stewart SF3-Ford (European GP)

190mph on the main straight. Damon Hill, who was exiting the pits at the time, described the resulting accident as 'the biggest shunt I have ever seen' but Herbert was uninjured.

Fast but fragile during the winter, the SF3 was a revelation. The revs were turned down for the first race in Australia, where Barrichello qualified fourth and might have won but for a catalogue of setbacks. Both cars simultaneously caught fire on the grid and caused the start to be aborted. Herbert took no further part and Barrichello started from the pitlane in the spare. He climbed through the field to fourth before pitting for the first time. Handed a 10sec stop-go for a restart infringement, he charged back to finish fifth with only Michael Schumacher setting a faster race lap.

That promise was confirmed at Barrichello's home race in São Paulo when he started third and, light-fuelled for a two-stop strategy, passed Mika Häkkinen for the lead on lap four. Barrichello was running third when hopes of a podium were dashed by engine failure. Herbert had climbed to seventh when his hydraulics failed. Barrichello started sixth at Imola and dedicated his third-place finish to Ayrton Senna, five years on from his countryman's death, while Herbert was two laps from claiming fifth when he suffered his latest blow-up. It was Barrichello's turn to face late disappointment in Monaco, where he qualified fifth and was running in that position when his suspension failed, as had Herbert's.

They were less competitive at Barcelona, where eighth-placed Barrichello was disqualified due to loose metal ballast in the plank being deemed dangerous. Having suffered another mechanical failure in Spain, Herbert finally saw the chequered flag when fifth in Canada

after a robust battle with Eddie Irvine. Barrichello started from that position but was hit by Jarno Trulli whose Prost-Peugeot crashed over him at the first corner of the race. He struggled on for 14 laps before retiring his battle-scarred SF3. The major news that weekend was that the Stewarts had sold their team to Ford, which later confirmed that it would be rebranded as Jaguar Racing in 2000. Jackie Stewart remained as chairman and team principal for the rest of 1999, with his son Paul now chief operating officer. David Ring left the company as Ford reorganised.

Fastest on Saturday morning at Magny-Cours, Barrichello set an early qualifying time that no one could beat when the rain intensified. Under pressure to improve performances, Herbert was forced to use the spare car and did well to set the ninth-quickest time when the conditions were at their worst. Barrichello led for 44 of the 72 laps, maintained that advantage at his first stop but dropped to third when he pitted again. Herbert had another disappointing day, losing second gear on the opening lap and all gears by the end of lap four. An upgrade was introduced for the British GP with new sidepods that were lower and had more conventional vertical intakes. The bargeboards, diffuser and wings were also revised. Both drivers challenged for points but did not score due to a puncture (Barrichello) and stop-go penalty for a safety car infringement (Herbert).

Upgraded engines and hydraulic differentials were introduced in Austria, where the cars were fitted with periscope exhausts that exited through the bodywork on either side of the airbox, similar to Ferrari's solution. They started from the third row of the grid but had contrasting opening laps as Barrichello snatched second after a great start while Herbert lost his rear wing when hit by Mika Salo's Ferrari. Barrichello was demoted in the pitstops and lay fourth when his engine failed once more. Herbert never recovered from the time lost in the pits and finished four laps down, albeit having set the race's second-fastest lap. Herbert suffered another rear-wing failure at 218mph during Saturday practice at Hockenheim and both cars retired on a disappointing day. Herbert had just taken fifth when his gearbox failed five laps from home.

With the SF3 fast but unreliable when testing at Silverstone during August, Barrichello was fifth in Hungary thanks to a one-stop strategy. Seventh on the grid for the next two races, the Brazilian lacked grip in Belgium but rebounded from a 204mph brake failure at Monza's Roggia chicane during testing to finish the Italian GP in fourth place. Herbert failed to score at all three races. Tenth at the Hungaroring where his car did not handle well, he lost his brakes and crashed in Belgium and had his third rear-wing failure of the season during the Monza test. He tangled with Olivier Panis at the first corner of the Italian GP and retired with clutch failure.

Fifth overall with three races to go, the young team enjoyed its 'day of days' at the Nürburgring. Only 14th and 15th on the grid for the European GP, with Herbert quicker for the first time, they took advantage of the chaos around them to climb through the field before changing tyres, Herbert choosing wets on lap 35 and Barrichello switching to dries two laps later. That gave the Englishman a crucial advantage in the rain and he was 25.032sec ahead of

his team-mate after changing to dry tyres. He took advantage of Giancarlo Fisichella's crash and Ralf Schumacher's puncture on successive laps to score Stewart Grand Prix's only GP victory, with Barrichello third at the finish.

Buoyed by that success, Herbert outqualified and outraced Barrichello at the last two GPs. They filled the fifth row in Malaysia and finished fourth and fifth respectively. Seventh and eighth at the final race in Japan, Stewart-Ford beat Williams-Supertec into fourth in the constructors' standings by a single point.

WINFIELD WILLIAMS

Williams usually retained at least one driver for technical continuity but there was an all-new line-up after Jacques Villeneuve moved to British American Racing and Heinz-Harald Frentzen was dropped. Alex Zanardi won the Champ Car World Series in 1997 and 1998 and Williams gambled on him transferring that winning form when he signed as team leader. There were talks with Rubens Barrichello before Stewart Grand Prix took up its option and the Brazilian was unable to match the buy-out clause. Williams considered promoting test driver Juan Pablo Montoya, who had just won the F3000 title, but appointed Ralf Schumacher once he settled a legal dispute with Jordan. Both drivers signed two-year contracts with an option to extend. It was the first time since 1977 that Williams entered a season without a GP winner in the team. Engines were unchanged

Alex Zanardi, Williams FW21-Supertec (Monaco GP)

Ralf Schumacher, Williams FW21-Supertec (Italian GP)

other than in name as Supertec, a new entity, supplied rebadged Mecachrome (*née* Renault) V10 units.

Race engineer Jock Clear resigned in September 1998 to follow Villeneuve to BAR and was initially replaced by Greg Wheeler. John Russell returned from the BMW sports car project as senior development engineer to work with Zanardi from the British GP. Craig Wilson continued to engineer the second car for Schumacher. Frank Williams was awarded a knighthood for services to motor racing in the New Year's honours list.

Launched in Barcelona on 25 January, the compact, light Williams FW21-Supertec was a radical departure for technical director Patrick Head, senior designer Gavin Fisher and head of aerodynamics Geoff Willis. Most notable was the switch from transverse to longitudinal gearbox, the narrow new six-speed having already been tried in a converted 1998 car (FW20C) in January. The result was an extremely slender body, from shapely raised nose to pointed low engine cover. The sidepods were also lowered with larger 'flip-ups' to the rear. Williams was the only team to still blow its exhausts into the central diffuser, its vee-shaped side channels each having a single vertical strake. Large bargeboards were tested at Silverstone on the eve of the season and fitted for Australia, only to be abandoned post-race after one fell off Schumacher's car during the closing stages without discernible loss of performance. The FW21 was shorter than its predecessor with new construction techniques used for the monocoque. The push-rod suspension was redesigned with front torsion bars and shock absorbers now mounted in front of the driver's feet. Zanardi's pedals were modified so he could right-foot brake, although he switched to left-foot braking in Hungary. The Supertec FB01 engine was approximately 60bhp shy of works

rivals although Williams did not suffer the vibrations that plagued BAR's season. The FW21 was unstable under braking and Williams struggled to make the hard tyres work. Attempting to fix poor initial pace, revised front aerodynamics and gearbox were taken to Brazil. A new diffuser was introduced at Monaco with stepped side channels.

The younger Schumacher enhanced his reputation in 1999. Fast but erratic in his F1 career so far, he outqualified Zanardi 11–5, scored three podium finishes and was sixth in the World Championship. He made a good start from eighth on the grid in Melbourne and inherited third place when both McLaren-Mercedes retired. A lapped fourth in Brazil, he lost another potential podium when his engine caught fire at Imola. He qualified poorly in Monaco and ran among the backmarkers after being hit by Damon Hill until he crashed at the hairpin. Fifth in Spain was 'best of the rest' behind pairs of McLaren-Mercedes and Ferraris. Despite compromised qualifying sessions in Canada and France, he was fourth both times, incurring an $11,500 fine in Montréal for speeding in the pitlane, and passing his brother at Magny-Cours to snatch fourth with three laps to go.

The FW21 was revised for the British GP with modified 'coke-bottle' rear and exhausts moved above the diffuser to improve stability and corner entry. Schumacher qualified eighth (his best grid position since Australia) and withstood pressure from Frentzen's Jordan to finish third. An early spin in Austria ended his points-scoring run but he registered another impressive fourth place at Hockenheim. Ninth in Hungary after Williams's worst weekend of the season, Schumacher qualified and finished fifth at Spa-Francorchamps having adopted a one-stop strategy. In low-downforce trim, the Williams-Supertecs qualified in the top five at Monza and battled during the early laps before Zanardi let Schumacher by. The German then set the fastest race lap as he finished in a fine second position on the team's best showing of 1999.

It could have been so much better at the chaotic Nürburgring, where Schumacher qualified fourth and had just taken the lead with 18 laps to go when his right-rear tyre punctured. A disappointed fourth that day, he spun out of the Malaysian GP and crashed heavily at Degner during qualifying for the Japanese GP. Ninth on the grid as a consequence, he recovered to finish fifth.

Zanardi had never driven a car with a semi-automatic gearbox or used left-foot braking and struggled to readapt to F1. Mechanical failures restricted track time at the first two rounds, where he qualified among the tailenders. He crashed out of the Australian GP and was sidelined by a troublesome differential at Interlagos, without threatening the top ten on either occasion. He qualified tenth at Imola (alongside his team-mate) and would have finished sixth but for a late spin. A loose seat caused him to spin on lap 14 of the Monaco GP and, struggling to reach the pedals thereafter, he was classified eighth, the last car still circulating at the finish.

Zanardi suffered mechanical failures at the next three races as his future was called into question. He outqualified Schumacher in Montréal but twice ran wide and served a stop-go penalty for a safety-car infringement before his gearbox failed. After finishing 11th at Silverstone, he ran out of fuel in Austria while dicing with Pedro Diniz (having not heard the instruction to pit). Languishing among the Arrows and Minardi-Ford backmarkers in Germany, he suffered race-ending differential failures at that race and the next. Eighth in Belgium despite a problem with the fuel rig, Zanardi's most competitive showing came at Monza where he qualified a career-best fourth (ahead of Schumacher) and ran third during the early stages. However, a loose floor caused him to slip out of the points and finish seventh. Eliminated from the European GP in an early contretemps with Pedro de la Rosa, he finished tenth in Malaysia after sustaining damage. His miserable campaign came to an end when his electrics shut down on the opening lap of Suzuka.

In its final season before a new works partnership with BMW, Williams were Supertec's best-placed team in fifth overall. Schumacher had scored all 35 points and he was rewarded with a pay rise and contract extension to the end of 2002. Zanardi was released a month after the season ended.

MILD SEVEN BENETTON PLAYLIFE

Benetton finished sixth overall in the constructors' standings as its tumble down the pitlane continued in 1999. Highlights were few and far between with an inconsistent and uncompetitive technical package as Benetton endured its worst season since 1986. Negotiations with Mecachrome were completed in May 1998 to continue with the rebadged Playlife V10s. A familiar face returned as Flavio Briatore was the chairman of a new company, Supertec Sport, that now marketed the former Renault units. Benetton angered its rivals when it approached Charlie Whiting for a senior management position but the FIA race director declined the advance.

Giancarlo Fisichella remained under contract and Alexander Wurz

was confirmed as his team-mate at the 1998 Canadian GP. Mild Seven extended its title sponsorship to the end of 2000 but Federal Express and Akai did not renew. A new wind tunnel opened in the winter was claimed to be the most advanced in F1. Laurent Redon joined from Minardi as test driver.

Benetton revealed the B199 at Enstone on 16 January as it aimed to re-establish itself in the top three. Described as 'brave and aggressive' by more than one in the organisation, technical director Pat Symonds and chief designer Nick Wirth promised innovation as they compensated for the lack of power from customer engines. Tested since September, the Front Torque Transfer (FTT) system connected the front wheels by driveshafts via a central viscous differential, which transferred energy from the inside wheel to the unloaded outside one under braking to improve stability and prevent locking up. It weighed 25lb and Wurz, who was the heavier Benetton driver, thought that was too much of a penalty. The front of the new car was extended by 5in and the monocoque was marginally higher to accommodate the FFT. A twin-clutch gearbox intended to improve acceleration was tested but not raced.

The driver was further reclined and the aerodynamics were reworked with a new front wing attached to the raised nose by two curved supports. The sidepods swooped down to the rear, in front of larger 'flip-ups'. The central diffuser was taller with vertical strakes in the outer channels set at an angle. The push-rod suspension reverted to horizontal torsion bars (with vertically mounted dampers) at the front with coil springs retained at the rear.

The B199 was initially too heavy so a weight-saving programme that included a lighter monocoque was implemented between the first two races. An aerodynamic flaw took until mid-season to identify, and the car lacked grip all season with the drivers often seen off the track. Chief executive Rocco Benetton soon looked to bolster the technical department. Reported approaches to Alan Jenkins, Gary Anderson and Gustav Brunner were unsuccessful but designer

Giancarlo Fisichella, Benetton B199-Playlife (Canadian GP)

Tim Densham, chassis specialist Chris Radage and aerodynamicist Ben Agathangelou all arrived from the disbanded Honda test team in September. Wirth resigned at the end of the season and did not return to F1 for another decade.

Wurz and Fisichella were disappointed to be off the pace when they tested the new car at Jerez. Three rear-wing failures were blamed on engine vibrations and another at Silverstone increased concern. Gearbox issues interrupted the Barcelona group test although Wurz was second behind Mika Häkkinen's McLaren-Mercedes, albeit after a low-fuel run.

They were the fifth fastest team in Melbourne, where Fisichella qualified seventh and finished fourth, despite a front-wing change after he ran into Jarno Trulli's Prost-Peugeot. Wurz, who raced without the FFT, climbed into the top six after a slow start until rear suspension failure. Fisichella qualified fifth in Brazil, where his clutch failed, and Wurz finished seventh despite a clash with Damon Hill damaging the balance of his car. Having struggled for grip, they qualified towards the back at Imola, where Wurz crashed into Pedro de la Rosa and Fisichella survived hitting Olivier Panis to salvage fifth.

With the FFT removed from both cars, they started the Monaco GP from the fifth row and finished fifth (Fisichella) and sixth (Wurz). The Spanish GP was compromised by lack of grip and more problems with the FFT, so the B199s were revised before Canada with the troublesome system removed and new front and rear wings fitted. Fisichella recovered from a heavy qualifying crash to score a surprise second place as faster rivals faltered, while Wurz's had a driveshaft breakage on the opening lap. They spun out of the French GP as rain fell and only Arrows and the Minardi-Fords were slower in qualifying

at Silverstone. Starting there from the worst combined grid position in Benetton's history, Fisichella finished seventh and Wurz tenth.

The B199 was better suited to the stop/start layouts at the A1-Ring and Hungaroring. Wurz outqualified his team-mate for the first time in Austria and scored a morale-boosting fifth place in front of his home fans. Fisichella damaged his diffuser in an altercation and was seventh when his engine failed with three laps to go. In Germany, Fisichella ran wide while trying to take eighth from Wurz and had to retire with damaged front wing and suspension. The wings were revised for the Hungarian GP where they qualified fourth (Fisichella) and seventh (Wurz). Having visited hospital on Saturday morning to have dirt removed from his eye, Fisichella ran third during his opening stint and would have finished in that position but for loss of fuel pressure; Wurz repeated his German GP seventh place.

Off the pace once again at Spa-Francorchamps and Monza, Benetton's inconsistency was highlighted by Fisichella qualifying sixth at the Nürburgring. Wurz was central to Pedro Diniz's barrel-roll, thankfully without injury. Fisichella climbed the lap charts as others hit trouble and inherited the lead when Ralf Schumacher pitted on lap 45, but a shock victory was lost when he spun five laps later at the chicane. 'I'm really sorry for the team,' the bitterly disappointed Italian said after the race. 'I went off the track because of my own error and if not I would have won… I threw away a unique opportunity.'

Wurz matched his best qualifying of the season (seventh) in Malaysia and finished eighth. Fisichella broke his front suspension in contact with Hill on the opening lap and lost four laps for repairs. They completed a disappointing season among the also-rans in Japan and finished outside the points. The Benetton family were looking to sell.

Alexander Wurz, Benetton B199-Playlife (Spanish GP)

Olivier Panis, Prost AP02-Peugeot (Brazilian GP)

GAULOISES PROST PEUGEOT

France's national team had a new car that was faster and more reliable than its unhappy predecessor but the Peugeot V10 engine now lagged behind the likes of Mercedes-Benz and Ferrari. The relationship between team and manufacturer grew increasingly strained with each blaming the other for poor results.

In disarray throughout 1998, Prost held talks John Barnard and Gary Anderson as it looked to strengthen its technical resources. Barnard visited Guyancourt in October of that year and his B3 Technologies was announced as exclusive consultants before Christmas. Loïc Bigois remained as chief designer despite the failure of the AP01 and retained overall responsibility for the new car. Prost's McLaren race engineer in the 1980s, Alan Jenkins replaced Bernard Dudot as technical director before the 1999 French GP. Sporting director Cesare Fiorio's contract was not renewed at the end of 1998.

An unchanged line-up of Olivier Panis and Jarno Trulli was announced at the 1998 Hungarian GP despite interest in both Jean Alesi and Heinz-Harald Frentzen. Stéphane Sarrazin was confirmed as test driver at the launch of the Prost AP02-Peugeot at the factory on 25 January. This straightforward design retained the Peugeot A18 72-degree V10 engine, longitudinal gearbox and rear suspension introduced on the AP01B at the 1998 Japanese GP. Barnard designed push-rod suspension with torsion bars front and rear. Ben Wood was responsible for the slippery bodywork, which included atypical

rounded sidepods with a double aerodynamic flick by each inlet. A new exhaust arrangement that exited through the top of the sidepods with 'flip-ups' to deflect the air over the tyres was tested in the autumn. The car was the longest in the field.

Trulli was fastest at Barcelona's Circuit de Catalunya at Prost's first major group test, raising expectations of challenging for points. The cars did not qualify in the top ten at the opening three races although there was promise. Trulli made a strong start in Australia only for a fuel-valve problem to force an extra stop, then spun off while avoiding Marc Gené at a restart. Panis had a nightmare as cooling issues plagued the team. Holes in the bodywork to alleviate overheating disturbed airflow and hurt performance. New wings were fitted to compensate for the extra vents required in Brazil, where Panis jumped the start and recovered from the resulting stop-go penalty to finish sixth; Trulli's gearbox failed. The Italian tangled with Pedro de la Rosa on lap one at Imola while Panis's engine failed after a controversial race. Delayed by a front-wing change following contact with Giancarlo Fisichella, he held up David Coulthard for four laps, prompting Ron Dennis to remonstrate with the Prost pit wall and drawing criticism from Alain Prost himself.

Having lost a points score at Monaco when he went up the Ste-Dévote escape road, Trulli finished sixth in Spain. Panis retired from both races as his relationship with the team deteriorated. Twelve months on from being involved in both first-corner accidents at the

Jarno Trulli, Prost AP02-Peugeot (German GP)

1998 Canadian GP, Trulli lost control under braking for the first corner in Canada, spun across the grass and eliminated Rubens Barrichello and Jean Alesi (for the second successive year). Panis was ninth after a stop-go penalty for ignoring blue flags once more.

At Magny-Cours, the Prost-Peugeots had a new front wing and revised suspension that aimed to reproduce the effects of an active system, plus an upgraded engine for qualifying. Prost sent its drivers out to qualify before the rain intensified and they delivered – Panis third and Trulli eighth on the grid. Panis made a slow start and faded to eighth by the finish, Trulli having passed him in the closing stages. They also finished outside the points at Silverstone and the A1-Ring, where Trulli came seventh after a solid race in Austria. The AP02 was better in low-downforce guise at Hockenheim, where both qualified in the top ten and Panis finished sixth despite another poor start. They were reliable but off the pace in Hungary and Belgium, where Panis had revised exhausts that blew out of the back of the sidepods and boosted power by 10bhp, with winglets deflecting the air over the rear tyres.

They hoped to be more competitive at Monza, especially after both drivers were in the top six on Friday, but were disappointed. They qualified in the midfield (Trulli having crashed his race car and the spare) and broke down during the race. Rammed by Johnny Herbert at the first corner, Panis had completed sufficient distance to be classified when his engine blew up on the last lap. Both drivers starred in changeable conditions at the Nürburgring. With his future uncertain, Panis qualified fifth only to change to wet tyres too early, compromising his race. Trulli took advantage of the chaos to hold off Rubens Barrichello and finish second.

The cars were uncompetitive in Malaysia and both suffered early engine failures, Trulli's on the formation lap. However, they were the surprise qualifying package for the final race in Japan, Panis sixth and Trulli seventh on the grid. The Frenchman made a great start (not normally his forte) and held third until his first pitstop but both cars had broken down by lap 20.

Trulli's second place at the Nürburgring contributed six of Prost-Peugeot's nine points and took the team to an improved seventh overall but all was not well behind the scenes. Prost questioned Peugeot's commitment to F1 throughout 1999 and his relationship with his drivers deteriorated as the season wore on.

RED BULL SAUBER PETRONAS

Sauber signed a one-year extension with Ferrari for a supply of 1998-specification engines, which continued to be rebadged as Petronas V10s. As these were supplied direct from Maranello, Osamu Goto's in-house department was not involved and Sauber's plans to build its own engine were on hold.

Jean Alesi was in the second year of his contract but Johnny Herbert left Sauber after three years. Rumours during the summer suggested Heinz-Harald Frentzen's return or an approach for either Ralf Schumacher or Rubens Barrichello. F3000 title challengers Juan Pablo Montoya and Nick Heidfeld were considered before Pedro Diniz signed in October 1998, with Parmalat joining Sauber's main sponsors Red Bull and Petronas. Jörg Müller remained as reserve driver despite being contracted to develop BMW's new Williams-bound engine. Porsche Supercup organiser Jost Capito joined as chief operating officer.

The Sauber C18-Petronas was launched on 19 January at a typically lavish ceremony at the Jean Tinguely museum in Basle. The latest offering from Leo Ress and his team at Hinwill was another evolution. Seamus Mullarkey was responsible for the aerodynamics and the team claimed that 20 weeks had been spent in the upgraded wind tunnel at Emmen. The new engine had a lower centre of gravity that was expected to improve handling. It drove through a new longitudinal semi-automatic gearbox that had seven gears at Alesi's behest. The brakes were redesigned and the steering rack lowered so horizontal torsion bars could be fitted to the front push-rod suspension. Coil springs replaced torsion bars at the rear, mounted horizontally under a low engine cover. There was much optimism before the season but poor reliability and inconsistent qualifying pace resulted in Sauber's worst points tally since entering F1.

A week after the launch, Alesi drove the C18 for the first time at Barcelona, where times were promising despite inevitable teething troubles. Gearbox and transmission issues made for a tough start to the season with just one finish from the opening five races. Diniz outqualified his new team-mate in Australia and was fourth before his gearbox failed. Competing in Brazil with 18 stitches in his knee following a mountain-bike accident, Diniz crashed out of that race and the next. Left on the grid in Australia, Alesi stormed into the top six at Interlagos after an early spin only for his gearbox to fail. The Frenchman then celebrated Sauber's 100th GP by finishing sixth at Imola thanks to a three-stop strategy.

They crashed within a lap of each other during the Monaco GP. Use of a new diffuser helped Alesi qualify in the top ten at the next four races although it was Diniz who scored points. Alesi was fifth on the grid in Barcelona but both retired once again. Armed with an upgraded engine in Montréal, Alesi was eliminated at the restart but Diniz recovered from a big shunt on Friday to finish sixth. Alesi had an eventful weekend at Magny-Cours: having rolled on Friday, he went out early to qualify second before rain fell, then lay third in the race when the heavens opened and aquaplaned into a gravel trap just as the safety car was deployed; Diniz suffered another transmission failure after five laps. The Brazilian finished sixth at Silverstone, where the fast-starting Alesi lost a lap rectifying a throttle issue. Poor handling ruined qualifying in Austria. Light-fuelled, Diniz made a great start from 16th and finished sixth for the third time in four races. Alesi adopted the same aggressive strategy and was ahead of Diniz when he did not hear the instruction to pit so ran out of fuel. Diniz was an inadvertent victim of the Marc Gené/Jacques Villeneuve first-corner shunt at Hockenheim, where Alesi finished a delayed eighth.

Alesi bruised his right ankle in a big accident on Saturday morning in Hungary. During the race he twice ran out of fuel as he pitted and was given a stop-go penalty when he exceeded the

Pedro Diniz, Sauber C18-Petronas (German GP)

Jean Alesi, Sauber C18-Petronas (Italian GP)

pitlane speed limit despite coasting. After running out of fuel for the third time with a couple of laps to go, the emotional Frenchman could not contain his frustration: 'I've had enough of this, we keep retiring, people are leaving like mad. I have lost faith in it.' Diniz spun out of the race after losing concentration when ordered to let Alesi pass, an instruction that drew criticism from the Brazilian's race engineer, Steve Clark, and resulted in his dismissal before the next race. It was the second such departure as Tim Preston had left earlier, to Alesi's annoyance, and head of research and development Andy Tilley departed at the end of the season.

Alesi was ninth in Belgium and Italy while Diniz spun out of both races. The Brazilian was fortunate to escape with bruising to his shoulder and knee when he rolled at Turn 2 on the opening lap at the Nürburgring. Launched when he hit Alexander Wurz's Benetton-Playlife, his roll-hoop broke as the car landed upside down and skidded along the grass. Alesi's transmission failed once more. Marketing director Fritz Kaiser sold his shares back to Peter Sauber in the autumn and left. Red Bull's Dietrich Mateschitz remained the majority shareholder with a 51 per cent stake.

The drivers demonstrated their cars beneath Kuala Lumpur's Petronas Towers to promote the Malaysian GP prior to the inaugural race. Diniz spun in qualifying at Sepang and three times during the race, his excursion on lap 45 proving final. A strong seventh after passing three cars in Malaysia, Alesi ended his Sauber career on a relative high by finishing sixth in Japan with Diniz 11th to complete a rare double finish. Sauber-Petronas scored just five points and was an unsatisfactory eighth overall.

ARROWS

Frustrated in attempts to hire Gary Anderson to replace John Barnard, Tom Walkinshaw promoted Mike Coughlan to technical director in January. Team manager John Walton left on 5 February with Rod Benoist chosen in his place. Eghbal Hamidy was hired as chief designer in August and reported to Coughlan.

The driver line-up was new despite Pedro Diniz having a contract for 1999 (he moved to Sauber amid the threat of legal action) and Arrows exercising its option on Mika Salo. The loss of title sponsor Danka led Arrows to seek well-funded replacement drivers. Pedro de la Rosa and Toranosuke Takagi tested alongside Salo at Barcelona in January and were announced as the drivers in February, with the Finn surplus to requirements. The newcomers brought backing from Repsol and PIAA respectively.

Financial restructuring was not confined to the cockpit, for Walkinshaw looked to sell a stake in the team. Rumours of Zakspeed's £30 million buyout ended on 13 January with the announcement of investment from Morgan Grenfell Private Equity and Nigerian Prince Malik Ado Ibrahim, with the deal due to be completed in July. The mysterious Prince, who was named as commercial director, was behind the T-minus brand that featured on the sidepods from the San Marino GP to the European GP. He disappeared from the sport after his resignation on 14 September amid tensions within the team.

With money even tighter than normal, the Leafield-based outfit relied on an updated version of the 1998 car and engine. The Arrows A20 was built around the A19's monocoque with new internals for the troublesome gearbox, revised aero package and suspension. The underpowered Arrows V10 engine was hardly updated so little was expected from, or achieved by, F1's perennial underachievers. There was little in the way of development or upgrades although a new undertray was introduced at the British GP and another at Monza following Hamidy's arrival.

The A20s shared the ninth row in Australia and ran together for much of that opening GP. De la Rosa beat his team-mate into sixth after a race of attrition on his F1 début but that was the only point Arrows would score. In Brazil, de la Rosa retired when eighth and Takagi finished in that position when last. They retired from three of the next four races – de la Rosa having been hit by Alexander Wurz at Imola – and finished at the back in Spain.

In the wet qualifying at Magny-Cours, they were a couple of seconds slower than the Minardi-Fords and outside the 107 per cent time required to make the field. However, the stewards allowed them start and even placed them ahead of the Italian cars due to times set in dry practice. De la Rosa was last after changing his front wing when he collided with Damon Hill. Takagi was disqualified for using a set of his team-mate's tyres. De la Rosa's gearbox broke on the British GP restart and Takagi was beaten by Marc Gené's Minardi-Ford in the race for last place.

The A20s were slow and unreliable during the second half of 1999 and were even outqualified by both Minardi-Fords at Hockenheim, Monza and the Nürburgring. De la Rosa's 15th place

Toranosuke Takagi, Arrows A20 (Brazilian GP)

in Hungary (where he ran ahead of Salo's Ferrari in the opening laps) and 13th at Suzuka were their only finishes in the last eight races. A braking issue caused the Spaniard to spin at the A1-Ring and he crashed at Hockenheim. The battle at the back became physical in Italy and caused Minardi boss Gabriele Rumi to accuse Arrows of deliberately crashing into his cars. Both Arrows drivers hit Marc Gené on the opening lap and Takagi crashed over the back of Luca Badoer when he locked up at the first chicane. Takagi continued with a new front wing but spun all on his own 12 laps later. During the chaotic European GP his slick-shod A20 crashed when the rain returned.

Pedro de la Rosa, Arrows A20 (German GP)

Luca Badoer, Minardi M01-Ford (Hungarian GP)

FONDMETAL MINARDI FORD

Minardi renewed its Cosworth contract for a supply of customer Ford Zetec-R V10 engines. There were three upgrades that revised the electronics (VJM1), saved weight and increased power (VJM2) and then lowered the crankshaft (VJM3).

Esteban Tuero remained under contract but quit in January. Whether that was due to his Suzuka neck injury or because his home race in Buenos Aires had been cancelled was a matter of conjecture. Marc Gené was quicker than test driver Laurent Redon and Italian F3 title winner Donny Crevels at Barcelona in December and the inaugural Spanish Open Fortuna by Nissan champion was confirmed at the launch of the Minardi M01-Ford (or M199) on 7 February. His place was secured by title sponsorship from Telefónica, the Spanish telecommunications giant, which negotiated with Gabriele Rumi to acquire the team although terms for the sale could not be agreed. Luca Badoer was Minardi's preferred team leader all winter and he

Stéphane Sarrazin, Minardi M01-Ford (Brazilian GP)

dovetailed that role with ongoing duties as Ferrari test driver. Cesare Fiorio joined as sporting director when his contract with Prost Grand Prix expired at the end of 1998.

Technical director Gustav Brunner began work on the M01 within days of his return from Ferrari on 1 February 1998, with George Ryton as chief designer. The M01 was totally new rather than another evolution of an existing design. A conventional high-nose machine, it had relatively short sidepods with 'flip-ups' in front of the rear wheels, push-rod suspension with torsion bars at the front, and Minardi six-speed sequential gearbox mounted longitudinally. Magneti Marelli supplied the electronics as before. Limited budget restricted time in the wind tunnel despite Rumi's interest in both Minardi and Fondmetal Technologies. The Minardi M01-Ford was a well-balanced car although it lacked aerodynamic grip and power.

Gené had a couple of spins during initial tests in Barcelona but stunned rivals by setting the fourth quickest time on day three, albeit with low fuel and soft tyres. Whether or not the car was on the weight limit was not revealed. The Australian GP was a more realistic guide to Minardi's true competitiveness as the cars were slowest in qualifying, Gené 1.697sec adrift of Badoer and outside the 107 per cent limit after a number of off-track excursions. Gené was allowed to start but spun at the second restart while Badoer climbed into the top six as others retired before his gearbox failed.

Badoer broke his hand when he crashed at Fiorano on 28 March following throttle failure. Test driver Gastón Mazzacane did not have a super licence so Prost reserve driver Stéphane Sarrazin deputised in Brazil. Without the benefit of driving the car before first practice, he outqualified Gené although his only F1 race is best remembered for a huge crash at the final corner. Gené finished ninth at that race and the next, with Badoer fit to return at Imola. The Italian drove

Marc Gené, Minardi M01-Ford (Monaco GP)

a long-wheelbase car that was extended by 2½in at the front by opening the angle of the suspension. Last on the grid, he beat his team-mate into eighth – the last two cars still circulating – with Gené lucky to survive contact with Toranosuke Takagi's Arrows.

Gené crashed four times on Saturday in Monaco, and at Ste-Dévote during the race, while Badoer's gearbox failed after ten laps. Having used the short-wheelbase car in Monte Carlo, the longer version was taken to Barcelona, scene of another shambles: in front of his sponsors and home crowd, Gené was left on the grid when unable to select a gear and Badoer spun out of last place. They qualified on the last row in Montréal but finished, Gené eighth and Badoer tenth after receiving a stop-go penalty for ignoring blue flags.

Revisions taken to Magny-Cours included new rear endplates and Badoer finished tenth after outracing both Arrows while Gené spun in the rain. The Spanish rookie beat Takagi at Silverstone, the first of five successive finishes; Badoer had already clashed with the Japanese driver when his gearbox broke after six laps. The first major aero upgrade was ready for the Austrian GP. A new diffuser and revised engine improved stability but they still finished outside the top ten. Unhappy that Ferrari chose Mika Salo to substitute for the injured Michael Schumacher, Badoer had to change his front wing after hitting Damon Hill's Jordan-Mugen.

Improved pace was reflected in Germany, where Gené qualified a season-best 15th. He survived separate opening-lap incidents with both BAR-Supertecs to finish ninth with Badoer tenth after his own spin. They were reliable but slow in Hungary and Gené was last in Belgium, where Badoer damaged his suspension by crashing over kerbs at the Bus Stop chicane. They outqualified both Arrows A20s at Monza but here the back-of-the-grid rivalry was too close for comfort: Gené was hit by both Arrows drivers on lap one and Takagi crashed

over Badoer when he lost control at the first chicane after 23 laps.

Rain turned the form book on its head at the Nürburgring and delivered Minardi's first point since 1995, Gené holding off Eddie Irvine's Ferrari to finish sixth. It could have been so much better as Badoer lay fourth after the final pitstops only to be left distraught when his gearbox failed with 13 laps to go. It was as close as he would come to scoring championship points. Gené was ninth after a great start in Malaysia and both retired from the final race at Suzuka, Badoer due to a smoky engine failure opposite the pits. Gené's sixth place at the European GP gave Minardi-Ford tenth in the constructors' championship and all-important FOCA benefits.

BRITISH AMERICAN RACING (BAR)

British American Racing entered F1 with lofty ambitions, the largest budget for a newcomer in history and a brash arrogance that antagonised the establishment. It finished its maiden campaign last in the constructors' championship having not scored a point and without vital prize and travel money for 2000.

The germs of the team dated back to 1994 on the day after Jacques Villeneuve drove a Forsythe-Green Reynard 94I-Ford to his breakthrough Champ Car victory at Elkhart Lake. His friend and manager Craig Pollock entertained Adrian Reynard and Rick Gorne of Reynard Cars at his house in Indianapolis and floated the idea of entering F1 together. Villeneuve, whose North American career had been backed by British American Tobacco's Player's brand, won the following year's Indianapolis 500 and Champ Car title before transferring to F1 in 1996 with Williams. Pollock continued to assemble a new 'super team' around his client, rumours of which dominated paddock gossip at the 1997 Brazilian GP.

Jacques Villeneuve, BAR 001-Supertec (Monaco GP)

A joint venture between British American Tobacco, Pollock and Reynard to form BAR was confirmed on 2 December 1997, with Tyrrell already acquired as a means to enter F1. Pollock was named as chairman, Reynard as technical director and Gorne as commercial director. It was at that press conference in London's BBC Radio Theatre that Reynard said 'our aim is to put the car on pole and win the first race', pointing out that his cars had won on début in every single-seater category to date. Villeneuve's team owner during his North American career, Jerry Forsythe joined the board of directors as a minority shareholder in September 1998.

With no works engine deal forthcoming, a two-year contract was agreed with Flavio Briatore's Supertec Sport for rebadged Renault V10 engines. The impressive new factory in Brackley was opened on 8 July 1998 and, after months of speculation, Villeneuve signed as lead driver a fortnight later. An approach was made to reigning Champ Car champion Alex Zanardi and Pollock held talks with Ralf Schumacher's manager Willi Weber at the German GP. With BAT South America influential, rookie Ricardo Zonta was preferred to Pedro Diniz as second driver and signed a one-year deal with options in October. Another old friend of Villeneuve, Patrick Lemarié was named as test driver on a long-term contract.

While the Tyrrell name was used for one final season in 1998, Pollock found resistance from the existing teams. The BAR name change was eventually ratified by the F1 Commission in September although a new rule suggested at that meeting presented the next obstacle. Central to BAT's plan was to promote separate tobacco brands on each car. However, the F1 Commission recommendation

that a team's livery on both cars must be 'substantially the same' was confirmed by the World Council on 15 October. Pollock contested the decision and dual liveries were revealed at the team's official launch on 6 January – red-and-white Lucky Strike for Villeneuve and blue-and-yellow 555 for Zonta. A committee of three independent lawyers at the International Chamber of Commerce in Lausanne sided with the FIA on 30 January so a compromise 'zip' livery featuring both brands was introduced on the eve of the season. The team was summoned to appear in front of the F1 World Council on 12 March to explain why it had lodged a parallel complaint with the European Commission, which was contrary to the Concorde Agreement for conflict resolution. It escaped without sanction when Pollock rescinded that action and apologised to the FIA.

A pair of high-tech motorhomes, acquired at a reputed cost of £2.5 million, combined to form a huge two-storey base. BAR was informed that only the top four teams in the constructors' standings were allowed two motorhomes in the paddock so the impressive facility was not used until the British GP. There was an aggressive recruitment programme during 1998 with key staff headhunted from rival teams, including Benetton's Greg Field as team manager and Villeneuve's Williams race engineer Jock Clear.

Reynard chief designer Malcolm Oastler had been responsible for successful F3000 and Champ Cars but had never designed an F1 car before. Wind-tunnel testing of a model began in May and Villeneuve gave the BAR 001-Supertec its shakedown at Barcelona on 15 December 1998, the all-new car finished in BAR's corporate livery. The engine, gearbox and electronics had been tried by Jean-

Christophe Boullion in a converted Tyrrell 026 in the autumn of 1998. The BAR 001 was a conventional design with 71-degree Supertec FB01 V10 engine mated to a BAR/Xtrac six-speed semi-automatic longitudinal gearbox. The Supertec engine had fallen further behind works rivals, lacked power and had excessive vibrations that virtually shook the fragile car to pieces. The double wishbone/push-rod suspension had vertical torsion bars at the front and coil springs to the rear. Villeneuve was occasionally quick but noted that 'reliability has been pathetic' after retiring from the first 11 events.

Testing was plagued by issues from day one when Villeneuve could not complete a flying lap due to gearbox and electronic gremlins. The problems continued throughout the winter, including losing a rear wing due to exhaust gases overheating the support. Individual components had to be beefed up, adding weight, and pace was not impressive when the car did run.

With rumours of tensions already behind the scenes, Villeneuve lay eighth in Australia when he crashed heavily following another wing failure. Zonta ran as high as fifth before stopping to check his rear wing as a precaution, then his gearbox failed late on. Villeneuve was among those to suffer a Supertec engine failure in Barcelona testing and Brazil was a disaster. Zonta was hospitalised with injured tendons in his left foot after crashing heavily at Ferradura during Saturday practice and Villeneuve was relegated to the back of the grid due to a fuel irregularity. Having missed a function to celebrate his 28th birthday in his frustration, Villeneuve had a hydraulic failure when running seventh in the race.

Villeneuve qualified a morale-boosting fifth at Imola but was left on the grid when the gearbox electronics failed. Mika Salo replaced Zonta and was classified seventh despite electrical failure with two laps to go. Both retired in Monaco as the recriminations began. Test team manager Robert Synge replaced Field and BAT's global sponsorship director Tom Moser was seconded to the team to look for new partners to supplement its budget. Gorne was moved into an operational role. There were signs of progress in Spain for Villeneuve jumped from sixth to third at the start and held that position despite Michael Schumacher's pressure throughout his first stint. He was jumped by the Ferraris in the pitstops and his transmission failed as he exited the pits for the second time. A BAR-Supertec finally saw the chequered flag for the first time when Salo finished eighth in Spain, his last appearance before Zonta's return.

The Canadian GP brought another dispiriting performance as the BAR-Supertecs languished among the backmarkers in qualifying and crashed out of the race. Having outqualified Villeneuve in France when tenth in the wet, Zonta registered his first finish – ninth. Villeneuve spun as he tried to catch the safety car after changing to wet tyres. Despite a disappointing season so far, testing was reduced to save money due to significant overspend that was reported to be in the region of £20 million.

Villeneuve's gearbox broke on the British GP starting grid. The red flag gave him a second chance but the gearbox on the spare car failed after 29 laps of the restarted race. Zonta crashed due to suspension failure. Criticised by Villeneuve in the press and having only attended three races thus far, Adrian Reynard was moved sideways into the new role of vice president with Oastler promoted to technical director. Villeneuve was punted off by Marc Gené's Minardi-Ford on the opening lap at Hockenheim and Zonta needed a new front wing when he tangled with the same driver. He was running last when his engine failed.

An untested aero upgrade was taken to Hungary, where Villeneuve qualified ninth but damaged his front wing at the start so made little impression before the clutch failed; Zonta finished 13th after an extra stop due to a faulty fuel rig. Both had huge shunts at Eau Rouge during Belgian GP qualifying. Villeneuve hit the barrier at Raidillon for the second successive year and Zonta rolled. Villeneuve registered his first finish on the next day but 15th was hardly cause for celebration. Zonta stalled at the start and ran at the back until another gearbox malfunction.

Villeneuve was eighth in Italy and qualified in that position at the Nürburgring, where he raced with a new clutch and differential for the first time. Having run on slicks throughout, he was fifth with four laps to go when the clutch broke to deny a vital score. That was all the more costly for Gené's sixth place relegated BAR-Supertec to last in the constructors' standings. Sidelined by a suspension problem at Monza, Zonta finished the European GP in eighth place. Villeneuve challenged for points in Malaysia, where both spun before mechanical failures caused another double DNF. They finished outside the points in Japan, the only time both cars completed a race, and BAR was the only team not to score a championship point all season.

Ricardo Zonta, BAR 001-Supertec (Australian GP)

Mika Salo, BAR 001-Supertec (Spanish GP)

DRIVER PERFORMANCE

DRIVER	CAR–ENGINE	AUS	BR	RSM	MC	E	CDN	F	GB	A	D	H	B	I	EU	MAL	J
Jean Alesi	Sauber C18-Petronas	16 R	14 R	13 6	14 R	5 R	8 R	2 R	10 14	17 R	21 8	11 16	16 9	13 9	16 R	15 7	10 6
Luca Badoer	Minardi M01-Ford	21 R	–	22 8	20 R	22 R	21 10	21 10	21 R	19 13	19 10	19 14	20 R	19 R	19 R	21 R	22 R
Rubens Barrichello	Stewart SF3-Ford	4 5	3 R	6 3	5 9	7 DSQ	5 R	1 3	7 8	5 R	6 R	8 5	7 10	7 4	15 3	6 5	13 8
David Coulthard	McLaren MP4-14-Mercedes-Benz	2 R	2 R	2 2	3 R	3 2	4 7	4 R FL	3 1	2 2	3 5 FL	3 2 FL	2 1	3 5	2 R	3 R	3 R
Pedro de la Rosa	Arrows A20	18 6	17 R	18 R	21 R	19 11	20 R	19 12	20 R	21 R	20 R	20 15	22 R	21 R	22 R	20 R	21 13
Pedro Diniz	Sauber C18-Petronas	14 R	15 R	15 R	15 R	12 R	18 6	11 R	12 6	16 6	16 R	12 R	18 R	16 R	13 R	17 R	17 11
Giancarlo Fisichella	Benetton B199-Playlife	7 4	5 R	16 5	9 5	13 9	7 2	7 R	17 7	12 12	10 R	4 R	13 11	17 R	6 R	11 11	14 14
Heinz-Harald Frentzen	Jordan 199-Mugen	5 2	8 3	7 R	6 4	8 R	6 11	5 1	5 4	4 4	2 3	5 4	3 3	2 1	1 R	14 6	4 4
Marc Gené	Minardi M01-Ford	22 R	20 9	21 9	22 R	21 R	22 8	22 R	22 15	22 11	15 9	22 17	21 16	20 R	20 6	19 9	20 R
Mika Häkkinen	McLaren MP4-14-Mercedes-Benz	1 R	1 1 FL	1 R	1 3 FL	1 1	2 1	14 2	1 R FL	1 3 FL	1 R	1 1	1 2 FL	1 R	3 5 FL	4 3	2 1
Johnny Herbert	Stewart SF3-Ford	13 R	10 R	12 10	13 R	14 R	10 5	9 R	11 12	6 14	17 11	10 11	10 R	15 R	14 1	5 4	8 7
Damon Hill	Jordan 199-Mugen	9 R	7 R	8 4	17 R	11 7	14 R	18 R	6 5	11 8	8 R	6 6	4 6	9 10	7 R	9 R	12 R
Eddie Irvine	Ferrari F399	6 1	6 5	4 R	4 2	2 4	3 3 FL	17 6	4 2	3 1	5 1	2 3	6 4	8 6	9 7	2 1	5 3
Olivier Panis	Prost AP02-Peugeot	20 R	12 6	11 R	18 R	15 R	15 9	3 8	15 13	18 10	7 6	14 10	17 13	10 11	5 9	12 R	6 R
Mika Salo	BAR 001-Supertec	–	–	19 7	12 R	16 8	–	–	–	–	–	–	–	–	–	–	–
	Ferrari F399	–	–	–	–	–	–	–	7 9	4 2	18 12	9 7	6 3	12 R	–	–	
Stéphane Sarrazin	Minardi M01-Ford	–	18 R														
Michael Schumacher	Ferrari F399	3 8 FL	4 2	3 1 FL	2 1	4 3 FL	1 R	6 5	2 R	–	–	–	–	–	–	1 2 FL	1 2 FL
Ralf Schumacher	Williams FW21-Supertec	8 3	11 4	9 R	16 R	10 5	13 4	16 4	8 3	8 R	11 4	16 9	5 5	5 2 FL	4 4	8 R	9 5
Toranosuke Takagi	Arrows A20	17 7	19 8	20 R	19 R	20 12	19 R	20 11	19 16	20 R	22 R	21 R	19 R	22 R	21 R	22 R	19 R
Jarno Trulli	Prost AP02-Peugeot	12 R	13 R	14 R	7 7	9 6	9 R	8 7	14 9	13 7	9 R	13 8	12 12	12 R	10 2	18 DNS	7 R
Jacques Villeneuve	BAR 001-Supertec	11 R	21 R	5 R	8 R	6 R	16 R	12 R	9 R	9 R	12 R	9 R	11 15	11 8	8 10	10 R	11 9
Alexander Wurz	Benetton B199-Playlife	10 R	9 7	17 R	10 6	18 10	11 R	13 R	18 10	10 5	13 7	7 7	15 14	14 R	11 R	7 8	15 10
Alex Zanardi	Williams FW21-Supertec	15 R	16 R	10 11	11 8	17 R	12 R	15 R	13 11	14 R	14 R	15 R	8 8	4 7	18 R	16 10	16 R
Ricardo Zonta	BAR 001-Supertec	19 R	NT DNP	–	–	–	–	17 R	10 9	16 R	15 15	18 R	17 13	14 R	18 R	17 8	18 12

FORMULA 1 RACE WINNERS

ROUND	RACE (CIRCUIT)	DATE	WINNER
1	Qantas Australian Grand Prix (Albert Park)	Mar 7	Eddie Irvine (Ferrari F399)
2	Grande Prêmio Marlboro do Brasil (Interlagos)	Apr 11	Mika Häkkinen (McLaren MP4-14-Mercedes-Benz)
3	Gran Premio Warsteiner di San Marino (Imola)	May 2	Michael Schumacher (Ferrari F399)
4	Grand Prix de Monaco (Monte Carlo)	May 16	Michael Schumacher (Ferrari F399)
5	Gran Premio Marlboro de España (Catalunya)	May 30	Mika Häkkinen (McLaren MP4-14-Mercedes-Benz)
6	Air Canada Grand Prix du Canada (Montréal)	Jun 13	Mika Häkkinen (McLaren MP4-14-Mercedes-Benz)
7	Grand Prix Mobil 1 de France (Magny-Cours)	Jun 27	Heinz-Harald Frentzen (Jordan 199-Mugen)
8	RAC British Grand Prix (Silverstone)	Jul 11	David Coulthard (McLaren MP4-14-Mercedes-Benz)
9	Grosser Preis von Österreich (Spielberg)	Jul 25	Eddie Irvine (Ferrari F399)
10	Grosser Mobil 1 Preis von Deutschland (Hockenheim)	Aug 1	Eddie Irvine (Ferrari F399)
11	Marlboro Magyar Nagydíj (Hungaroring)	Aug 15	Mika Häkkinen (McLaren MP4-14-Mercedes-Benz)
12	Grand Prix Foster's de Belgique (Spa-Francorchamps)	Aug 29	David Coulthard (McLaren MP4-14-Mercedes-Benz)
13	Gran Premio Campari d'Italia (Monza)	Sep 12	Heinz-Harald Frentzen (Jordan 199-Mugen)
14	Grosser Preis Warsteiner von Europa (Nürburgring)	Sep 26	Johnny Herbert (Stewart SF3-Ford)
15	Petronas Malaysian Grand Prix (Sepang)	Oct 17	Eddie Irvine (Ferrari F399)
16	Fuji Television Japanese Grand Prix (Suzuka)	Oct 31	Mika Häkkinen (McLaren MP4-14-Mercedes-Benz)

DRIVERS' CHAMPIONSHIP

	DRIVERS	POINTS
1	Mika Häkkinen	76
2	Eddie Irvine	74
3	Heinz-Harald Frentzen	54
4	David Coulthard	48
5	Michael Schumacher	44
6	Ralf Schumacher	35
7	Rubens Barrichello	21
8	Johnny Herbert	15
9	Giancarlo Fisichella	13
10	Mika Salo	10
11=	Damon Hill	7
	Jarno Trulli	7
13=	Pedro Diniz	3
	Alexander Wurz	3
15=	Jean Alesi	2
	Olivier Panis	2
17=	Marc Gené	1
	Pedro de la Rosa	1

CONSTRUCTORS' CHAMPIONSHIP

	CONSTRUCTORS	POINTS
1	Ferrari	128
2	McLaren-Mercedes-Benz	124
3	Jordan-Mugen	61
4	Stewart-Ford	36
5	Williams-Mecachrome	35
6	Benetton-Playlife	16
7	Prost-Peugeot	9
8	Sauber-Petronas Ferrari	5
9=	Arrows	1
	Minardi-Ford	1

Ferrari won its first constructors' title since 1983

INDEX

Activa Technology 61
Adams, Philippe 159–160, 163
Advanced Composites 71, 95, 188
Agathangelou, Ben 242, 277, 288
Agip (fuel and oil) 201
Agnelli, Gianni 55, 201
AGS (Automobiles Gonfaronaise Sportive) 10, 28, 32–33, 61, 68–70, 72, 92, 102
  JH24-Ford 32–33
  JH25-Ford 32–33, 68–70
  JH25B-Ford 69–70
  JH26-Ford (not built) 68
  JH27-Ford 69–70
Aïello, Laurent 180
Akagi, Akira 21, 22, 63, 64, 93
Alboreto, Michele 24–25, 31, 32, 64–67, 90–91, 97, 124, 131, 138, 152, 155–156, 186
Alesi, Jean 10, 12, 16, 19–21, 30, 32, 45, 47–49, 52, 54, 62, 73, 83, 84, 85–87, 89, 98, 113, 116–117, 123, 136, 143–145, 148, 162, 169, 171, 172, 173, 174–175, 179, 184, 199, 200, 202–204, 207, 213, 227, 228–229, 231, 232, 255, 257, 261, 262–263, 268, 289, 290–292
Alesi, José 169
Alliot, Philippe 28–29, 128–129, 146–147, 156, 158
Aloi, Giovanni 72
Alolique 99
Amati, Giovanna 99–100
Anderson, Gary 52, 126, 147, 180–181, 207, 208, 209, 232, 258, 259, 260, 282, 283, 287, 289, 292
Anderson, Ken 35
André, Charles-Pierre 63
Andrea Moda 79, 95, 102–103, 129
  S192-Judd 103, 161
Andretti, Mario 85, 199
Andretti, Michael 44, 85, 112–113, 116, 117, 122, 124, 127
AP (Associated Products) (clutches) 14, 46, 58
Apicella, Marco 29, 30, 72, 127, 223
Arnott, Rob 197
Arnoux, René 28
Arrows 21, 24–25, 31, 32, 34, 44, 64, 153, 183, 207, 209, 213, 214, 225, 232, 234, 238–239, 240, 258, 263–265, 283, 287, 288, 292–293, 295
  A11-Ford 24–25
  A11B-Ford 24–25
  A11C-Porsche (test chassis) 64, 65
  A18-Yamaha 238–239
  A19 264–265, 292
  A20 292–293
Arrows engines
  V10 (3-litre) 264, 293
    C-spec 265
    D-spec 265

Ascanelli, Giorgio 13, 16, 81, 112, 174
Ashmore, Bruce 62
Astauto 101, 217
Audetto, Daniele 72, 156, 214
Audi 184
Ayari, Soheil 256

B3 Technologies 226, 265, 268, 289
Baccini, Giancarlo 175
Badoer, Luca 125, 130, 131, 138, 146, 155, 186–187, 199, 215, 216–217, 254, 281, 293, 294–295
Baghetti, Giancarlo 199
Bailey, Julian 58–59, 100
Baldi, Mauro 72
Balestre, Jean-Marie 10, 43, 62, 108
Banassi, Umberto 13
BAR (British American Racing) 269, 270, 277, 285, 286, 295–297
  001-Supertec 296–297
Barbazza, Fabrizio 68–70, 118, 122–123, 124, 158
Barbosa, João 243
Barilla, Paolo 29–30
Barlesi, Laurent 158
Barnard, John 13, 14, 16, 48, 49, 50, 79, 84, 85, 87, 116, 117, 124, 130, 143, 144, 145, 172, 174, 201, 202, 226, 239, 264, 265, 268, 289, 292
Barrichello, Rubens 113, 122, 125–128, 136, 143, 145, 146, 147–149, 176, 177, 179, 180–181, 201, 202, 207–209, 225, 226, 232, 238, 240–241, 265–267, 282, 283–285, 290
Bartels, Michael 58–59, 162
Battaglino, Daniele 37
Bauer, Jo 223
Beaujon, Michel 67, 118
Becker, Thomas 122
Belco-Avia 190
Bell, Bob 90
Belli, Tino 70, 71, 95, 128
Belmondo, Jean-Paul 71, 93
Belmondo, Paul 71, 93–94, 114, 128, 163, 189
Benetton 13, 16–18, 20, 28, 44, 46, 49–51, 53, 57, 81, 82, 83–85, 86, 88, 89, 99, 110, 112, 113, 114–115, 116, 120, 121, 122, 123, 137, 138–140, 142, 143, 145, 149, 150, 153, 154, 157, 158, 162, 163, 168, 169, 170–171, 172, 174, 175, 176, 178, 181, 191, 199, 200, 202–204, 209, 210, 213, 226, 228–229, 232, 233, 234, 243, 244, 253, 258, 259, 260–261, 271, 277, 287–288, 292, 296
  B189B-Ford 16
  B190-Ford 16–18, 84
  B190B-Ford 50–51
  B191-Ford 50–51
  B191B-Ford 84
  B192-Ford 84–85
  B193-Ford 114
  B193B-Ford 114–115
  B194-Ford 138–140
  B195-Renault 170–171, 178, 203

B196-Renault 203–204, 228
B197-Renault 228–229
B198-Playlife 260–261
B199-Playlife 287–288
Benetton, Alessandro 170
Benetton Formula
  — see 'Benetton'
Benetton, Rocco 261, 287
Benoist, Rod 292
Benson & Hedges Jordan Mugen Honda — see 'Jordan'
Benson & Hedges Total Jordan Peugeot — see 'Jordan'
Beresford, Nigel 186
Beretta, Olivier 156–158, 163, 190
Berger, Gerhard 12–13, 14, 20, 44–45, 47, 50, 79, 81, 81–83, 85, 87, 95, 111, 112, 113, 116–117, 118, 119, 120, 143–145, 174–175, 182, 191, 199, 200, 201, 202–204, 228–229, 233
Bernard, Éric 27–28, 35, 61–63, 117, 138, 147, 149–150, 158, 160
Berri, Claudio 144
Bertaggia, Enrico 102, 103
Bez, Ulrich 64, 67
Bigois, Loïc 152, 209, 234, 267, 289
Bilstein (shock absorbers) 86, 91, 157, 176
Birrane, Martin 245
Blanchet, Mike 244
Blash, Herbie 26, 61, 196
Blundell, Mark 34, 45, 59–61, 81, 82, 99, 117–119, 142, 150–151, 153, 176–178, 180, 181, 185, 210
BMS Scuderia Italia
  — see 'Scuderia Italia'
BMW 34, 102, 103, 120, 152, 161, 183, 191, 286, 287, 290
  M1
    Group 5 120
    Procar 120
Boldrini, Andrea 243
Bosch (electronics) 36, 59
  Motronic 65
Bouchut, Christophe 158
Boudy, Jean-Pierre 145
Bouillon, Jean-Christophe 172, 182–183, 184, 198, 296–297
Boulter, Ray 99
Boutsen, Thierry 13, 18–19, 34, 67–68, 85, 91–92, 117, 121, 126–127
Bowen, Paul 90
Brabham 19, 20, 25–26, 33, 35, 57, 59–61, 79, 81, 88, 98, 99–100, 101, 103, 129
  BT58-Judd 25–26
  BT58Y-Yamaha 59
  BT59-Judd 26
  BT59Y-Yamaha 59–60
  BT60Y-Yamaha 60–61
  BT60B-Judd 99–100
Brabham, David 26, 30, 58, 145, 161–162, 191
Brabham, Gary 35, 37
Brabham, Jack 11, 26, 161
Bräck, Kenny 209, 213
Braun Tyrrell Honda — see 'Tyrrell'

Brawn, Ross 6, 24, 51, 84, 114, 138, 170, 204, 226, 228, 238, 280
Brembo (brakes) 46
Briatore, Flavio 16, 49, 50, 51, 79, 83, 138, 140, 149, 178, 186, 191, 202, 204, 209, 228, 229, 243, 270, 287, 296
Bridgestone 214, 222, 234, 235, 238, 239, 240, 241, 243, 244, 245, 250, 251, 252, 255, 261, 267, 270, 276
British Aerospace 201, 283
British American Racing
  — see 'BAR'
Broadley, Eric 62, 95, 244
Brown, Andy 60, 63, 100
Brown, David 142, 198, 205, 277
Brown, Paul 162, 163
Brown, Sam 160
Brun, Walter 34
Brundle, Martin 25, 52, 57, 60–61, 83–85, 89, 99, 110, 111, 113, 114, 117–119, 122, 129, 142, 146–147, 149, 154, 172, 173, 174, 175, 176, 178–180, 205, 207–209, 211, 215, 238
Brunner, Gustav 21, 63, 64, 93, 94, 98, 122, 144, 145, 202, 226, 270, 287, 294
Bruynseraede, Roland 196
Bugatti, Giuseppe 102
Burgess, Paul 36, 102, 129
Burt, Kelvin 147, 180, 209
Burti, Luciano 283
Bussey, Paul 88, 119
Byrne, Rory 6, 49, 51, 84, 114, 163, 170, 204, 226, 228, 254, 280

Caffi, Alex 24–25, 28, 31, 64–67, 102, 103
Cagiva 103
Calmels, Didier 96
Calvert, Jacques 207
Camel Benetton Ford
  — see 'Benetton'
Camel Team Lotus
  — see 'Lotus'
Campos, Adrián 161
Cane, Michael 46
Canon Williams Team
  — see 'Williams'
Canon Williams Renault
  — see 'Williams'
Cantú, Patrizio 31, 68
Capelli, Ivan 15, 21–22, 63–64, 85–87, 95, 126
Capito, Jost 290
Carletti, Tommaso 101
Carman, George QC 140
Casola, Romeo 25
Castelli, Pierguido 85
Castrol (oil) 88, 119, 158
Central Park Venturi Larrousse
  — see 'Larrousse'
Challis, Alan 46
Chamberlain, Jo 25
Chapman, Clive 22
Chapman, Colin 22
Chaves, Pedro 73
Cheever, Eddie 24
Chevron 162
Chiesa, Andrea 99, 101–102
Chirac, Jacques 234

Chiti, Carlo 29, 36
Chrysler 156
Chrysler engines 128, 145
  V12 (3.5-litre) 113, 145
Cipriani, Giuseppe 79
Clark, Steve 91, 118, 292
Clear, Jock 158, 198, 286, 296
Cochin, Henri 32, 68
Collard, Emmanuel 28, 149, 158, 170, 172, 189, 209, 212, 235, 242, 264
Collins, Peter 57, 88, 119, 120, 158, 160
Coloni 10, 31, 32, 36–37, 73, 79, 102
  C3B-Ford 36
  C3B-Subaru 36
  C4-Ford 73
  C4B-Judd (test chassis) 102, 103
Coloni, Enzo 36, 73
Comas, Érik 67–68, 91–92, 117, 118, 128–129, 156–158
Comtec (Composite Technics) 88
Commissione Sportiva Automobilistica Italiana (CSAI) 85
Comstock Group 95, 96
Cooper, Adam 113, 128, 130
Cooper, Julian 244
Cooper, Neil 160
Coppuck, Frank 22, 57, 58, 188
Coppuck, Gordon 22, 63
Corsmit, Jan 78, 196
Costa, Aldo 29, 55, 96, 122, 186, 215, 226
Costa, Michel 32, 36, 68, 102
Cosworth Engineering 16, 63, 88, 98, 112, 138, 156, 157, 158, 181, 183, 186, 190, 210, 215, 217, 242, 243, 251, 266, 269, 270, 283, 294
Coughlan, Mike 16, 22, 49, 50, 54, 89, 116, 129, 130, 226, 265, 292
Coulthard, David 110, 140–143, 145, 151, 158, 170, 171, 172–173, 174, 175, 176, 179, 198, 201, 202, 205–207, 208, 223, 227, 229, 230–231, 233, 236, 248–249, 250, 252–254, 256, 257, 260, 261, 263, 276, 278–279, 280, 281, 289
Cowperthwaite, Nigel 29, 56
Cresson, Édith 62
Crevels, Donny 294
Crooks, Paul 162, 191, 209
Crypton Engineering 31, 68

Daewoo 183
Daimler-Benz
  — see 'Mercedes-Benz'
Dallara 29, 31–32, 72, 86, 90, 94–95, 131, 235, 277
  F189-Ford 32
  F190-Ford 31–32, 56
  F191-Judd 56–57
  F192-Ferrari 94–95
Dallara, Gian Paolo 31, 56
Dalmas, Yannick 32–33, 146, 157–158
DAMS (Driot Arnoux Motor Sport) 158, 197
  GD01 (not completed) 186
Danka Arrows Yamaha
  — see 'Arrows'

Danka Zepter Arrows
— see 'Arrows'
David Price Composites 121,
152, 161
David, Darren 283
Davis, John 57, 58, 89, 92, 117
Dawson, Ian 162
de Cesaris, Andrea 20, 29,
31–32, 52–53, 55, 56, 57,
64, 68, 73, 89–90, 96,
118, 123, 129–130, 148,
152–153, 159
de Chaunac, Hugues 32, 234
de Cortanze, André 121, 152,
182, 209, 234
de Ferran, Gil 209
de Marco, Riccardo 216
de la Rosa, Pedro 258, 287, 288,
289, 292–293
de Rouvre, Cyril 32, 68, 92, 117,
118, 149
de Simone, Fabrizio 207
Delco Electronics 223
Délétraz, Jean-Denis 158, 178,
188–189
Denekamp, Johan 35
Dennis, Ron 44, 80, 81, 111,
112, 114, 145, 146, 176,
205, 206, 230, 252, 253,
279, 289
Densham, Tim 26, 60, 99, 129,
277, 288
Depardieu, Gérard 203
Dernie, Frank 22, 57, 67, 68,
91, 92, 114, 149, 178, 209,
214, 238
Dhainhaut, Frédéric 95,
102–103, 215
di Montezemolo, Luca 6, 85, 87,
116, 117, 145, 175, 200, 202,
243, 254, 281
Diniz, Pedro 190–191, 199, 207,
208, 209–210, 216, 227, 237,
238–239, 242, 264–265, 283,
287, 288, 290–292, 296
Divila, Richard 29, 37, 67, 71,
96
Djeliri, Daniel 68
Doi, Yasuhiro 62, 72
Dome 109, 223
Dome F105-Mugen 223
Donnelly, Martin 22–23, 57,
58, 137
Doohan, Mick 257
Douglas, Michael 252
Dowe, Tony 149, 178, 209, 214
Driot, Jean-Paul 158, 197
Ducarouge, Gérard 62, 68, 92,
117, 149
Dudot, Bernard 18, 138, 267,
289
Dufour, Jérémie 209
Duncan Lee, W. 22, 49
Durand, Henri 12, 15, 44, 82,
176, 205
Dynamic Suspension (shock
absorbers) 95

Earle, Mike 25, 34–35
Ecclestone, Bernie 138, 168
Eddie Jordan Racing 52
Edwards, Guy 88, 160
Ehrlinspiel, Herbert 270
Elf (fuel and oil) 28, 42, 46, 79,
89, 112, 114, 178, 209
Emiliani, Vincenzo 29

Engine Developments
— see 'Judd engines'
Équipe Ligier Gitanes
— see 'Ligier'
Escuderia Bravo F1 España 161
ESPO Larrousse — see 'Lola'
EuroBrun 10, 19, 34
ER189-Judd 34
ER189B-Judd 34
Évin, Claude 108

Fangio, Juan Manuel 11
Fantuzzi, Gianfranco 85, 270
Fast Group 157
Fauconnier, Pierre-Michel 207
Faure, Patrick 138
Ferrari 10, 12, 13–15, 16, 18,
19, 22, 28, 31, 35, 37, 44,
45, 46, 47–49, 54, 55, 56,
62, 73, 81, 83, 85–87, 89,
91, 95, 96, 98, 101, 109,
111, 112, 113, 116–117, 120,
121, 122, 123, 124, 126, 131,
137, 143–145, 162, 169, 171,
174–175, 179, 182, 184, 186,
191, 200–202, 203, 204,
206, 207, 210, 213, 214,
216, 222, 224, 225, 226–227,
228, 233, 234, 236, 238,
240, 243, 244, 244, 251,
252, 253, 254–256, 264,
265, 270, 271, 276, 278,
279, 280–281, 284, 285,
286, 293, 295, 297
312T 55
640 14
641 14
641/2 14–15
642 47–49
643 48–49
645 116
F92A 85–87, 201
F92AT 86–87
F93A 116–117
412T1 143–145, 181,
201, 205
412T1B 144–145
412T2 172, 174–175, 201
F310 200–202, 226
F310B 226–227
F300 254–256, 280
F399 278, 280–281
Road cars
512 174
F40 85
F355 174
Ferrari engines 18, 42, 94, 131,
256, 289, 290
V12 (3.5-litre) 10, 55, 95, 116,
131, 143
037 14
V12 (3-litre) 174
V10 (3-litre) 174, 196, 201,
226, 236, 262
046/2 226
Evo 2 226
047 254
048B 281
048C 281
Ferrari Design & Development
(UK facility)
Ferrari, Enzo 48, 226
Ferrari, Piero 48, 85
FFSA (Fédération Française
du Sport Automobile)
108, 223

FIA (Fédération Internationale
de l'Automobile) 6, 10, 108,
136, 137, 139, 140, 142, 145,
147, 161, 168, 171, 178, 196,
197, 207, 213, 216, 222–223,
227, 237, 250, 251, 252, 255,
265, 276, 277, 279, 281,
287, 296
Fiat 47, 55, 85, 102, 201
Field, Greg 57, 88, 99, 296
Finfirst Group 217
Fiorio, Cesare 13, 15, 48, 149,
178, 209, 216, 234, 289, 294
FIRST
189 37
FISA (Fédération Internationale
du Sport Automobile) 12, 28,
42, 43, 48, 49, 56, 61, 62, 67,
78, 81, 85, 89, 108, 110, 129
Fisher, Gavin 224, 256, 286
Fisichella, Giancarlo 186, 206,
215–216, 232–233, 242, 243,
257, 258, 260–261, 263, 271,
283, 285, 287–288, 289
Fittipaldi, Christian 96–98, 111,
117, 122–123, 125, 139,
153–155, 181
FOCA (Formula One
Constructors' Association) 18,
26, 59, 61, 64, 65, 67, 137,
153, 187, 238, 269, 270
Foitek, Gregor 25–26, 27, 31,
35, 101
Foitek, Karl 35
Fomet 1 70–71, 95, 101
FA1Me-Ford 71
F1-Ford 71, 101
Fondmetal 70–71, 79, 96, 99,
101–102, 122, 243
GR01-Ford 101–102
GR02-Ford 101–102
Fondmetal Minardi Ford
— see 'Minardi'
Fondmetal Osella — see 'Osella'
Fondmetal Technologies 150,
186, 203, 212, 243, 270, 294
Fontana, Norberto 181, 210,
236–237, 245, 262
Footwork 24, 64–67, 90–91, 97,
112, 115, 124–125, 128, 129,
147, 149, 153–155, 183–185,
187, 189, 213–214, 216, 238
A11C-Porsche 65, 67
FA12-Porsche 65–67
FA12-Ford 66–67, 90
FA13-Mugen 90–91
FA13B-Mugen 124–125
FA14-Mugen 124–125, 154
FA15-Ford 154–155
FA16-Hart 183–185
FA17-Hart 213–214
Footwork Arrows
— see 'Arrows'
Footwork Arrows Racing
— see 'Arrows'
Footwork Ford — see
'Footwork'
Footwork Hart — see 'Footwork'
Footwork Mugen Honda
— see 'Footwork'
Footwork Porsche —
'Footwork'
Ford 16, 52, 98, 112, 114, 138,
180, 210, 240, 283, 284
Ford engines 88, 158, 180, 181,
183, 236, 240

V8 (3.5-litre) 36
DFR 19, 24, 29, 30, 32, 35,
36, 52, 54, 61, 67, 68,
70, 71, 73, 101
HB 16, 56, 79, 84, 89, 98,
101, 112, 122, 138, 153,
155, 186
Series IV 17, 52, 101
Series V 50, 88, 101,
161
Series VI 84
Series VII 85, 156
Series VIII 113, 114, 156
Zetec-R 138
V8 (3-litre)
DFV 88
Zetec-R 181, 216, 245
ED 186, 188, 190, 191,
215, 216, 243
ED2 215
ED3 215
ED4 216, 242
ED5 242
V10 (3-litre) 196, 210, 243,
266
Zetec-R 240, 241, 266,
269, 270, 294
VJM1 294
VJM2 294
VJM3 294
CR-1 283
Forghieri, Mauro 22, 27, 72
Forsythe-Greene 295
Forsythe, Jerry 296
Forti 190–191, 199, 209, 214,
216–217
FG01-Ford 190–191
FG01B-Ford 216–217
FG03-Ford 217
Forti, Guido 190, 216, 217
Foster, Trevor 52, 119, 126, 160,
207, 260
Fouche, Hans 190
Franchitti, Dario 205
Frazer Nash (electronics) 88
Frentzen, Heinz-Harald 141,
152–153, 173, 176, 177,
181–183, 198, 199, 202,
210–211, 224–225, 227, 241,
243, 255, 256–258, 259, 260,
261, 271, 276, 277, 282–283,
285, 286, 289, 290
Frison, Nino 70
Fry, Pat 84, 112, 114, 230
Fusaro, Piero 48, 85, 94

Gachot, Bertrand 25, 31, 36–37,
52–53, 62–63, 95–96, 163,
188–189, 191
Galmer 100
Galopin, Claude 28, 67, 197
Ganassi, Chip 113
Gancia, Carlo 190
Gardella, Pierpaolo 31, 95
Gascoyne, Mike 121, 150, 152,
186, 212, 259, 260, 269, 282
Gauloises Prost Peugeot
— see 'Prost'
Gavin, Oliver 163, 189
Gené, Marc 289, 291, 293,
294–295, 297
Gentry, John 63, 93
George, Tony 78
Gerriet, Gérard 91
Ghedini, Sante 85, 144
Giacomelli, Bruno 37

Gillitzer, Peter 210
Gnutti, Enrico 155
Golay, Michel 157
González Luna Associates 72
Goodyear 10, 14, 16, 35, 36, 42,
52, 55, 71, 79, 89, 108, 214,
222, 223, 225, 228, 229, 235,
239, 240, 242, 250, 251, 252,
253, 254, 255, 257, 258, 259,
261, 269, 276
Gorne, Rick 295, 296, 297
Goto, Osamu 44, 144, 201, 236,
262, 290
Gotoh, Ko 188
Gounon, Jean-Marc 94,
122–123, 130, 161, 162
GP Motorsport 100
Grand Prix Drivers' Association
(GPDA) 137
Grand Prix Engineering 122,
186
Greco, Marco 34
Green, Andrew 52
Grouillard, Olivier 18, 26, 28,
30–31, 69, 70–71, 89–90,
94, 95, 96
Gruber, Johannes 109
Guerrero, Carlos 100
Gugelmin, Maurício 15, 21–22,
63–64, 98–99, 102, 125
Guildford Technical Office 13,
47, 73, 81, 87, 116,
Guilloud, Éric 95
Gurney, Dan 131

Haberfeld, Mario 283
Häkkinen, Mika 6, 57, 58–59,
88–89, 108, 110, 112–113,
117, 119, 140, 141, 146–147,
148, 153, 171, 176–178, 181,
189, 202, 205–207, 225, 228,
230–231, 235, 236, 239,
248–249, 250, 252–254, 255,
256, 260, 263, 274–275, 276,
278–279, 280, 281, 284, 288
Hall, Peter 159
Hall-VDS Racing 209
Hallam, Steve 44, 57, 81
Hamidy, Eghbal 240, 283, 292,
293
Hamilton, Maurice 186
Harrison, Alan 184
Harrison, Ian 110, 172
Hart engines 125, 180, 214, 243,
244, 270
V10 (3.5-litre)
1035 125
V8 (3-litre) 183, 243
V10 (3-litre) — see 'Arrows
engines'
Hart, Brian 19, 24, 35, 61, 67,
70, 73, 125, 183, 243, 263,
264
Hasegawa, Takehiro 98
Hattori, Naoki 73
Hawtal Whiting 197
Hayashi, Minoru 223
Hayes, Nick 283
Head, Patrick 18, 42, 45, 46,
137, 140, 172, 173, 198,
225, 286
Heath, Darren 230
Heer (née Ziegler), Carmen 121,
152
Heidfeld, Nick 230, 278, 290
Henry, Alan 91, 112, 198

Herbert, Johnny 22, 23, 52, 58–59, 88–89, 119–120, 140, 146, 149, 150, 158–160, 168, 170–171, 172, 175, 181, 208, 210–211, 212, 226, 231, 233, 236–237, 239, 254, 259, 262–263, 277, 281–285, 290
Hercules Aerospace (carbon-fibre) 12
Herd, Robin 70, 95, 157, 180
Hewland (gearboxes) 32, 52, 56, 163
Hilhorst, René 29, 55, 96, 182, 186, 210, 215
Hill, Damon 6, 45, 80, 100, 109, 110–111, 113, 115, 117, 119, 137, 140–143, 145, 147, 153, 168, 170, 171, 172–173, 174, 175, 180, 181, 194–195, 196, 198–200, 202, 203, 204, 206, 210, 224, 225, 230, 232, 235, 238–239, 240, 250, 252, 256, 258–260, 261, 262, 264, 267, 282–283, 284, 286, 288, 293, 295
Hill, Georgie 194–195
Hill, Graham 200
Hindenoch, Dany 91, 149
Hitco (brakes) 101
Hodges, David 143
Holloway, Tim 22, 70, 71, 95, 128, 180, 208
Honda 269, 277
Honda engines 6, 14, 18, 42, 56, 64, 83, 89, 90, 109, 112, 116, 144, 147, 201, 236, 258, 260, 288
    V10 (3.5-litre) 10, 54
        RA100E 12
    V12 (3.5-litre) 65, 78, 81, 116
        RA121E 44
        RA122E 81
Honda Marlboro McLaren
    — see 'McLaren'
Honda Racing Development 277
Honda, Soichiro 45
Hubbert, Jürgen 205
Hulme, Denny 11
Hunt, David 160, 185, 188, 189
Hunt, James 11, 115, 160

Ibrahim, Prince Malik Ado 292
Ikuzawa
    HW001 (cancelled) 197
Ikuzawa, Tetsu 197
Il Barone Rampante 47, 79, 89, 91
Iley, John 282
Ilien, Mario 63, 122, 152
Ilmor Engineering 6, 63, 64, 89, 120, 152, 153, 176, 230, 252
    V10 (3.5-litre) 42, 63, 64, 93, 120, 163
        2175A 63, 121
    V10 (3-litre) — see 'Mercedes engines'
Inoue, Taki 162, 184–185, 215
Intertechnique 140
Irvine, Eddie 113, 125, 127–128, 138, 143, 147–149, 149, 160, 177, 180–181, 201–202, 203, 204, 206, 207, 210, 211, 213, 214, 224, 225, 226–227, 229, 236, 239, 244, 250, 253, 254–256, 257, 261, 271, 276, 279, 280–281, 282, 284, 295

Isuzu engines
    V12 (3.5-litre)
        P799WE 59

Jabouille, Jean-Pierre 145, 156, 207
Jacques, David 58
Jaguar 57, 88, 122, 284
    XJR-14 100
Jaguar Racing — see 'Jaguar'
Jeffreys, Matthew 82
Jenkins, Alan 24, 35, 65, 90, 124, 154, 184, 213, 240, 266, 283, 287, 289
Jenkinson, Denis 22
Johansson, Stefan 34, 35, 66–67, 68–69
Jones, Len 19
Jordan 51, 52–53, 55, 56, 57, 68, 79, 88, 89, 90, 95, 98–99, 100, 102, 113, 119, 125–128, 129, 138, 145, 146, 147–149, 151, 152, 179, 180–181, 196, 207–209, 213, 215, 227, 232–233, 236, 238, 240, 243, 250, 252, 258–260, 261, 262, 263, 264, 267, 269, 270, 276, 277, 280, 282–283, 286, 295
    191-Ford 52–53
    191Y-Yamaha (test chassis) 99
    192-Yamaha 98–99
    192B-Hart 125
    193-Hart 126–127
    194-Hart 147–149
    194-Peugeot (test chassis) 180
    195-Peugeot 180–181, 205
    196-Peugeot 207–209, 232
    197-Peugeot 232–233
    197-Mugen (test chassis) 258
    198-Mugen 258–260
    199-Mugen 282–283
Jordan, Eddie 51, 52, 148, 161, 180, 201, 207, 232, 234, 258, 260, 282
Juan Carlos, King of Spain 252
Judd engines 88, 161, 238
    V8 (3.5-litre) 22
        CV 26, 34, 37
        EV 21, 26, 57
    V10 (3.5-litre) 42, 94, 99, 129
        GV 56, 102
Judd, John 21, 56, 99, 150
Julien, Henri 32

Kaiser, Fritz 292
Kaneda, Hiro 99
Katayama, Ukyo 60, 95–96, 120, 129–130, 150–151, 185–186, 187, 212–213, 214, 215, 242, 243–244
Keeble, Simon 21, 22, 63, 64
Kimball, Gordon 12, 44, 50, 51
Koni (shock absorbers) 95
Konrad, Franz 102, 109
Kranefuss, Michael 52
Kristensen, Tom 162, 245, 270
Kumpen, Sophie 214

Laffite, Jacques 178
Lagorce, Franck 150, 156, 178
Lambo — see 'Modena Team'
Lamborghini 27, 31, 58, 61, 62, 72, 73, 109, 128, 156

Lamborghini engines 22, 23, 27, 57, 67, 72, 95, 96, 98, 101, 122, 145, 153
    V12 (3.5-litre) 95, 113
        3512 22
        LC01 128
Lammers, Jan 94
Lamy, Pedro 120, 136, 139, 158–159, 181, 187, 189, 208, 212, 214, 215–216, 243
Lancia 48
Landhurst Leasing 99, 100
Lane-Nott, Roger 196, 223
Langes, Claudio 34
Langford & Peck (engines) 19, 36, 73
Larini, Nicola 18, 28–29, 72–73, 85, 87, 144–145, 201, 226, 236–237
Larrousse 10, 22, 27–28, 61–63, 67, 68, 70, 73, 91, 95–96, 101, 117, 128–129, 131, 156–158, 162, 163, 180
    Larrousse LC92-Lamborghini 95–96
    Larrousse LH93-Lamborghini 128–129
    Larrousse LH94-Ford 156–158
Larrousse, Gérard 61, 62, 72, 95, 145, 149, 156, 158
Larrousse UK 157
Lauda, Niki 85, 175, 280, 281
Lavaggi, Giovanni 188–189, 216
Le Fleming, Andy 89, 124, 129, 240
Lechner, Reinhard 121
Lehto, J.J. 34, 35, 56–57, 61, 94–95, 119, 121–122, 124, 127, 136, 138–139, 152, 153, 158
Leloup, Philippe 95
Lemarié, Patrick 296
Leoni, Lamberto 37
Leyton House 15, 19, 21–22, 26, 28, 32, 37, 43, 60, 63–64, 70, 93, 161, 224
    CG891-Judd 21
    CG901-Judd 21–22, 63
    CG901-Ilmor (test chassis) 63
    CG911-Ilmor 63–64
Leyton House Racing
    — see 'Leyton House'
Life 10, 37
    F190 37
    F190-Judd 37
Life engines
    W12 (3.5-litre) 36, 37
Ligier 18, 28–29, 57, 61, 62, 67–68, 71, 89, 91–92, 96, 111, 112, 114, 117–119, 128, 129, 138, 149–150, 151, 152, 156, 160, 161, 162, 170, 172, 174, 176, 178–180, 186, 207, 209–210, 214, 216, 234, 238, 243, 244, 260
    JS33B-Ford 28–29
    JS35-Lamborghini 67–68
    JS35B-Lamborghini 67–68
    JS35R-Renault 91
    JS37-Renault 91–92
    JS39-Renault 117–119
    JS39B-Renault 149–150
    JS41-Mugen 178–180, 209, 214
    JS43-Mugen 209–210, 234, 238

JS45-Mugen 234
Ligier Gauloises Blondes
    — see 'Ligier'
Ligier Gitanes Blondes
    — see 'Ligier'
Ligier, Guy 28, 67, 92, 209, 234
Liverpool Data Research Associates 139
Lola 22, 27–28, 35, 49, 61–63, 70, 95, 125, 130, 131, 242, 244–245, 251
    LC89-Lamborghini 27
    90-Lamborghini 27–28
    L91-Ford 61–63
    T93/30-Ferrari 131
    T97/30-Ford 244–245
Lola BMS Scuderia Italia
    — see 'Lola'
Lombardi, Claudio 48, 85, 86, 87, 144
Longanesi, Francesco 48, 85
Longines (timing) 78
Lotus 16, 22–23, 26, 44, 50, 56, 57–59, 67, 88–89, 92, 99, 102, 108, 110, 112, 114, 119–120, 126, 128, 139, 140, 146, 150, 154, 158–160, 185, 189, 207
    49-Ford 88
    101-Judd 22, 58
    102-Lamborghini 22–23
    102B-Judd 57–59
    102C-Isuzu 59
    102D-Ford 88–89
    107-Ford 88–89
    107B-Ford 119–120
    107C-Mugen 158–159
    109-Mugen 159–160
    112-Mugen (not completed) 160
Lowe, David 214
Lowe, Paddy 110, 112
Lucas (electronics) 126
Lucchini, Beppe 31, 94, 96, 131, 155, 243
Luna, Fernando González 72

MacDonald, John 60, 100
Mader, Heini 29, 30, 32, 35, 68, 120, 163, 189
Magneti Marelli (engine management) 36, 46, 87, 122, 170, 186, 244, 270, 294
Magnussen, Jan 177–178, 205, 226, 229, 235, 236, 237, 240–241, 265–267, 271
Mäkinen, Tommi 257
Mallya, Vijay 203
Mansell, Nigel 6, 13–15, 21, 29, 42, 45–47, 50, 54, 61, 63, 64, 67, 76–77, 78, 80–81, 83, 85, 87, 110, 141–143, 145, 158, 170, 172, 176–177, 181, 184, 232
Manwaring, Rupert 54, 57, 89, 186, 277
March 21, 22, 63, 70, 79, 86, 93–94, 161, 162, 224
    CG911-Ilmor 93–94
Marelli, Gianni 37
Marlboro McLaren
    — see 'McLaren'
Marlboro McLaren Mercedes
    — see 'McLaren'
Marlboro McLaren Peugeot
    — see 'McLaren'

Marlow, Rolf-Peter 34
Marniga, Dino 155
Marques, Tarso 208, 215–216, 243–244, 270
Marrable, Ken 93, 94
Martinelli, Paolo 144, 201, 280
Martini, Giancarlo 55
Martini, Oliver 270
Martini, Pierluigi 20, 27, 29–30, 55–56, 90, 95, 96, 123, 155–156, 158, 186–187, 190
Massai, Paolo 14, 85
MasterCard Lola F1 Team
    — see 'Lola'
Mateschitz, Dietrich 182, 236, 292
Mazzacane, Gastón 294
Mazzola, Luigi 13, 47, 121, 144
McCarthy, Perry 103
McDonald, Alan 213
McLaren 6, 10, 12–13, 17, 20, 22, 34, 44–45, 47, 48, 50, 57, 64, 80, 81–83, 84, 85, 87, 92, 108, 110, 111, 112–113, 114, 115, 116, 117, 119, 138, 142, 144, 145–147, 149, 152, 153, 156, 158, 172, 174, 176–178, 180, 181, 181, 184, 189, 191, 198, 200, 201, 205–207, 223, 224, 225, 226, 228, 230–231, 236, 240, 242, 250, 251, 252–254, 255, 257, 259, 260, 261, 263, 276, 278–279, 280, 283, 286, 288, 289
    F1 GTR 177
    MP4/5B-Honda 12–13, 14, 44, 45
    MP4/6-Honda 44–45
    MP4/6B-Honda 81–82
    MP4/7A-Honda 81–83
    MP4/7B-Honda 82
    MP4/8-Ford 112–113, 125
    MP4/8-Lamborghini (test chassis) 145
    MP4/9-Peugeot 145–147, 176
    MP4/10-Mercedes 176–177
    MP4/10B-Mercedes 177–178, 205
    MP4/10C-Mercedes 177–178
    MP4/11-Mercedes 205–207
    MP4/11B-Mercedes (unofficial designation) 206
    MP4-12-Mercedes 230–231
    MP4-13-Mercedes 248–249, 252–254, 261, 278, 279, 283
    MP4-14-Mercedes 278–279
    MP4-98T-Mercedes 252
McLaren International
    — see 'McLaren'
McNish, Allan 12, 44, 81, 82, 114, 244
McTaggart, Les 70
MCD Consultants 245
    V10 (3-litre) 245
Mecachrome engines 91, 117, 256, 257, 260, 287
    V10 (3-litre) 286
        GC37/01 256
Megatech 156
Melling, Al 245
Mendel, Harry 21
Menem, Carlos 137
Mercedes-Benz 53, 64, 120, 121, 122, 152, 176, 178, 196, 252, 278

Mercedes-Benz engines 6, 176, 181, 256, 289
  V10 (3.5-litre) 152, 182
  V10 (3-litre) 176, 205, 230, 231
    FO110 176
    FO110F 230
    FO110G 252
    FO110H 278
Mertens, Alan 100
Message, Gordon 50, 83, 138
Messaoudi, Jean 158
Mezger, Hans 65
Michael, Sam 258
Michel, Bruno 178, 234
Middlebridge 25, 59, 60, 99
Migeot, Jean-Claude 19, 47, 48, 54, 85, 116, 150, 186, 203, 270
Mild Seven Benetton Ford
  — see 'Benetton'
Mild Seven Benetton Playlife
  — see 'Benetton'
Mild Seven Benetton Renault
  — see 'Benetton'
Miles, John 88
Minardi 20, 27, 29–30, 36, 47, 55–56, 94, 95, 96–98, 101, 110, 117, 118, 122–123, 124, 130, 131, 144, 154, 155–156, 178, 182, 183, 186–187, 189, 206, 208, 212, 215–216, 223, 232, 235, 242, 243–244, 254, 257, 259, 261, 269, 270–271, 280, 287, 288, 293, 294–295, 297
  M189-Ford 29–30
  M190-Ford 29–30
  M191-Ferrari 55–56
  M191B-Lamborghini 96–97
  M192-Lamborghini 96–98
  M193-Ford 122–123
  M193B-Ford 155–156
  M194-Ford 155–156
  M195-Ford 186–187
  M195B-Ford 215–216, 243
  M197-Hart 243–244, 270
  M198-Ford 270–271
  M01-Ford 294–295
Minardi, Giancarlo 55, 155, 215–216, 243, 270
Minardi Scuderia Italia
  — see 'Minardi'
Minardi Team — see 'Minardi'
Minassian, Nicolas 256
Mitterand, François 67
Mobil 1 (oil) 158, 176
Modena, Stefano 25–26, 33, 46, 54–55, 56, 64, 85, 89, 95, 98–99, 125
Modena Team 62, 68, 72–73
  Lambo 290 72
  Lambo 291 72–73
Moneytron 34, 35
Montermini, Andrea 47, 48, 56, 85, 95, 96, 114, 136, 138, 162, 188–189, 190, 216–217
Monteverdi
  ORE2-Ford 35
Monteverdi, Peter 35
Monteverdi Onyx — see 'Onyx'
Monteverdi Onyx Formula One
  — see 'Onyx'
Montoya, Juan Pablo 256, 285, 290
Moody, Charlie 21, 94, 162

Morbidelli, Giancarlo 96
Morbidelli, Gianni 13, 30, 32, 47, 49, 55–56, 85, 96–98, 147, 149, 154–155, 156, 177, 183–185, 190, 207, 216, 226, 235, 236–237, 241
Moreno, Roberto 17–18, 34, 46, 50–51, 52–53, 56, 63, 103, 120, 190–191
Morgan, Dave 72, 99
Morgan, Paul 63
Moser, Tom 297
Mosley, Max 6, 43, 103, 108, 109, 110, 161, 171, 222, 252, 279
Mosnier, Jean-François 161
Motor Racing Developments
  — see 'Brabham'
Motori Moderni engines
  Flat-12 (3.5-litre) 36
MTV Simtek Ford — see 'Simtek'
Mugen engines 90, 99, 124, 153, 160, 178, 180, 186, 210, 234, 238, 258, 260, 277
  V10 (3.5-litre) 124, 158, 159
    MF-351H 90
  V10 (3-litre) 223, 234, 235, 258, 282
    MF-301HA 210
Mullarkey, Seamus 262, 291
Müller, Jörg 238, 262, 290
Murphy, Chris 22, 27, 28, 29, 62, 63, 64, 88, 158, 159, 160
Murray, Gordon 12
MVS Venturi 62, 95

Nagata, Yoshihiko 24
Naher, Walter 152
Nakajima, Satoru 12, 19–21, 22, 25, 28, 54–55, 68, 89, 242
Nakano, Shinji 227, 234–235, 239, 241, 259, 261, 270–271, 282
Nakauchi, Kohji 25
Nakaya, Akihiko 99
Nannini, Alessandro 13, 16, 19, 20, 25, 243
Nardon, Maurizio 13, 47, 91, 118
Naspetti, Emanuele 93–94, 101, 127, 190
Neerpasch, Jochen 120, 121
Neilson, David 82
Neotech engines 34
  V12 (3.5-litre) 34
Newey, Adrian 19, 21, 22, 42, 46, 140, 142, 172, 173, 198, 200, 224, 230, 231, 252, 278
Newman-Haas Racing 85, 110
Nichols, Steve 12, 13, 47, 48, 85, 121, 126, 147, 158, 176, 180, 205, 230
Niefer, Werner 120
Nielsen, Steve 186, 277
Nimrod Aston Martin 60
Nissen, Kris 181
Noda, Hideki 157–158, 191
Nokia Tyrrell Yamaha
  — see 'Tyrrell'
North, David 44, 82
Nursey, Dennis 99, 100

Oastler, Malcolm 296, 297
Oatley, Neil 12, 44, 82, 112, 176, 205, 230
Oda, Yasutada 64
Ohashi, Wataru 24, 64, 153

Oku, Akiyoshi 223
Oliver, Jackie 24, 153, 183, 184, 213, 214, 238
Onyx 24, 25, 27, 34–35, 64, 90
  ORE1-Ford 35
  ORE2-Ford 35
ORECA 32, 234
Osella 10, 18, 25, 30–31, 70, 79, 190
  FA1M-Ford 31
  FA1Me-Ford 31
Osella, Enzo 30, 70
Owen, David 230

Pacific 160, 162–163, 178, 182, 185, 188–189, 190, 191
  PR01-Ilmor 162–163
  PR02-Ford 188–189
Pacific Grand Prix — see 'Pacific'
Pacific Team Lotus — see 'Pacific'
Palazzani, Vittorio 155
Palmer, Jonathan 12, 44
Panis, Olivier 149–150, 151, 154, 156, 178–180, 181, 197, 202, 206, 209–210, 227, 231, 234–235, 239, 244, 267–269, 279, 280, 285, 288, 289–290
Paoli, Jean-Pierre 91, 118
Papenreulo, Vaso 43
Papis, Max 184–185
Parmalat Forti Ford — see 'Forti'
Patrese, Riccardo 18–19, 31, 45–47, 50, 80–81, 83, 85, 92, 95, 110, 114–115, 121, 122, 123, 125, 152
Patrucco, Sergio 72, 73
Paul Stewart Racing 25, 154, 213, 240
Pavanello, Paolo 34
Pedrotta, Giuseppe 47
Penske 90, 124, 186
  PC21-Chevrolet (Indycar) 112
Penske, Roger 63
Penske (shock absorbers) 26, 48, 86, 95, 157, 176
Perrin, Didier 209
Petronas engines
  V10 (3-litre) 236, 262, 290
Peugeot 44, 113, 117, 121, 126, 128, 145, 156, 207, 208, 267, 290
Peugeot engines 145–147, 180, 183, 232, 234, 267, 289
  V10 (3.5-litre) 145
    A4 145
    A6 145
    Evo2 147
  V10 (3-litre) 181, 207, 268
    A10E 181
    Evo2 181
    A14 232
    A18 269, 289
Phillips, Ian 21, 52, 63
Piano, Renzo 201
Piccinini, Marco 31, 48, 85
Pininfarina 72
Piquet, Nelson 11, 16, 20, 22, 28, 50–51, 88, 91, 120, 152
Pirelli 10, 14, 16, 19, 26, 29, 30, 31, 32, 34, 42, 50, 54, 55, 56, 60, 71, 79, 89
Pirro, Emanuele 31–32, 56–57, 94, 95
Playlife engines 260, 287
  V10 (3-litre) 260, 287

Pollock, Craig 198, 256, 269, 270, 295, 296
Porsche 34, 64, 65
  962 34
Porsche engines 24, 34, 60, 64, 65, 90
  TAG Turbo 65
  V12 (3.5-litre) 34, 42
Postlethwaite, Harvey 19, 54–55, 85, 87, 117, 120, 121, 130, 150, 186, 212, 242, 269, 276–277
Pratt, Hugo 119
Precision Composites 52
Preston, Tim 198, 262, 292
Prewitt, Dave 100
Price, David 60
Princess Anne, HRH 267
Prodrive 229
Prost 225, 232, 234–235, 239, 244, 258, 260, 261, 265, 267–269, 270, 279, 284, 288, 289–290, 294
  JS45-Mugen 234–235
  AP01-Peugeot 267–269, 289
  AP01B-Peugeot 269, 289
  AP02-Peugeot 289–290
Prost, Alain 6, 8–9, 10, 12, 13–15, 16, 17, 18, 22, 32, 34, 43, 46, 47–49, 56, 80, 81, 85, 91, 106–107, 110–111, 113, 114, 115, 117, 121, 140, 146, 177, 205, 210, 234, 258, 267, 289, 290
Prost Gauloises Blondes
  — see 'Prost'
Prost Grand Prix — see 'Prost'

Queen, HM Elizabeth II 46
Quinn, Richard 99

Radage, Chris 217, 277, 288
Rafanelli, Gabriele 68
Ragnotti, Jean 185
RAM Racing 60
Rampf, Willi 152
Randall, Alan 100
Ratzenberger, Roland 6, 136, 140, 161–162
Red Bull Racing 99
Red Bull Sauber Ford
  — see 'Sauber'
Red Bull Sauber Petronas
  — see 'Sauber'
Redon, Laurent 270, 287, 294
Reed, Ian 149, 178
Rees, Alan 24, 64, 153, 210
Renault engines 6, 42, 45, 67, 79, 92, 121, 138, 141, 149, 150, 170, 172, 175, 178, 198, 206, 207, 222, 224, 228, 256, 260, 267, 286, 287, 296
  V10 (3.5-litre) 78, 91, 112
    RS02 18
    RS03 46, 91
    RS03B 46
    RS03C 80, 92
    RS04 80
    RS05 111, 117
    RS06 140
    RS06B 140
    RS06C 140
  V10 (3-litre) 170
    RS07 170, 172
    RS07B 171
    RS08 198, 203

RS08B 199
RS09 224, 228
Ress, Leo 120, 121, 152, 181, 236, 262, 290
Ressler, Neil 283
Reutemann, Carlos 199
Reynard 49, 51, 52, 73, 79, 162, 295, 296
  89D-Mugen (F3000) 52
  941-Ford (Indycar) 295
Reynard, Adrian 295, 296, 297
Reynard Composites 163
Rial 10, 94
Richards, David 229, 261
Ring, David 283, 284
Rinland, Sergio 19, 25, 26, 60, 73, 99, 101, 131, 190, 203, 217
Robin Herd Limited 70, 95, 101
Robinson, James 24, 44, 198
Rocchi, Franco 37
Rodgers, Fred 161
Roebuck, Nigel 32, 87
Rolls-Royce 251
Rosa, Riccardo 71, 102, 103
Rosberg, Keke 57, 59, 85, 190
Rose, Jeffrey 108
Rosset, Ricardo 210, 212, 213–214, 216, 242, 245, 269–270, 271
Rothmans Williams Renault
  — see 'Williams'
Rouelle, Claude 32
Royal Automobile Club (RAC) 108, 168
Royce, Mike 95
Rudd, Tony 22, 57
Rumi, Gabriele 30, 70, 71, 101, 102, 212, 243, 270, 293, 294
Russell, John 142, 286
Ryan, Dave 12
Ryton, George 19, 34, 54, 55, 89, 116, 216, 217, 223, 234, 270

Sakai, Tenji 258
Sala, Luis Pérez 25, 35
Sala, Maurizio Sandro 63
Salo, Mika 160, 179, 185–186, 189, 202, 203, 206, 212–213, 241, 242–243, 244, 264–265, 279, 281, 285, 292, 293, 295, 297
Salvarini, Walter 37
Sardou, Max 101
Sarrazin, Stéphane 289, 294
Sasol Jordan — see 'Jordan'
Sasol Jordan Yamaha
  — see 'Jordan'
Sassetti, Andrea 73, 102, 103
Sauber 85, 93, 112, 114, 119, 120–122, 126, 144, 147, 150, 152–153, 156, 170, 181–183, 184, 186, 189, 198, 210–211, 224, 233, 236–237, 239, 241, 254, 259, 261, 262–263, 268, 290–292
  C12-Ilmor 121–122
  C12 121–122
  C13-Mercedes 152–153
  C14-Ford 181–183
  C15-Ford 210–211
  C16-Petronas 236–237
  C17-Petronas 262–263
  C18-Petronas 290–292

Sauber engines 122
V10 (3.5-litre) 122, 152
2175B 122
Sauber-Mercedes (sports cars)
54, 64, 120
C6-Ford 120
Sauber Mercedes (F1)
— see 'Sauber'
Sauber, Peter 120, 121, 152,
262, 292
Sauber Petronas Engineering
236
Saunders, Chris 244
Saward, Joe 22
Scalabroni, Enrique 13, 14, 15,
57, 79, 88, 197
Scapini, Franco 37
Schiattarella, Domenico 162,
191
Schlesser, Jo 234
Schmidt Motor Sport 161
Schneider, Bernd 24–25, 30, 37,
52, 58, 64, 67, 205
Schübel, Horst 57
Schumacher, Corinna (née
Betsch) 171
Schumacher, Michael 6, 43,
51, 52–53, 79, 81, 83–85,
113, 114–115, 118, 120, 122,
134–135, 136, 137, 138–140,
141, 142, 143, 145, 147, 148,
151, 154, 166–167, 168, 169,
170–171, 172, 173, 174, 175,
176, 181, 196, 197, 198, 199,
200–202, 204, 205, 206,
208, 210, 220–221, 222, 224,
225, 226–227, 229, 231, 233,
234, 239, 241, 250, 251, 253,
254–256, 257, 260, 261, 265,
271, 276, 278, 279, 280–281,
284, 295, 297
Schumacher, Ralf 205, 222, 227,
232–233, 237, 241, 258–260,
266, 270, 281, 282, 285,
285–287, 288, 290, 296
SCM Minardi Team
— see 'Minardi'
Scott Russell Engines 21
Scott, Tim 100
Scuderia Ferrari — see 'Ferrari'
Scuderia Ferrari Marlboro
— see 'Ferrari'
Scuderia Italia 28, 31–32, 36,
56–57, 68, 85, 94–95, 96,
131, 155, 244
Senna, Ayrton 6, 8–9, 10, 11,
12–13, 14, 15, 17, 19, 20, 22,
40–41, 42, 43, 44–45, 46,
47, 49, 52, 53, 78, 80, 81–83,
84, 85, 90, 94, 108, 110,
111, 112–113, 114, 115, 118,
119, 128, 134–135, 136, 138,
140–141, 144, 145, 146, 157,
200, 284
SEP (brakes) 101
Shadow 184
Shannon Racing Team 217
Shell (fuel and oil) 112, 176, 201
Shimizu, Norio 60
Shirai, Hiroshi 160
Showa (suspension) 82
Sims, Brian 131
Simtek 102, 103, 145, 161–162,
170, 191
S941-Ford 161–162
S951-Ford 191

Smith, Dominic 184
Smith, Mark 52
Smith, Mike 63, 64, 93
Sospiri, Vincenzo 203, 209,
212, 245
Stanford, Dickie 46, 172
Stanzani, Paolo 56, 155
Stefan Grand Prix 223
Stefanovi, Zoran 223
Stepney, Nigel 50, 57, 88, 116
Stevens, Peter 59
Stewart 210, 213, 229, 236, 238,
240–241, 260, 263, 265–267,
269, 270, 271, 276, 277,
283–285
SF1-Ford 240–241
SF2-Ford 265–267
SF3-Ford 283–285
Stewart Ford — see 'Stewart'
Stewart Grand Prix
— see 'Stewart'
Stewart, Jackie 11, 153, 240,
277, 283, 284
Stewart, Paul 153–154, 240,
277, 283, 284
Stirano, Giorgio 190
Streiff, Philippe 10, 32
Stroud, Nigel 158
Stubbs, Dave 25, 240
Stuck, Hans-Joachim 120
Subaru 36
Subaru-Coloni — see 'Coloni'
Subaru engines
Flat-12 (3.5-litre) 29
1235 36
Sukhoi (composites) 58
Summerhayes, Paul 189
Superpower Engineering 71
Supertec engines 286, 287
V10 (3-litre) 286, 296
FB01 286, 297
Suzuki, Aguri 25, 27–28, 30, 32,
49, 50, 61–63, 70, 90–91,
122, 124–125, 127, 147, 153,
170, 178–180, 186, 214
Suzuki, Toshio 129
Swift Cars 240
Symonds, Pat 49, 51, 84, 114,
170, 228, 287
Synge, Robert 297

TAG Electronics 82, 112, 125,
154, 244, 264
TAG Heuer (timing) 78
TAG/McLaren Marketing
Services 19, 54
Takagi, Toranosuke 242, 266,
269–270, 292–293, 295
Takaoka, Yoshio 36
Tambay, Patrick 156
Tarquini, Gabriele 32–33, 68–70,
71, 101–102, 186, 270
Team 7UP Jordan — see 'Jordan'
Team Lotus — see 'Lotus'
Tétu, Michel 62
Texaco Havoline (fuel and oil)
240
Thompson, Ian 121
Thynne, Sheridan 45, 110
Tickford (engines) 30
Tilke, Hermann 276
Tilley, Andy 158, 208, 262, 292
Todt, Jean 6, 117, 145, 175, 201,
254, 280, 281
Toet, Willem 49, 51, 174, 202,
226

Toleman 16
Tolentino, Mario 31, 68, 70,
72
Tomaini, Antonio 31, 70
TOM's (Tachi Oiwa Motorsports)
79
Toso, Dino 258
Total (fuel and oil) 180
Total Jordan Peugeot
— see 'Jordan'
Tourtel Larrousse F1
— see 'Larrousse'
Toyota 79, 234
Tracy, Paul 140, 186
Trebron 109
Tredozi, Gabriele 96, 215,
243, 270
Tremayne, David 56
Trulli, Jarno 225, 234–235,
243–244, 261, 263, 267–269,
284, 288, 289–290
Tuero, Esteban 215, 243, 257,
270–271, 294
TWR (Tom Walkinshaw Racing)
51, 88, 155, 178, 209, 213,
214, 226, 238
Tyrrell 11, 12, 13, 16, 19–21, 22,
25, 42, 50, 54–55, 57, 58, 64,
79, 89–90, 94, 95, 96, 118,
120, 129–130, 142, 150–151,
153, 185–186, 187, 212–213,
215, 223, 241, 242–243, 244,
259, 267, 269–270, 271,
277, 296
018-Ford 19, 20
019-Ford 19–21, 47
020-Honda 54–55
020B-Ilmor 89–90
020C-Yamaha 129–130
021-Yamaha 116, 130
022-Yamaha 150–151
023-Yamaha 185–186
023B-Yamaha (test chassis)
212
024-Yamaha 212–213
025-Ford 242–243
026-Ford 269–270, 297
Tyrrell, Bob 19, 269
Tyrrell, Ken 19, 54, 196, 242,
269
Tyrrell Ford — see 'Tyrrell'
Tyrrell Racing Organisation
— see 'Tyrrell'
Tyrrell Yamaha — see 'Tyrrell'

Unser, Al Jr 80, 114
Urbinelli, Luigi 85

Vale, Pete 56
van de Poele, Eric 35, 72–73,
99–100, 102
van der Grint, Kees 34
van Rossem, Jean-Pierre 34, 35
Vanderpleyn, Christian 31, 36,
56, 68, 70
Venturi — see 'MVS Venturi'
Venturi Larrousse —
'Larrousse'
Verstappen, Jos 137, 138–140,
147, 149, 153–154, 169, 170,
171, 191, 202, 206, 213–214,
225, 236, 238, 239, 242–243,
244, 260, 266–267, 269,
277, 283
Verstappen, Max 243
Vickers 16, 98, 251

Villadelprat, Joan 13, 19, 50, 54,
84, 138
Villeneuve, Gilles 198
Villeneuve, Jacques 6, 196, 197,
198–200, 202, 203, 204,
206, 210, 217, 220–221, 222,
224–225, 226, 227, 231, 233,
234, 235, 238, 239, 251, 253,
256–258, 269, 270, 271, 278,
285, 286, 291, 295–297
Visconti, Amedeo 47, 85, 144
Vita, Ernesto 37
Volkswagen 251
Vollenberg, Henny 93
von Brauchitsch, Manfred 230
Vortex (F3000 team) 93

Walker, Murray 252
Walkinshaw, Tom 25, 50–51, 57,
83, 149, 159, 170, 178, 209,
213, 214, 234, 238, 263, 264,
265, 292
Walters, Martin 210
Walton, John 126, 207, 213,
292
Walz, Klaus 96
Warr, Peter 22, 78
Warwick, Derek 22–23, 24,
57, 110, 112, 115, 124–125,
128
Warwick, Paul 25
Wass, Dave 16, 49, 51
Watson, Dave 188
Watson, John 52
Weber (fuel injection) 36
Weber, Willi 296
Welti, Max 64, 182, 262
Wendlinger, Karl 53, 64, 86,
93–94, 112, 119, 120–122,
125, 136, 152, 156,
181–183, 189
West McLaren Mercedes
— see 'McLaren'
West, Richard 110
Wheatcroft, Tom 10, 109
Wheeler, Greg 286
Whitaker, Martin 210
White, Paul 208
Whiting, Charlie 78, 109, 136,
196, 198, 207, 223, 287
Whitmarsh, Martin 230
Wickham, John 24, 65, 184
Wiggins, Keith 162, 163,
188, 189
Williams 6, 13, 18–19, 21, 44,
45–47, 50, 58, 63, 67, 80–81,
82, 83, 85, 89, 91, 95, 100,
110–111, 112, 113, 115, 117,
118, 119, 137, 139, 140–143,
144, 146, 151, 153, 169, 170,
171, 172–173, 175, 176, 179,
183, 196, 198–200, 202,
203, 204, 205, 210, 222,
223, 224–225, 227, 230, 231,
234, 240, 241, 243, 244, 252,
256–258, 262, 271, 280,
281, 282, 283, 285–287, 290,
295, 296
FW13-Renault 26, 46
FW13B-Renault 18–19
FW14-Renault 45–46
FW14B-Renault 78, 80–81,
111
FW15-Renault 80, 110
FW15B-Renault 110
FW15C-Renault 110–111

FW15D-Renault (test chassis)
140
FW16-Renault 140–141, 172
FW16B-Renault 142–143
FW17-Renault 171, 172–173
FW17B-Renault 173, 198
FW18-Renault 196, 198–200,
203, 226
FW18B-Renault (test chassis)
224
FW18C-Renault (test chassis)
224
FW19-Renault 224–225, 231
FW19-Mecachrome 257
FW20-Mecachrome 256–258
FW20C-Supertec (test chassis)
286
FW21-Supertec 285–287
Williams, Frank 19, 45, 110, 140,
172, 198, 286
Williams, Mark 62
Willis, Geoff 224, 286
Wilson, Craig 286
Wilson, Max 256
Windsor, Peter 13, 46, 110,
197
Winfield Williams —
see 'Williams'
Wirth, Nick 103, 161, 170, 191,
228, 260, 287
Wood, Ben 242, 267, 289
Wright, Peter 57, 88, 92, 158
Wright, Tim 12, 44, 126, 147,
152, 170
Wurz, Alexander 228–229, 237,
253, 255, 259, 260–261, 271,
287–288, 292, 293
Wyss, Peter 32, 70, 72

Xtrac (transmissions) 61, 71, 89,
90, 91, 154, 161, 184, 186,
238, 240, 244, 297

Yamaha 59, 60, 61, 79, 125,
196, 212, 213, 238, 239, 242
Yamaha engines 59–61, 98, 99,
129–130, 185, 212, 263, 264
V8 (3.5-litre)
OX88 59
V10 (3.5-litre)
OX10A 129, 150
V12 (3.5-litre) 42
OX99 60, 98
V10 (3-litre) 238
OX11A 212, 215
OX11D 238
Yamamoto, Katsumi 189
Yasuoka, Akimasa 44
Ypsilon Technology 60, 129

Zakspeed 10, 30, 59, 162, 292
Zanardi, Alex 51, 53, 83,
89, 97–98, 99, 111, 114,
118, 119–120, 140, 154,
158–160, 232, 267, 285–287,
296
Zargo, Sergio 103
Zehnder, Beat 152
Ziegler, Carmen — see
'Heer, Carmen'
Zoboli, Vittorio 147
Zoellner, Heinz 181
Zonta, Ricardo 232, 252,
296–297
Zorzi, Renzo 190
Zytek (engine management) 63